Communication En

Communication Engineering

M.N. Bandyopadhyay
Director
National Institute of Technology
Calicut
Ex-Director, National Institute of Technology
Kurukshetra

PHI Learning Private Limited
Delhi-110092
2013

₹ 295.00

COMMUNICATION ENGINEERING
M.N. Bandyopadhyay

ISBN-978-81-203-3962-0

The export rights of this book are vested solely with the publisher.

Second Printing ... ... **January, 2013**

Published by Asoke K. Ghosh, PHI Learning Private Limited, Rimjhim House, 111, Patparganj Industrial Estate, Delhi-110092 and Printed by Baba Barkha Nath Printers, Bahadurgarh, Haryana-124507.

To
Debendra Nath Bandyopadhyay
Grandson

Contents

Preface

This book is designed to present a comprehensive treatment of communication engineering. It is intended for use as a textbook for the undergraduate students of electrical, electronics, and telecommunication engineering. It explains the basic theory of operation and applications; the objective being to provide the students with a thorough understanding of communication and telecommunication engineering.

The text has been organized into *eight chapters* and *one appendix*.

Chapter 1 elucidates the introductory part of communication engineering. Chapter 2 elaborately discusses the concepts of modulation and demodulation. It provides a thorough knowledge of amplitude modulation and demodulation, frequency modulation, phase modulation, and pulse modulation. Chapter 3 deals with the details of radio communication. It discusses high level broadcast transmitters, the main components of radio transmitters, radio receivers, automatic volume control, automatic frequency control, antenna, microphone and loudspeaker. Chapter 4 provides an in-depth coverage of telecommunication, Strowger automatic dialling, cross bar switch, mobile telephone communication, application of fibre optic lines, telegraphy, telecommunication in power system, telemetering, and picture telegraph system. Chapter 5 deals with radar. The pulse radar, effects of noise on radar, moving target indicator, blind speed are explained briefly. Chapter 6 is devoted to the detailed study of television. It provides an in-depth coverage of TV transmitter and receiver, horizontal and vertical scanning, interlaced scanning, monochrome picture tube, and different types of camera. A brief description of cable television and colour television is also provided. Chapter 7 describes the network management in communication. It discusses switched network, data transmission, network protocols satellite communication, and facsimile services. Chapter 8 deals with advanced communication. It is devoted to the solid state radio system, multi-access radio telephone system, high definition television, satellite tracking through earth station technology, speech processing technology, and telecommunication application with multiprocessor system.

It has been my earnest endeavour to present the entire text in a simple and lucid manner, so that the students acquire a comprehensive knowledge on the subject.

The book contains some solved examples in some chapters. The objective type questions (around 400) are provided in the Appendix.

I am deeply indebted to my Guide Professor late Dr. S.K. Nag of Jadavpur University. His blessings have been the major driving force in writing this book.

I would like to express my deep respect to my beloved father and mother, late Shri Tarak Nath Bandyopadhyay, and late Shrimati Susoma Bandyopadhyay. As always, I am grateful to my wife, Ila, our son, Dr. Soumendra, and our daughter-in-law, Rumi, for their loving understanding throughout the countless hours I spent working on the manuscript.

It would be my pleasure to welcome suggestions from readers aimed at making this book more readable.

Finally, I would like to shower my gratitude on the Staff of PHI Learning for leaving no stone unturned to publish this book.

M.N. Bandyopadhyay

1 ▪▪▪ Introduction

1.1 TELECOMMUNICATION

Telecommunication is the transmission over a distance for the purpose of communication. In ancient times, telecommunication involved the use of smoke signals, drums, semaphore, flags or heliograph. These days, telecommunication involves the use of electronic devices such as the telephone, television, radio and computers. Alexander Graham Bell, Guglielmo Marconi, Jagadish Chandra Bose, and John Logie Baird were early inventors in the field.

The basic communication engineering consists of the three elements:

- A transmitter that takes information and converts it into a signal
- A transmission medium that carries the signal
- A receiver that receives the signal and converts it back into logical and usable information. Suppose, in a radio broadcast the broadcast tower is the transmitter, free space is the transmission medium and radio is the receiver. Generally, communication systems are two-way with a single device acting as both a transmitter and a receiver or transreceiver. The ideal example of this is a mobile phone. Telephone line service can be termed point-to-point communication since this happens between one transmitter and one receiver. The important point of telecommunication is the flow of signals.

1.2 ANALOGUE OR DIGITAL SIGNALS

Signals are classified as analogue or digital. In case of analogue signal, the signal is varied continuously according to the information. But, in case of digital signal, the information is encoded with a set of discrete values. These are 1 and 0. Usually, analogue signals get degraded by noise. On the other hand, the information contained in digital signals does not change unless the noise exceeds a certain level. The main advantage of digital signals over analogue signals is noise resistance. The next important point which appears in communication is network.

1.3 NETWORK

The transmitters, receivers, transreceivers communicate with one another through network. An analogue network has one or more switches and those switches establish a connection between two or more users. Whereas, in case of digital network routers are available in place of switches and those routers help in transmitting information to the intended user. Whether it is analogue or digital signal, repeaters are essential for amplifying the signal, if the transmission is for long distances. This helps to avoid attenuation and the signal cannot be lost in the noise. When signal moves from one end to the other, some transmitting medium is essential.

1.4 CHANNELS

A channel is a division in a transmission medium for sending multiple streams of information. The medium is divided by frequency and each channel receives a separate frequency to broadcast on. Sometimes, a channel is allocated for a recurring segment of time for broadcasting. That is termed *time-division multiplexing,* which is used in digital communication.

1.5 MODULATION

To convey information, the shaping of signal is termed *modulation.* Modulation can be utilised for representing a digital message as an analogue waveform. This is termed *keying.* Several keying techniques are available, e.g., phase-shift keying, frequency-shift keying, amplitude-shift keying. Modulation can allow the transmission of information of analogue signals at higher frequencies. Low frequency analogue signals cannot be properly transmitted over free space and that is why low frequency analogue signal is superimposed on higher frequency signal which is known as carrier wave.

1.6 HISTORY OF TELECOMMUNICATION

Sir Charles Wheatstone and Sir Willian Fothergill Cooke invented the electric telegraph in 1837. Samuel Morse independently developed a version of the electrical telegraph. His code was an important advance over Wheatstone's signalling method. The first transatlantic telegraph cable was completed on 27 July 1866.

The conventional telephone was invented by Alexander Bell and Elisha Gray in 1876. Antonio Meucci invented the first device that made the electrical transmission of voice over a line in 1849. The first commercial telephone services were developed in 1878–79 on both the sides of the Atlantic in the cities of New Haven and London. In 1832, James Lindsay gave the concept of wireless telegraphy. Afterwards, he demonstrated a transmission across the Firth of Tay from Dundee, Scottand to Woodhaven. The distance was two miles. The transmission medium was water. Nobel prize winner Guglielmo Marconi developed wireless communication between St John's, New found land (Canada) and Poldhu, Cornwall (England). Of course, Nikola Telsa, in 1893, presented a small-scale radio communication in the National Electric Light Association. On 25 March, 1925, John Logie Baird demonstrated the transmission of moving pictures at the London department store Selfridges. Karl Braun discovered the cathode ray tube (CRT). The twentieth-century televisions depended upon the CRT.

On 11 September, 1940, George Stibitz was successful to transmit problems utilising teletype to his complex number calculator in New York and received the calculated outcome back at Dartmouth college in New Hampshire. This concept of centralized computer or mainframe with remote dumb terminals remained popular throughout the 1950s. Then the research continued to investigate packet switching. In the long run, that allowed chunks of data to be sent to different computers without first passing through a centralized main frame. The ARPANET (Advanced Research Project Agency Network) developed by ARPA of United States department of defence during the Cold War, was the first operational packet switching network and the predecessor of the global internet. The packet switching was the dominant basis for both data and voice communication worldwide. It was an important concept in data communication. Previously, data communication was based on the idea of circuit switching as in the old typical telephone circuit, where a dedicated circuit was tied up for the duration of the call. With the packet switching, a system could use one communication link to communicate with more than one machine by disassembling data into data graphs, then gather these as packets The ARPANET would merge with other networks to form the internet and many of the protocols of the internet relied upon today were specified through the request for comment process.

1.7 MODERN TECHNOLOGY IN COMMUNICATION

Mobile phones made a significant impact on telephone networks. Mobile phone subscriptions now out-number the fixed line subscriptions in many countries. There have also been unimaginable changes in telephone communication behind the scenes. Starting with the operation of TAT-8 in 1988 (8th transatlantic telephone cable), there is widespread adoption of system based on optic fibres from 1990. TAT-8 carried initially 40,000 telephone circuits between the USA, the UK and France. It was constructed in 1988 by a consortium of companies led by AT & T, France Telecom and British Telecom. It served the three countries with a single trans-atlantic crossing with the use of an innovative branching unit located underwater on the continental shelf off the coast of Great Britain. The cable exists are in Tuckerton, New Jersey, USA, Widermouth Bay, England and Penmarch, France. This was first transatlantic cable to use optical fibres.

TAT-8 was able to carry ten times as many telephone calls as the last copper cable laid at that time. Of course, today's optic fibre cable can carry twenty five times as many telephone calls as TAT-8. The main factors for the increase in data capacity are as follows:

(i) Optic fibres are physically much smaller than computing technologies,
(ii) They do not suffer from cross talk which means several hundreds of them can be easily bundled together in a single cable,
(iii) Improvements in multiplexing have led to an exponential growth in the data capacity of a single fibre. Assisting communication across many modern fibre networks is protocol termed *asynchronous transfer mode* (ATM). It is suitable for public telephone networks since it develops a pathway for data through the network and associates a traffic contract with that pathway. There are a few competitors to ATM, for example, multiprotocol label switching (MPLS).

1.8   DEVELOPMENT IN RADIO AND TELEVISION

The broadcast media industry is at a critical turning point in its achievement, with many countries moving from analogue to digital broadcasts. This is only possible because of the production of cheaper, faster and more capable integrated circuits. The main advantage of digital broadcasts is that they prevent a number of complaints with traditional analogue broadcasts. In case of television, this helps in eliminating the problems, for example snowy pictures, ghosting and other distortions.

In analogue transmission, there occurs perturbations on account of noise and in the final outcome it is visualised. But, digital transmission gets rid of that problem since digital signals are reduced to discrete values upon reception and small perturbations do not create problems in the final output. For example, suppose there is a binary message 1011. It is transmitted with signal amplitudes [1.0 0.0 1.0 1.0] and received with signal amplitudes [0.9 0.2 1.1 0.9]. The decoding to the binary message will be again 1011. Thus, the sending message will be receiving message. But, in case the noise is very large, then the signal will be altered in a large scale at the time of decoding. In digital television broadcasting, there are three competing standards which are likely to be adopted worldwide. These are ATSC, DVB and ISDB standards. All these standards use MPEG-2 for video compression. The MPEG-2 is the standard for "the genetic coding of moving pictures and associated audio information". It actually describes a combination of lossy video compression and lossy audio data compression methods which allow storage and transmission of movies utilising currently available storage media and transmission bandwidth. The ATSC uses Dolby Digital AC-3 for audio compression, ISDB uses Advanced Audio Coding (MPEG-2 Part 7) and DVB has no standard for audio compression but typically uses MPEG-1 Part 3 Layer 2.

In digital audio broadcasting, standards are much more unified with practically all countries choosing to adopt the Digital Broadcasting standard. But, the USA has chosen to adopt HD Radio. HD Radio technology is a system used by AM and FM radio stations to digitally transmit audio and data in conjunction with their analog signals. Up to October 2008, 1800 stations covering approximately 84% of the United States are broadcasting with this technology. If digital signal reception is lost, the HD receiver will revert to the analogue signal, thus providing seamless operation between the newer and older transmission methods. HD radio is simply a brand name. The earlier whitepaper documents refer to "Hybrid Digital" radio technology. Of course, there is no connection with high definition television (HDTV), except in the sense that both HDTV and HD radio are digital formats. Analogue television is still transmitted in practically all countries. The United States had hoped to end analogue broadcasts on 31 December, 2006; but this was recently pushed to 17.2.2009. For analogue, television, there are three standards in practice. These are termed PAL, NTSC and SECAM.

1.9   THE INTERNET

The Internet is a world wide network of computers and computer networks. These can communicate with one another utilising the Internet Protocol. Any computer on the internet can send a message to any other computer utilising its IP address. The internet is an exchange of messages between computers. An Internet Protocol (IP) address is a numerical identification (logical address) that is assigned to devices participating in a computer network using the Internet Protocol for communication between its nodes. The role of the IP address is explained a follows:

- A name indicates what we seek;
- An address indicates where it is; and
- A route indicates how to get there.

Due to the tremendous growth in the internet and the resulting depletion of the address space, a new addressing system (IPV6) using 128 bits for the address has been developed. Till 2008, an estimated 21.9% of the world population has access to the internet with the highest access rates in North America (73.6%) Oceania/Australia (59.5%) and Europe (48.1%). These are measured as percentage of the population. In connection with broadband access, Iceland (26.7%), South Korea (25.4%) and Netherlands (25.3%) led the world. In case of the internet, the physical medium and data link protocol can vary many times as packets traverse the globe. In general, most intercontinental communication will use the Asynchronous Transfer Mode (ATM) protocol on the top of optic fibre. This is due to the reason that for most intercontinental communication the internet shares the same infrastructure as the public switched telephone network. Presently, the most largely used version of the internet protocol is version four but a move towards version six is imminent. In spite of the growth of the internet, the characteristics of local area networks (LANs) which run at most a few kilometres, remain distinct. *Ethernet* and *Token ring* are typical data link protocols for local area networks. In spite of modest popularity of Token Ring in the 80s and 90s virtually all local area networks now use wired or wireless Ethernet. Most wired Ethernet implementations use copper twisted pair cables. But some previous implementations used co-axial cables. On the other hand, some recent implementations use optic fibres. In case of optic fibre, both multimode fibre and single mode fibre can be used. Multimode fibre is obviously thicker optical fibre. It is also cheaper to manufacture. But it suffers from less usable bandwidth and greater attenuation. Therefore, the performance becomes poor for long distances.

2 ∎∎∎ Modulation and Demodulation

2.1 NEED FOR HIGH FREQUENCY COMMUNICATION

For perfect radiation and reception of electromagnetic wave, the height of the antenna should be quarter of the wavelength of the electromagnetic wave. So, for 20 kHz frequency of electromagnetic wave, the wave length will be $\dfrac{3 \times 10^8}{20 \times 10^3}$ = 15000 metre. Hence, the height of the vertical antenna will be 15000/4 metre = 3750 metre. This is totally impracticable. Hence, to make the system feasible, the communication signal should be high. Therefore, we have to generate high frequency signal for communication. Suppose, if we generate 1.5 MHz electromagnetic wave, then, as per above principle, the required height of antenna will be $\dfrac{3 \times 10^8}{1.5 \times 10^6 \times 4}$ = 50 metre. This height is quite practicable. All sorts of sounds in the earth lie between 20 Hz to 20 kHz, in general. Hence, the transmitting signal frequency is to be enhanced. To separate the various signals in the earth, it is essential to convert them all to various portions of electromagnetic spectrum.

2.2 MODULATION

How do we modify the audio signal? The answer is modulation. Modulation is nothing but the process of superimposition of a low frequency voice information component on a high frequency carrier signal. Therefore, by virtue of modulation, voice information component is carried by high frequency carrier signal. It is just like a load being carried by a vehicle. Load cannot move alone. Similarly the voice signal cannot be transferred from a place to a distant place without any carrier signal. Otherwise, it will get mixed up with other audio signals and the very essence of it will not be received at the receiving end. It will be lost on the way. Now the question comes how this voice signal keeps its identity even after superimposition with a high frequency carrier signal at its receiving end?

With the modulation process, some of the characteristics, usually amplitude, frequency, phase of a voltage are varied. In other words, the voltage, frequency and phase of carrier waveform are changed with instantaneous values of audio signal voltage. The voltage of voice signal is termed modulating voltage. The voltage of carrier signal is termed unmodulated voltage. When amplitude is being changed, the process is termed amplitude modulation, when frequency is changed, the process is termed frequency modulation. When the phase is changed, the process is termed phase modulation. The signal which is developed after modulation is termed as modulated signal, or it is termed translated signal.

2.3 AMPLITUDE MODULATION

The amplitude modulation is the amplitude of a carrier signal that varies with the modulating voltage whose frequency is much lower than that of the carrier. In case of amplitude modulation, the amplitude of carrier is made proportional to the instantaneous amplitude of modulating voltage. Let the carrier voltage and modulating voltage be represented by

$$v_c = V_c \sin \omega_c t, \text{ and } v_m = V_m \sin \omega_m t$$

Then the amplitude modulated voltage will be expressed as

$$V_c + V_m \sin \omega_m t = V_c + m V_c \sin \omega_m t$$
$$= V_c (1 + m \text{ sing } \omega_m t)$$

V_m is considered equal to mV_c where 'm' is constant and the 'm' is termed modulation index.

The instantaneous voltage of the resulting amplitude modulated wave is

$$V_c(1 + m \sin \omega_m t) \sin \omega_c t$$

Figure 2.1 describes the above.

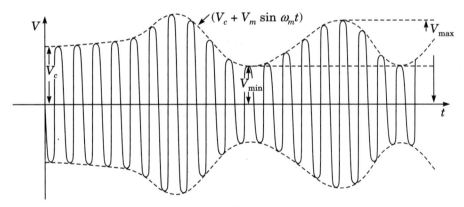

Figure 2.1 Amplitude modulation.

If the voltage equation is synthesized, then we get

$$V_c (1 + m \sin \omega_m t) \sin \omega_c t$$

$$= V_c \sin \omega_c t + m V_c \sin \omega_m t \sin \omega_c t$$

$$= V_c \sin \omega_c t + \frac{m V_c}{2} [\cos (\omega_c - \omega_m) t - \cos (\omega_c + \omega_m) t]$$

The process of amplitude modulation has added two sidebands of frequency $\omega_c + \omega_m$ and $\omega_c - \omega_m$ with the unmodulated carrier frequency ω_c. The lower sideband consists of frequency $(\omega_c - \omega_m)$ (i.e. $f_c - f_m$) and the upper sideband consists of frequency $(\omega_c + \omega_m)$ (i.e. $f_c + f_m$). Hence the bandwidth of the system becomes $f_c + f_m - (f_c - f_m) = 2f_m$.

From Figure 2.1, it is quite clear that the maximum voltage,

$$V_{max} = V_c + V_m$$

Similarly, minimum voltage becomes,

$$V_{min} = V_c - V_m$$

$$\frac{V_{max} - V_{min}}{2} = \frac{V_c + V_m - V_c + V_m}{2}$$

$$= V_m$$

$$V_c = V_{max} - V_m$$

$$= V_{max} - \frac{(V_{max} - V_{min})}{2}$$

$$= \frac{V_{max} + V_{min}}{2}$$

Again,

$$V_m = mV_c$$

$\therefore$

$$m = \frac{V_m}{V_c}$$

$$= \frac{V_{max} - V_{min}}{V_{max} + V_{min}}$$

The above ratio (i.e. m) is termed modulation index.

2.3.1 Circuit Diagram of Amplitude Modulation

Figure 2.2 describes the circuit diagram of amplitude modulation. It is also known as collector modulation. Here,

$$C_1 = C_2, \; C_3 = C_4, \; r_1 = r_2$$

The basic circuit of the collector modulation consists of class 'C' amplifier. Modulation is done at the last *RF* amplifier stage. The modulated amplifier is a push pull amplifier. The bias is used as a leak type. The base modulation is also possible. But the collector modulation is better than the base modulation. The reasons are:

    (a) the modulation is much more linear;
    (b) the collector circuit efficiency is higher;
    (c) the power output per transistor is higher;

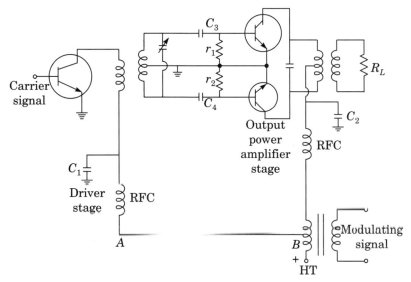

Figure 2.2 Amplitude modulation.

The problem of the collector modulation is that it requires higher modulating power. Moreover, a hundred per cent modulation cannot be obtained in collector modulation system on account of collector saturation. The connection *AB* develops collector modulation of the output *RF* amplifier and the driver (Figure 2.2). We can also use simultaneously collector modulation and base modulation of the same stage. But at the same time, power output may drop because bias may become excessive. However, simultaneous base and collector modulation are also sometimes preferred in the same principle to that of collector modulation. In certain case, simultaneous drain and gate modulation of FET amplifier is also utilized.

2.4 DOUBLE SIDEBAND SUPPRESSED CARRIER MODULATION

The double sideband suppressed carrier modulation is that type of modulation in which the transmitted wave consists of the upper and lower sideband. The carrier wave is suppressed and the transmission power is saved. The channel bandwidth will remain twice the frequency of the modulating signal. In other words, the double sideband suppressed carrier modulation (DSB-SC) consists of the product of modulating signal and carrier wave signal. Let us assume that the carrier voltage is $V_c \cos \omega_c t$ and modulation voltage is $V_m \cos \omega_m t$. Hence, the product of the carrier voltage and modulating voltage is

$$V_c \cos \omega_c t \cdot V_m \cos \omega_m t = \frac{V_c V_m}{2} [2\cos \omega_c t \cos \omega_m t]$$

$$= \frac{V_c V_m}{2} [\cos(\omega_c - \omega_m)t + \cos (\omega_c + \omega_m)t]$$

Figure 2.3(a) shows the modulating signal voltage waveform and Figure 2.3(b) shows the DSB-SC voltage waveform.

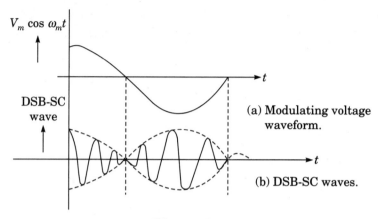

(a) Modulating voltage waveform.

(b) DSB-SC waves.

Figure 2.3

2.5 SINGLE SIDEBAND MODULATION

The terminology indicates that after modulation, one sideband will exist. In other words, we have to eliminate both the carrier and one of the sidebands. The single sideband halves the bandwidth needed for transmission. The single sideband saves the power in the practical application. The SSB is used mostly for the following:

(a) point-to-point communication
(b) land, air and maritime mobile communication
(c) television
(d) telemetry
(e) military communication
(f) radio, navigation and amateur radio

2.5.1 To Develop SSB Signal

The SSB signal is developed in stages. Suppose, an SSB signal is to be generated with a carrier signal of 10 MHz. If a passband filter provides a certain attenuation within 600 Hz, then it is very difficult to construct a filter of sharp selectivity having a percentage frequency change of $\dfrac{600 \times 100}{10 \times 10^6} = 0.006\%$. That is why, it is wise to develop the SSB signal in stages.

Figure 2.4 shows the block diagram describing the stages being carried for production of SSB signal. Say, for example, the carrier frequency for the Ist stage is f_{c1} (= 100 kHz) and in the second stage, the carrier frequency is kept f_{c2} (= 10 MHz). Now, the carrier signal and the base band signal (modulating signal) are passed through a balanced modulator to produce DSB-SC signal. If the modulating signal is of 600 Hz, then the upper sideband of the modulated

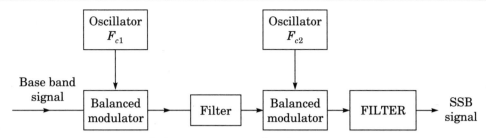

Figure 2.4 Block diagram for development of SSB signal.

signal will have the frequency $100 + \dfrac{.6}{2} = 100.3$ kHz. After filtration, say, we get the signal 100.3 kHz.

Let us assume that the output of the balanced modulator ranges from 100.3 kHz to 103 kHz. The selectivity percentage for the first stage will be $\dfrac{600}{100 \times 10^3} \times 100 = 0.6\%$. This percentage is quite practicable to design a filter. With this output, the signal is passed to the next balanced modulator. The frequency of the two sideband signals of the output of the balanced modulator will be 10 MHz + 100.3 kHz and 10 MHz – 100.3 kHz. Hence, for the fixed attenuation, the bandwidth will be

$$100.3 - (-100.3) = 200.6 \text{ kHz}$$

This is nothing but $\dfrac{200.6 \times 10^3}{10 \times 10^6} \times 100 = 2\%$ of the carrier frequency. The filter design at this stage is also practicable. Thus, the range of the upper sideband signal will lie between 10 MHz + 100.3 kHz to 10 MHz + 103 kHz, since the second balanced modulator ranges from 100.3 kHz to 103 kHz. Similarly, if it is desired, lower sideband signal can be obtained by using a proper filter.

Concept of balanced modulator

Figure 2.5(a) and 2.5(b) show the two circuits of balanced modulator. Figure 2.5(b) describes push-pull amplifier. Both the carrier signals of voltage V_2 and the modulating signal of voltage V_1 are fed into the push-pull amplifier as input. In the gates of the FET circuit, the carrier voltage is applied in phases. Whereas the modulating voltage is applied on the two gates at 180° phase difference with each other. Hence, the voltage applied on one gate is $V_1 + V_2$ and to the other gate the voltage applied is $V_1 - V_2$.

In Figure 2.5(a), two diodes are applied instead of FET. Even Class A amplifiers utilising transistors can also be applied. Considering the perfect symmetry, the two drain currents of Figure 2.5(b) will be

$$i_{d1} = C_1 + C_2(V_1 + V_2) + C_3(V_1 + V_2)^2$$
$$i_{d2} = C_1 + C_2(V_1 - V_2) + C_3(V_1 - V_2)^2$$
$$i_{d1} = C_1 + C_2 V_1 + C_2 V_2 + C_3 V_1^2 + 2C_3 V_1 V_2 + C_3 V_2^2$$
$$i_{d2} = C_1 + C_2 V_1 - C_2 V_2 + C_3 V_1^2 - 2C_3 V_1 V_2 + C_3 V_2^2$$

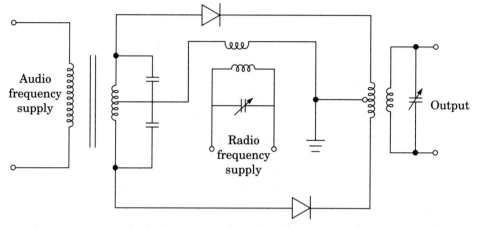

(a)   Balanced modulator utilising the diode.

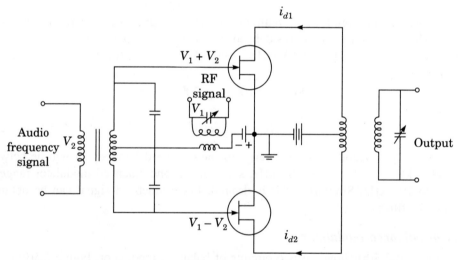

(b)   Balanced modulator utilising the field effect transistor.

Figure 2.5

where C_1, C_2 and C_3 are constants. Therefore, the primary current will be

$$i_p = i_{d1} - i_{d2}$$
$$= 2C_2V_2 + 4C_3V_1V_2$$

Let $V_1 = V_c \sin \omega_c t$

and $V_2 = V_m \sin \omega_m t$

The output voltage will be,

$$= ki_p \quad \text{(where } k \text{ is constant of proportionality)}$$
$$= k[2C_2V_m \sin \omega_m t + 4C_3V_cV_m \sin \omega_c t \sin \omega_m t]$$

$$= 2kC_2V_m \sin \omega_m t + 4C_3kV_cV_m \sin \omega_c t \sin \omega_m t$$

$$= 2kC_2V_m \sin \omega_m t + 2kC_3V_cV_m [\cos(\omega_c - \omega_m)t - \cos(\omega_c + \omega_m)t]$$

$$= A \sin \omega_m t + B \cos(\omega_c - \omega_m)t - B \cos(\omega_c + \omega_m)t$$

where $A = 2kC_2V_m$

$B = 2kC_3V_cV_m$

Thus, in the ideal symmetrical condition, the carrier signal is eliminated. The two sidebands and modulating frequencies exist in the output of balanced modulator.

2.6 VESTIGIAL SIDEBAND MODULATION (VSB)

The doubled sideband system is usually large. There is a way to reduce the bandwidth by considering the fact that the entire signal information exists in each of the two sidebands of the modulated carrier. Figure 2.6 describes the same. Here, we are only using the upper sideband, the carrier and suppress the lower sideband.

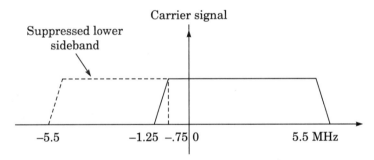

Figure 2.6 Vestigial sideband.

Hence, Figure 2.6 is an example of vestigial sideband signal modulation. Therefore, in case of vestigial sideband, a part of one sideband is suppressed. In practice also, removal of one sideband from the modulated signal is also practically impossible. Over and above, the outcome of the vestigial sideband is the effective saving of bandwidth and also the design of filter becomes much more easier for removal of the part of the sideband instead of the full sideband.

2.6.1 Mathematical Analysis of Vestigial Sideband Modulation

Let a carrier signal of angular frequency ω_c be amplitude modulated by a sinusoid of angular frequency ω_m. The resultant waveform will be

$$f(t) = A(1 + m \cos \omega_m t) \cos \omega_c t$$

$$= A \cos \omega_c t + mA \cos \omega_c t \cos \omega_m t$$

$$= A \cos \omega_c t + \frac{mA}{2} [\cos(\omega_c + \omega_m)t + \cos(\omega_c - \omega_m)t]$$

If one of the sidebands is removed, then the resultant waveform will be

$$f_1(t) = A \cos \omega_c t + \frac{mA}{2} \cos (\omega_c + \omega_m)t$$

$$= A \cos \omega_c t + \frac{mA}{2} [\cos \omega_c t \cos \omega_m t - \sin \omega_c t \sin \omega_m t]$$

$$= A \left(1 + \frac{m}{2} \cos \omega_m t\right) \cos \omega_c t - \frac{mA}{2} \sin \omega_m t \sin \omega_c t$$

Let
$$A(t) \cos \alpha = A(1 + \frac{m}{2} \cos \omega_m t)$$

$$A(t) \sin \alpha = \frac{mA}{2} \sin \omega_m t$$

$$= A(t) \cos \alpha \cos \omega_c t - A(t) \sin \alpha \sin \omega_c t$$

$$= A(t) \cos (\omega_c t + \alpha)$$

where
$$A(t) = \sqrt{A^2 \left(1 + \frac{m}{2} \cos \omega_m t\right)^2 + \left(\frac{mA}{2} \sin \omega_m t\right)^2}$$

$$= \sqrt{A^2 (1 + \frac{m^2}{4} \cos^2 \omega_m t + 2\frac{m}{2} \cos \omega_m t) + \frac{m^2 A^2}{4} \sin^2 \omega_m t}$$

$$= \sqrt{A^2 \left(1 + \frac{m^2}{4}\right) + A^2 m \cos \omega_m t}$$

$$A(t) \approx \sqrt{A^2 + A^2 m \cos \omega_m t}$$

$$= A(1 + m \cos \omega_m t)^{1/2}$$

$$\approx A \left(1 + \frac{m}{2} \cos \omega_m t\right)$$

But practically, if is very difficult to get the above value by filtering out the entire lower sideband without affecting the amplitude and phase of the lower frequencies of upper sideband and carrier.

2.7 MULTIPLEXING

Multiplexing is the method by virtue of which many individual messages can be transmitted simultaneously over a single communication channel. This is made possible by translating each message to a different position in the frequency spectrum. That is why, the same is also called frequency multiplexing. Afterwards, each and individual message is separated by filtering. There are two types of multiplexing techniques:

   (i) Frequency-division multiplexing
   (ii) Time-division multiplexing.

The frequency-division multiplexing utilises analogue modulation systems. But the time-division multiplexing utilises pulse modulation system. The pulse modulation will be explained in detail in a Section 2.19. This helps in the reduction of channel and ultimately the cost of installation and maintenance of more channels is reduced.

2.8 HETERODYNING

The meaning of heterodyning is to mix. The heterodyning process indicates a simple change or translation of carrier frequency. This change in carrier frequency is obtained by heterodyning or mixing the modulated carrier voltage with a locally generated high frequency voltage in a nonlinear device to have at the output a similarly modulated carrier voltage at the different carrier frequency, which is termed the intermediate frequency.

2.9 RECOVERY OF TRANSLATED SIGNAL AND DEMODULATION

The recovery of a translated signal can be made by reverse translation. The reverse translation can be achieved by multiplying the translated signal with $\cos \omega_c t$ where ω_c is the angular frequency of the carrier signal. Suppose, $m(t) \cos \omega_c t$ is a translated signal. Translated signal means the modulated signal. Say, $A_1 \cos \omega_m t$ is the modulating signal and $A_2 \cos \omega_c t$ is the carrier signal. The modulated signal is $A_1 A_2 \cos \omega_m t \cos \omega_c t$. $A_1 A_2 \cos \omega_m t$ is considered as function by $m(t)$. If we separately obtain $m(t)$, then automatically, we will be able to recover translated signal. Mathematically, how can we do it? Multiply $\cos \omega_c t$ with $m(t) \cos \omega_c t$.

$$[m(t) \cos \omega_c t] \cos \omega_c t$$

$$= m(t) \cos^2 \omega_c t$$

$$= m(t) \left[\frac{1}{2} + \frac{1}{2} \cos 2\omega_c t \right]$$

$$= \frac{m(t)}{2} + \frac{m(t)}{2} \cos 2\omega_c t .$$

Thus $m(t)$ is separated. Sometimes, a problem may occur that the auxiliary signal (i.e $\cos \omega_c t$) differs in phase from the auxiliary signal used in the initial translation. If the auxiliary signal used in the initial translation differs by a phase angle θ from the auxiliary signal used in the recovery translation, then the outcome will be as follows:

$$[m(t) \cos \omega_c t] \cos (\omega_c t - \theta)$$

$$= \frac{m(t)}{2} 2 \cos \omega_c t \cos (\omega_c t - \theta)$$

$$= \frac{m(t)}{2} [\cos(2\omega_c t - \theta) + \cos\theta]$$

$$= \frac{m(t)}{2} \cos(2\omega_c t - \theta) + \frac{m(t)}{2} \cos\theta$$

So, we cannot separate $m(t)$ truly because it will be $\dfrac{m(t)}{2} \cos\theta$. Hence, the baseband signal strength will vary except at $\theta = 0°$. Hence, the question stands how we can recover the signal without any loss of its strength.

This is only possible if the auxiliary signal at the recovery point, i.e. the second multiplication point is made synchronous with the auxiliary signal at the first multiplication point.

Suppose, the modulated signal is $A \cos \omega_m t \cos \omega_c t$, where ω_c is the carrier frequency. We have to obtain $\cos \omega_c t$ at the receiving end without any phase difference. The above signal is to be passed to a squaring circuit. The output of the squaring circuit will be,

$$A^2 \cos^2 \omega_m t \cos^2 \omega_c t$$

$$= A^2 \left\{ \frac{1}{2} + \frac{1}{2} \cos 2\omega_m t \right\} \left\{ \frac{1}{2} + \frac{1}{2} \cos 2\omega_c t \right\}$$

$$= \frac{A^2}{4} (1 + \cos 2\omega_m t)(1 + \cos 2\omega_c t)$$

$$= \frac{A^2}{4} \left\{ 1 + \frac{1}{2} \cos 2(\omega_c + \omega_m)t + \frac{1}{2} \cos 2(\omega_c - \omega_m)t + \cos 2\omega_m t + \cos 2\omega_c t \right\}$$

The above output of the squaring circuit is passed to a filter circuit which selects the component $\dfrac{A^2}{4} \cos 2\omega_c t$. Then the same is passed to a frequency divider. The bistable multivibrator can be used as frequency divider. The output of the divider is utilised as the auxiliary signal at the receiving end to demodulate the incoming signal, i.e. the modulated signal. In other words, we can also state that a DSB–SC signal (i.e. $A \cos \omega_c t \cos \omega_m t$) is passed to the squaring synchronizer and the output of the same is utilised at the time of demodulation of modulated wave to have baseband signal. Figure 2.7 shows the Block-Diagram of the same.

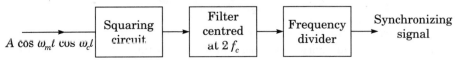

Figure 2.7 Block diagram of development of auxiliary signal at receiver end.

2.10 DEMODULATION OF THE AMPLITUDE MODULATED SIGNAL

The reason for modulation has already been described. Here, we discuss the method of amplitude modulation. When the amplitude modulated wave reaches at the receiving end, then we have to get back the modulating signal or baseband signal. In other words, we have to make it free from carrier signal. The detectors for demodulation are classified as follows:

(a) Square law diode detector.
(b) Linear diode detector.

2.10.1   Square Law Diode Detector

Figure 2.8 shows the basic circuit of square law diode detector.

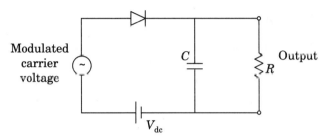

Figure 2.8   Square law diode detector.

The diode is biased positively so that zero signal operating point will work in the non-linear region of dynamic current-voltage characteristic. Figure 2.9 shows the following:

(a) superposition of modulated carrier voltage over the dynamic characteristic of diode, and
(b) output current of diode-detector with resistance load. The dynamic current and voltage characteristic of the diode follows approximately the square law relation.

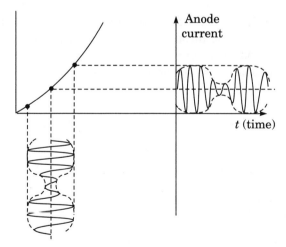

Figure 2.9   Output current of diode detector.

$$i_{\text{anode}} = K_1 \, v_{\text{anode voltage}} + K_2 v^2_{\text{anode voltage}}$$

where

$$v_{\text{anode voltage}} = V_c[1 + m \cos \omega_m t] \cos \omega_c t$$

'm' is the modulation index of amplitude modulated signal, V_c is the amplitude of the carrier voltage. From the expression of the i_{anode}, it is observed that the output current will consist of the frequencies $2\omega_c$, $2(\omega_c + \omega_m)$, $2(\omega_c - \omega_m)$, ω_m and $2\omega_m$. The radio frequency components will be bypassed through the shunt capacitor 'C' as shown in Figure 2.8. The components with frequency ω_m and $2\omega_m$ will appear across the load resistance R as shown in Figure 2.9. The components with frequencies ω_m and $2\omega_m$ will be developed across the load resistance R. The components with frequency 'ω_m' will be the desired output whereas the term with frequency '$2\omega_m$' will develop distortion.

2.10.2 Linear Diode Detector

Figure 2.10 shows the circuit diagram for demodulation by linear diode detector. The modulated carrier voltage should have very high carrier voltage. As a result, with high carrier voltage, the operation may be easily assumed to have taken place over the linear region of the dynamic current-voltage characteristic of the diode. Hence, the rectification characteristic of the diode can easily be utilised.

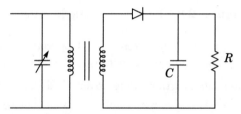

Figure 2.10 Linear diode detector.

Figure 2.11 shows the dynamic characteristic of the diode at linear region. The superposition of modulated carrier voltage on the linear $i_{anode} - v_{anode}$ characteristic of diode is shown. The output voltage with linear diode detector is shown in Figure 2.11. Also, the output voltage with linear diode detector and capacitor is shown in the same figure.

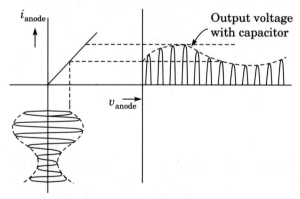

Figure 2.11 Demodulation with linear diode detector.

During the positive half cycle diode conducts and the capacitor will be charged and in the negative half cycle, the capacitor discharges through the resistance. Finally, the output voltage curve with capacitor almost traces the baseband signal. In other words, demodulated voltage will come as output at the end of terminal. Of course, filter is to be provided to smoothen the output voltage.

2.10.3 Mathematical Analysis of Demodulation

In case of square law demodulator or detector, let us consider that the applied signal is

$$A_o + A_c[1 + m(t)] \cos \omega_c t$$

The output of the squaring circuit will be

$$k\{A_o + A_c(1 + m(t)) \cos \omega_c t\}^2$$

$$= k[A_o^2 + A_c^2 (1 + 2m(t) + (m(t^2))) \cos^2 \omega_c t + 2A_o A_c(1 + m(t)) \cos \omega_c t]$$

$$= k\{A_o^2 + A_c^2 \cos^2 \omega_c t + 2A_c^2 m(t) \cos^2 \omega_c t$$

$$+ A_c^2 (m(t))^2 \cos^2 \omega_c t + 2A_o A_c \cos \omega_c t + 2A_o A_c m(t) \cos \omega_c t]$$

$$= k\{A_o^2 + A_c^2 \frac{1}{2}(1 + \cos 2\omega_c t) + 2A_c^2 \frac{m(t)}{2} (1 + \cos 2\omega_c t)$$

$$+ A_c^2 m(t)^2 \frac{1}{2}(1 + \cos 2\omega_c t) + 2A_o A_c \cos \omega_c t + 2A_o A_c m(t) \cos \omega_c t\}$$

$$= k\{A_o^2 + \frac{1}{2}A_c^2 + \frac{1}{2}A_c^2 \cos 2\omega_c t + A_c^2 m(t) + A_c^2 m(t) \cos 2\omega_c t + A_c^2 \frac{(m(t))^2}{2}$$

$$+ A_c^2 \frac{(m(t))^2}{2} \cos 2\omega_c t + 2A_o A_c \cos \omega_c t + 2A_o A_c m(t) \cos \omega_c t\}$$

The dc component and spectral component having frequencies ω_c and $2\omega_c$ are filtered out. The output signal will be

$$k\left(A_c^2 m(t) + \frac{A_c^2 m^2(t)}{2} \right)$$

If $\left| \dfrac{1}{2} m^2(t) \right| \ll m(t)$ or $|m(t)| \ll 2$, then the recovered signal will be distortion free.

2.11 FREQUENCY MODULATION

Frequency modulation is a system in which the amplitude of modulated carrier is kept constant while its frequency varies with the modulating signal. Suppose, an unmodulated or carrier wave is represented by $A \sin (\omega t + \phi)$. If the frequency of it varies with the help of another signal normally of a lower frequency, then the frequency of the carrier will develop a frequency modulated wave. In other words, the carrier signal will be frequency modulated by the modulation signal or baseband signal of lower frequency.

Figure 2.12(a) shows the low frequency voltage waveform and that is nothing but the base band signal or modulating signal. Figure 2.12(b) shows the high frequency carrier signal voltage. Figure 2.12(c) shows the frequency modulated signal voltage.

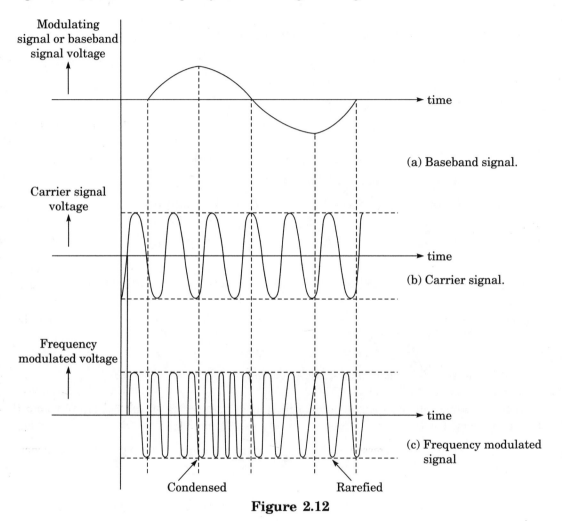

(a) Baseband signal.

(b) Carrier signal.

(c) Frequency modulated signal

Figure 2.12

When the baseband signal voltage is nearby positive peak, the frequency modulated voltage waveform is found condensed, i.e. the frequency of the waveform is increased. Similarly, when the baseband signal voltage is nearby negative peak, the frequency modulated voltage is found rarefied. In this way, frequency modulated signal is developed.

Figure 2.13 describes the waveform of the frequency vs. time at the time of frequency modulation.

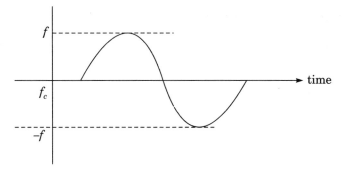

Figure 2.13 Variation of frequency during frequency modulation.

Here, f_c is considered as the carrier frequency. The frequency varies from $f_c + f$ to $f_c - f$ sinusoidally when the frequency of the baseband sinusoidal signal is f.

2.12 MATHEMATICAL EXPRESSION FOR FREQUENCY MODULATED SIGNAL

The frequency modulation is expressed mathematically as follows.

$$f = f_c(1 + kV_m \cos \omega_m t)$$

Figure 2.13 shows the frequency variation with respect to time. The frequency reference for the carrier frequency f_c is taken at the origin. k is proportionality constant. $V_m \cos \omega_m t$ is the instantaneous modulating voltage.

The maximum deviation of the frequency of the particular signal occurs when the instantaneous frequency will be

$$f = f_c (1 \pm kV_m)$$

In other words, the maximum frequency deviation will be $kV_m f_c$.

The instantaneous value of frequency modulated voltage can be determined as follows.

Let us assume the instantaneous value of the amplitude of FM signal is $A \sin \theta$, where θ is the function of carrier angular frequency ω_c and modulating signal angular frequency is ω_m.

Mathematically 'θ' is expressed as $\theta = \int \omega \, dt$ where 'ω' is the modulated angular frequency, represented by

$$\omega = \omega_c (1 + kV_m \cos \omega_m t)$$

since $f = f_c (1 + kV_m \cos \omega_m t)$ at the time of frequency modulation.

$\therefore$

$$\theta = \int \omega_c (1 + kV_m \cos \omega_m t) \, dt$$

$$= \omega_c t + \frac{kV_m \, \omega_c \sin \omega_m t}{\omega_m}$$

$$= \omega_c t + \frac{kV_m f_c \sin \omega_m t}{f_m}$$

Hence, the instantaneous value of the FM voltage is

$$A \sin \left(\omega_c t + \frac{kV_m f_c}{f_m} \sin \omega_m t \right)$$

The modulation index for frequency modulation is the ratio of maximum frequency deviation and modulating frequency. Hence, the modulation index

$$= \frac{kV_m f_c}{f_m}$$

where k—proportionality constant
   V_m—maximum modulating signal voltage
   f_c—carrier frequency

The solution to the instantaneous value of the FM voltage can be made by using BESSEL function. If the instantaneous value of the FM voltage is

$$A \sin (\omega_c t + m_f \sin \omega_m t)$$

where m_f is the modulation index, then the above can be written by using BESSEL function.

$$V = A[J_0(m_f) \sin \omega_c t + J_1(m_f) \{\sin (\omega_c + \omega_m)t$$
$$- \sin (\omega_c - \omega_m)t\} + J_2(m_f) \{\sin (\omega_c + 2\omega_m)t$$
$$+ \sin (\omega_c - 2\omega_m)t\} + J_3(m_f) \{\sin (\omega_c + 3\omega_m)t - \sin (\omega_c - 3\omega_m)t\}$$
$$+ J_4(m_f) \{\sin (\omega_c + 4\omega_m)t + \sin (\omega_c - 4\omega_m)t\} + \cdots$$

where $J_n(m_f)$ is the solution to the equation of form

$$(m_f)^2 \frac{d^2 V}{dm_f^2} + m_f \frac{dV}{dm_f} + (m_f^2 - n^2) V = 0$$

and the solution is

$$J_n(m_f) = \left(\frac{m_f}{2}\right)^n \left[\frac{1}{\lfloor n} - \frac{\left(\frac{m_f}{2}\right)^2}{1!(n+1)!} + \frac{\left(\frac{m_f}{2}\right)^4}{2!(n+2)!} - \frac{\left(\frac{m_f}{2}\right)^6}{3!(n+3)!} + \cdots \right]$$

The results of the above equation in a tabular form are readily available for different values of n. Hence, the values of carrier and different pair of sidebands can be easily determined if the Bessel function of the first kind is found out from its tabular form result.

2.13   GENERATION OF FREQUENCY MODULATION

Consider a basic reactance modulator. It uses an FET and behaves as a three-terminal reactance that may be connected across a tank circuit of oscillator to be frequency modulated. Under certain conditions, the impedance z shown in Figure 2.14 between the terminals kk_1 becomes entirely reactive. It can be made capacitive or inductive by just interchanging one component. The value of the reactance is proportional to the transconductance of the device, which in turn depends upon the gate bias and its variation. The FET shown in Figure 2.14 can be replaced by a bipolar transistor.

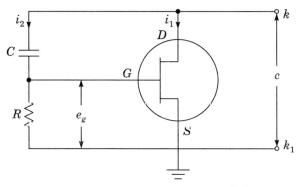

Figure 2.14 Basic reactance modulation.

2.13.1   Mathematical Analysis of Reactance Modulator

A voltage 'e' is applied to the terminal kk_1. The resulting current is calculated as follows.

$$e_g = i_2 R = \frac{Re}{R - jX_c}$$

The FET drain current will be

$$i_1 = g_m\, e_g = \frac{g_m Re}{R - jX_c}$$

The impedance seen at the terminals kk_1 will be

$$z = \frac{e}{i_1} = \frac{e}{\dfrac{g_m Re}{R - jX_c}}$$

$$= \frac{R - jX_c}{g_m R}$$

$$= \frac{1}{g_m}\left(1 - j\,\frac{X_c}{R}\right)$$

Assuming $X_c \gg R$,

$$z = -\frac{jX_c}{g_m R}$$

Hence, the value of reactance 'X_e' $= \dfrac{X_c}{g_m R} = \dfrac{1}{2\pi f g_m CR} = \dfrac{1}{2\pi f C_s}$ where $C_s = g_m RC$

Usually X_c is made 5 to 10 times of R. Let us assume the factor to be n, then $X_c = nR$ at carrier frequency.

$$X_c = \frac{1}{\omega C} = nR$$

or

$$C = \frac{1}{\omega n R} = \frac{1}{2\pi f\, nR}$$

Hence,

$$C_s = g_m RC = \frac{g_m}{2\pi f n}$$

2.14 PRACTICAL ILLUSTRATION OF FM GENERATION

FM can be generated utilising direct method or indirect method. In the *direct method*, the tank circuit parameters are varied by the modulating voltage. The reactor modulator and varactor modulator are illustrations of this method. The instantaneous frequency deviation is directly proportional to the modulating signal in case of direct FM. The frequency of oscillation is not, of course, directly varied in case of *indirect method*.

Figure 2.15 describes how FM signal is generated using reactance modulator. There are two major components of the circuit. One is colpits oscillator and the other is reactance modulator.

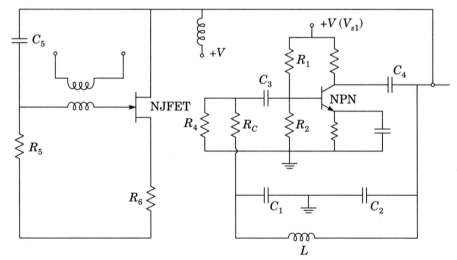

Figure 2.15 Practical circuit of FM generator.

The main components of colpits oscillator are:

(a) V_{s1}
(b) NPN transistor

(c) R_1 and R_2

(d) $C_1 = C_2$

(e) L

(f) R_3 and R_4

The main components of the reactance modulator are

(a) C_5

(b) R_5

The value of the reactance for C_5 is very much higher than the resistance R_5.

2.15 COMPARISON BETWEEN FREQUENCY AND AMPLITUDE MODULATION

The merits and demerits of frequency modulation and amplitude modulation can be compared as follows (Table 2.1)

Table 2.1 Merits and demerits of frequency modulation and amplitude modulation

Frequency modulation	Amplitude modulation
The amplitude of the frequency modulated wave is constant. Hence, it is independent of the modulation depth.	The amplitude of the amplitude modulated wave is varying and the modulation depth governs the transmitted power
For FM transmitters low level modulation may be used and all the subsequent amplifiers are class C and therefore it is not possible to handle large power compared to average power.	In AM transmitter power up to four times the average power can be handled
The FM is more efficient due to class 'C' amplifiers and all these amplifiers handle constant power.	AM is not so efficient compared to FM
All the transmitted powers in FM are useful.	Most of the powers are transmitted carrier. Hence, there is no chance of modulation changes for those powers
The amplitude variations in FM receivers can be removed with amplitude limiters. Hence, FM reception is not much affected by noise	The AM reception is more affected by noise.
In case of FM, the noise can be reduced further by increasing the deviation	In case of AM, the noise cannot be reduced by increasing the deviation since it is not possible 100% modulation without causing severe distortion.
There is less adjacent channel interference in FM stations in case of FM broadcasts	The adjacent channel interference in AM stations is more as compared to FM stations
FM broadcasts operate in the upper VHF and UHF frequency ranges. Hence the noise is less.	AM broadcasts operate in the MF and HF ranges. Hence the noise is more.
It is possible to operate several independent transmitters on the same frequency with less interference	Interference is more in case of AM for operating several independent transmitters on the same frequency.

(Contd.)

Table 2.1 Merits and demerits of frequency modulation and amplitude modulation *(Contd.)*

Frequency modulation	Amplitude modulation
A wide channel is required by FM. It is about ten times as large as AM	A wide channel is not required
FM transmitting and receiving equipments are more complex for modulation and demodulation.	AM transmitting and receiving equipments are not so complex for modulation and demodulation.
The area of reception for FM is small.	The area of reception for AM is large.

2.16 DEFINITION OF PRE-EMPHASIS AND DE-EMPHASIS

Pre-emphasis is the boosting of the higher modulating frequencies in accordance with a pre-arranged curve. *De-emphasis* is the cutting of the artificially boosted higher modulating frequencies at the receiver, i.e. compensation at the receiver. The pre-emphasis and de-emphasis are essential because the noise has a greater effect on the higher modulating frequencies than the lower ones. Suppose, two modulating signals have the same amplitude. One of them is pre-emphasized to twice the amplitude and the other is kept constant.

Obviously, the receiver has to de-emphasize the first signal by a factor two. Before demodulation, the noise interference will affect both the modulating signals, hence, after de-emphasizing, the noise sideband voltages of the pre-emphasized signal will be reduced to a great extent compared to that of the non-pre-emphasized signal. Therefore, pre-emphasis process in an FM-transmitter amplifies high frequency more than the low frequency audio-signal to reduce the effect of noise. On the other hand, de-emphasis process in an FM receiver reduces the amplitudes of high frequency audio signals down to their original value to counteract the effect of pre-emphasis network of transmitter.

Figure 2.16 shows the pre-emphasis circuit. The standard value of L/R of the output circuit is 75 µs. Figures 2.17 and 2.18 show the two de-emphasis circuits. In Figure 2.18, the time constant of the output circuit is 75 µs.

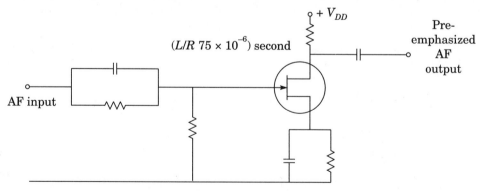

Figure 2.16 Pre-emphasis circuit.

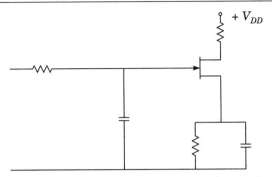

Figure 2.17   De-emphasis circuit no. 1.

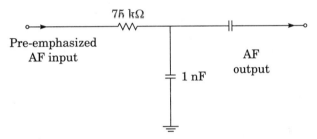

Figure 2.18   De-emphasis circuit no. 2.

2.17   PHASE MODULATION

The phase modulation is the system where the phase of the carrier is varied but the amplitude of the same remains constant. If the phase ϕ in the equation $A \sin (\omega_c t + \phi)$ is varied so that its magnitude is proportional to the instantaneous amplitude of the modulating voltage, the wave is termed the phase modulated wave. The general expression of the phase modulated wave is $A \sin (\omega_c t + \phi_m \sin \omega_m t)$ where $\phi_m \sin \omega_m t$ is the modulating signal. For uniformity, the modulation index for phase is taken equal to ϕ_m, i.e. the maximum value of phase change. Hence, the phase modulated wave can be represented as

$$A \sin (\omega_c t + m_p \sin \omega_m t)$$

where m_p is the modulation index for phase modulation.

2.18   COMPARISON BETWEEN FREQUENCY AND PHASE MODULATIONS

The comparison between frequency modulation and phase modulation can be tabulated as follows (Table 2.2).

Table 2.2 Comparison between frequency modulation and phase modulation

Frequency modulation	Phase modulation
The frequency deviation is proportional to the amplitude of the modulating voltage.	The phase deviation is proportional to the amplitude of the modulating signal.
The frequency modulation is a form of phase modulation since the FM vector has a phase lead or lag with respect to the carrier frequency reference rotating with a constant angular velocity.	Although the phase deviation is independent of the frequency, yet the phase modulated vector sometimes leads and sometimes lags the reference carrier vector and its instantaneous angular velocity is continuously changing. Thus, it can also be concluded that the some form of frequency change occurs here also.
The modulation index is inversely proportional to the modulation frequency.	The modulation index is proportional to the instantaneous amplitude of the modulating voltage.
With the change of modulating frequency, the FM modulation index will be changed.	With the change of the modulating frequency, the PM modulation will remain constant.

2.19 PULSE MODULATION

The pulse modulation is a method by virtue of the which continuous waveforms are sampled at regular intervals and the information regarding the signal is transmitted at the sampling times. The classification of pulse modulation can be described as follows.

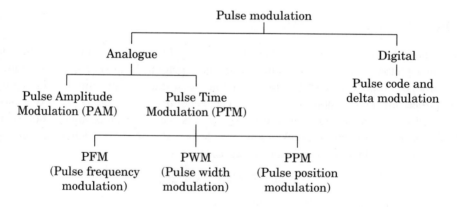

2.19.1 Pulse Amplitude Modulation

The pulse amplitude modulation (PAM) system is the pulse modulation system in which the signal is sampled at regular intervals and each sample is kept proportional to the amplitude of the signal at the instant of sampling. Generally, the pulse amplitude modulation is of two types:

(a) Double polarity PAM.
(b) Single polarity PAM.

Figure 2.19(a) shows the waveform of the signal. Figure 2.19(b) shows the double polarity PAM. Figure 2.19(c) shows the single polarity PAM. In case of single polarity PAM, the fixed

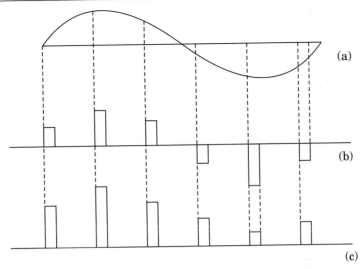

Figure 2.19 Generation of PAM signals.

dc level is added to the signal for ensuring the pulses positive all the time. The main problem is that it does not develop constant amplitude pulses and that is why, it is not frequently used.

Generation and demodulation of PAM pulses

The PAM pulses are generated by applying the signal to be converted to PAM as input of an 'AND' gate and pulses at the sampling frequency as the input of the same AND gate. The output of the gate will be the pulses at the sampling rate being equal to the amplitude of the signal voltage at each instant. The pulses are then passed through a pulse shaping network which provides flat-tops of the pulses. To develop constant amplitude pulse, frequency modulation is employed and the system becomes PAM–FM. In the receiver, the pulses are first of all recovered with a standard FM demodulator. Then the output is sent to the diode detector and low pass filter.

The cut-off frequency of the filter is to be made high enough to pass the highest signal frequency, but at the same time, it is to be made low enough to remove the sampling frequency ripple. Then the original will be reproduced.

Figures 2.20(a) and 2.20(b) describe the circuit diagrams of natural sampling and flat top sampling. The PAM demodulator is an envelope detector. It detects the shape of the input envelope. The variations in the output voltage increase and decrease proportionally, the output waveform follows the shape of the input envelope.

Figure 2.21 shows the circuit for PAM demodulation.

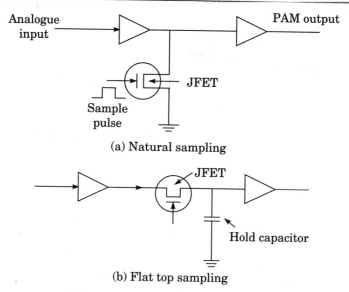

(a) Natural sampling

(b) Flat top sampling

Figure 2.20 PAM generation.

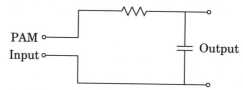

Figure 2.21 Circuit for PAM demodulation.

2.20 PULSE TIME MODULATION

The pulse time modulation (PTM) is a pulse modulation system in which the signal is sampled and each sample has constant amplitude. Usually, it is of three types:

(a) Pulse frequency modulation
(b) Pulse width modulation
(c) Pulse position modulation.

Pulse frequency modulation has no significant practical application. Pulse width modulation and pulse position modulation are the systems which are generally used in practice.

2.20.1 Pulse Width Modulation

In case of pulse width modulation, the starting time and amplitude of each pulse are kept fixed but the width of each pulse is made proportional to the amplitude of the signal at that instant.

Figure 2.22(a) shows the signal. The amplitude of the signal at points A, B, and C are assumed 0.9 volt, 0.5 volt and –0.4 volt. If the width corresponding to zero amplitude is considered 1 μs, then the pulse widths corresponding to the points A, B, and C are considered

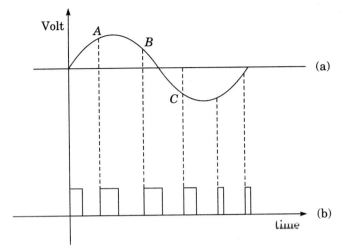

Figure 2.22 Pulse width modulation.

1.9 μs, 1.5 μs and 0.6 μs. It is also considered that the signal amplitude will vary between +1 volt to –1 volt. Hence, width will vary between 2 μs to 0 μs. On the above assumption, it is quite obvious that negative pulse width will not exist.

Generation and demodulation of pulse width modulation

The pulse width modulation is generated by trigger pulses at the sampling rate by controlling the starting time of pulses from a monostable multivibrator and by feeding the signal for controlling the duration of the pulses.

Figure 2.23 shows the circuit for monostable multivibrator generating pulse width modulation. The pulse width at the output depends on the voltage at which the capacitor C is charged. If the voltage is varied with the signal voltage, a series of rectangular pulses of different widths will be found out.

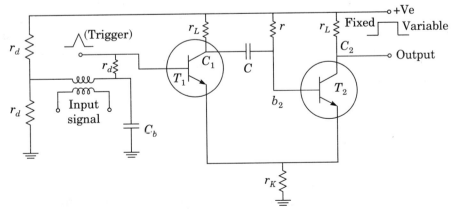

Figure 2.23 Development of PWM signal by monostable multivibrator.

The circuit in Figure 2.23 serves the purpose of sampling as well as developing PWM. The function of the circuit can be explained as follows:

(a) The stable state of multivibrator is T_1 off and T_2 on.
(b) The switch T_1 is on by applying trigger pulse.
(c) The voltage at C_1 falls as T_1 begins to draw collector current.
(d) The voltage at b_2 falls and T_2 is switched off.
(e) Now capacitor 'C' starts charging through resistance r.
(f) After a time depending on the supply voltage and rc time constant, b_2 will be sufficiently positive to switch on T_2.
(g) T_1 is simultaneously switched off.
(h) The period of time during which T_2 is off is the pulse duration. The pulse duration is very short compared to the highest frequencies and as a result no real distortion arises through changes in signal amplitude while T_2 is off.

The demodulation of pulse width modulation is done by passing the same in an integrating circuit from which the signal that is developed will have an amplitude at any time being proportional to the pulse width at that time.

2.20.2   Pulse Position Modulation

The pulse position modulation (PPM) is the system where the amplitude and width of the pulses are kept constant but the position of each pulse in relation to the position of the recurrent reference pulse is varied by each instantaneous sampled value of the modulating wave. The recurrent reference pulse is provided by the transmitter which sends synchronizing pulses to operate timing circuits in the receiver.

Generation and demodulation of pulse position modulation

The pulse position modulation can be generated very easily from pulse width modulation.

Figures 2.24(b) shows the PWM signal corresponding to a modulating signal as shown in Figure 2.24(a). The train of pulses as shown in Figure 2.24(b) may be differentiated and the pulse will be as shown in Figure 2.24(c). Thus, there will be positive going narrow pulses corresponding to leading edges and negative going pulses corresponding to trailing edges. Here, the position of the trailing edges of an unmodulated pulse is counted as zero displacement and the other trailing edges arrive earlier or later so that the width of the pulse will remain constant. (The unmodulated pulse is nothing but the pulse obtained when the signal value is zero.) Therefore, there will be time displacement other than zero and this time displacement is proportional to the instantaneous value of the signal voltage. The differential pulses corresponding to leading edges are removed with a diode clipper or rectifier and the remaining pulses as shown in Figure 2.24(d) are position modulated.

In case of demodulation, the PPM is first of all converted to PWM. This is done by a flip-flop or bistable multivibrator. One input of the multivibrator triggers receives trigger pulses from a local generator and that is synchronized by trigger pulses obtained from the transmitter. These triggers are utilised to switch off one of the stages of the flip-flop. The PPM pulses are applied to the other base of the flip-flop and that stage is switched 'ON'. The period of time

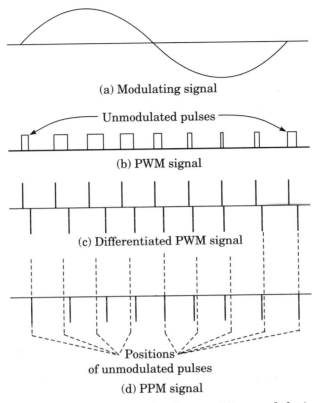

(a) Modulating signal

Unmodulated pulses

(b) PWM signal

(c) Differentiated PWM signal

Positions
of unmodulated pulses

(d) PPM signal

Figure 2.24   Process of pulse position modulation.

during which the particular stage is 'OFF' will depend on the time displacement of each individual PPM pulse. The PPM pulse is to be demodulated as per usual procedure.

2.20.3   Practical Circuit Diagrams for PAM, PWM, PPM

Figures 2.25 to 2.30 describe the practical circuit diagrams. In Figure 2.25 for PAM modulation FET is used as a switching device. The switches are generally made of diodes, transistors, FETs or ICs. The signal to be modulated must be fed to a switch which is operated by sampling signal. In this circuit component and equipments required are FET, Diode, resistors, capacitors and CRO signal generators. In Figure 2.26 PAM demodulation circuit is shown. PAM demodulator is an envelope detector. Figure 2.27 describes the modulation circuit of PWM. IC 555, diode, resistors, capacitors and pots are used for developing this circuit. A square wave is passed to pin no. 2 of the 555 IC through a differentiator. The timer is configured in the monostable mode. When the modulating input is zero, the monostable multivibrator produces mono pulses. But when the voltage at pin 5 (controlling voltage) is applied, the width of the pulse changes according to the amplitude of the input signal. Figure 2.28 circuit diagram describes PWM demodulation.

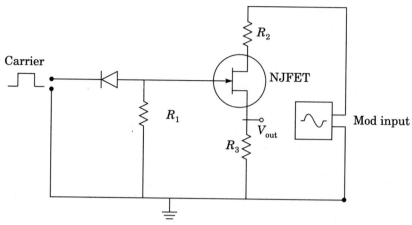

Figure 2.25 Circuit diagram for pulse amplitude modulation.

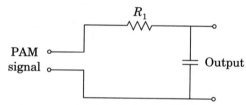

Figure 2.26 Circuit diagram for PAM demodulation.

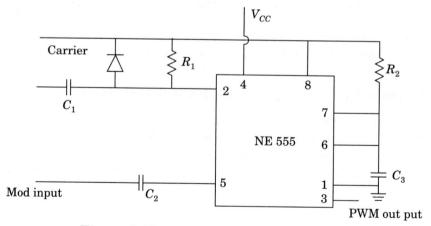

Figure 2.27 Modulation circuit of PWM.

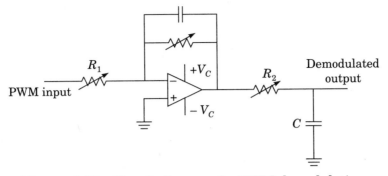

Figure 2.28 Circuit diagram for PWM demodulation.

The pulse width modulated signal is demodulated using an integrator. The integrator is designed in such a way that its passband gives the modulating signal in the output. The filter at the output reduces the high frequency noise in the output. Figure 2.29 shows the circuit diagram of PPM modulation. IC 7400, IC 7486 and capacitors are required for generation of PPM signal.

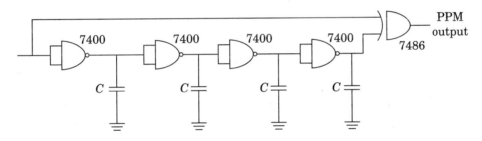

Figure 2.29 Circuit diagram for PPM modulation.

In pulse position modulation the position of a pulse with respect to the reference pulses in each cycle changes proportional to the modulating input signal. Here, the PWM input is given to an XOR directly and also through a delay circuit. The output of the XOR gate will be the PPM signal. Figure 2.30 shows the circuit diagram of PPM demodulation. The demodulation circuit of a PPM is a single toggle flip-flop. The clock input to the flip-flop is obtained by passing PPM through a NOT gate. This produces a PWM wave at the output.

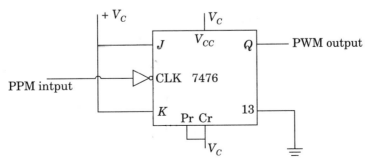

Figure 2.30 Circuit diagram for PPM demodulation.

2.20.4 Pulse Code Modulation

The pulse code modulation is the system in which the signal is subdivided into a number of standard levels. The levels are transmitted in a binary code. The process which is applied, is called quantization. For example, a signal amplitude 6.8 volt at any time will not be sent as 6.8 volt pulse just like PAM nor as 6.8 μs wide pulse as PWM but it will be sent as the digit 7 since 7 volt is the standard amplitude nearest to 6.8 volt. The digit '7' will be expressed in the binary coding schemes. The binary coding schemes are tabulated as follows (Table 2.3).

Table 2.3 Binary coding scheme

Ordinal number of representation level	Level number as sum of power of 2	Binary number
0		0000
1	2^0	0001
2	2^1	0010
3	$2^1 + 2^0$	0011
4	2^2	0100
5	$2^2 + 2^0$	0101
6	$2^2 + 2^1$	0110
7	$2^2 + 2^1 + 2^0$	0111
8	2^3	1000
9	$2^3 + 2^0$	1001
10	$2^3 + 2^1$	1010
11	$2^3 + 2^1 + 2^0$	1011
12	$2^3 + 2^2$	1100
13	$2^3 + 2^2 + 2^0$	1101
14	$2^3 + 2^2 + 2$	1110
15	$2^3 + 2^2 + 2^1 + 2^0$	1111

The digit '7' is sent as a series of pulses corresponding to number '7' that means for 16 levels (2^4), 4 binary places are required. '7' digit will be equal to 0111. Usually, it is sent as 0PPP, where P is termed pulse and 0 is termed no pulse.

Pulse code modulation and demodulation

Figure 2.31 shows the block diagram of generation of PCM signal.

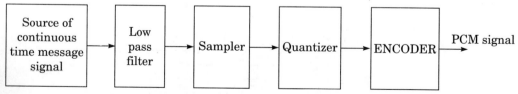

Figure 2.31 Generation of PCM signal.

Figures 2.31, 2.32 and 2.33 show the block diagrams of transmitter, transmission and the receiver of the PCM system. The generation of the PCM signal is made by sampling, quantizing and encoding in a sequential manner. A low pass filter is provided prior to sampling for preventing aliasing of the message signal. The quantizing and encoding are made on the analogue to digital converter. The PCM signal is regenerated in the transmission path due to distortion on account of noise. The demodulation of the PCM is performed as follows. The impaired signals are regenerated and the same are decoded. The reconstruction of train of quantized samples is made by reconstruction filter. An integrating RC circuit is used for reconversion in the receiver.

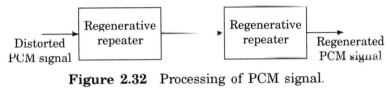

Figure 2.32 Processing of PCM signal.

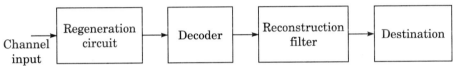

Figure 2.33 Demodulation of PCM signal.

Basic idea about regenerative repeater: The regenerative repeater is a device by virtue of which the effects of distortion and noise are controlled during the transmission of PCM signal through a channel. Figure 2.34 describes the three basic functions which are done by a regenerative repeater. Those are equalisation, timing and decision making. The equalizer shapes the received pulses for compensating the amplitude and phase distortions developed by the transmission characteristics of the channel. The timing circuit provides a periodic pulse train, derived from the received pulses by sampling the equalized pulses at the instant of time where the signal to noise ratio is maximum. The sample is compared to the predetermined threshold in the decision making device. In each bit interval a decision is made, whether the received symbol is 1 or 0, whether the threshold is exceeded or not. Thus the accumulation of distortion and noise in a repeater is entirely removed.

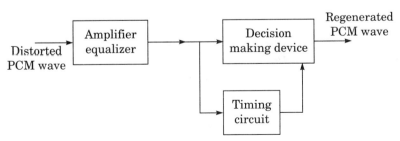

Figure 2.34 Regenerative repeater.

2.20.5 Need for Sampling Theorem in Pulse Modulation

The sampling theorem describes that, if the sampling rate in any modulation system exceeds twice the maximum signal frequency, the original signal can be developed in the receiver with minimal distortion.

Figure 2.35(a) describes the baseband signal. $m(t)$ is the baseband signal. The periodic train of pulses $s(t)$ of unit amplitude and period T_s is shown in Figure 2.35(c). The baseband signal $m(t)$ is multiplied with the train of pulses as shown in Figure 2.35(b). The pulses are of narrow width 'dt'. The above two pulses are applied to a multiplier providing output $s(t)\,m(t)$ as shown in Figure 2.35(d). The multiplier output will be the same as $m(t)$ when the train of pulses occurs, otherwise the multiplier output will be zero. The train of pulses $s(t)$ can be expressed mathematically with the help of Fourier series.

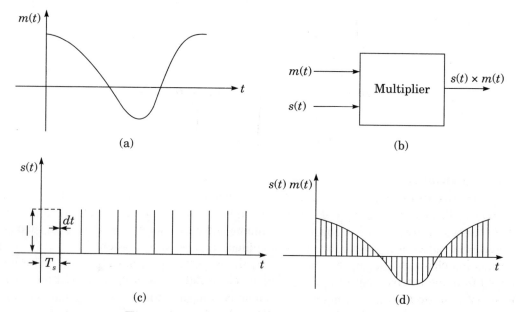

Figure 2.35 Generation sampled pulses.

$$s(t) = \frac{dt}{T_s} + \frac{2dt}{T_s}\left(\cos 2\pi \frac{t}{T_s} + \cos 2 \cdot \frac{2\pi t}{T_s} + ...\right)$$

[**Note:** Value of Ist component is derived as follows:

$$\frac{1}{T_s}\int_0^{dt} 1 \cdot dt = \frac{dt}{T_s}$$

where T_s the time period of sampling and 'dt' is the width of the pulse.]

If f_m is the signal frequency, then the value of $T_s = \dfrac{1}{2 f_m}$.

$$s(t)\ m(t) = \frac{dt}{T_s}\ m(t) + \frac{dt}{T_s}\ [2m(t)\ \cos\ 2\pi\ (2f_m)t + 2m(t)\ \cos\ 2\pi\ ((4f_m)t) + \cdots]$$

From the above equation, it is clear that the spectrum of first term extends 0 to f_m and the spectrum of the second term extends from $(2f_m - f_m)$ to $(2f_m + f_m)$. Figure 2.36(a) shows the magnitude of spectral density of signal and Figure 2.36(b) shows the amplitude of spectrum of sampled signal. From Figure 2.36(b), it is quite clear that if the value of sampling frequency is greater than $2f_m$, then the sampled signal can be recovered properly, whereas if f_s is less than $2f_m$, then there will be overlapping of double sideband suppressed carrier signal with the exact sampled signal. Thus, it is proved that if the sampling rate in any pulse modulation system exceeds twice the maximum signal frequency, the original signal can be developed in the receiver with minimal distortion. This is nothing but the sampling theorem.

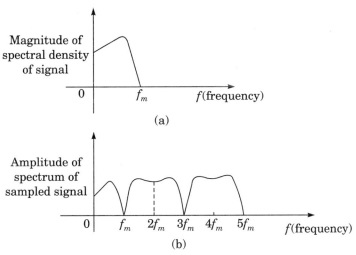

Figure 2.36   Frequency spectrum.

2.21   EXAMPLES OF MODULATION

EXAMPLE 2.1   A 300 watt carrier is modulated to a depth of 80%. Find out the total power in the modulated wave.

Solution
$$P_t = P_c\left(1 + \frac{m^2}{2}\right)$$

where carrier power $P_c = 300$ watt $m =$ modulation index $= 0.80$

$\therefore$ Total power in the modulated wave $= 300\left(1 + \frac{0.8^2}{2}\right) = 300(1.32) = 396$ watt.

EXAMPLE 2.2 The radiation of a broadcast radio transmitter is 12 kW when the modulation percentage is 65%. What is the value of carrier power?

Solution
$$P_c = \frac{P_t}{1 + \frac{m^2}{2}} = \frac{12}{1 + \frac{(0.65)^2}{2}} = \frac{12}{1.21125} = 9.907 \text{ kW}.$$

EXAMPLE 2.3 The antenna current of an AM transmitter is 7 amperes at the time of sending the carrier only. But it enhances to 7.8 ampere when the carrier signal is modulated by a sine wave. Determine the percentage modulation. Also, find out the antenna current when the percentage modulation is changed to 0.85.

Solution
$$\left(\frac{I_t}{I_c}\right)^2 = 1 + \frac{m^2}{2}$$

where I_c is the carrier current I_t is the current at the time of modulation. m is the modulation index.

$$\frac{m^2}{2} = \left(\frac{I_t}{I_c}\right)^2 - 1$$

or
$$m^2 = 2\left\{\left(\frac{I_t}{I_c}\right)^2 - 1\right\}$$

or
$$m = \sqrt{2\left\{\left(\frac{I_t}{I_c}\right)^2 - 1\right\}}$$

$$= \sqrt{2\left\{\left(\frac{7.8}{7}\right)^2 - 1\right\}}$$

$$= \sqrt{2\{1.24 - 1\}}$$

$$= \sqrt{.48} = 0.69$$

Hence, the percentage modulation = 69%

$$I_t = I_c\sqrt{1 + \frac{m^2}{2}}$$

$$= 7\sqrt{1 + \frac{(.85)^2}{2}} \text{ ampere} = 8.16 \text{ A}$$

EXAMPLE 2.4 A particular transmitter radiates 9.5 kW with the carrier unmodulated and 10.5 kW when the carrier is sinusoidally modulated. Find out the modulation index. If another sine wave having 45% modulation is transmitted simultaneously, find out the total radiated power.

Solution

$$\frac{m^2}{2} = \frac{P_t}{P_c} - 1 = \frac{10.5}{9.5} - 1 = 1.105 - 1 = .105$$

$$m^2 = .210$$

$$m = .458$$

For the second part, the modulation index will be

$$m_t = \sqrt{m^2 + m_1^2}$$

where $m = .458$, $m_1 = .45$

$$\therefore \qquad m_t = \sqrt{(.458)^2 + (.45)^2}$$

$$= \sqrt{0.209764 + 0.2025}$$

$$= \sqrt{.412264}$$

$$= .642$$

$$\therefore \qquad P_t = P_c \left(1 + \frac{m_t^2}{2} \right)$$

$$= 9.5 \left(1 + \frac{(.642)^2}{2} \right)$$

$$= 9.5 \times 1.205$$

$$= 11.45 \text{ kW}$$

EXAMPLE 2.5 The antenna current of a transmitter is 11.5 ampere when it is modulated to a depth of 45% by an audio sine wave. It enhances to 12.5 ampere on account of simultaneous modulation by another audio sine wave. Find out the modulation index on account of the second wave.

Solution

$$I_c = \frac{I_t}{\sqrt{1 + \frac{m^2}{2}}} = \frac{11.5}{\sqrt{1 + \frac{(0.45)^2}{2}}}$$

$$= \frac{11.5}{\sqrt{1 + \frac{0.2025}{2}}} = \frac{11.5}{\sqrt{1.10125}}$$

$$= \frac{11.5}{1.0494} = 10.9586 \text{ ampere}$$

$$m_t = \sqrt{2\left[\left(\frac{I_t}{I_c}\right)^2 - 1\right]}$$

$$= \sqrt{2\left[\left(\frac{12.5}{10.9586}\right)^2 - 1\right]}$$

$$= 0.776$$

Modulation index due to the second wave $= \sqrt{(0.776)^2 - (0.45)^2}$

$$= \sqrt{.602176 - .2025}$$

$$= \sqrt{0.399676}$$

$$= .632$$

EXAMPLE 2.6 Find out the percentage power saving when the carrier and one of the sidebands are suppressed in an AM wave modulated to a depth of 70%.

Solution

$$P_t = P_c\left(1 + \frac{m^2}{2}\right)$$

$$= P_c\left(1 + \frac{.7^2}{2}\right) = P_c\left(1 + \frac{.49}{2}\right)$$

$$= P_c \times 1.245$$

Sideband power $= P_c \dfrac{m^2}{4} = P_c \times \dfrac{.7^2}{4} = P_c \times \dfrac{.49}{4} = P_c \times .1225$

Saving percentage

$$= \frac{1.245\, P_c - P_c\, .1225}{1.245\, P_c} \times 100\%$$

$$= \frac{1.1225}{1.245} \times 100\%$$

$$= 90.16\%$$

EXAMPLE 2.7 A frequency modulation system is provided with the following data.
  (a) Audio frequency = 550 Hz.
  (b) Audio frequency voltage = 2.5 volt.
  (c) Deviation = 5 kHz.

If the audio frequency voltage is increased to 7.5 volt, what will be the new deviation? If the audio frequency voltage is raised to 12 volt when the audio frequency is dropped to 250 Hz, find out the deviation at that stage. Also, determine the modulation index in each case.

Solution We know, in FM deviation, $\delta = kV_m f_c$.
That means, for a carrier frequency $\delta \propto V_m$

$$\therefore \qquad \frac{\delta}{V_m} = \frac{5}{2.5} = 2 \text{ kHz/volt}$$

Since deviation = 5 kHz and audio frequency voltage = 2.5 volt
When V_m = 7.5 volt, the deviation 'δ' will be 2 × 7.5 = 15 kHz
When V_m = 12 volt, δ = 2 × 12 = 24 kHz
   Change in modulating frequency to 250 Hz will not make any impact on deviation since it is independent of modulating frequency.
The modulation index in the first case will be

$$m_{f_1} = \frac{\text{Deviation}}{\text{Modulating frequency}} = \frac{5}{.55} = 9.09$$

The modulation index in the second case $\dfrac{\text{Deviation}}{\text{Modulating frequency}} = \dfrac{15}{.55} = 27.27$

The modulation index in the third case $\dfrac{\text{Deviation}}{\text{Modulating frequency}} = \dfrac{24}{0.25} = 96$.

EXAMPLE 2.8 A voltage equation is expressed as follows.

$$V = 15 \sin (6.5 \times 10^8 t + 5.55 \text{ in } 1260t)$$

In the above FM wave voltage expression, determine the following:

(a) Carrier frequency
(b) Modulating frequency
(c) Modulation index
(d) Maximum deviation

   Also, determine the power to be dissipated in a 12 Ω resistor applying the above FM wave.

Solution From the voltage equation of FM wave $V = 15 \sin (6.5 \times 10^8 t + 5.5 \sin 1260t)$

We can write the following, carrier frequency $= \dfrac{6.5 \times 10^8}{2\pi} = 1.035 \times 10^8$ Hz

$$\text{Modulating frequency} = \frac{1260}{2\pi} = 200.64 \text{ Hz.}$$

$$\text{Modulation index} = 5.5$$

$$\text{Deviation} = \text{modulation index} \times \text{modulating frequency}$$

$$= 5.5 \times 200.64$$

$$= 1103.52 \text{ Hz}$$

Power to be dissipated

$$= \frac{(V_{rms})^2}{resistance}$$

$$= \frac{(15/\sqrt{2})^2}{12} = \frac{225}{24} = 9.375 \text{ watt}$$

EXAMPLE 2.9 What is the bandwidth required for an FM signal in which the modulating frequency is 3 kHz and the maximum deviation is 15 kHz.

Solution Modulation index $= m_f = \dfrac{\delta}{f_m} = \dfrac{15}{3} = 5$

x (m_f)	J_0	J_1	J_2	J_3	J_4	J_5	J_6	J_7	J_8	J_9	J_{10}	J_{11}	J_{12}	J_{13}	J_{14}	J_{15}	J_{16}
0.00	1.00	—	—	—	—	—	—	—	—	—	—	—	—	—	—	—	—
0.25	0.98	0.12	—	—	—	—	—	—	—	—	—	—	—	—	—	—	—
0.5	0.94	0.24	0.03	—	—	—	—	—	—	—	—	—	—	—	—	—	—
1.0	0.77	0.44	0.11	0.02	—	—	—	—	—	—	—	—	—	—	—	—	—
1.5	0.51	0.56	0.23	0.06	0.01	—	—	—	—	—	—	—	—	—	—	—	—
2.0	0.22	0.58	0.35	0.13	0.03	—	—	—	—	—	—	—	—	—	—	—	—
2.5	−0.05	0.50	0.45	0.22	0.07	0.02	—	—	—	—	—	—	—	—	—	—	—
3.0	−0.26	0.34	0.49	0.31	0.13	0.04	0.01	—	—	—	—	—	—	—	—	—	—
4.0	−0.40	−0.07	0.36	0.43	0.28	0.13	0.05	0.02	—	—	—	—	—	—	—	—	—
5.0	−0.18	−0.33	0.05	0.36	0.39	0.26	0.13	0.05	0.02	—	—	—	—	—	—	—	—
6.0	0.15	−0.28	−0.24	0.11	0.36	0.36	0.25	0.13	0.06	0.02	—	—	—	—	—	—	—
7.0	0.30	0.00	−0.30	−0.17	0.16	0.35	0.34	0.23	0.13	0.06	0.02	—	—	—	—	—	—
8.0	0.17	0.23	−0.11	−0.29	−0.10	0.19	0.34	0.32	0.22	0.13	0.06	0.03	—	—	—	—	—
9.0	−0.09	0.24	0.14	−0.18	−0.27	−0.06	0.20	0.33	0.30	0.21	0.12	0.06	0.03	0.01	—	—	—
10.0	−0.25	0.04	0.25	0.06	−0.22	−0.23	−0.01	0.22	0.31	0.29	0.20	0.12	0.06	0.03	0.01	—	—
12.0	0.05	−0.22	−0.08	0.20	0.18	−0.07	−0.24	−0.17	0.05	0.23	0.30	0.27	0.20	0.12	0.07	0.03	0.01
15.0	−0.01	0.21	0.04	−0.19	−0.12	0.13	0.21	0.03	−0.17	−0.22	−0.09	0.10	0.24	0.28	0.25	0.18	0.12

n or Order Table

From Table, it is seen that the highest 'J' coefficient included for this value of m_f is J_8. This means that for a modulation index all higher values of Bessel functions which have values less than 0.01 may be ignored. Considering the eighth pair of sidebands, the bandwidth required will be

$$\Delta = f_m \times \text{highest needed sideband} \times 2$$

$$= 3 \times 8 \times 2 = 48 \text{ kHz.}$$

EXAMPLE 2.10 A 30 MHz carrier is modulated by a 500 Hz audio sine wave. If the carrier voltage is 5 volt and the maximum deviation is 12 kHz. Develop the voltage expression of the modulated wave for (a) FM and (b) PM. If the modulating frequency is now changed to 2500 Hz, develop the expression of FM and PM maintaining the other factors constant.

Solution Carrier frequency

$$\omega_c = 2\pi \times 30 \times 10^6$$

$$= 60\pi \times 10^6 \text{ rad/second}$$

Modulating signal frequency

$$\omega_m = 2\pi \times 500 = 1000\pi$$

The modulation index will be

$$m = m_f = m_p = \frac{\delta}{f_m} = \frac{12000}{500}$$

$$= 24$$

Hence, the voltage expression for FM wave is

(a) $V_1 = 5 \sin (60\pi \times 10^6 t + 24 \sin 1000\pi t)$

The voltage expression for PM wave is

(b) $V_2 = 5 \sin (60\pi \times 10^6 t + 24 \sin 1000\pi t)$

Now, when the modulating frequency is changed to 2500 Hz, then the modulation index for FM will be (12000/2500) = 4.8. But for PM, modulation index will remain the same.

Hence, the voltage expression for FM will be

$$V_3 = 5 \sin (60\pi \times 10^6 t + 4.8 \sin 1000\pi t)$$

The voltage expression for PM will be,

$$V_4 = 5 \sin (60\pi \times 10^6 t + 24 \sin 1000\pi t)$$

EXAMPLE 2.11 Find out the value of capacitive reactance from a reactance modulator FET having g_m of 12 ms. The gate to source resistance is one-seventh of the reactance of the gate to drain. The frequency of operation is 5 MHz.

Solution We have already derived that the capacitive reactance of a reactance modulator FET

is $\dfrac{g_m}{2\pi\,fn}$.

∴

$$C_s = \frac{g_m}{2\pi\,fn}$$

or

$$2\pi f C_s = \frac{g_m}{n} = \frac{1}{X_{cs}}$$

∴

$$X_{cs} = \frac{n}{g_m} = \frac{7}{12 \times 10^{-3}} = 0.583 \times 10^3$$

$$= 583 \ \Omega$$

EXAMPLE 2.12 A FET is utilized as a capacitive reactance modulator. The gate to source resistance is one-eleventh of gate to drain resistance. Mutual conductance of the FET utilized, swings linearly with gate voltage between the limits 0 to 12 ms. The tank circuit of the oscillator is turned to 50 MHz using to 45 pF fixed capacitor.

Determine the total frequency variation when g_m of the FET is varied from zero to maximum by the modulating voltage.

Solution   Let f_1 = minimum frequency

f_2 = maximum frequency

f = average frequency

δ = maximum deviation

C_1 = minimum equivalent capacitance of FET

C_2 = maximum equivalent capacitance of FET

Form the given data $C_1 = 0$ since $g_m = 0$

and
$$C_2 = \frac{g_m}{2\pi fn} = \frac{12 \times 10^{-3}}{2\pi \times 50 \times 10^6 \times 11} = 3.474 \text{ pF}$$

$$\frac{f_2}{f_1} = \frac{\dfrac{1}{2\pi\sqrt{LC}}}{\dfrac{1}{2\pi\sqrt{L(C+C_2)}}}$$

$$= \frac{1}{2\pi\sqrt{LC}} \cdot 2\pi\sqrt{L(C+C_2)}$$

$$= \sqrt{\frac{L(C+C_2)}{LC}}$$

$$= \sqrt{1 + \frac{C_2}{C}}$$

$$= \sqrt{1 + \frac{3.474}{45}} = \sqrt{1.0772} = 1.0379$$

Now,
$$\frac{f_2}{f_1} = \frac{f+\delta}{f-\delta}$$

$\therefore$
$$f + \delta = 1.0379 \, (f - \delta)$$

or
$$f + \delta = 1.0379f - 1.0379\delta$$

or
$$2.0379\delta = .0379f$$

or
$$\delta = \frac{.0379}{2.0379} \times 50 \times 10^6$$

$$= 0.92988 \text{ MHz}$$

$\therefore$ Total frequency variation $= 2 \times .92988 = 1.86$ MHz

EXAMPLE 2.13   The centre frequency of an *LC* oscillator to which a capacitive reactance FET modulator is connected is 75 MHz. The g_m of the FET varies linearly from 1.5 to 2.5 ms, and the bias capacitor reactance is eleven times the resistance of the bias resistor. If the fixed tuning capacitor across the oscillator tank circuit is 26 pF, determine the maximum frequency deviation possible.

Solution

$$C_1 = \frac{1.5 \times 10^{-3}}{2\pi \times 75 \times 10^6 \times 11} = 0.2895 \text{ pF}$$

$$C_2 = \frac{2.5 \times 10^{-3}}{2\pi \times 75 \times 10^6 \times 11} = 0.4825 \text{ pF}$$

$$\therefore \quad \frac{f_2}{f_1} = \sqrt{\frac{C + C_2}{C + C_1}} = \sqrt{\frac{26 + 0.4825}{26 + 0.2895}} = \sqrt{\frac{26.4825}{26.2895}} = 1.0036$$

Now, $$\frac{f_2}{f_1} = \frac{f + \delta}{f - \delta}$$

or $$1.0036 = \frac{f + \delta}{f - \delta}$$

or $$f + \delta = 1.0036f - 1.0036\delta$$

or $$2.0036\delta = .0036f$$

or $$\delta = \frac{.0036}{2.0036} f$$

$$= \frac{.0036}{2.0036} \times 75 \times 10^6$$

$$= .134757 \times 10^6 \text{ MHz}$$

$$= 134.757 \text{ kHz.}$$

EXAMPLE 2.14 A sinusoidal signal is to be transmitted utilizing PCM so that the output signal to quantizing noise ratio is 49.8 dB. Determine the minimum number of representation level L and binary code word length 'n' to obtain the above performance.

Solution The signal to quantizing noise ratio in decibels for PCM system utilizing sinusoidal signal is $(SNR)_{dB} = 1.8 + 20 \log_{10} L$

For a quantizer of midtread type, we may write

$$L = 2^n - 1$$

$$\approx 2^n \text{ for large } n.$$

The signal to quantizing noise therefore, can be written as

$$(SNR)_{dB} = (1.8 + 6n)_{dB}$$

Substituting the given value of the signal to quantization ratio, we get

$$49.8 = 1.8 + 6n$$

$$n = 8$$

EXAMPLE 2.15 A sinusoidal modulating signal of amplitude A_m uses all the representation levels provided for quantization in case of full load condition. Determine the signal to noise ratio in dB assuming number of quantization levels to be 512.

Solution

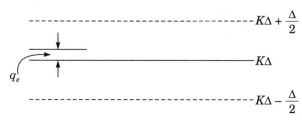

Figure 2.37

Suppose,

L = No. of quantization level

Δ = quantizer step size

n = Code word length

Suppose, quantizing noise is uniformly distributed when the error may take on a sample value q_e anywhere in the interval $(-\Delta/2, \Delta/2)$ with equal likelihood. Under the circumstances, the average power of the quantizing noise, can therefore, be written as

$$P_q = \frac{1}{\Delta} \int_{-\Delta/2}^{+\Delta/2} q_e^2 \, dq_e$$

$$= \frac{\Delta^2}{12}$$

The sinusoidal modulating signal swings between $+A_m$ and $-A_m$. Therefore, the peak to peak excursion of the quantizer input is $2A_m$.

Assuming that L number of quantization levels are provided, the quantizer step size can be obtained as,

$$\Delta = \frac{2A_m}{L}$$

The average quantizing noise power is given by

$$P_q = \frac{\Delta^2}{12} = \frac{(2A_m)^2}{(L)^2} \times \frac{1}{12}$$

$$= \frac{A_m^2}{3L^2}$$

Therefore, the output signal to quantizing noise ratio of the PCM system, for a full load test is given by

$$\text{SNR} = \frac{\dfrac{A_m^2}{2}}{\dfrac{A_m^2}{3L^2}} = \frac{3L^2}{2}$$

Expressing the signal to quantizing noise ratio in decibels, we get

$$(\text{SNR})_{dB} = 10 \log \frac{3}{2} + 20 \log_{10} L$$

$$= 1.8 + 20 \log_{10} L$$

Since, in the problem $L = 512$

$$(\text{SNR})_{dB} = 1.8 + 54.19 = 55.99.$$

EXAMPLE 2.16 How would you develop sampling and reconstruction of low pass signals?

Solution The low pass signal can be sampled by using CD4016 and then it can be reconstructed using an Op-Amp. CD4016 is an analog switch. The analog input signal is sampled utilizing a train of pulses which is equally placed. The sampling produces an output pulse train in which the amplitudes of each pulse correspond to instantaneous amplitude of the modulating signal at the sampling instant. Thus, the switch CD4016 produces the PAM output corresponding to the input given to it. The original signal can be reconstructed at the receiver end if the sampling is done as per the sampling theorem. The reconstruction is an evelope detector.

Figures 2.38 and 2.39 describe the sampling circuit and reconstruction circuit.

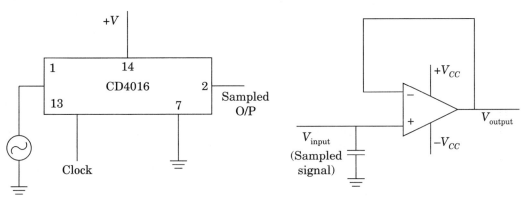

Figure 2.38 Sampling circuit.   **Figure 2.39** Reconstruction circuit.

■ SUMMARY ■

Need for high frequency communication has been explained. Feasibility of the system will be under question if high frequency signal is not developed for communication. For practicable height of an antenna, signal frequency is to be enhanced. Automatically, the concept of modulation arises. Process of superimposition of a low frequency voice information component on a high frequency carrier signal is also described. In this connection, the concept of amplitude modulation is described. In case of amplitude modulation, the amplitude of carrier is made proportional to the instantaneous amplitude of modulating voltage. Amplitude modulated voltage expression is developed. The outcome of amplitude modulated wave is discussed. Two sidebands with the unmodulated carrier frequency are explained. The collector modulation circuit is also shown to explain the amplitude modulation. The concept of double sideband suppressed carrier modulation is discussed with diagram. The concept of single sideband modulation is further discussed. The reason for stagewise development of SSB signal is also explained. An idea is also given about balanced modulator utilizing diode and also field effect transistor. The mathematical expression for the above is also shown.

The concept of vestigial sideband modulation is also given. Mathematical analysis of the same is also described. Transmitting many individual messages over a single communication channel is explained by the concept of multiplexing. Both frequency division multiplexing and time division multiplexing are defined. Definition of heterodyning is also given. The recovery of the translated signal can be made by reverse translation. With mathematical expression the same is explained. Practical methodology is further discussed. Demodulation of the amplitude modulated signal is discussed. Both the procedures of square law detector and linear diode detector are explained with diagrams. Mathematical analysis of demodulation is also shown.

The concept of frequency modulation is discussed in detail. Baseband signal, carrier signal and frequency modulated signal are defined clearly in the context. Mathematical expression of frequency modulated signal with BESSEL function is explained clearly. Basic reactance modulator is explained from the point of view of generation of frequency modulation. Mathematical expression of reactance modulator is also shown. The practical circuit of FM generation is also illustrated. A detailed comparison of frequency and amplitude modulation is tabulated. The merits and demerits of frequency modulation and amplitude modulation are compared effectively. Pre-emphasis and de-emphasis have been defined, circuits of both are also shown.

The concept of phase modulation is discussed. A detailed comparison of frequency and phase modulation is also tabulated.

Pulse modulation is classified in both perspective, i.e. analogue and digital. Analogue is further classified as pulse amplitude modulation and pulse time modulation. Pulse time modulation is again classified as pulse frequency modulation, pulse width modulation and pulse position modulation. Pulse code and delta modulation are described at digital pulse modulation. Pulse amplitude modulation (PAM) is explained with a diagram. Both double polarity PAM and single polarity PAM are discussed. Generation and demodulation of PAM pulses are explained. PAM generation circuits are shown. Both the circuit diagrams of natural sampling and flat top sampling are explained through diagrams. Circuit diagram of PAM demodulation is also discussed. In case of pulse width modulation, it is shown that the starting time and amplitude of each pulse are kept fixed but width of each pulse is made proportional to the amplitude of the signal at that instant. Generation and demodulation of pulse width modulation are explained in detail. Even the diagram of the development of PWM signal by monostable multivibrator is also described. It is also narrated that demodulation of pulse width modulation is done by passing the same in an integrating circuit from which the signal that is developed will have an amplitude at any time being proportional to the pulse width at that time. Pulse position modulation is also defined. The generation and demodulation of pulse modulation are described with a diagram. Various practical circuit diagrams of PAM, PWM, PPM are also shown and explained. The principle of pulse code modulation is discussed. The generation and processing of pulse code modulation (PCM) are explained by block diagrams. The demodulation of PCM signal is also shown and explained through block diagrams.

An idea is also given about the regenerative repeater. It is further explained that the effects of distortion and noise are controlled during the transmission of PCM signal through a channel. Need for sampling theorem in pulse modulation is explained. Sampling theorem is defined. Generation of sampled pulses are described through diagrams. Frequency spectrum is shown with proper diagrams.

Some solved numerical examples of modulation are also provided to reinforce the concepts.

■ QUESTIONS ■

1. Why is the high frequency communication desirable?

2. What do you mean by modulation? Why is it needed? How would you develop modulated signal?

3. What do you mean by amplitude modulation? What is the modulation index of amplitude modulation? Describe the circuit diagram of an amplitude modulation.

4. What do you mean by the double sideband suppressed carrier modulation? Explain in detail.

5. What is single sideband modulation? How would you develop SSB signals?

6. Describe balanced modulator with a diagram. Also deduce the mathematical expression for balanced modulator.

7. Explain the vestigial sideband modulation.

8. What is multiplexing? How is it classified?

9. What do you mean by heterodyning?

10. What do you mean by demodulation? Show the mathematical expression for recovery of translated signal.

11. How do you demodulate amplitude modulated signal? What are the different methods of demodulation of amplitude modulated signal?

12. What do you mean by frequency modulation? Explain in detail.

13. Explain the mathematical expression for frequency modulated signal.

14. What is a reactance modulator? Develop the mathematical expression for reactance modulator?

15. Explain the practical circuit of FM generator.

16. Compare the amplitude modulation with frequency modulation.

17. Define the pre-emphasis and de-emphasis.

18. What do you mean by phase modulation?

19. Compare the frequency modulation with phase modulation.

20. What is the pulse modulation? Classify the pulse modulation.

21. How many types of pulse amplitude modulation are there? Explain with a diagram.

22. How do you generate and demodulate PAM pulses? Explain with a circuit diagram.

23. What is pulse width modulation? Describe with a diagram.

24. How do you generate and demodulate PWM signal? Explain with a circuit diagram.

25. What do you mean by pulse position modulation? Describe how will you generate and demodulate pulse position modulation.

26. Draw some practical circuit diagram of PAM, PWM and PPM.

27. What is pulse code modulation? How do you generate and demodulate PCM signals?

28. What is regenerative repeater? What is its use?

29. What is the need for sampling theorem in pulse modulation? Explain in detail.

3 ∎∎∎ 　Radio Communication

3.1 INTRODUCTION

The radio communication system consists mainly of three items.

    (a) Transmitters,

    (b) Receivers, and

    (c) Channels.

Figures 3.1 and 3.2 show the block diagrams of transmitter and receiver. If the information source is in the form of a phonograph record, the mechanical output of which is passed into a magnetic pick up cartridge type of transducer. The electronic signals will be the final outcome after the transmission of the output of the transducer through a frequency compensation network.

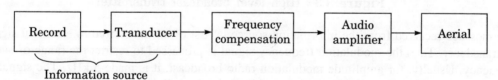

Figure 3.1 Transmitter block diagram.

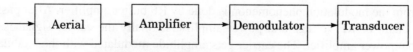

Figure 3.2 Receiver block diagram.

The signal is boosted up by an audio amplifier and then the main function of the transmitter is made, i.e. modulation. The modulated wave is passed through a cable up to the aerial which transforms the electrical energy to electromagnetic form and is passed to the earth's atmosphere which is nothing but the atmospheric channel. The signal strength is reduced on account of spherical dispersion of the radiated signal and on account of interaction with air and moisture particles. The function of the radio receiver is nothing but to get the signal back. At the receiver, the aerial takes the energy from the electromagnetic wave. The signal thus received from the electromagnetic wave is passed to demodulator after being strengthened by the amplifier. The demodulated signal is then passed to the transducer, e.g. loudspeaker so that the actual voice can be listened.

3.2 HIGH LEVEL BROADCAST TRANSMITTER

The high level broadcast system requires high level modulation system and for which high gain, narrow band and efficient amplifiers are used on the carrier to achieve the desired power level. Figure 3.3 shows the block diagram of high level broadcast transmitter.

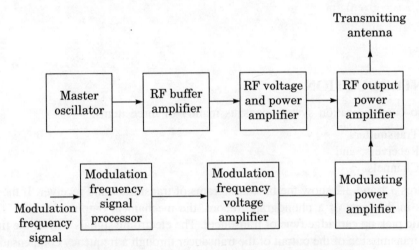

Figure 3.3 High level broadcast transmitter

The message received from the information source is first of all transferred to electrical signal by transducer. Then the modulation frequency signal is processed to restrict the range of audio frequency. Usually, for amplitude modulation radio broadcast, it is made 5 kHz. The signal in the radio transmitter is amplified in several stages of small signal amplifiers (i.e. voltage amplifiers) and large signal amplifiers (i.e. power amplifiers). The stable carrier voltage of desired frequency is generated in a master oscillator (e.g. crystal oscillator). Isolation of the oscillator from the modulation phenomenon is done by RF buffer amplifier. After passing carrier signal to a chain of RF voltage and power amplifiers, finally the carrier signal is brought to the RF output power amplifier. The carrier gets amplitude modulated with the modulating signal at RF output power amplifier and the modulated signal is transmitted through the antenna or aerial.

3.3 NEED FOR HIGH CARRIER FREQUENCY

The high carrier frequency is desired in the radio communication on account of the following facts.

(a) The transmitting antenna radiates efficiently and it radiates large fraction of the total power fed to it if the dimensions of the transmitting antenna are comparable with the carrier wavelength. The size of the antenna conductor is inversely proportional to the carrier frequency. Hence, the size of the antenna will be smaller if the carrier frequency is made high. Therefore, it will be economical if the carrier frequency is made high.

(b) If the carrier frequency is high, the selection of the signal in the receiver will be better.

3.4   MAIN COMPONENTS OF RADIO TRANSMITTER

A radio transmitter has the following main components:

- Master Oscillator
- Buffer amplifier or Isolating amplifier
- Harmonic Generators
- Class 'C' amplifiers
- Modulated amplifier
- Modulating amplifier

3.4.1   Master Oscillator

It is an oscillator which generates oscillations of desired frequency maintaining frequency constant. Even for voltage variation, ambient temperature variation and variation of temperature components of load, the generated frequency is needed to remain constant within close limits. Frequency variations with time and age of the transistor are to be avoided.

An optimum care is taken in the design and operation of the oscillator for reducing frequency drift and scintillation if an ordinary L–C oscillator is used as master oscillator. Proper precautions are to be taken for master oscillator.

(a) The oscillator is to be kept in a constant temperature chamber so that values of tank circuit L and C should not vary with temperature.

(b) Stable power supply is very important so that the electrode voltages do not vary.

(c) Effective Q of the tank circuit is to be maintained very high.

(d) The amplifying device must have high ratio of mutual conductance to interelectrode capacitance.

(e) The arrangement of the oscillator circuit should be such that there is small coupling from the tank circuit to the base and collector of the oscillator transistor.

(f) Master oscillator must operate at sub-harmonic of the carrier frequency.

(g) Oscillator circuit must have close coupling between different parts of tapped coil, for example, in Hartley Oscillator Circuit.

(h) Residual variation of supply voltage is to be eliminated entirely. Suitable reactances are to be inserted in the leads going from the tank circuit to the transistor electrodes.

(i) Harmonic generation is to be made minimum by proper operating conditions.

(j) At the buffer amplifier stage, the negligible power from the oscillator circuit is to be drawn.

Presently, crystal oscillator is the best choice as master oscillator for maintaining frequency stability.

The most important points of crystal oscillator as master oscillator are the following.

(i) Zero-temperature coefficient cut crystal is to be utilized.

(ii) The crystal oscillator must operate at a reasonable low frequency. It should not exceed a few maga-hertz. The oscillator frequency will be a sub-harmonic of the final carrier frequency.

(iii) The whole oscillator circuit or at least the crystal assembly is to be kept in constant temperature chamber in case of extreme frequency stability of the order of 1 in 10^7 or 10^8.

(iv) Buffer amplifier or isolating amplifier must be used after the master oscillator circuit.

(v) In case of frequent changes in carrier frequency, it is not advisable to use crystal oscillator, because at that time there is necessity of changing the crystal and to retune all the RF stages.

3.4.2 Buffer Amplifier or Isolating Amplifier

The buffer amplifier does not draw any input current and as a result there will be no loading of the master oscillator. The changes in the carrier frequency on account of variations in loading are avoided. On the other hand, if the master oscillator directly drives a harmonic generator or class C power amplifier, then the class 'C' power amplifier may draw the input current (i.e. base current in CE amplifier) and obviously the power is drawn from the master oscillator. The outcome is that there occurs loading of master oscillator and as a result there will be variation of effective resistance of the tank circuit of the oscillator. That ultimately creates variation in the frequency.

3.4.3 Harmonic Generators

The master oscillator generates voltage at a frequency which is submultiple of the carrier frequency. The harmonic generators are class C tuned amplifiers. The RF output voltage is first of all disforted through class 'C' operation. Finally, the tuned circuit in the output circuit of amplifier selects the required harmonic frequency. In other words, for deriving harmonic frequency from a pure sine voltage, the pure sine voltage is first of all distorted by some means to produce harmonic and then the output tank circuit is tuned to the required harmonic for rejecting all frequency components except the needed one. Different harmonic generators adopt different ways to distort the pure sine voltage.

Pure sine wave can be distorted by feeding it to a half wave rectifier. A tuned circuit being tuned to any desired harmonic frequency can be placed in series with the rectifier. Figure 3.4 describes the same.

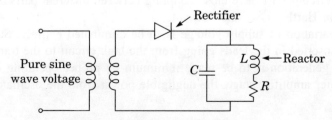

Figure 3.4 Harmonic generator.

The reactor is tuned to any desired harmonic frequency. The demerit of this harmonic generator is that the low impedance of the tuned circuit at the input develops a very heavy damping on the input circuit.

Let the frequency at which the system is tuned is equal to ω_h where $\omega_h = n\omega$ ('ω' is the fundamental angular frequency).

The Q of the circuit will be

$$Q_h = \frac{\omega_h L}{R} = \frac{1}{\omega_h CR}$$

Tank circuit impedance at fundamental frequency 'ω' will be

$$z = \frac{\dfrac{1}{j\omega C}(R + j\omega L)}{\dfrac{1}{j\omega C} + R + j\omega L}$$

$$= \frac{R + j\omega L}{1 + j\omega C(R + j\omega L)}$$

$$= \frac{\dfrac{R}{j\omega CR} + \dfrac{j\omega L}{j\omega CR}}{\dfrac{1}{j\omega CR} + \dfrac{j\omega C}{j\omega CR}(R + j\omega L)}$$

$$= \frac{\dfrac{1}{j\omega C} + \dfrac{L}{CR}}{\dfrac{1}{j\omega CR} + 1 + \dfrac{j\omega L}{R}}$$

$$= \frac{\dfrac{1}{j\omega C} + \dfrac{L}{CR}}{\dfrac{Q_h \omega_h}{j\omega} + 1 + j\dfrac{\omega Q_h}{\omega_h}}$$

$$= \frac{\dfrac{1}{j\omega C} + \dfrac{L}{CR}}{1 + Q_h\left(j\dfrac{j\omega_h}{j\omega} + j\dfrac{\omega}{\omega_h}\right)}$$

$$= \frac{\dfrac{1}{j\omega C} + \dfrac{L}{CR}}{1 + jQ_h\left(-\dfrac{\omega_h}{\omega} + \dfrac{\omega}{\omega_h}\right)}$$

If Q_h is of higher value, then

$$z = \dfrac{\dfrac{1}{j\omega C} + \dfrac{L}{CR}}{jQ_h\left(\dfrac{\omega}{\omega_h} - \dfrac{\omega_h}{\omega}\right)}$$

$$= \dfrac{\dfrac{1}{\omega C} + j\dfrac{L}{CR}}{Q_h\left(\dfrac{\omega_h}{\omega} - \dfrac{\omega}{\omega_h}\right)}$$

$$= \dfrac{\dfrac{1}{Q_h\omega C} + j\dfrac{L}{Q_h CR}}{\dfrac{\omega_h}{\omega} - \dfrac{\omega}{\omega_h}}$$

Since, $\qquad \dfrac{L}{CR} > \dfrac{1}{\omega C}$

$$= \dfrac{j\dfrac{L}{CR \cdot Q_h}}{\dfrac{\omega_h}{\omega} - \dfrac{\omega}{\omega_h}}$$

when $\omega_h = n\omega$ and $n = 2$.

Magnitude of $\qquad z = \dfrac{j\dfrac{L}{CR} \cdot \dfrac{1}{Q_h}}{\dfrac{\omega_h}{\omega} - \dfrac{\omega}{\omega_h}}$

$$= \dfrac{j\dfrac{L}{CR}\dfrac{1}{Q_h}}{2 - \dfrac{1}{2}} = j\dfrac{2}{3}\dfrac{L}{CR}\dfrac{1}{Q_h}$$

when $n = 3$

$$z = \dfrac{j\dfrac{L}{CR}\dfrac{1}{Q_h}}{3 - \dfrac{1}{3}}$$

$$= j\dfrac{L}{CR}\dfrac{1}{Q_h} \cdot \dfrac{3}{8}$$

when $n = 4$

$$z = \dfrac{j\dfrac{L}{CR}\dfrac{1}{Q_h}}{4 - \dfrac{1}{4}}$$

$$= j\frac{L}{CR}\frac{1}{Q_h}\cdot\frac{4}{15}$$

when $Q_h = 10$,

Then the magnitude of impedance,

$$z = \frac{1}{15}\frac{L}{CR} \quad \text{(for } n = 2)$$

$$z = \frac{3}{80}\frac{L}{CR} \quad \text{(for } n = 3)$$

$$z = \frac{2}{75}\frac{L}{CR} \quad \text{(for } n = 4)$$

From the above, it is also clear that as n is increasing, the impedance of the tuned circuit is being decreased. With the increase in order of harmonics, the impedance of the tuned circuit is reduced.

Figure 3.5 is the circuit diagram of class 'C' harmonic generator.

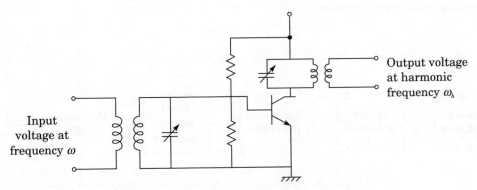

Figure 3.5   Class C harmonic generator.

The tuned circuit on the input side is tuned to the fundamental angular frequency ω. The tuned circuit on the output side is tuned to the harmonic angular frequency ω_h. The emitter is reverse biased beyond the cut-off for obtaining Class 'C' operation so that the collector current flowing in the form of pulses will possess sufficient amount of harmonics. The cut-off emitter bias is fixed corresponding to a given collector supply voltage V_{CC}. The value of emitter bias and the input drive find the angles of base current flow and collector current flow. Again, relative proportions of different harmonics depend upon the angle of collector flow. Therefore, for the generation of a given harmonic, certain value of angle of collector flow provides optimum output, collector supply voltage, cut-off emitter bias voltage and emitter voltage V_{EE}. The input drive voltage is to be adjusted to obtain the optimum value of angle of collector flow.

3.4.4   Class C Amplifier

The radio frequency voltage is of very small power. It is of the order of a few watts. The power level is needed to be increased to the final high value in the chain of class 'C' amplifier having high output circuit efficiency which is of the order of 70%. To speak the truth, first few stages of class 'C' amplifier work as harmonic generators.

3.4.5 Modulated Amplifier

This is class 'C' tuned amplifier. It is push-pull type. It is modulated by audio modulating voltage from modulating amplifier. High efficiency series plate modulation is generally utilized in high power radio broadcast and radio telephone transmitters. In small transistorised radio transmitter, collector modulation or base modulation or both may be utilized.

3.4.6 Modulating Amplifier

This is a Class B push-pull amplifier. It feeds audio power in the modulation amplifier in the plate circuit, control grid circuit or suppressor grid circuit on the basis of the method of modulation used. The reason for the use of the Class B operation is the high plate circuit efficiency. Sometimes Class 'A' modulating amplifier is used for low power transmitters.

Figure 3.6 describes the block diagram of amplitude modulation radio transmitter utilizing modulation at high carrier power level.

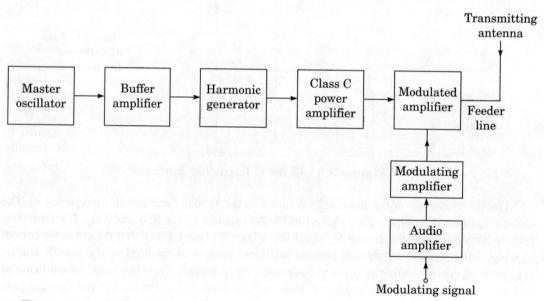

Figure 3.6 High carrier power level amplitude modulation radio transmitter.

Figure 3.7 describes the low power level modulation system block diagram. Here, it modulates the carrier at low power level. Then the carrier power is enhanced to the desired level in Class B tuned power amplifiers. Now-a-days, of course, high power level modulation system is mostly utilized.

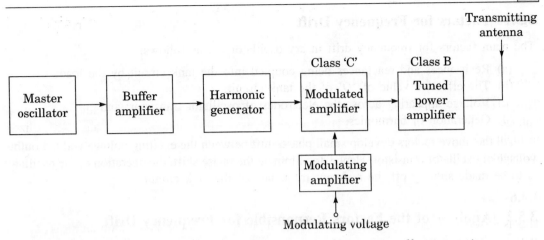

Figure 3.7 Low power level modulation system for radio transmitter.

3.5 TYPE OF CARRIER FREQUENCY NEEDED IN RADIO TRANSMISSION

The following are three main requirements of radio transmitter from the point of view of the carrier frequency.

(a) The generated carrier frequency should be at the specified value. It is essential for avoiding sidebands of one station completely or partially overlapping in frequency spectrum with the sidebands of the other radio station. The master oscillator which determines the carrier frequency generates sub-harmonic of the final carrier frequency and the frequency is taken to the final value by harmonic generators.

(b) Readily adjustable carrier frequency is one of the most important requirements. In general, crystal controlled master oscillator is used for radio transmitters. Readily adjustable carrier frequency cannot be achieved by the same. That is why, the crystal is changed in the master oscillator and tuning of all the tuned amplifiers and harmonic generators are made accordingly.

(c) Frequency drift and frequency scintillation should be made as small as possible. The maximum frequency drift allowed for radio transmitters is ± 20 Hz for medium wave transmitters and the same is ± 0.002% for short wave and UHF transmitters.

When there is abrupt variations in load, there occurs abrupt changes in frequency. That is nothing but frequency scintillation. Wide change in the load creates change in the resistance and reactance of the tank circuit and that automatically changes the frequency of oscillator. The scintillation is avoided as follows.

The master oscillator is to be made to drive buffer amplifier. The adjustment is to be made such that the buffer amplifier will draw little power from the master oscillator. Thus, the master oscillator loading is reduced. Hence, at the time of the change of the load of transmitter, very little effect will appear on the master oscillator. The assembly of master oscillator and buffer amplifier is termed MOPA (Master Oscillator Power Amplifier).

3.5.1 Factors for Frequency Drift

The main factors for frequency drift in ary oscillator are as follows:

(a) Resistances and reactances being coupled into the tank circuit by the load;
(b) The effective value of 'Q' of the tank circuit;
(c) Voltage appearing across the electrodes of oscillator transistor; and
(d) Generation of harmonics.

All the above factors develop small phase shift between the exciting voltage and the output voltage of oscillator transistor. Hence, to eliminate the phase shift, the operation of the oscillator is to be made slightly off the resonant frequency of the tank circuit.

3.5.2 Analysis of the Factors Responsible for Frequency Drift

When the ambient temperature and temperature of the components change, the outcome will be the variations of the tank circuit inductance and capacitance and the inter electrode capacitance. As a result, there will occur the change in resonant frequency and the frequency of oscillation.

The inductance and capacitance variations of the tank circuit can be reduced by keeping the tank circuit in closed constant temperature chamber. The variation of inter electrode capacitance can be compensated by providing some means so that the electrostatic energy stored in inter electrode capacitances becomes negligible as compared with the total electrostatic energy stored in resonant circuit.

The means are the following:

(i) To use high circuit 'Q'.
(ii) To keep high ratio of mutual conductance to variations in inter electrode capacitances.
(iii) To allow small coupling from the tank circuit to the base and collector of the oscillator transistor.
(iv) To use low resonant frequency.

(That means to generate by master oscillator a frequency which is sub multiple of the frequency of transmitter.)

The frequency variations on account of transistor voltage, load impedance, harmonics produced vary inversely with the effective 'Q' of the tuned circuit. That is why 'Q' is to be maintained as high as possible. A high effective 'Q' is found through a very loosely coupled load. This is made by providing the ratio of L/C of the tank circuit low or by coupling the collector to a small part of the tank circuit and as a result the collector–emitter voltage becomes very small part of the voltage across the tank circuit.

The outcome of the variations in collector voltage is the variations in the ac currents which flow between the tank circuit, the base and the collector electrodes of the oscillator transistor. That ultimately affects the frequency. Here, also by providing large 'Q' tank circuit, frequency variation can be reduced. By using very close spacing between different parts of the tapped coil, it can be reduced. In this case, preference can be given to Hartley oscillator. Of course, the effect of variation of the collector voltage on the frequency of oscillation can be totally eliminated by inserting reactances in series with the leads going from the tank circuit to the collector. This is shown in Figures 3.8(a) and (b) for Hartley oscillator.

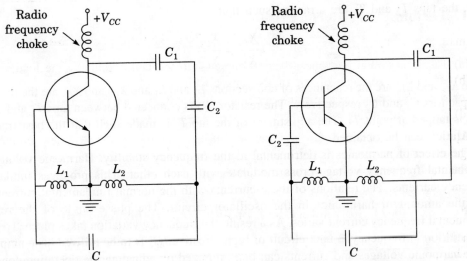

Figure 3.8(a) Collector reactance stabilization on Hartley oscillator.

Figure 3.8(b) Base reactance stabilization on Hartley oscillator.

Figure 3.8(a) describes the Hartley oscillator with stabilizing capacitor C_2 being inserted in the collector circuit. On the other hand, Figure 3.8(b) describes the Hartley oscillator with stabilizing capacitor C_2 being connected in the base circuit. In some cases, two stabilizing capacitors are connected, one in the collector circuit and the other the base circuit. Stabilization can also be arranged on Colpitts oscillator, tuned collector oscillator, tuned base oscillator, etc. Frequency variations on account of variations in load can also be eliminated if the load is purely resistive and is connected across collector–emitter circuit or across base emitter circuit.

Figure 3.9 describes frequency stabilization of oscillator in spite of variations in electrode voltages.

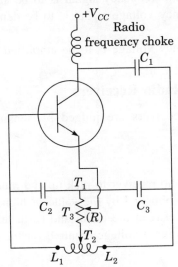

Figure 3.9 Frequency stabilization of oscillator.

Here, the taps T_2 and T_1 are arranged such that

$$\frac{X_{L_2}}{X_{L_1}} = \frac{X_{C_3}}{X_{C_2}}$$

where X_{L_2} and X_{L_1} are the reactances of coil sections L_2 and L_1 and X_{C_3} and X_{C_2} are the reactances of capacitors C_3 and C_2 respectively. The resistor (R) is connected between taps T_2 and T_1. The same is tapped at point T_3. The adjustment of the tap T_3 is made such that the best frequency stabilization can be obtained.

The effect of harmonics is detrimental to the frequency stability. Harmonic voltages and fundamental frequency voltage cross modulate with each other. This produces fundamental frequency currents. The relations of these currents with the normal fundamental currents vary with the amount of harmonics in the oscillator circuit. The phase angle of the resultant fundamental frequency current varies. As a result, the frequency variation takes place. To reduce this variation in frequency, a tank circuit of high effective 'Q' is to be utilized. The amplitudes of the harmonic voltages and currents can be minimized by adjusting the operating conditions in the above manner.

3.6   RADIO RECEIVER

A radio transmitter transmits a modulated carrier voltage and that is accepted by the antenna of a radio receiver. The received signal is generally found very weak. Therefore, this signal is amplified first in a radio frequency amplifier stage. The unwanted noise signals are to be eliminated. Then the radio frequency carrier should be demodulated for obtaining the main modulating signal. The detected signal is to be amplified finally.

The functions of the radio receiver can be enumerated as follows.

(a) The required radio frequency modulated carrier is to be received by the antenna.
(b) The unwanted noise signals are to be eliminated for the selection of the required signal.
(c) The above selected radio frequency signal is to be amplified.
(d) The modulation frequency voltage signal is to be demodulated from radio frequency signal.
(e) The modulation frequency voltage is to be amplified.

3.6.1   Characteristics of Radio Receivers

The characteristics of radio receivers are judged by sensitivity, selectivity, fidelity and stability.

Sensitivity

Sensitivity is the ability of a radio receiver to pick up and reproduce weak radio signals. The sensitivity of a radio receiver is obtained by the value of high frequency voltage which must be fed to its input circuit, i.e. between the aerial and earth terminals, for securing a normal output power. The lower is such input voltage required for the normal reception, the higher is the receiver sensitivity. The sensitivity of modern radio receivers has ranges from several microvolts to several millivolts.

It depends upon the number of amplification stages and upon their quality.

Selectivity

Selectivity is the ability of the radio receiver to separate the signal of a required radio station from the signals of unwanted stations. That means, the selectivity of a radio receiver is its ability of receiving radio signals within a comparatively narrow frequency band. The selectivity of radio receivers is very important aspect when a large number of radio stations operate on nearly equal frequencies. The selectivity of radio receiver depends upon the number and the quality of tuned circuits utilized by the receiver. The greater the number of tuned circuits being adjusted to resonance in a radio receiver and the higher the quality (Q) of such tuned circuits, the higher is the selectivity of such a receiver.

Fidelity

Fidelity is the quality or precision with which the output is reproduced. The lower the distortion is introduced by a radio receiver, the higher is the quality of reproduction on fidelity of such a receiver.

Stability

Stability is the ability of radio receiver to deliver a constant amount of output for a given period of time when the receiver is supplied with a signal of constant amplitude and frequency. This is categorised by mechanical stability and electrical stability.

3.6.2 Classification of Radio Receivers

The radio receivers are classified mainly as follows:

(a) Tuned radio frequency receiver (TRF)
(b) Super heterodyne receivers.

Tuned radio frequency receiver

Figure 3.10 describes the TRF receiver. It is a straight receiver in which the incoming signal is first of all amplified in one or more tuned radio frequency amplifier stages. As a result, the

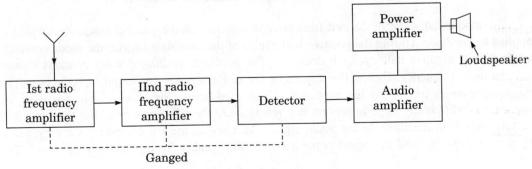

Figure 3.10 Radio receiver.

magnitude of the signal is increased and the sensitivity of the receiver is improved. Then, output amplified signal is fed to the detector for obtaining the original modulation frequency signal. After that the modulation frequency signal is amplified in one or more stages of audio frequency amplifiers. Finally, it is fed to the loudspeaker. One or two tuned R–F amplifier stages are sufficient for TRF receiver from the points of view of sensitivity and selectivity, otherwise the circuit becomes too selective. That may lower the fidelity of the receiver. Another very important point of TRF receiver is that its selectivity decreases as the carrier frequency increases.

Superheterodyne receiver

Figure 3.11 describes a superheterodyne receiver. The radio waves from various broadcasting stations are intercepted by the receiving antenna and the RF stage selects the desired radio wave and raises the strength of the wave to the desired level. The amplified output of RF amplifier is fed to the mixer stage where it is combined with a local oscillator. The intermediate frequency is the difference between oscillator frequency and incoming radio frequency. The intermediate frequency (IF) is always 455 kHz regardless of the frequency to which the receiver is tuned. The locally generated oscillations in a superheterodyne receiver are usually of a frequency higher than the incoming signals. The output of the IF is fed to the fixed tuned IF amplifiers. These amplifiers are tuned to 455 kHz frequency and render nice amplification. The output from the IF amplifier stage is coupled to the input of the detector stage. The audio signal is extracted from the IF output. The diode detector is used because of its low distortion and excellent audio fidelity.

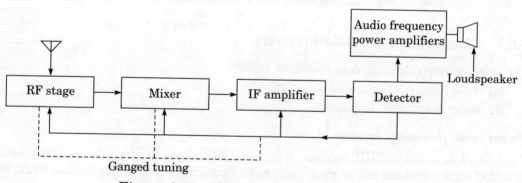

Figure 3.11 The superheterodyne receiver.

The modulated wave of desired frequency is selected by the parallel tuned circuit and is applied to the diode. During the positive half cycles of the modulated wave, the diode conducts while during negative half cycles it does not. The rectified modulated wave contains signals and the radio frequency. Hence, this cannot be fed to the speaker for sound reproduction. The RF component is filtered by the capacitor 'C' shunted across the speaker. The value of the capacitor is sufficiently large to present low reactance to the RF component. But the same will be relatively high reactance to the audio signal. As a result, the RF components are bypassed by the capacitor 'C' and the signal is passed on to the speaker for reproduction of sound. The audio signal output of detector stage is fed to the multistage audio amplifier. The signal is amplified until it is strong enough to drive the speaker. The speaker finally converts the audio signal into sound waves corresponding to the original sound at the broadcasting station.

Comparison between superheterodyne receiver and tuned radio frequency receiver: The comparison between tuned radio frequency receiver and superheterodyne receiver is tabulated below (Table 3.1).

Table 3.1

Superheterodyne receiver	TRF receiver
Its sensitivity is very high.	Its sensitivity is less.
The gain is attained very high due to the IF Amplifier.	The gain is not so high.
The selectivity is also high due to greater number of tuned circuits.	The selectivity is not so high.
The constancy of sensitivity and selectivity can be maintained better over the entire tuning range of the receiver.	The constancy of sensitivity and selectivity cannot be maintained so efficiently.
Due to the high gain, various improvements can be adapted, for example automatic gain control, utilisation of optical tuning indicators.	Since gain is not so high, there is less scope for improvement.

The main reason for high sensitivity of superheterodyne receiver is that the signal is amplified at a single and convenient frequency after the frequency conversion. The reason for high selectivity of superheterodyne receiver is that the IF amplifier use tuned stages with good selectivity and required bandwidth. The fidelity of the receiver becomes better as the bandwidth of the IF amplifier is of the required value. The radio frequency amplifier stage improves signal to noise ratio, reduces IF interference and it offers a better coupling between antenna and the input of the receivers.

3.6.3 Automatic Volume Control (AVC)

AVC is the automatic volume control or automatic gain control. It is a device by virtue of which fading of the amplitude of IF carrier at the detector can be restricted. The AVC is used in all broadcast and radio telephone receivers. It reduces the amplitude variation on account of fading from a high value of 30 to 40 dB to a small value of 3 to 4 dB. The AVC derives a dc voltage by rectification of carrier voltage in a linear diode detector and this dc voltage is proportional to the carrier amplitude. Then it applies the dc voltage as reverse bias at the input of the RF amplifier, frequency mixer and the IF amplifier. When the carrier amplitude increases, the AVC bias increases and the gains of all the tuned stages decrease. The outcome is the reduction in carrier amplitude at the input of the detector and it turns back to its normal value. In case of sudden decrease of carrier amplitude, reverse action takes place.

Figure 3.12 shows the example of the automatic gain control with the help of unipolar transistor. For the unipolar transistor g_m is calculated by the following formulae.

$$|A| = g_m r_D$$

$$A = \frac{v_{\text{output}}}{v_{\text{input}}} = \frac{i_D r_D}{v_{\text{in}}}$$

$$g_m r_D = \frac{i_D r_D}{v_{\text{in}}} \text{ or } g_m = \frac{i_D}{v_{\text{in}}}$$

$$g_m = g_{mo} \left[1 - \frac{V_{GS}}{V_{GS}(\text{off})} \right]$$

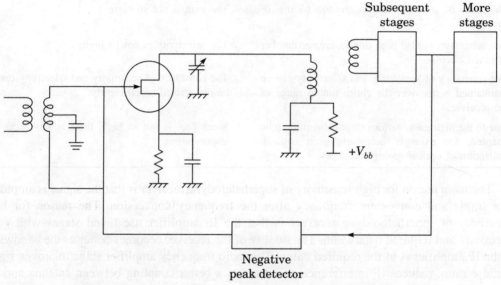

Figure 3.12 Automatic volume control or gain control.

Figure 3.13 describes the graphical representation of the above equation.

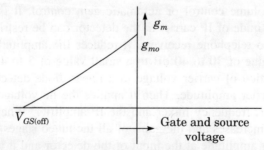

Figure 3.13 g_m vs. voltage between gate and source.

There are various schemes of automatic volume control.

(a) Linear diode detector with capacitor filter and simple AVC
(b) Linear diode detector with π filter and simple AVC
(c) Linear diode detector with amplified and delayed AVC
(d) Detector circuit using transistor
(e) Tone compensated volume control
(f) Tone control
(g) Tuning control

Figure 3.14(a) describes linear diode detector with capacitor filter and simple AVC. The rectified voltage is developed across R. The radio frequency components are filtered by the capacitor C. The dc and modulation frequency voltage are developed across the load resistor R.

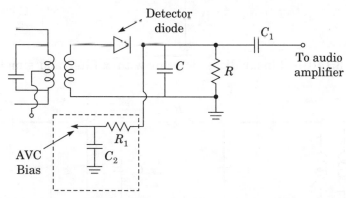

Figure 3.14(a)   Linear diode detector with capacitor filter and simple AVC.

The capacitance 'C_1' will not accept the dc component. AVC will pick up dc component but the modulation frequency component will be bypassed through capacitor C_2. Important factors of the design of this circuit are the following.

(a) Time constant of AVC filter is to be chosen such that all modulation frequency components are eliminated. The value of $R_1 C_2$ will be very large so that the lowest modulation frequency components can even be removed.
(b) The typical value of the above time constant lies within 0.1 second to 0.2 second.
(c) The positive AVC bias is applied to the base of PNP transistor of preceding tuned stages.
(d) In case of NPN transistor, negative bias is applied.

Figure 3.14(b) describes linear diode detector with π-filter and simple AVC. π filter is more reliable from the point of view of removal of radio frequency components.

Figure 3.14(c) describes linear diode detector with delayed AVC. The delayed AVC is required due to the fact that the AVC system suffers from the drawback that the AVC becomes operative even for weak signals. An ideal AVC system should not be operative until the input carrier voltage reaches a reasonably large predetermined voltage and after the operation it will maintain output level constant in spite of variation in input carrier level. Here, in Figure 3.14(c), the delay diode conducts for zero and small signals and as a result, the potential of AVC bias is just equal to the potential of cathode of the diode. Hence, the AVC remains fixed at low

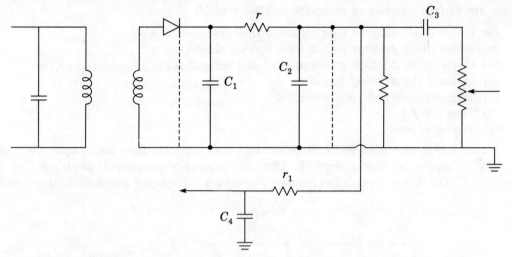

Figure 3.14(b) Linear diode detector with π filter and simple AVC.

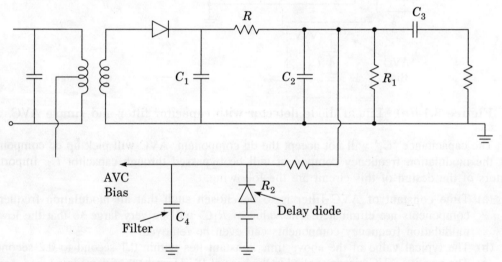

Figure 3.14(c) Linear diode detector with delayed AVC.

positive value. When the input carrier voltage enhances, the AVC bias voltage exceeds the magnitude of the positive cathode voltage of delay diode. The delay diode stops conducting. Therefore, the normal functioning of AVC system starts.

Figure 3.14(d) compares the different methods of AVC.

Figure 3.14(e) describes the linear diode detector with amplified and delayed AVC.

The speciality of this circuit is that a separate IF amplifier drives the AVC diode. Figure 3.14(f) describes detector circuit using transistor. Here, a transistor is used as a Class B power detector instead of a diode. The transistor is biased at or near the cut-off. It is operating over the nonlinear region of its I_b vs. I_c characteristics. The V_c is kept constant. The intermediate

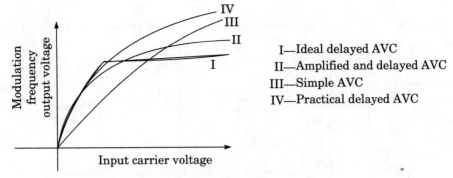

Figure 3.14(d) AVC characteristics.

I—Ideal delayed AVC
II—Amplified and delayed AVC
III—Simple AVC
IV—Practical delayed AVC

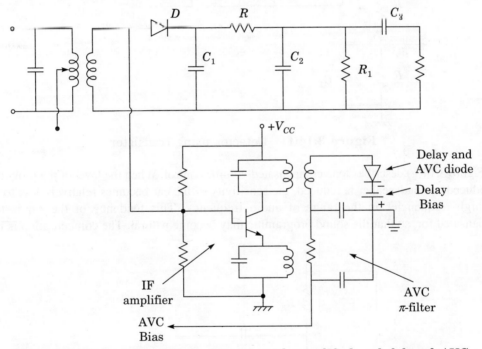

Figure 3.14(e) Linear diode detector with amplified and delayed AVC.

frequency signal from the last IF amplifier is sent to the base of the NPN transistor 'T' as shown in Figure 3.14(f). The resistor R_3, R_2, R_1 and R_4 develop a potential divider across the $+V_{CC}$ supply. At the bias just equal to the cut-off value, the flow of output current occurs during the positive half cycles of the available IF signal. The collector current will be the combined dc component, modulation frequency component and RF component. The capacitor C_2 will eliminate the RF component. Through the load resistance R_6, there will be flow of dc component and modulation frequency component. The dc component will be blocked by capacitor 'C_3'. Hence, the modulation frequency component will flow to the audio amplifier stage.

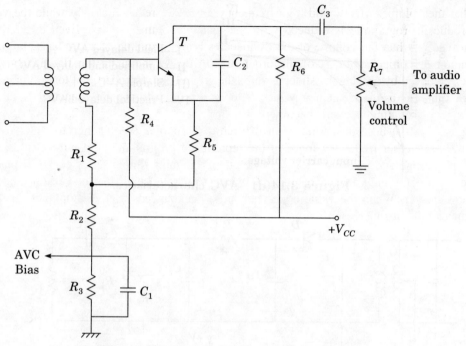

Figure 3.14(f) Detector using transistor.

Figure 3.14(g) describes tone compensated volume control. When the level of the programme reproduced by loudspeaker is reduced, the sensitivity of the ear becomes relatively less for low and high frequencies in the range of audio frequency. This tendency of the ear is to be compensated for, so that the sound programme may become natural. The compensation is made

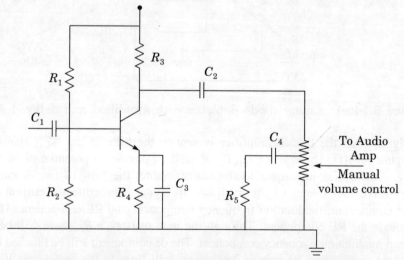

Figure 3.14(g) Tone compensated volume control.

such that the volumes of low and high frequency terms are reduced slowly while the volume of reproduced programme is reduced with the manual volume control. Even this reduction becomes slower than the volume of the frequencies lying in middle of audio band. In general, the amount of compensation is of the order of 20 dB. As shown in the figure 3.14(g), the volume is reduced by moving the slider towards the ground end. Impedance of tone compensating network enhances as the frequency reduces and, as a result, at lower frequencies, the shunting effect of compensating network becomes low.

Figure 3.14(h) describes tone control circuit. It enables the listener to adjust relative amplitudes of higher frequency tones in the reproduced programme as per the characteristics of the programme and individual's taste. The circuit contains simple series combination of the fixed capacitor C_2 and variable resistor R_5 placed in parallel with the load resistor and audio voltage amplifier. When the value of resistance R_5 is enhanced, relative amplitudes of higher frequency terms are increased.

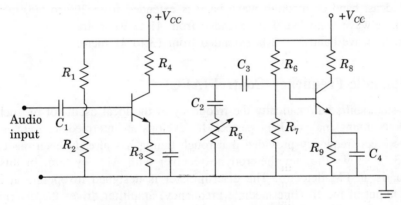

Figure 3.14(h)   Tone control circuit.

Figure 3.14(i) shows the tune circuits arrangement.

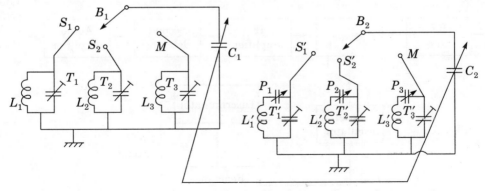

Figure 3.14(i)   Tuned circuits in 3 band superheterodyne receiver.

The following are the components of the circuit.

L_1, L_2, L_3 — Radio frequency tuned circuit coils

C_1, C_2 — Ganged tuning condenser

L_1', L_2', L_3' — Oscillator tuned circuit coils

T_1, T_2, T_3 — Radio frequency circuit trimmers

T_1', T_2', T_3' — Oscillator circuit trimmers

P_1, P_2, P_3 — Oscillator circuit padders

In this capacitor tuning, for each band of receiver, separate coils are used. One coil is for each RF circuit and one coil is in oscillator circuit.

All the coils related to any band of frequencies may be selected in or out at the same time by dint of a band switch. Therefore, in Figure 3.14(i) 3 band receiver has the following 3 bands.

(i) Broadcast band or medium wave band is extended from 200 to 500 metres.

(ii) A short wave band No. 1 is extended from 41 to 91 metres.

(iii) A short wave band No. 2 is extended from 13 to 31 metres.

3.6.4 Automatic Frequency Control (AFC)

The AFC system shifts automatically the frequency of the local oscillator by such an amount that continuous tuning may be kept perfect. It develops an intermediate frequency signal at exactly the correct frequency provided that rough tuning has already been made.

Figure 3.15 shows the superheterodyne receiver with AFC system. In this figure, the discriminator is an FM detector. The discriminator is designed to operate at intermediate frequency. Output of the IF (Intermediate Frequency) amplifier drives the discriminator. The AFC control voltage from the discriminator is applied across the varactor diode (reactance tube) as reverse bias. The varactor diode is connected across the tank circuit of the local oscillator. Due to the drift of the local oscillator frequency or on account of improper tuning made in

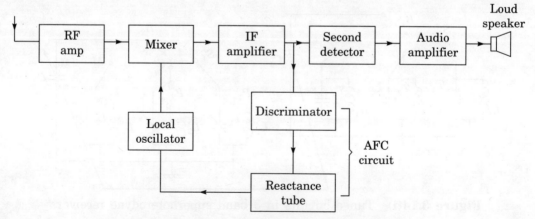

Figure 3.15 Automatic frequency control.

presence of automatic voltage control, the frequency of the IF voltage fed to the discriminator becomes different than the standard value. The outcome is the development of dc voltage across the output of the discriminator. The magnitude of the AFC control voltage depends upon the frequency difference and the polarity of this voltage depends upon the fact that the frequency of IF voltage is above or below the standard value. Truly speaking, the capacitance offered by the varactor diode to the local oscillator tuned circuit changes with the change in the magnitude of AFC voltage. The polarity of capacitance change will, of course, depend upon the AFC control voltage. Thus, the frequency of local oscillator will be changed in magnitude and direction in such a way that the intermediate frequency will be obtained.

Principle of varactor diode

It is already known to us that any semiconductor diode has a junction capacitance and when the same is reverse biased, the junction capacitance varies with the applied back bias. If such a diode is developed in a microwave system, then it is called varactor diode. The characteristics of varactor diode are shown in Figures 3.16 and 3.17.

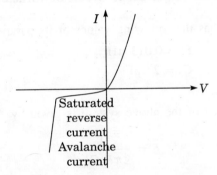

Figure 3.16   Current vs. voltage characteristic of varactor diode.

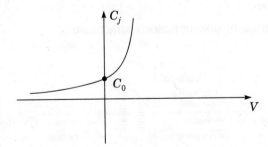

Figure 3.17   Junction capacitance vs. voltage of varactor diode.

Figure 3.16 describes the current vs. voltage characteristics of the varactor diode. Figure 3.17 describes the junction, i.e. the depletion layer capacitance vs. voltage characteristic. From the Figure 3.17, it is very much clear that C_0 is the junction capacitance for zero bias voltage.

Figure 3.18 describes the equivalent circuit diagram of varactor diode. The components of the equivalent circuit are the following:

L_s — Stray lead inductance.
C_s — Stray fixed capacitance between cathode and anode.
R_b — Series resistance
C_j — Junction capacitance.

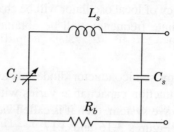

Figure 3.18 Equivalent circuit of varactor diode.

The typical silicon varactor has the following values of its parameters

$$C_s = 1.4 \text{ pF}, \quad L_s = 0.013 \text{ } \mu H$$
$$R_b = 1.3 \text{ } \Omega, \quad C_0 = 25 \text{ pF}$$
$$C_{min} = 5 \text{ pF}$$

The resistive cut-off frequency of the above system is given by

$$f_c = \frac{1}{2\pi R_b C_{min}}$$

From gallium arsenide varactors, the value of f_c is found more than 1000 GHz.

Discriminator characteristic

Figure 3.19 describes nature of discriminator characteristics.

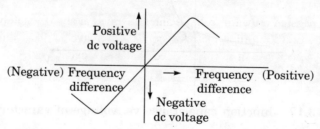

Figure 3.19 Discriminator characteristic.

3.6.5 Image Frequency and Rejection Ratio

If the signal received in the antenna of the superheterodyne receiver is f_s and the intermediate frequency is f_i, then the frequency which is generated at local oscillator is $f_s + f_i$. Now, by chance any signal received at the antenna is equal to $f_s + 2f_i$, then at the mixer, there is probability of development of [$(f_s + 2f_i)$ – local oscillator frequency], i.e. f_i, the intermediate frequency. That is why, this $(f_s + 2f_i)$ frequency is termed the image frequency. The ratio of strength or gain of signal frequency (f_s) and strength or gain of image frequency $(f_s + 2f_i)$ is termed rejection ratio. The value of the same is $\sqrt{1 + Q^2 P^2}$

where

$$P = \frac{f_s + 2f_i}{f_s} - \frac{f_s}{f_s + 2f_i}$$

and Q is the Q-factor of the tuned circuit of IF stage amplifier.

3.6.6 Aerials or Antenna

An aerial is a system of wires utilized for the transmission of radio waves by transmitting station and for the reception of waves by receiving stations. The aerial converts high frequency alternating current into the energy of radio waves. Similarly, the radio wave energy is converted to high frequency alternating current energy. The transmitting equipment generates the signal, then it amplifies to a high power level. Afterwards, the same is applied to an antenna which radiates the same into space. Similarly, at the receiving end the antenna intercepts a portion of the radiated energy and then develops signal in the form of ac current. Antenna is nothing but a length of conductor which acts as a conversion device and the radio waves are simply the electromagnetic waves. Hence, this conversion device converts an electrical signal into electromagnetic energy and electromagnetic energy into and electric signal. The same antenna can often be utilized either for transmitting or receiving. This type of system is termed 'antenna reciprocity'.

The major factors of the antenna system are the following:

- Wavelength
- Antenna impedance
- Directivity.

Wavelength

The radio waves propagated outward from an antenna travel at approximately the speed of light (186000 miles/second or 300 million metres/second). The wavelength of this radio wave is the distance travelled by the wave in the time needed for one cycle.

$$\lambda = c/f$$

where c = 300,000, 000 metres/second = speed of light

f = frequency of wave in cycles/second

λ = wavelength in metres

Antenna Impedance

The antenna impedance is made resistive between any two points equidistant from the centre along the antenna length, because, when the half wave dipole is resonant, the capacitive reactance and inductive reactance cancel each other leaving resistance only as the net impedance.

Directivity

During emission of radio waves, radiation emitted by a point source radiator will spread outward equally in all directions. But, in case of practical antennas, this phenomenon does not occur. Rather, all antennas radiate more energy in some directions. Again, in some directions, the radiation becomes very weak and even in some direction, it is found totally zero. Hence, every antenna has a characteristic radiation pattern. Graphs, termed polar diagrams, are generally utilized to provide a pictorial representation of these radiation patterns. The pictorial representation of the pattern of radiation is termed the directivity pattern. This is applied both for reception and transmission

Important terms related to antenna are

- Bandwidth
- Beamwidth
- Polarization

Bandwidth

This is the frequency over which the operation is found satisfactory. This is generally taken between the half power points. This is a width of frequency over which the antenna keeps certain required characteristics, for example, gain, standing wave ratio, shape or direction, polarization and impedance.

Beamwidth

The beamwidth of the antenna is defined as the angular separation between the two half power points in the power density radiation pattern. It is actually the angular separation between the two 3-dB down points on the field strength radiation of the antenna. It is generally expressed in degrees.

Polarization

The polarization is the direction of the electric field component of the wave with respect to the ground. Wave travels through the space and its electric field is vertical with respect to the ground. Wave is termed vertically polarized. If the electric field is horizontal with respect to the ground, then it is termed horizontally polarized. Vertically positioned antennas develop vertically polarized waves and horizontally positioned antennas develop horizontally polarized waves.

Dipole antenna

The fundamental radio antenna is a metal rod or tubing that has a physical length approximately equal to one half wavelength in free space at the frequency of operation. This type of structure of antenna is termed a half wave dipole. It is termed a symmetrical antenna in which the two ends are at equal potential relative to the midpoint. A half-wave dipole is generally positioned horizontally relative to earth's surface. The half wave dipole antenna is also termed "zero-dB gain antenna". The half wave dipole is the equivalent of a resonant circuit. It has distributed L, C and R where 'L' is the inductance in the metallic elements when current flows and R is resistance developed mostly due to the electrical losses associated with the radio frequency currents. The half wave dipole antenna can be made resonant to one frequency, i.e. the frequency for which it has been cut. The resonant frequency can be changed by changing the length of elements.

Figure 3.20 describes half wave dipole. Voltage is fed to the antenna and current flows to the open end. It cannot go further, therefore it attains its zero value. The magnetic field collapses back into the antenna and makes the voltage maximum at the ends. Thus, a fixed pattern of standing waves forms in the half wave dipole till the energy is supplied to the antenna. In the half wave metal rod of antenna, the standing wave pattern of voltage and current possesses the maximum voltage at the ends and minimum at the centre. At the same time, the current is found maximum at the centre and minimum at the ends. The standing wave of voltage and current is independent of the orientation of the antenna, the amount of energy supplied to the antenna and diameter of the element.

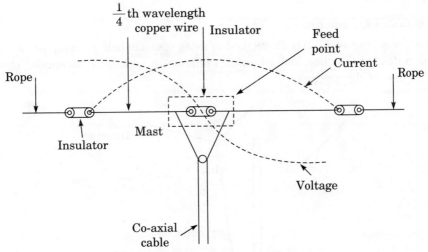

Figure 3.20 Half wave dipole.

'Inverted V' Antenna

Figure 3.21 describes an 'Inverted V' antenna. It is a non-directional antenna. It is also called 'drooping doublet'. It exhibits more or less omnidirectional radiation characteristics while it is used for a single band. The multiband version is directional above 7 MHz off the ends of the antenna. The reason is that the legs of the 'V' are long in terms of wavelength at 14, 21 and 28 MHz. In case of single band operation, the 'V' is cut to the same length as a half wave length doublet. It is fed with 52 Ω coaxial line. Its centre, i.e. the feed point is made as high above the ground as possible. Generally, it is one quarter wavelength or more at the operating frequency. The apex angle is generally made very near 90° because angle less than 90° creates trouble of excessive cancellation of the signal. Although metal mast or tower provides satisfactory result, yet it will be wiser to utilise a wooden mast for keeping the field of antenna unobstructed. Even the outcome is good if the supporting of the centre of antenna is made from a limb on a tall tree provided that the area below the limb is entirely open.

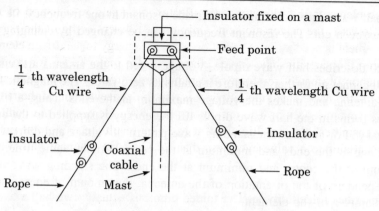

Figure 3.21 'Inverted V' antenna.

Parasitic array (Yagi antenna)

The parasitic array (Figure 3.22) is the method of using resonant half wave dipoles to concentrate radiation in a desired direction and minimize radiation in undesired directions. This helps to enhance the gain of the antenna.

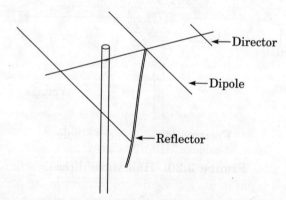

Figure 3.22 Parasitic array (yagi antenna.)

The parasitic array or beam antenna consists of following elements.

(a) resonant half wave dipole

(b) director

(c) reflector

The resonant half wave dipole receives power from the transmitter. It also delivers the received power to the receiver. It is also termed the driven element. The metal rod in front of this driven element is termed director. The director is kept parallel to the driven element at the same "line of sight" level. Sometimes two or more directors are utilized. *The rod in back of the driven* element is termed reflector. In case of transmission, energy is delivered to the driven element. It radiates energy towards the front and the rear. Actually, some of the energy induces current in the parasitic elements, i.e. director and reflector and again re-radiation of mostly all the energy occurs towards the driven element. Only proper dimensioning of the parasitics relative to the driven element is needed for re-radiation of all the energy to the driven element. Electrical distance between the parasitics and driven element is also major factor for proper design. The above phenomenon ultimately reinforces the radiation in front of the antenna and cancels the radiation towards the *rear*. Thus, the outcome is that the concentration of the radiation towards the front of the antenna occurs. The current in the driven element is the combination of the effect of the transmitter and parasitic element and as a result the feed point impedance of the driven element attains to a value even less than 72 Ω of the resonant half wave dipole.

Folded dipole

Figure 3.23 describes folded dipole. The folded dipole is actually two half wavelength dipole. One is a continuous rod and the other is split in the centre connected in parallel.

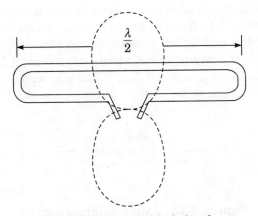

Figure 3.23 Folded dipole

The transmission line is connected to the split dipole. The directivity of the folded dipole is bidirectional but, on account of the distribution of currents in the parts of the folded dipole, its input impedance is very much high. When all parts of the antenna are made of like diameter rod of tubing, the feed point impedance is found 288 Ω. So, there occurs a variation in the folded dipole in comparison to a conventional half wave dipole. It is actually an excellent match for 300 Ω twin lead transmission line.

Rhombic antenna

Figure 3.24 describes rhombic antenna which is very efficient one for broad frequency capability. It is also prominent in all radio communication facilities where the space required for a large structure is available. It can be termed to be a double 'V'. In that case it appears as a diamond shaped structure existing in the horizontal plane.

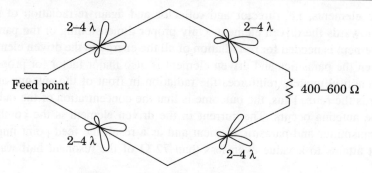

Figure 3.24 Rhombic antenna.

3.6.7 Microphone

Microphone is a device which converts the variations in air pressure developed by the human voice or a musical instrument into the electrical voltage or current of the same frequency and corresponding amplitude. It is nothing but an electroacoustic transducer for converting acoustic energy into electric energy. It converts speech signals into electrical signal and then the signal is transmitted or processed in some way and then the same is reproduced. The simple example of application of the microphone is the public address system as shown in Figure 3.25.

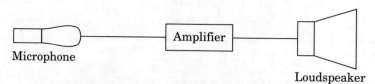

Figure 3.25 Public address system.

Different types of microphones are as follows:

(a) Carbon Microphone
(b) Crystal Microphone
(c) Moving Coil Microphone
(d) Electrostatic Microphone

Carbon Microphone

Figure 3.26 describes the carbon microphone. Sound wave striking the diaphragm sets up vibrations which vary the pressure on the button. Hence, the pressure on the carbon granules varies. As a result, the resistance of the carbon granules varies. Since the granules are in series with a battery and primary of the transformer, the varying resistance develops a corresponding variation in the circuit current. The outcome of the pulsating dc in the *primary* develops an alternating voltage in the *secondary*. The transformer is utilized to step up the voltage and to match the low impedance microphone with the high impedance grid circuit. Usually, the microphone current varies from 10 to 100 mA and the resistance varies from 50 to 90 Ω.

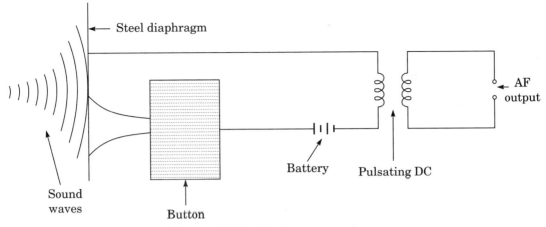

Figure 3.26 Carbon microphone.

Crystal Microphone

The crystal microphone utilises the property of certain crystal such as rochell salt termed piezo electric crystals. The bending of the crystal, resulting from the pressure of sound wave develops an emf across the faces of the crystals. This emf is applied to the input circuit of the amplifier. Even man-made crystal Barium titanate can be utilized for piezoelectric microphones. The barium titanate is developed in the form of a ceramic wafer similar to the crystal wafer. Its frequency response is flat over the whole audio frequency range. It is non-directional and hence may be utilized at any angle. Other benefits are that it is light in weight. Maintenance is also easy. Over and above, it does not require any external power source.

Crystal microphones are utilized in high quality public address system, broadcasting station, recording equipment. Special precautions are to be taken so that the crystal does not get exposed to high temperature and it should not also absorb moisture from air. Otherwise, the crystal will not remain effective.

Moving coil microphone

The moving coil electromagnetic microphone is also termed dynamic or electrodynamic microphone. This has high sensitivity. This is utilized in broadcasting work and specially it is applied where long cables are needed. In extreme conditions of temperature and humidity, this microphone can be easily used.

Electrostatic microphone

The electrostatic types of microphones are generally utilized for measurement of sound for the high fidelity pick up of music.

3.6.8   Loudspeaker

Figures 3.27, 3.28, 3.29 and 3.30 describe various types of loudspeakers. Figure 3.27 shows permanent magnet type of dynamic loudspeaker. Audio frequency signal current passes through voice coil. Interaction takes place between the above signal current and the permanent magnetic

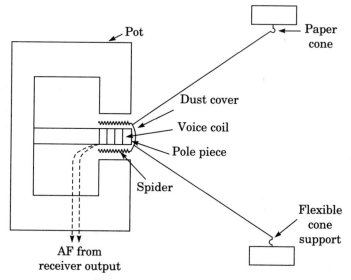

Figure 3.27 PM type dynamic loudspeaker.

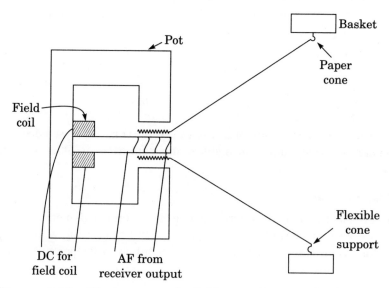

Figure 3.28 Electromagnetic field type dynamic loudspeaker.

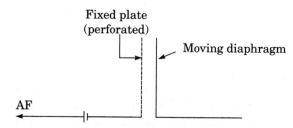

Figure 3.29 Simple electrostatic loudspeaker.

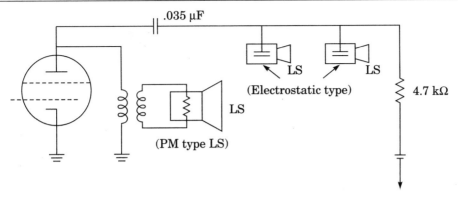

Figure 3.30 Connection of PM type and electrostatic type loudspeakers.

field. The outcome is vibration and the same is transmitted to the paper cone via spider. Figure 3.28 describes Electromagnetic field type dynamic loudspeaker. Here, instead of permanent magnet, magnetic field is provided by electromagnet. DC supply is fed to the electromagnet. Figure 3.29 shows simple electrostatic loudspeaker.

Here, variation in current develops varying electrostatic force and as a result vibration of diaphragm is communicated through loudspeakers. Figure 3.30 shows the connection of PM type and electrostatic loudspeakers.

3.7 SOLVED EXAMPLES

EXAMPLE 3.1 In a broadcast superheterodyne receiver, the loaded Q of the antenna coupling circuit is 100. It is at the input to the mixer. If the intermediate frequency is 455 kHz, calculate

(i) The image frequency and its rejection ratio at 950 kHz.
(ii) The image frequency and its rejection ratio at 30 MHz.

Consider that the receiver has no RF amplifier.

Solution
(i) Image frequency = 950 + 2 × 455

$$= 1860 \text{ kHz}.$$

Rejection ratio calculation:

$$\rho = \frac{1860}{950} - \frac{950}{1860}$$

$$= 1.447$$

$$\alpha = \sqrt{1 + 100^2 \times 1.447^2} = 144.703$$

(ii) Image frequency = 30 + 2 × .455

$$= 30.91 \text{ MHz}$$

$$\rho = \frac{30.91}{30} - \frac{30}{30.91} = 0.05977$$

$$\alpha = \sqrt{1 + 100^2 \times .05977^2} = 6.06$$

EXAMPLE 3.2 For making the image frequency rejection of the receiver of Example 3.1 as good at 30 MHz as it was at 950 kHz, determine

(i) The loaded Q which an RF amplifier for this receiver would have to apply.
(ii) The new intermediate frequency that would be required if the RF amplifier is not to be applied.

Solution

(i) Since the mixer possesses a rejection ratio of 6.06, the image rejection of the RF stage will be

$$\alpha' = \frac{144.703}{6.065} = 23.878$$

∴ $$(Q')^2 = \frac{(23.878)^2 - 1}{0.05977}$$

or $$Q' = \sqrt{9522.484256} = 97.58$$

As well-designed receiver should have the same 'Q' for both the tuned circuits. Here, it will be geometric mean of 100 and 97.58, i.e., 98.78.

(ii) If the rejection is to be the same as initially through a change in the intermediate frequency, it is clear that ρ will have to be the same because Q is also the same.

Hence, $$\frac{f'_{si}}{f'_s} - \frac{f'_s}{f'_{si}} = \frac{1860}{950} - \frac{950}{1860} = 1.447$$

∴ $$\frac{f'_{si}}{f'_s} = \frac{1860}{950} = 1.95789$$

$$\frac{30 + 2f'_i}{30} = 1.95789$$

or $$30 + 2f'_i = 58.7367$$

or $$2f'_i = 28.7367$$

or $$f'_i = 14.36835 \text{ MHz.}$$

EXAMPLE 3.3 Three speakers each of 20 Ω impedance are connected to an amplifier with a 550 ohms line. The speakers power handling capacity are 22 watt, 16 watt and 12 watt. Determine the turns ratio of output transformer to meet the above requirement.

Solution The total power delivered by the amplifier = 22 + 16 + 12 = 50 watts. Voltage developed across the 550 Ω line

$$\frac{V_1^2}{R} = 50$$

or $\qquad V_1 = \sqrt{50 \times 550} = 165.83$ volt

voltage across secondary for no 1

$$E_1 = \sqrt{22 \times 20} = 20.976 \ \text{volt}$$

since speaker impedance is 20 Ω.
Voltage across secondary for no 2

$$E_2 = \sqrt{16 \times 20}$$

$$= 17.89 \ \text{volt}$$

Voltage across secondary for no 3

$$E_3 = \sqrt{12 \times 20}$$

$$= \sqrt{240} \ = 15.49 \ \text{volt}$$

Thus ratio for no 1

$$\frac{N_2}{N_1} = \frac{20.976}{165.83} = 0.1265$$

Turns ratio for no 2

$$\frac{N_2}{N_1} = \frac{17.89}{165.83} = 0.108$$

Turns ratio for no 3

$$\frac{N_2}{N_1} = \frac{15.49}{165.83} = 0.093$$

EXAMPLE 3.4 The power output from a microphone is 1.2 milliwatt into a line 650 Ω resistance. The attenuation is 3 dB. Find out the voltage at the distant end of line.

Solution $\qquad \text{Power} = \dfrac{V^2}{R}$

$$V = \sqrt{1.2 \times 10^{-3} \times 650}$$

$$= .883 \ \text{volt}$$

Attenuation in dB

$$3 = 20 \log_{10} \frac{E_1}{E_2} = 20 \log_{10} \frac{.883}{E_2}$$

or $\qquad \dfrac{3}{20} = \log_{10} \dfrac{.883}{E_2}$

$$\text{or} \qquad 10^{\frac{3}{20}} = \frac{.883}{E_2}$$

$$\text{or} \qquad E_2 = \frac{.883}{10^{3/20}}$$

$$= \frac{.883}{1.412537545} = 0.625 \text{ volt}$$

EXAMPLE 3.5 The sensitivity of a crystal microphone is 45 dB below 1 volt. Determine the output voltage when the microphone is an open circuit.

Solution
$$-45 = 20 \log_{10} \frac{E_{\text{output}}}{E_{\text{input}}}$$

$$\text{or} \qquad 45 = 20 \log_{10} \frac{E_{\text{input}}}{E_{\text{output}}}$$

$$\text{or} \qquad 45 = 20 \log_{10} \frac{1}{E_{\text{output}}}$$

$$\text{or} \qquad \frac{45}{20} = \log_{10} \frac{1}{E_{\text{output}}}$$

$$\text{or} \qquad \frac{1}{E_{\text{output}}} = 10^{\frac{45}{20}}$$

$$\text{or} \qquad E_{\text{output}} = \frac{1}{10^{\frac{45}{20}}}$$

$$= \frac{1}{177.827941}$$

$$= 5.623 \times 10^{-3} \text{ volt}$$

EXAMPLE 3.6 The output of a microphone is 70 dB below one volt in a resistance 6 Ω. Determine the gain to be provided by an amplifier to develop an output of 3 watt into 3000 Ω.

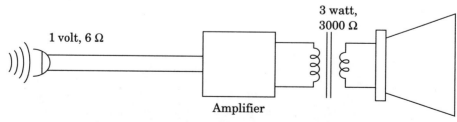

1 volt, 6 Ω

3 watt, 3000 Ω

Amplifier

Figure 3.31 Microphone with loudspeaker.

Solution $10 \log_{10} \dfrac{P_2}{P_1} = -70$

or $\log_{10} \dfrac{P_2}{P_1} = -7$

or $\log_{10} \dfrac{P_1}{P_2} = 7$

or $\dfrac{P_1}{P_2} = 10^7$

or $\dfrac{P_2}{P_1} = 10^{-7}$

Power input to the microphone

$$P_1 = \frac{E_1^2}{R_1} = \frac{1 \times 1}{6} = \frac{1}{6} \text{ watt}$$

Now, $\dfrac{P_2}{P_1} = 10^{-7}$

where $P_1 = \dfrac{1}{6} \text{ watt}$

$\therefore$ $P_2 = P_1 \times 10^{-7} = \dfrac{1}{6} \times 10^{-7} \text{ watt.}$

Hence, the gain to be provided by the amplifier

$$= 10 \log_{10} \frac{3}{\dfrac{1}{6} \times 10^{-7}}$$

$$= 10 \log_{10} 18 \times 10^7$$

$$= 10 [\log_{10} 18 + 7]$$

$$= 10 [1.2553 + 7]$$

$$- 10 [8.2553]$$

$$= 82.553 \text{ dB}$$

■ SUMMARY ■

Transmitters, Receivers and channels are three important items in radio communication. Block diagrams of transmitter and receiver are shown and explained. High level broadcast transmitter block diagram is also described. Need for high carrier frequency is explained. Main components of radio transmitter are narrated. Master oscillator is defined. Proper precautions to be taken for master oscillator are described. It is also mentioned that the crystal oscillator is the best choice as master oscillator for maintaining frequency stability. Most important points of crystal oscillator as master oscillator are discussed. The concept of buffer amplifier is explained. Since the buffer amplifier does not draw any input current, there will be no loading of the master oscillator. An idea is also given about harmonic generators. For deriving harmonic frequency from a pure sine voltage, the pure sine voltage is first of all distorted by some means to produce harmonic and then the output tank circuit is tuned to the required harmonic for rejecting all frequency components except the needed one. The mathematical expression for harmonic generator is also expressed. The circuit diagram of Class C harmonic generator is also described. An idea for the use of Class C amplifier is also explained. The modulated amplifier, i.e. Class C tuned amplifier is also discussed. The need for modulating amplifier, i.e. Class B push-pull amplifier is also explained. Both the block diagrams for high carrier power level amplitude modulation radio transmitter and low per level modulation system for radio transmitter are shown. The type of carrier frequency needed in radio transmission is elaborately discussed. Three main requirements of radio transmitter from the point of view of the carrier frequency are focused. In this connection, the factors for frequency drift are also mentioned. Analysis is also made on the factors responsible for frequency drift. The remedy for avoiding the problem is also suggested. Collector reactance stabilization on Hartley oscillator and base stabilization on Hartley oscillator are shown by circuit diagrams. Frequency stabilization of oscillator in spite of variations in electrode voltages is also shown through circuit diagram.

Elaborate discussion is made on radio receiver. The characteristics of the radio receivers, i.e. sensitivity, selectivity, fidelity, stability are defined. The classifications of radio receivers are made. Tuned radio frequency receiver with diagram is elaborately discussed. Superheterodyne receiver is explained in detail with a diagram. A tabular comparison is made between superheterodyne receiver and tuned radio frequency receiver. An idea is also given about automatic volume control (AVC). Automatic volume control circuit diagram is also explained. Various schemes of AVC are also narrated. Circuit diagrams of the following are shown with explanation.

(a) Linear diode detector with capacitor filter and simple AVC;
(b) Linear diode detector with π filter and simple AVC;
(c) Linear diode detector with delayed AVC;
(d) Linear diode detector with amplified and delayed AVC;
(e) Detector using transistor;
(f) Tone compensated volume control;
(g) Tone control circuit;
(h) Tuned circuits in the 3-band superheterodyne receiver.

The graphical representation of AVC characteristics is also shown.

Automatic frequency control (AFC) is discussed. With a block diagram, the AFC is shown in superheterodyne receiver. In this connection, the principle of varactor diode is also described. Equivalent circuit of the same is also discussed. An idea is also given on discriminator characteristic graphically. The concept of image frequency and rejection ratio in connection with superheterodyne receiver is also explained. The concept of aerial or antenna is also given. The major factors of the antenna system are narrated, i.e. wavelength, antenna impedance and directivity. Some ideas have been given on wavelength, antenna impedance and directivity.

Important terms related to antenna, e.g. bandwidth, beamwidth and polarization are discussed. The dipole antenna is defined. The half wave dipole antenna is described with diagram. Inverted 'V' antenna is also discussed with a diagram. An idea is also given about parasitic array or Yagi antenna It is also mentioned that the parasitic array or beam antenna consists of the elements like resonant half wave dipole, director and reflector.

Folded dipole is also described. An idea is also given about rhombic antenna with a diagram.

The concept of microphone is also given. Different types of microphones, e.g. carbon microphone, crystal microphone, moving coil microphone, electrostatic microphone are shown.

Loudspeakers of various types, e.g. permanent magnet type dynamic loudspeaker, electromagnetic field type dynamic loudspeaker, electrostatic loudspeaker and permanent magnet type and electrostatic type loudspeakers are shown through diagrams.

Some solved examples on superheterodyne receiver, loudspeaker, microphone are also given.

■ QUESTIONS ■

1. What are the main parts of radio communication? Explain by a block diagram.

2. What is high level broadcast transmitter? Explain with the help of a block diagram.

3. What are the main components of radio transmitter? What is a master oscillation? What is its role in radio communication?

4. Why crystal oscillator is the best choice for master oscillator?

5. Why buffer amplifier is used in radio transmission?

6. What is harmonic generator? Why is it used in radio transmission?

7. Prove that, with the increase of order of harmonics, the impedance of the tuned circuit is reduced?

8. What type of amplifier is used for modulated amplifier for radio transmission? What is the reason for that?

9. What type of amplifier is used for modulating amplifier for radio transmission? What is the reason behind that?

10. What are the main requirements of radio transmitter from the point of view of the carrier frequency?

11. What are the main factors for frequency drift in any oscillator?

12. What are the ways of compensation against the variation in inter electrode capacitances?

13. What are the functions of radio receiver?

14. How do you judge the characteristic of radio receivers?

15. Write a short not on

    (a) Selectivity of radio receivers

    (b) Sensitivity of radio receivers

    (c) Fidelity of radio receivers

    (d) Stability of radio receivers

16. How would you classify the radio receivers? Describe them.

17. How do you compare tuned radio frequency receiver and superheterodyne receiver?

18. What is automatic volume control of radio receiving system? Why is it needed?

19. Describe different types of automatic volume control?

20. What is automatic frequency control? Why is it needed?

21. What are the major factors of antenna system? Describe them.

22. Write a short note on

    (a) Bandwidth of antenna

    (b) Beamwidth of antenna

    (c) Polarization of antenna

23. What is dipole antenna? Describe it.

24. What is inverted V antenna? Describe it with a diagram.

25. What is Yagi antenna? What is its speciality?

26. What is folded dipole? Describe it.

27. What are the different types of microphones being used in radio transmission? Describe them.

28. What are the different types of loudspeakers in radio receiving system? Describe them.

4 ■■■ Telecommunication

4.1 INTRODUCTION

Let us first of all start with a telephone set. The inset transmitter and receiver are mounted in a carefully designed moulding which is termed hand microtelephone or handset. The insets are contained in a suitable compartment provided with a mouthpiece and earpiece respectively. The handset which is used is the 700 type telephone. The conductors are connected directly to the insets. The transmitter consists of an enclosure containing a powder of small carbon granules. One side of the enclosure is flexible and is mechanically attached to a diaphragm, on which sound waves impinge. The sound vibrates the diaphragm, the diaphragm makes the carbon granules to compress or allow them to expand and consequently there is a decrease or increase in the resistance of the carbon granules in the box. When the same is connected with an external battery, the change in resistance produces corresponding change in current. The receiver is an electromagnet. It is provided with a magnetic diaphragm. The received changes in the current form changes in the force of the electromagnet and that ultimately causes corresponding displacements of the receiver diaphragm. The above concept starts the telephone system. Now, we will proceed stage by stage to the modern telecommunication system.

4.2 TELEPHONE COMMUNICATION SYSTEM BETWEEN TWO STATIONS

Figure 4.1 shows the telephone communication system between the two stations. The sound incident on the transmitter at station 1 will not only be heard at receiver 2, but also at the receiver at station 1. The sound which is heard at the sound generating station is termed side tone. The inductor 'L' offers no dc resistance but is usually an open circuit at voice frequencies. There is a quiescent current flowing even in the absence of sound. This is generally useful for faithful sound reproduction.

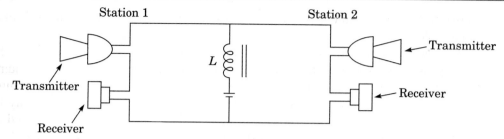

Figure 4.1 Telephone communication between two stations.

4.3 MODIFICATION OF THE TELEPHONE

Figure 4.2 shows the modern station set being used by the telephone subscriber. The major points pertaining to the modern station set are as follows.

(a) The minimum current required for proper operation of modern carbon microphone is 23 mA.

(b) The battery utilized in the system is 50 volt.

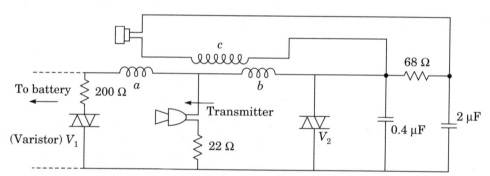

Figure 4.2 Modified telephone circuit.

(c) The maximum resistance allowable in the battery station set loop is $\dfrac{50}{23} \times 10^3 \approx 2200\ \Omega$.

(d) A resistance of approximately 400 Ω is kept at the battery for protecting against short circuits in the wire between the local office and subscriber. This is termed 'loop'. The station set resistance is generally 200 Ω. Hence, the Cu wire loop which connects battery to the station set will possess resistance approximately 1600 Ω (2200 Ω – 400 Ω – 200 Ω).

(e) Telephone connections are made with wire whose size lies between 19 to 26 gauge.

(f) A loop distance of about 4 miles is possible for 26 gauge wire, whereas a loop distance of about 18 miles is possible for 19 gauge wire.

(g) V_1 is a varistor which is nothing but a semiconductor. The resistance of the varistor decreases with the increase in current. When the resistance between the battery and station set decreases, the current shunted through V_1 will increase and therefore, the current passing through the transmitter will not increase. As the transmitter current and the signal strength generated and received by a station set is the function of the distance between the battery and the station set, the varistor V_1 maintains the variability within acceptable bounds.

(h) The sidetone of the station is also reduced. When a signal is developed by the microphone in the transmitter, the signal current flows through the transformer winding 'a' and 'b' in opposite directions. The parameters of 'V_2' and the associated circuitry of 'V_2' are made in such a manner that the currents in 'a' and 'b' will not only be oppositely directed but also of equal magnitude. Therefore, the voltage induced in winding 'c' on account of the current in 'a' and 'b' will oppose one another. As a result, the sidetone can be maintained within reasonable limits. When the signal is received from battery side, i.e. from the transmitter of another station set, the current will flow through 'a' and 'b' in the same direction and the signal received by the secondary winding 'c' of the transformer will provide the receiving earpiece the exact signal without attenuation.

4.4 METHOD OF SWITCHING

The methods of switching which can be applied to the telephone connection are as follows.

(a) A switching system in which each station has its own switching.

(b) A central exchange system.

From Figure 4.3, it is quite clear that any station can talk with other stations keeping provision the remaining two stations to communicate at the same time if they desire. Each station is provided with two inputs. One input is the signal received that the call is being allowed and

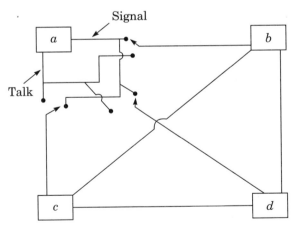

Figure 4.3 Own switching system.

the other input is nothing but the signal that means speaker can talk. In the figure, only the switches are shown in station 'a' for simplicity, but the switches are to be provided on all the four stations. This scheme is nothing but the switching system in which each station provides its own switching. In the above scheme more modifications are needed to make the system practically feasible.

(i) At least two wires are required for interconnection between stations. Moreover, for multiple connections between stations, more wires are required.

(ii) When there is no conversation, all switches will be in the signalling position and at that time any party can call the other. When there is conversation, both parties will switch to talk position. If there are 'N' stations, then the number of switching is required $N(N-1)$ and the number of interconnecting wires needed is $N(N-1)/2$.

With the help of central switching, improvement with respect to the total length of the interconnecting wires and the number of switches can be made. Thus, the concept of switching exchange comes. All the switches are located at one central location. The control can be made by a human operator or by automatic machinery. By central switching, the number of long interconnecting wires is reduced form $N(N-1)/2$ to N and the number of switches are reduced from $N(N-1)$ to $N(N-1)/2$ and this is very much clear from Figure 4.4.

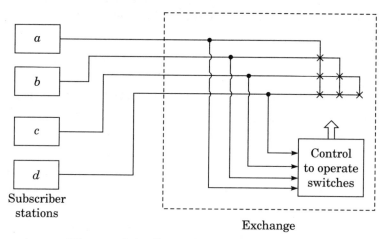

Figure 4.4 Central exchange system.

4.5 IDEA OF SIMPLE EXCHANGE SYSTEM

Figure 4.5 describes a simple exchange system. A simple exchange system is controlled by an operator.

During the starting of a call, the subscriber I lifts the transmitter-receiver from the cradle. The cradle switch is generally in open condition by the weight of the transmitter-receiver. But as it is lifted, the transmitter-receiver gets connected with subscriber loop. The ring key is normally connected to the points p and r. The current flows through the line lamp relay coil I. When the cradle switch closes, the capacitor C_1 will not allow the bell B_1 to ring because the battery supply is dc. The excitation in the line lamp relay Coil I causes the lamp switch on and the line lamp I glows. The lamp indicates the caller and the operator will be in action seeing the illuminated line lamp I, the operator will close the speak key I and ask the number from the speaker. Suppose the speaker wants to talk with a person in station II. The operator will throw the Ring key II towards the ringing generator side. The key is spring loaded and it will remain in the ringing position only when it will be in the hold position. The ring generator will provide an ac supply and the bell B_2 will ring. If the subscriber II does not pick up the phone, the operator informs the subscriber I, that the call is not being responded. If the subscriber II

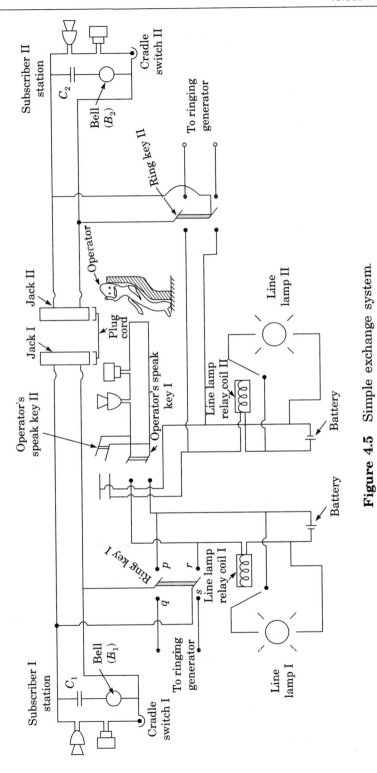

Figure 4.5 Simple exchange system.

lifts his phone from the cradle, the operator will find that the line lamp II is illuminated. The operator will then simply connect Jack I with Jack II with the help of plug cord as shown in Figure 4.5. Then the operator will advise subscriber I to talk with subscriber II. The speak keys are spring loaded and provide connection only when they are being held. When the conversation between I and II continues, both the line lamps I and II will glow. When both the subscribers place the phone on the cradle switch, the lamps will be off and the operator will disconnect the jacks.

4.6 STROWGER AUTOMATIC DIALING SYSTEM

Strowger automatic dialing system is the utilisation of some electo-mechanical switching devices.

The main switching device is shown in Figure 4.6. An array of 100 terminals are arranged in ten rows. The rows are stacked vertically. Each row has ten contacts. The terminals are placed

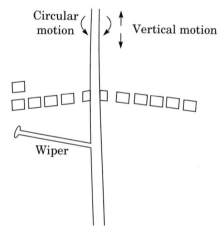

Figure 4.6 Strowger switch.

in a circular fashion at a constant distance from a shaft on which the wiper arm is fixed. The shaft and the wiper can be moved both in vertical and circular manners. The Strowger switch is arranged to operate in three modes as follows.

(a) In this mode, the shaft automatically searches out the right row and then it will start rotating to land the wiper on the mark. Receiving an external signal, it can search out a specific terminal distinguished by some voltage differential.

(b) It responds to an external signal by an advance of just a single row in the vertical direction. Then it advances step by step and an advance to row '*n*' needs '*n*' individual signals. Afterwards, the circular motion is self driven to a mark.

(c) It advances step by step both in the vertical direction and circular direction receiving response of individual circular or vertical driving signals from the external source.

Once the wiper reaches its desired terminal, it does not require any power to remain at that position. When a knock-down signal is received, it will automatically come back to its original position. The shaft is rotated back by its spring tension and then falls down on account of gravity.

4.6.1 Process of Strowger Switching System

Figure 4.7 shows the arrangement of Strowger switches for establishing a connection against dialing. There are four switches with respective control (as shown in Figure 4.7). The switches are:

(a) Line finder switch
(b) Two selector switches
(c) Connector switch.

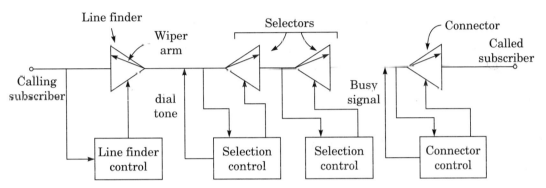

Figure 4.7 Strowger switching telephone system.

In the line finder, the terminal bank faces the calling subscriber. Whereas for all other three switches, the terminal bank faces the called subscriber. When the phone is lifted from its cradle, then it is termed "off hook". The current starts flowing in the subscriber's loop. The current also gives signal to the line finder control mechanism. As a result, the line finder switch is set on a self driven search for finding the terminal on its bank at which the connection is to be made. The switch starts moving upwards until it selects the proper row and then rotates until if finds its mark. In practice, the line finders are equipped with two parallel hundred terminal banks. The wiper arm is then provided with two contacts and an extra relay is required to distinguish one bank from the other. Moreover, it is essential that an incoming subscriber line is to be connected to a number of line finders because at a particular moment, an arbitrary line finder may be busy. Hence, the selector which is lying in the home position is not busy and the same will be connected with the calling party. If such free selector is available, then the calling party will receive the dial tone indicating that he can dial. Suppose, the caller has to dial 6123. The caller first of all will dial 6 at the rotary station set dial. When the dial returns to the rest position due to spring tension, a cam mechanism opens the line 6 times. As a result, the waveform will be developed as shown in Figure 4.8. The response of the first selector to these 6 pulses is to advance vertically one step for each pulse and finally it reaches the 6th row of the Strowger. Therefore, all the terminals in this row are now ready to connect through other Strowger switch to phones whose first digit number is 6. The first selector will connect the incoming line to a second connector which can respond to the second digit. The second selector is to be found out and that should not be busy. The first connector on row 6 rotates and goes on testing terminal to terminal on that 6th row until it finds a switch which is not busy. Now

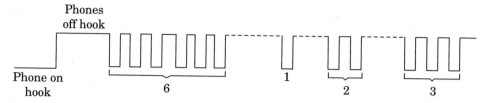

Figure 4.8 Waveform developed in Strowger switching telephone system.

the second stage selector will respond to the second dialed digit, i.e. 1 in number 6123. The last switch usually takes care of the last two digits, i.e. 23 because there are 100 terminals on the switch. That means, the dialing of '2' makes the switch advanced to row '2' and then dialing of '3' makes the switch rotated to the 3rd column. Hence, the call is completed.

If the amount of switching equipment is limited, then it is not possible for the automatic system to complete the call connection on account of non-availability of idle switching gear. At that scenario, the call is blocked.

4.7 THE CROSS BAR SWITCH

The cross bar switch arrangement is also another type of telephone exchange system. In many cases, it has replaced the Strowger switching arrangement. Figure 4.9 describes the same. It has an array of horizontal and vertical wires (shown by firm lines in Figure 4.9). These wires are connected to initially separated contact points of switches. Horizontal and vertical bars (shown as dashed lines in Figure 4.9) are mechanically connected to these contact points. The bars are connected to electromagnets. An excitation of a bar magnet creates a slight rotation of the bar and as a result, the contact points connected to the bar move closer to its facing contact points. The motion is not, of course, large to cause contact.

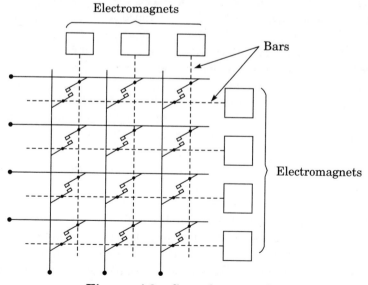

Figure 4.9 Cross bar switch.

On the other hand, an electromagnet connected to a horizontal bar and an electromagnet connected to a vertical bar are activated simultaneously, the contact of the intersection of the two bars will be nearer since both of the contact points will move towards each other. There lies a mechanical latching provided with cross bar switches in such a way that in case of activation of horizontal and vertical bars, a contact is made and that contact exists even in case of release of activation of horizontal bar. The contact will only open when both the vertical and horizontal activations are withdrawn.

4.8 MOBILE TELEPHONE COMMUNICATION

The main concept of developing mobile communication lies on the following basic points.

  (a) To provide telephone communication to thousands of mobile users within a greater metropolitan area,
  (b) To achieve the above target, minimum amount of the frequency spectrum is to be used;
  (c) When the demand increases, the subscriber can use the same throughout the country;
  (d) To allow hand-held portable operation and vehicle operation of the telephone;
  (e) To provide regular telephone services and quality of service.

To satisfy the above objectives, a cellular radio network concept was developed. Usually, in this type of network each geographical area is subdivided into small regions termed cells. Within a cell, all communications are performed utilising a given bandwidth and centre frequency.

In Figure 4.10 a cellular layout is shown. In cell a centre frequency f_a is used. Similarly in cell b, centre frequency f_b is used. If two cells are separated largely, then the receiving antenna in one cell cannot identify the signal being transmitted from other cell. Then both cells can be allocated the same centre frequency. Some idea of choosing the centre frequency is shown in Figure 4.10. For example, a_1 and a_2 have the same centre frequency; b_1 and b_2, c_1 and c_2, d_1 and d_2 have the same centre frequency. This method of conserving the frequency is termed frequency reuse. The bandwidth provided with each cell is divided into n channels. Hence, if the bandwidth of a cell is b_c, then the bandwidth provided with each user is $b_u = b_c/n$.

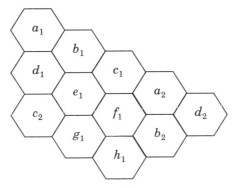

Figure 4.10 Cellular layout.

4.8.1 Mobile Service

There are three methods of mobile calls in practice.

- (a) Mobile to mobile calls
- (b) Mobile to fixed subscriber calls
- (c) Fixed to mobile subscriber calls.

Mobile to mobile calls

Figure 4.11 describes mobile to mobile call procedure. When a mobile subscriber wants to make a call, the mobile unit first of all enquires about the availability of channel and its centre frequency. There exist 21 special set-up channels for this purpose.

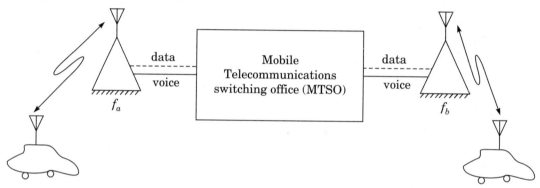

Figure 4.11 Mobile to mobile call.

After the determination of centre frequency, the unit then sends a data message which consists of the user's identification and the number to be called. The bit rate of the message is 10 kb/second. Over and above, an error correcting code is utilised and the message is repeated five times with majority-rule logic employed to reduce errors in signal amplitude fluctuation. The data message is transmitted to a mobile telecommunication switching office (MTSO) as shown in Figure 4.11. The MTSO analyzes identification insuring that the same is proper. Afterwards it also analyzes the called number. It checks whether it is a mobile or fixed subscriber. If the call is a mobile unit, the MTSO sends the data message containing the called number to each cell site. Each mobile subscriber's unit starts scanning. The unit finally responds to the cell site in which the unit is located and then the cell site responds to the MTSO. The MTSO then makes the caller's cell and the called unit's cell with voice line connections. Then the conversation starts. When the conversation is finished and any one of the users hangs up, the MTSO releases both the voice lines.

Mobile to fixed subscriber calls

When the mobile subscriber calls a fixed subscriber, the MTSO recognizes the number called as being fixed. The cell is then routed to the class '5' switching office (local switching office). There the arrangement is made to send the call to the destination. Figure 4.12 describes mobile fixed call connection.

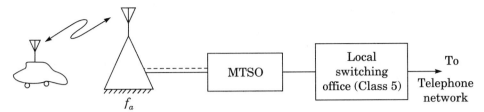

Figure 4.12 Mobile to fixed call connection.

Fixed to mobile subscriber calls

When a fixed subscriber calls a mobile subscriber, the call is routed to the particular toll office. That is found out from the area code of the called number. The toll office routes the call to the local office and MTSO. The MTSO then finally completes the connection.

4.8.2   The Concept of Cellular Telephone System

Since the invention of radio systems, the goal of telephone engineers is to provide personal telephone service to individuals by using radio systems to link the phone line with persons in their cars or on foot. In the past this type of personal telephone service was not possible because limited spectrum space did not permit the assignment of a "private line" radio channel for each subscriber. In addition, the existing radio equipment was bulky and expensive. However, with the development of integrated circuit technology, radio equipment can now be miniaturized and relatively sophisticated operations can be implemented at low cost.

The cellular radio concept is illustrated in Figure 4.13. Each user communicates via radio from a cellular telephone set to the cell site base station. This base station is connected via telephone lines to the mobile telephone switching office (MTSO). The MTSO connects the user to the called party. If the called party is land based, the connection is via the central office (CO)

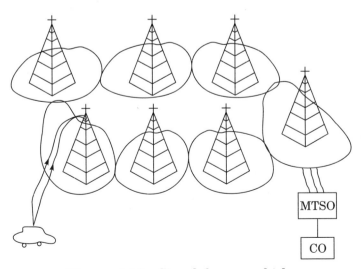

Figure 4.13 Signal from a vehicle.

to the terrestial telephone network. If the called party is mobile, the connection is made to the cell site that covers the area in which the called party is located using an available radio channel in the cell associated with the called party.

Theoretically, this cellular concept allows any number of mobile users to be accommodated for given set of radio channels. That is, if more channels are needed, the existing cell sizes are decreased and additional small cells are inserted so that the existing channels can be reused more efficiently. As the mobile user travels from one cell to another, the MTSO automatically switches the user to an available channel in the new cell and the telephone conversation continues uninterrupted.

Each cellular telephone contains a PROM (programmable read-only memory) or EPROM (erasable programmable read-only memory). This is called a numeric assignment module (NAM). This is programmed to contain the following:

(a) The telephone number which is termed the electronic service number (ESN) of the phone.
(b) The serial number of the phone as assigned by the manufacturer.
(c) Personal codes that can be used to prevent unauthorized use of the phone.

When the phone is "on the air", it automatically transmits its serial number to the MTSO.

The serial number is used by the MTSO to lock out the phone that has been stolen. This feature, of course, discourages theft of the units. The MTSO uses the telephone number of the unit to provide billing information. When the phone is used in a remote city, it can be placed in the roaming mode so that calls can be initiated or received and the service will be billed via the caller's "hometown" company.

The following sequence of events occurs at the time of placing a call.

(a) The cellular subscriber initiates a call by keying in the telephone number of the called party and then presses the send key.
(b) The MTSO verifies that the telephone number is valid and that the user is authorized to make the call.
(c) The MTSO issues instructions to the user's cellular phone indicating which radio channel to use.
(d) The MTSO sends out a signal to the called party to ring his phone. All of these operations occur within ten seconds of initiating the cell.
(e) When the called party answers, the MTSO connects the trunk lines for the two parties and initiates billing information.
(f) When one party hangs up, the MTSO frees the radio channel and completes the billing information.

While a call is in progress, the cellular subscriber may be moving from one cell area to another, so the MTSO performs the following operations.

(i) The MTSO monitors the signal strength from the cellular telephone as received at the cell base station. If the signal drops below some designed level, the MTSO initiates a hand-off sequence.
(ii) For 'hand-off' the MTSO inquires about the signal strength as received at adjacent cell sites.

(iii) When the signal level becomes sufficiently large at an adjacent cell site, the MTSO instructs the cellular radio to switch over to an appropriate channel for communication with that new cell site. The switching process takes less than 25 ms and is usually unnoticed by the subscriber.

4.8.3 Application of Fibre Optic Lines

The optical source has a wavelength in the range of 0.85 to 1.6 μm which is about 77,000 GHz. The optical sources can be classified into two categories.

- Light emitting diodes (LED) that produce noncoherent light.
- Solid state lasers that produce coherent light (single carrier frequency.)

Figure 4.14 shows the application of fibre optic line in the telecommunication. Figure 4.15 has described specifically the remote terminal (RT).

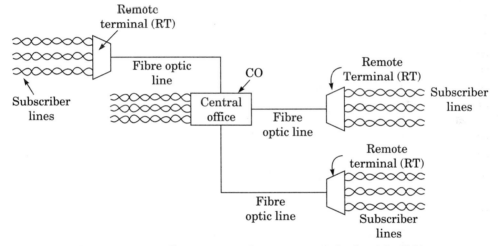

Figure 4.14 Connection of remote terminal with 'CO'.

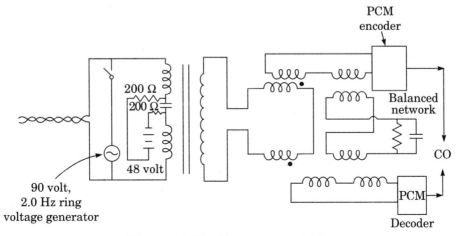

Figure 4.15 Remote terminal.

Digital fibre optic system utilizes modulation of an optical source to produce a modulated light beam. Optical fibre is a piece of very thin highly pure glass with an outside cladding of glass that is similar but because of a slightly different chemical composition it has a different refractive index. The fibre optical cable is the channel of transmission medium. The receiving end of the fibre consists of optical detector. The optical detectors are generally pin diode, avalanche photo diode. Pin diode is a low cost detector. The optical source is Indium gallium Arsenide phosphide. Usually, the optical diode is Avalanche Germanium photodiode (APD). Most of the fibre applications for telephony have utilized digital signals. Of course, analog transmission is not impossible. Analog FM modulation of optical signals is also used in the feeder applications of CATV system. Over and above, systems that carry 80 channels of AM video on fibre to residences have been produced. This is the capability that permits analog television sets to receive fibre based cable TV without a digital video decoder.

4.8.4 Fibre Optic Elements in Transmission System

Figure 4.16 describes the fibre optic transmission system block diagram. The components are as follows:

(a) Electrical to optical transducer
(b) Optical fibre
(c) Optical to electrical transducer
(d) Signal processing circuitry
    (i) amplification
    (ii) clock recovery
    (iii) data detection.

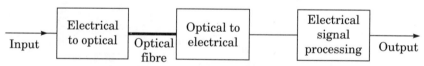

Figure 4.16 Fibre optic transmission system block diagram.

Regenerative repeaters require optical to electrical conversion for the signal processing functions and conversion back to optical for transmission. Direct optical amplification with erbium doped fibre amplifiers (EDFAs) are used instead of repeaters specially for wavelength division multiplexing (WDM) transmission links.

4.8.5 Fundamentals of Optical Fibre

Figure 4.17 describes the basic construction of an optical fibre.

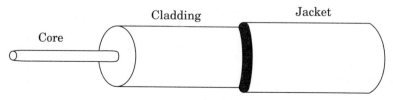

Figure 4.17 Optical fibre construction.

Here, the core and the cladding are transparent to the desired light signal. The design of the cladding is made with lower index of refraction. That causes most of the light waves in the core to be reflected back into the core. This reflection back of the ray totally depends at which the ray strikes the core cladding boundary. If the angle is very sharp, the ray is not reflected but passes through the cladding. Then the same ray is absorbed by the opaque protective jacket. Generally, the sharp angles occur at two places.

(a) One is near the source where all of the output of the source is not focused into the centre of the fibre.

(b) Second is at splices, bends or other imperfections in the fibre.

Figure 4.18 describes fibre with multimode propagation. A typical multimode fibre has a 50 μm core diameter and a 125 μm cladding diameter. This fibre is termed 50/125 fibre. The bandwidth distance product (BDP) of a typical step index multimode fibre is 13 Mbps-km. The step index fibre is the fibre whose index of refraction in the core is constant with a step change in the index occurring at the core-cladding boundary. Multimode dispersion can be reduced by changing the index of refraction within the core so that a high value occurs in the centre and a low value occurs at the edge. We know that the speed of propagation of light is higher in lower indices of refraction. Therefore, the rays which reflect back and forth within the core travel at an average speed. This average speed is greater than a primary ray. The primary ray remains entirely within the centre. Hence, if the index of refraction is graded within the core, all rays can be made to reach at the receiver with the same amount of delay. This fibre is termed graded-index fibre. The BDP of the graded index fibre is 2 Gbps-km.

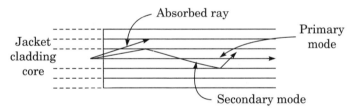

Figure 4.18   Multimode propagation on fibre.

4.8.6   Electrical to Optical Transducer

The following semiconductor devices convert electrical signals into optical signals.

(a) Laser Diode ((LD)

(b) Light emitting diode (LED)

The advantages of a laser diode are as follows:

• A laser diode provides better performance in terms of higher output power

• It provides better performance in terms of greater bandwidth

• It provides better performance in terms of narrower signal spectrum.

The advantages of an LED are as follows:

• A LED is less expensive

• It requires simple interface circuitry

- It is more tolerant to environmental conditions
- It is more reliable

Mainly the laser diodes are used for long transmission distances. The LED is used when ruggedness and interface costs are more vital than performance.

4.8.7 Optical to Electrical Transducer

The photodetectors are used as transducers to convert the optical energy at the receiver to electrical energy for amplification and other processing for example clock recovery, data detection. The photodetectors are of two types.

- Silicon based p-i-n diode
- Avalanche photodiode (APD)

Silicon based p-i-n diodes

The silicon based p-i-n diode operates in systems having wavelength of 800–900 nm. The advantages of these diodes are as follows:

(a) Silicon based p-i-n diode is inexpensive;
(b) It is reliable; and
(c) It is good at performance.

The demerits are as follows

(a) It does not operate at higher wavelength where fibre loss is minimized.
(b) If the germanium devices are used, we may get higher wavelength but the same will be more temperature dependent and less reliable.

Avalanche photodiode (APD)

The advantages of the APD are as follows:

(a) Avalanche photodiode enhances the receiver sensitivity since it operates with internal gain.
(b) The APD can be 10–15 dB more sensitive in detecting low level signals at a given error rate.

The demerits of APD are:

(a) Avalanche photodiode requires a high supply voltage to operate.
(b) It is very sensitive to temperature.
(c) APD has somewhat lower data rate.

4.9 TELEGRAPHY

The telegraphy is a kind of communication that utilizes a typewriter like machine being operated at a maximum speed of about sixty words per minute for sending messages from one place to another. A person submits a written message at a telegraph or postoffice and that is subsequently transmitted to the office nearest to the address and finally the same is delivered in written form to the appropriate place.

The main difference between the telegraph and telex is the signalling method and the procedure of sending the message. The telex combines the telegraph system with the subscriber dialing techniques. The originator of the message composes the message and the message is automatically routed to the concerned person and the same is printed out by the machine. The telegraphy system works in the following manner:

(a) When the key of the transmitting teletypewriter is tapped, a set of coded pulses are developed.

(b) At the receiving end, just the reverse happens. The same machine prints out the appropriate letter when a given code is reversed.

The different typewriters in the telegraphy system are as follows.

- Page printer form.
- Tape printer form.

The message in the telegraphy system is typed out in advance on perforated tape to avoid limitations on account of the maximum typing speed and efficiency. Thus, the capacity of the channel and machine can be fully utilized.

4.9.1 Code of the Telegraphy System

Code is a coherent system of rules, which develops some particular object or purpose. Hence, a signalling code comprises the system of rules. With the help of these rules, the letters or figures to be signalled are defined. The telegraph codes which are largely utilized are the five unit codes and its variants, the Morse code and the cable code.

Morse code and five unit codes are termed two condition codes. The Morse code and five unit codes are binary codes. That means, they depend on the utilization of two signalling conditions. These conditions are either "current on" and "current off" or "positive current" and "negative current". In other words, they are single current working or double current working. Both ac and dc signalling systems are for two condition signalling.

Cable code is a type of dc signal utilized for transoceanic submarine cable working. Here, three signalling conditions are utilized.

(a) Negative voltage to line represents "Dots".

(b) Positive voltage to line represents "Dashes".

(c) No voltage represents spaces between words and letters.

Line is earthed at the transmitter for the duration of spacing signal elements.

Morse code

Radiotelegraphy by Morse code is named after its inventor Samuel Finley Breese Morse (1791 1872). He was an American artist and promoter of the telegraph.

Morse code is the efficient means of radio communication. Radiotelegraphy in itself is a language. Every person does not understand English; but, through recognized systems and combination of dots and dashes, every person converses in a common language—the Morse code. Amateur radio is one of the most important applications of Morse code. A majority of public service, health, welfare and emergency messages can be handled quickly and with greater accuracy on Morse code.

The advantages of Morse code are as follows:

(a) Morse code is economical;
(b) It is compact;
(c) It uses low power;
(d) It has global coverage; and
(e) It is free from disturbances.

Timing of Morse code

The basic unit of time in Morse code is the length of the dot. The duration of the dash is three times that of the dot. The term 'element' is used to indicate both dots and dashes. The space between two elements forming the same character is also the length of the dot.

The space between letters is equal to three dots and the space between words is equal to five dots.

* Dot (one unit)   — Dash (Three units)
  or Dit (one unit)   or Dah (Three units).

The character to character is generally called one Dit (unit). The letter to letter is called three Dits (units). The word to word is called five Dits (units). The Morse code is built up of three elements. The dit, a short signal, the dash, a long signal and the space are the international Morse Alphabet. Letters and figures are represented by various combinations of dots and dashes.

```
A  · —
B  — · · ·
C  — · — ·
D  — · ·
E  ·
F  · · — ·
G  — — ·
H  · · · ·
I  · ·
J  · — — —
K  — · —
L  · — · ·
M  — —
N  — ·
O  — — —
P  · — — ·
Q  — — · —
R  · — ·
S  · · ·
T  —
U  · · —
V  · · · —
```

W   · — —
X   — · · —
Y   — · — —
Z   — — · ·
1   · — — — —
2   · · — — —
3   · · · — —
4   · · · · —
5   · · · · ·
6   — · · · ·
7   — — · · ·
8   — — — · ·
9   — — — — ·
10   — — — — —

Full stop	.	· — · — · —
Semi colon	;	— · — · — ·
Comma	,	— — · · — —
Question mark	?	· · — — · ·
Hyphen	–	— · · · · —
Double dash	=	— · · · —

Five unit code

Five unit code is preferable than Morse code. The main problem of the Morse code is that the unequal lengths of the code combinations represent different characters and thus it creates problem for direct printing of the received messages from the line signals. That is why, five unit code and its variants are mainly used in the telegraphy system and specially in the teleprinter system.

"International Telegraph Alphabet No 2"

"International Telegraph Alphabet No 2" is the most important standardized form of the code. In the five unit code, 2^5 (= 32) is the total number of combinations available. That is why 32 numbers of codes are found in the International Alphabet No 2.

No.	Letter case	Figure case	Start signal	5 unit code	Stop signal
1	A	—	○	● ● ○ ○ ○	●
2	B	?	○	● ○ ○ ● ●	●
3	C	:	○	○ ● ● ● ○	●
4	D	WRU	○	● ○ ○ ● ○	●
5	E	3	○	● ○ ○ ○ ○	●
6	F	Note (1)	○	● ○ ● ● ○	●
7	G	Note (1)	○	○ ● ○ ● ●	●
8	H	Note (1)	○	○ ○ ● ○ ●	●
9	I	8	○	○ ● ● ○ ○	●

(Contd.)

(Contd.)

No.	Letter case	Figure case	Start signal	5 unit code	Stop signal
10	J	Audible signal	○	● ● ○ ● ○	●
11	K	(	○	● ● ● ● ○	●
12	L	)	○	○ ● ○ ○ ●	●
13	M	.	○	○ ○ ● ● ●	●
14	N	,	○	○ ○ ● ● ○	●
15	O	9	○	○ ○ ○ ● ●	●
16	P	0	○	○ ● ● ○ ●	●
17	Q	1	○	● ● ● ○ ●	●
18	R	4	○	○ ● ○ ● ○	●
19	S	,	○	● ○ ● ○ ○	●
20	T	5	○	○ ○ ○ ○ ●	●
21	U	7	○	● ● ● ○ ○	●
22	V	=	○	○ ● ● ● ●	●
23	W	2	○	● ● ○ ○ ●	●
24	X	/	○	● ○ ● ● ●	●
25	Y	6	○	● ○ ● ○ ●	●
26	Z	+	○	● ○ ○ ○ ●	●
27	Carriage RETN		○	○ ○ ○ ● ●	●
28	LINE FEED		○	○ ● ○ ○ ○	●
29	LETTERS*		○	● ● ● ● ●	●
30	Figures*		○	● ● ○ ● ●	●
31	SPACE		○	○ ○ ● ○ ○	●
32	Not used**		○	○ ○ ○ ○ ○	●

4.10 TELEGRAPH KEY

The telegraph key is a means of making and breaking a connection. Figure 4.19 describes the telegraph key. The key is mounted firmly on the operating table. The contacts are adjusted until

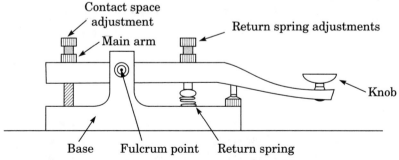

Figure 4.19 Telegraph key.

the handle moves about 1/16th inch when it is pressed. Fixing and adjustments are to be done to reduce side to side sway.

Finally, the spring tension is adjusted to a comfortable feel. The wrist is to be kept off the table. The message is to be sent with the help of the wrist, but not through the fingers. A gentle grip is needed around the knob. A smooth up and down motion makes for clean and effortless sending.

4.10.1 Morse key

Figure 4.20 describes the Morse key. Here (3) and (4) are the front and back stops. The tips of both the stops are made of platinum. (2) is the pivot. (1) is the brass lever. (5) is a spring. Terminal screws are mounted on the brass plates which carry the front stop, bridge and the back stop.

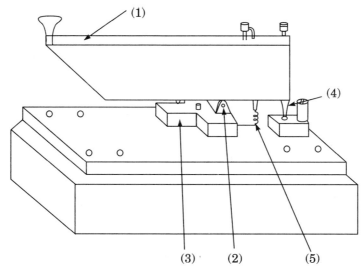

Figure 4.20 Morse key.

4.10.2 Non-polarized Sounder

Figure 4.21 shows the non-polarized sounder. The components of the non-polarized sounder are as follows:

1. Soft iron armature
2. Bell crank lever
3. Pivot
4. Soft iron cores
5. Soft iron yoke
6. Stop (lever is held against the stop)
7. Stop (preventing the armature from touching the cores)
8. Spring

9. Milled headed screw
10. Elbow.

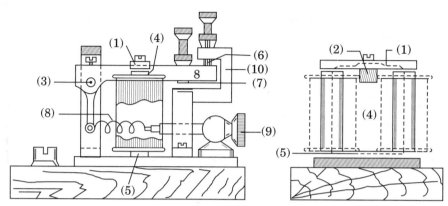

Figure 4.21 Non-polarized sounder.

The soft iron armature (1) is carried on a bell crank lever (2) pivoted at (3). The armature is kept just above the two iron cores (4) placed in two opposite ends. The bell crank lever is held by the stop (6) with the help of the tension of the spring (8). The tension of the spring is adjusted by a milled headed screw (9). (7) is another stop which prevents the armature from touching the cores and being stuck at elbow (10). When the current is passed through the coils, which are wound on the soft iron cores and are joined in series as well as connected to two terminal screws, the armature will move towards the cores against the spring action. Therefore, stop (7) will strike elbow (10) since it prevents the armature from touching the cores. Thus, their becomes indication of starting the Morse signal by the striking sound. Similarly, the sound made by the lever (2) striking the stop (6) will be the indication of the end of the signal when the current is stopped.

In this type of sounder, the coil resistance is 21 Ω and the same is shunted by a resistance of 420 Ω and operating current required is 55 mA. The shunt resistance reduces the effect of inductance. Otherwise, this may cause sparking at the contacts.

4.10.3 Telegraph Relay

The telegraph relay is a device which is being used in place of sounders. Since the sounders are not very much sensitive, it is not wise to use sounders on long lines. That is why relays are used in place of sounders over a wide range handling small value of current.

The relays generally utilized in the telegraph system are as follows:

(a) Non-polarized relay.
(b) Polarized relay.

Figure 4.22 shows non-polarized relay. The components of the non-polarized relay are as follows:

1. Two soft iron armatures mounted on the pivoted brass spindle;
2. Spring;

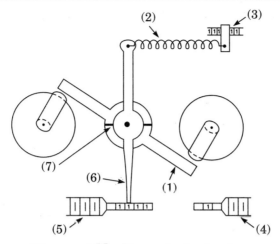

Figure 4.22 Non-polarized relay.

3. Screw to adjust the tension of the spring;
4. Platinum tipped contacts termed 'marking';
5. Platinum tipped contacts termed 'spacing';
6. German silver tongue moving between two adjustable platinum tipped contacts;
7. Brass-strip.

The two soft iron armatures are mounted on a pivoted brass spindle. They are split by a brass strip, as a result there will be no magnetic saturation. A light German silver tongue (6) is attached at the upper end of the spindle. The tongue (6) can move between two adjustable platinum tipped contacts (4) and (5). The screw (3) is utilized to adjust the tension of the spring (2) that makes the tongue (6) to hold over to the spacing stop. This relay has a range from 6 to 15 mA operating current. In case of polarized relay, the armatures and cores are polarized by a strong permanent horseshoe magnet.

Figure 4.23 shows the circuit diagram of polarized relay. When the current passes through the coil, the flux is strengthened on the one side and weakened on the other. Hence, the armature moves to one side or the other depending on the direction of the current.

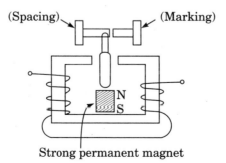

Figure 4.23 Polarized relay.

4.11 TELECOMMUNICATION IN POWER SYSTEM

The high voltage power transmission line can be coupled with the telecommunication line. The coupling of the high frequency apparatus with the power transmission line is usually made possible with the help of coupling condensers. These condensers block the power frequency current but permit the *hf* currents at frequencies of 50 kHz–300 kHz to pass practically without attenuation. On the other hand, the wave traps block the *hf* currents presenting only very little impedance to the passage of power frequency current with a frequency of 16.67–60 Hertz.

Figure 4.24 describes the coupling with power transmission line.

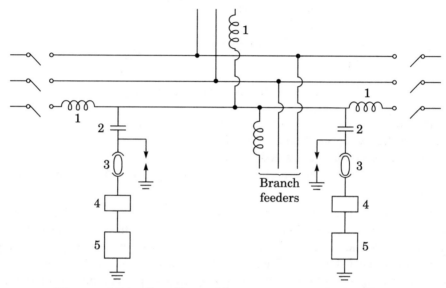

Figure 4.24 Coupling with power transmission line.

The components of the coupling with power transmission line are as follows:

1. Carrier trap unit
2. Coupling condenser
3. Protective apparatus
4. Impedance matching unit
5. HF cable.

In case of disturbance in the transmission line for travelling wave, the coupling circuit is to be improved further. Figure 4.25 describes the above.

The components of the detailed coupling system are as follows:

1. Carrier trap unit
2. Coupling condenser
3. Combined fuse and isolating switch
4. High frequency cubicle
5. High frequency cubicle
6. Line earthing switch

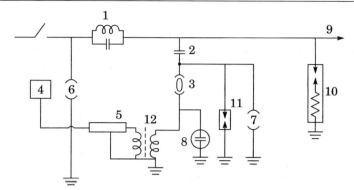

Figure 4.25 Detailed coupling system with power transmission line.

7. Earthing switch
8. 350 V arrestor
9. Power transmission line
10. Resorbit arrestor
11. Resorbit arrestor for protection of high frequency apparatus
12. Impedance matching transformer.

4.11.1 Description of the Components of the Circuit

Coupling condenser

The coupling condenser is oil immersed, paper insulated type. It is designed for all standard voltages. It may be of indoor or outdoor type.

Carrier trap units

The wave traps are used to block the high frequency currents with values of frequencies between 50 kHz and 300 kHz, but to allow the power frequency current to pass without losses. The blocking effect depends on the value of inductance in the wave trap. Higher the inductance in the wave trap, the larger the blocking effect will occur. Wave traps are designed as resonant circuit tuned to block the carrier wave. In the wave trap, inductance and condenser are connected in parallel. Arrangement can be made such that a wave trap is able to tune two different carrier frequencies. The addition of a second inductance and a second condenser can do this. The wave traps are connected directly in one phase of the power transmission line. It is also essential to design the inductances in such a way that they can carry the current flowing in the line. Wave traps are standardized for currents of 200 ampere, 400 ampere and 700 ampere. The variation in the tuning frequency in the wave trap is possible due to the variable condensers. The inductance unit is made of copper or aluminium windings. The condenser units are mounted on a moisture proof casing.

Protective and matching equipment

The protective equipment prevents any surge voltage, which may occur on the high tension line, from reaching the high frequency part of the plant and creating a dangerous voltage on the low tension side of the coupling condenser. Resorbit arrestor with a striking voltage of

1500 volt and a fuse with a rating of 1 ampere is mounted in the immediate vicinity of the coupling condenser. This helps as a protective device. Earthing switch also helps the low tension section of the high frequency installation to be completely isolated. The primary windings of the impedance matching transformer is protected by a low voltage arrestor. The primary and secondary windings of the impedance matching transformer are insulated from each other for a voltage of 10 kV. For reducing the high frequency power losses to a minimum, the impedance of the low voltage side of the installation is matched to the impedance of the high voltage side impedance.

4.11.2 Various Methods of Coupling

Two methods of coupling are generally utilized in case of three phase transmission line.

(a) Coupling to one phase and earth
(b) Coupling to two phases.

Figure 4.26 describes phase to earth coupling in power line carrier system. The equipments required for this system are as follows.

- Carrier trap unit (1) as shown in Figure 4.26
- Coupling condenser (2)
- Protective apparatus (3)
- Impedance matching unit (4)
- H.F. cubicle (5)

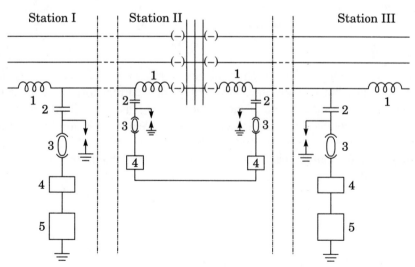

Figure 4.26 Phase to earth coupling in power line carrier system.

Figure 4.27 describes phase to phase coupling in power line carrier systems. The equipments required for this system are as follows.

- Carrier trap unit (1)

- Coupling condenser (2)
- Combined fuse and isolating switch (3)
- HF cubicle (4)
- HF cubicle (5).

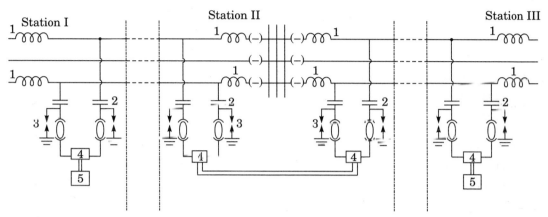

Figure 4.27 Phase to phase coupling in power line carrier systems.

Comparative study of the above two systems:

Phase to earth coupling in power line carrier system	Phase to phase coupling in power line
The characteristic impedance is of the order 400 Ω.	The characteristic impedance is of the order 800 Ω.
The attenuation for transmission is high.	The attenuation for transmission is low.
This method is cheap.	This method is costly.
Generally, this system is used.	In special cases such as extra high voltage lines of great length, danger of hoar frost etc., this is used.

4.11.3 Equipments Used in the Power Transmission Line

The equipments required are as follows:

- Low voltage equipment
- High frequency equipment
- Current supply

Low voltage equipment

The equipment mainly consists of transmitter and receiver. The transmitter consists of

- Oscillator for generating the carrier wave
- 10–W amplification stage
- Modulator

The receiver consists of

- Detector
- Amplifier stages with automatic gain control.

High voltage equipment

High voltage equipment consists of

- Transmitter
- Receiver
- Accessories such as filters, relays, rectifiers
- Panels for mounting the above
- Test panel

Current supply

The necessary equipments are

- Rectifier for supplying the voltage needed for heater and other circuits.
- Automatic change over to an emergency set with a rating of about 400 volt ampere.

4.11.4 Applications

Telephony

Figure 4.28 describes the integrated system of power line carrier system and telephone exchange system without automatic exchange.

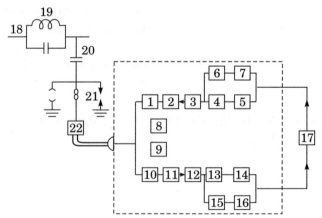

Figure 4.28 Integrated system of power line carrier system and telephone exchange.

The components are:

1. Transmitter filter
2. HF transmitter
3. Modulator

4. Band pass filter
5. Microphone amplifier
6. Low pass filter
7. AF oscillator for calling
8. Power supply unit
9. Testing and checking unit
10. Receiver filter
11. Automatic volume control
12. HF receiver
13. Band pass filter
14. Telephone amplifier
15. Low pass filter
16. Call receiver amplifier
17. Telephone
18. Power transmission line
19. Carrier trap unit
20. Coupling condenser
21. Protective apparatus
22. Impedance matching unit.

Two carrier waves are needed for the establishment of telephonic communication. In the state of rest only the receivers are in operation. As a result, each set is at every instant capable of receiving a call. At the time of lifting the telephone receiver, the transmitter is switched on and sends through the transmission line a carrier wave with a frequency F_1 that operates the calling receiver at the other end. While the receiver at the called end is lifted, it interrupts the calling and initiates in its turn the transmission of a second carrier wave with the frequency F_2. The connection between the two station is thus made. Microphone currents modulate the respective carrier waves. Good quality telephony claims the transmission of the frequency band between 300 to 2500 Hertz.

If the system is provided with automatic change, the following components are required further.

1. AF oscillator for dialling instead of AF oscillator for calling
2. Hybrid transformer
3. HF cable.

Telemetering

Figure 4.29 describes the telemetering facilities in power line carrier systems. The main components are

1. Carrier trap unit
2. HF transmitter
3. Modulator
4. High pass filter
5. Telemetering transmitter
6. Telemetering transmitter

7. Band pass filter
8. Low pass filter
9. Microphone amplifier
10. AF oscillator (call checking)
11. Control meter for telemetering
12. Control meter for telemetering
13. Telephone
14. Coupling condenser
15. Automatic volume control
16. HF receiver
17. Low pass filter
18. Band pass filter
19. Call receiver amplifier
20. Telephone amplifier
21. Indicating or recording meter
22. Telemetering receiver

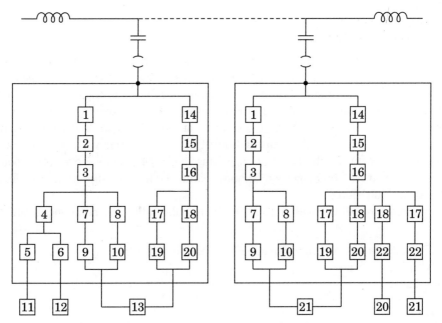

Figure 4.29 Telemetering facilities in power line carrier systems.

The telemetering system is the transmission of meter values over large distances. This transmission is made possible with high frequency transmitting and receiving apparatus. Six different sets of readings can be simultaneously telemetered with the help of a single carrier wave. The various audio frequencies are used for modulation. Of course, if the telephone connection is provided with the help of carrier, the three sets of readings can be transmitted simultaneously and continuously. But if meter reading is required for a short period of time, then the number of readings can be telemetered unlimited because telephone conversation will be interrupted very little during the short period of time for meter reading. When the carrier equipment is used only for telemetering, the apparatus of the h.f. cubicle will be reduced to a high frequency transmitter at one end and high frequency receiver at the other end. At the high frequency transmitter end, the components of the actual telemetering equipment are mounted. At the receiving end, indicating or recording instruments are connected in series. The total resistance of the instruments and connections should not exceed 5000 Ω. Since, resistance of a normal milliammeter is only 200 Ω approximately, a large number of instruments can be installed in series.

Supervisory and remote regulation in a power line carrier system

Figure 4.30 describes supervisory and remote regulation in the power line carrier system. The equipments needed are described as follows.

    3 —Coupling condenser
    4 —Protective apparatus
    5 —Impedance matching unit
    6 —H.F. cubicle
    7 —Supervisory control equipment
    8 —Control panel
    9 —Telephone
  10 —Indicating or recording meters
  11 —Control contactors
  12 —Switchgear
  13 —Telemetering transmitter
  14 —Carrier trap unit

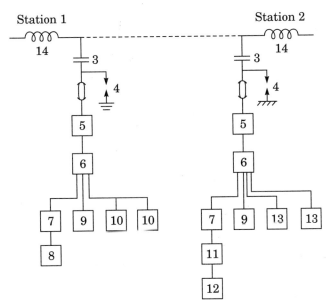

Figure 4.30 Supervisory and remote regulation in the power line carrier system.

For the supervisory control power houses and substations, the arrangements are made as shown in Figure 4.30. These installations are equipped with an impulse combination system. Here, the number of signals is unlimited.

The impulse series corresponding to each signal is transmitted one after another. A storage and a checking circuit automatically supervise the correct transmission in the proper order of control and corresponding return signals.

Protection of power transmission lines

Figure 4.31 describes the power line carrier system protection. The equipments needed are described as follows.

    3 —Breaker tripping coil
    4 —impedance matching unit
    5 —H.F. transmitter receiver
    6 —Transmitting relay
    7 —Receiving relay.

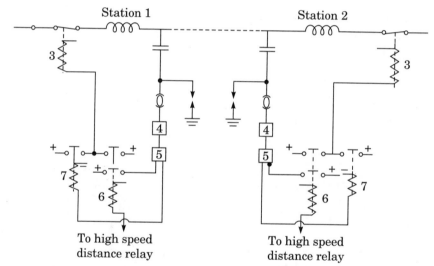

Figure 4.31 Power line carrier system protection.

In this scheme, it is essential that the breakers at both ends of the line are to be protected. They should open and reclose simultaneously. To perform the same, the carrier equipment in conjuction with apparatus for line protection is adopted as shown in Figure 4.31.

4.12 PICTURE TELEGRAPH SYSTEM

Figure 4.32 shows a schematic diagram of a picture telegraph system. The main features of the operation are as follows:

- The picture is wrapped round a cylinder.
- The cylinder is rotated and made to move transversely.

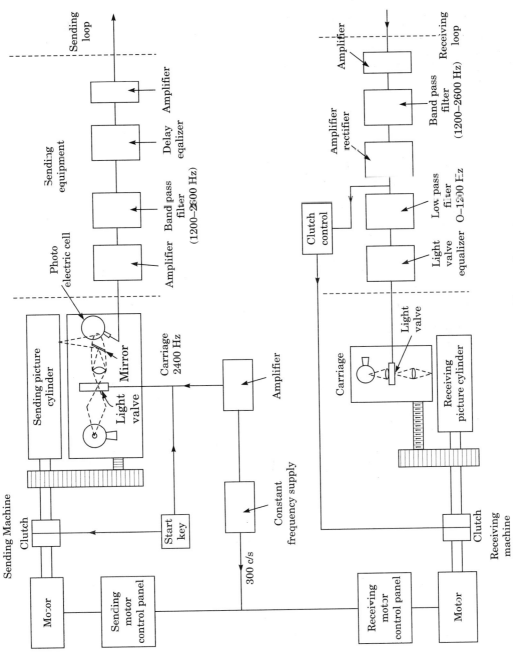

Figure 4.32 Picture telegraph system.

- A beam of light that has been interrupted 2400 times a second, is made to scan a series of parallel and slightly slanting lines over the picture.
- Usually 100 lines are traversed per inch.
- A photoelectric cell collects the scattered light.
- The output from the cell is amplified.
- Then the same is filtered.
- Then it is equalized for delay by delay equalizer.
- Then it is again amplified.
- Finally, the signal is sent out.
- At the receiving end, the transmitted signals are amplified.
- Then the same is filtered and rectified.
- Then it is equalized.
- Then the same is applied to the light valve.
- The beam of light is passed on, through the valve, to a photographic paper.
- The photographic paper is wrapped on a rotating and moving cylinder.
- Finally the original picture is reproduced at the receiving end.

The details of the photo-telegraph equipments can be described through transmitter and receiver in a photo-telegraph system.

4.12.1 Transmitter in Photo-telegraph System

Figure 4.33 describes a transmitter in a photo-telegraph system. The main features of the operation of the transmitter are as follows.

- The chopper disc is rotated by an induction motor.
- It is made to chop the reflected light from the picture at a frequency of 7200 Hz.

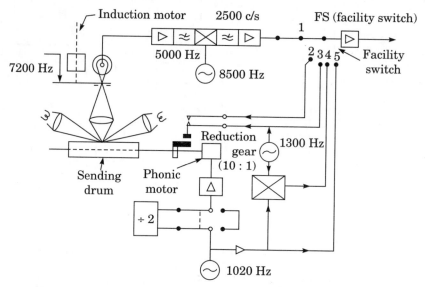

Figure 4.33 Transmitter in a photo-telegraph system.

- An amplitude modulated signal with 7200 Hz as carrier frequency and picture base band as modulating signal is developed.
- The high pass filter of (f_c = 5000 Hz) following the amplifier eliminates the unwanted low frequency modulation product.
- The amplitude modulated signal is translated by a product modulator of carrier frequency 8500 Hz.
- The lower sideband is selected by the low pass filter (f_c = 2500 Hz) following the modulator.
- The picture signal will have the carrier frequency (8500–7200) = 1300 Hz.
- The signal is amplified further and transmitted over the line.
- The 'facility switch' has five positions to transmit over the lines with other signals needed for synchronization and other adjustments to be carried out at the receiving station.
- The 1020 Hz synchronizing tone is transmitted either in the pure form or as a modulated tone depending on the need of the transmission path before the commencement of the transmission.
- The phasing signal is transmitted to start the receiver drum at the proper phase after the receiver end oscillator has been synchronized.
- The phasing contacts of the drum remain closed for a period of 30 milliseconds during each revolution.
- 1300 Hz tone appears at position 2 of the facility switch.
- This signal is known as phasing signal and is used to start the receiver drum.
- The phase difference between the paper clips on the sending and receiving drum does not exceed 3.6°.
- When a steady white portion of the picture is being scanned, the picture signal on the line will be a tone of 1300 Hz with constant amplitude.
- For steady black portion of the picture, the signal is also a 1300 Hz tone with constant amplitude but at a level 30 dB below the steady white signal.
- The auxiliary oscillator of 1300 Hz is applied to give an artificial white or black signal as per necessity.

4.12.2 Receiver in Photo-telegraph System

Figure 4.34 shows the receiver in photo-telegraph system. The main features of the operation of the receiver are as follows:

- The synchronizing tone of 1020 Hz is received either directly (position PP) or through a demodulator and bandpass filter (position QQ).
- The second case happens when the picture signal has to come through carrier telephone circuits. This will be in the form of a modulating signal on a carrier with a frequency of 1300 Hz. This signal is applied on the z-terminal of a cathode ray oscilloscope. The CRO is arranged to produce a circular trace by the locally generated 1020 Hz oscillator.
- The effect of the incoming synchronizing signal is to blank out a portion of circular trace.

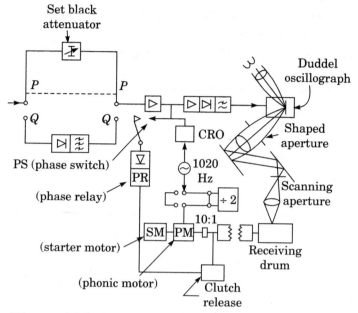

Figure 4.34 Receiver in a photo-telegraph system.

- When the two frequencies are identical, then the blank out portion remains stationary.
- If there is any difference between the two frequencies, the trace moves.
- The local oscillator frequency is adjusted until the two signals are synchronized.
- The receiver drum is started by closing the phase relay switch when the sender is transmitting the phasing signal. 30 milliseconds pulse of 1300 Hz is available at position 2 of the facility switch. (Figure 4.34).
- A rectified dc is obtained from the pulse and is used to trip the clutch release mechanism. When the constantly rotating tooth of the phonic motor acts with the stationary tooth clutch of the drum.
- The drum starts rotating with the correct speed.
- The picture signal passes through amplifier, the demodulator and then through the low pass filter having f_c = 1000 Hz.
- The same actuates a Duddel oscillograph.
- The movement of the oscillograph's mirror follows the amplitude and frequency of the picture signal.
- The light beam which is reflected by the mirror and focussed on the receiving drum, generates the picture.

■ SUMMARY ■

A telephone set is described. The operation of the same is introduced. Telephone communication system between two stations are described. Modified telephone circuit is discussed. Major points pertaining to the modern station set are described. Methods of switching of telephone switching are mentioned. Both the schemes, i.e., (a) each station has its own switching; (b) a central exchange system, are described. The importance of central exchange system is elaborately discussed. A simple exchange system with operator is explained through a diagram. Strowger automatic dialing system is described. Electro-mechanical switching devices are shown in Strowger automatic dialing system. The arrangement of Strowger switches for establishing a connection against dialing is narrated.

Cross bar switch arrangement is also discussed.

Most modern telephone communication such as mobile telephone communication has been elaborately described. The cellular radio network concept is explained. The concept of cell is also shown in cellular layouts. It is also mentioned that if the bandwidth of a cell is b_c, then the bandwidth provided to each user is $b_u = b_c/n$, where n is the number of channels. Mobile to mobile calls, mobile to fixed subscriber calls, fixed to mobile subscriber calls are elaborately explained. The concept of cellular telephone system is discussed in detail. The roles of base station, mobile telephone switching office, central office and terrestial telephone network are narrated.

The importance of PROM (programmable read-only memory), EPROM (erasable programmable read only memory), NAM (numeric assignment module) is discussed. The sequences of events are explained stage by stage at the time of placing a call. Application of fibre optic lines are also described with the connection of remote terminal with CO. A detailed study is made on fibre optic elements in transmission system. An idea about optical fibre fundamentals is also given. The semiconductor devices converting electrical signals into optical signals are discussed. Both laser diode and light emitting diodes are described.

The advantages of laser diodes and LED are narrated. Mainly, the laser diodes are used for long transmission distances. The LEDs are used when ruggedness and interface costs are more vital than performance. The photodetectors being used as transducers to convert the optical energy at the receiver to electrical energy for amplification and other processing are discussed. Two types of photodetectors, i.e. silicon based p-i-n diodes and avalanche photodiode are mentioned. The advantages and disadvantages of the both the above types are narrated.

The concept of telegraphy is also introduced. The main difference between the telegraph and telex is discussed. The working system of telegraphy is explained. Code of the telegraphy system is also discussed elaborately. Five unit codes and its variants, Morse code and the cable code are mentioned. Morse code and five unit codes are binary codes. These depend on the utilization of two signalling conditions. Both ac and dc signalling systems are for two condition signalling. Cable code is a type of dc signal utilized for transoceanic submarine cable working. Three signalling conditions are utilized for cable code. Morse code is an efficient means of radio communication. Amateur radio is one of the most important applications of Morse code. The advantages of Morse code are described. Timing of Morse code is discussed. Morse, letters and figures are shown with dots and dashes. The importance of five unit code over Morse code is discussed and 'International Telegraph Alphabet NO2' is described and it is further tabulated.

The telegraph key is a means of making and braking connection. The same is described. The Morse key diagram is also shown. The components of the non-polarized sounder are shown with diagram. The detailed description of its operation is also narrated. Telegraph relay is also discussed. Non-polarized relay and polarized relay are shown and explained through diagrams.

Detailed discussion is made on telecommunication in power system. Coupling with power transmission line is described with a diagram. The components of the detailed coupling system are explained one by one. Various methods of coupling are also narrated. Comparative study of phase to earth coupling and phase to phase coupling are also tabulated. Integrated system of power line carrier system and telephone exchange is also introduced. Telemetering facilities in power line carrier systems are also shown. Supervisory and remote regulation in a power line carrier system is discussed. Protection of power transmission lines is explained in detail. Picture telegraph system is explained with a diagram. In this connection, transmitter in photo telegraph system and receiver in photo-telegraph system are narrated with diagrams.

■ QUESTIONS ■

1. Describe a telephone system.

2. What is the need of central exchange system in telephone communication? Explain in detail.

3. Describe a simple manual exchange system.

4. What is Strowger automatic dialing system? Explain with a diagram.

5. What is cross-bar switch arrangement? Explain with a diagram.

6. What is the main concept of mobile telephone communication?

7. What are the different methods of mobile services? Explain in detail.

8. What are the salient features of cellular telephone system?

9. Describe the application of fibre optic line.

10. Explain the optical fibre construction.

11. What are the devices by virtue of which electrical signals can be converted into optical signals. Explain their advantages.

12. What are the optical to electrical transducers? What are the advantages and disadvantages of them?

13. Write a short note on 'telegraphy'.

14. What do you mean by code of the telegraphy system?

15. Describe the Morse code.

16. What do you mean by "International Telegraph Alphabet No 2"?

17. Write a short note on
    (a) Telegraph key
    (b) Morse key
    (c) Non-polarized sounder
    (d) Telegraph relay.

18. The high voltage power transmission line can be coupled with the telecommunication line. Explain the statement with a diagram.

19. What are the various methods of coupling?

20. Compare the phase to earth coupling in power line carrier system and phase to phase coupling in power line.

21. Describe the integrated system of power line carrier system and telephone exchange system without automatic exchange.

22. What is telemetering? Describe the telemetering facilities in power line carrier system.

23. What is supervisory and remote regulation in a power line carrier system? Explain with a diagram.

24. Explain with a diagram the protection of power transmission lines.

25. What is a picture telegraph system? State the salient features of a picture telegraph system.

26. Describe the main features of transmitter in photo-telegraph system.

27. Describe the salient features of the receiver in photo-telegraph system.

5 ∎∎∎ Radar

5.1 INTRODUCTION

The word Radar is an acronym for **Ra**dio **d**etection **and r**anging. The radar system uses radio waves. Then it detects and finally fixes the position of objects or targets at a distance. The development of radar was made during world war II. The basic fact that electromagnetic waves are reflected from objects is encashed by the Radar system. If the radio wave comes across sudden change in conductivity, permittivity and permeability in the medium, a portion of electromagnetic energy is absorbed by the second medium and is reradiated. The sudden changes in the electrical properties of the medium constitute the target. When the re-radiated energy is received back at the radar station, it provides the information about the location of the target. The energy needed to be radiated by the radar transmitting antenna is very large because the power received back should be sufficient so that the location of the target can be distinctly identified. Such large amounts of power at high frequencies are developed through high power magnetrons.

Radar systems are subdivided into two categories

- Continuous wave radar.
- Pulsed radar.

When detection of moving targets is made through unmodulated continuous wave energy, then the radar system is termed continuous wave radar. But in case of pulsed radar system, periodic pulses of high power but short duration are developed. Pulsed radar is practically used for detection of targets in most of the cases.

5.2 PULSED RADAR

The block diagram of the pulsed radar is described in Figure 5.1.

The pulsed radar consists of the following components.

(a) Transmitter
(b) Antenna system
(c) Trans-receive switch (T.R. switch) or Duplexer

(d) Timer
(e) Receiver
(f) Indicator
(g) Scanner.

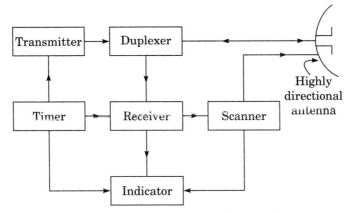

Figure 5.1 Block diagram of pulsed radar system.

Transmitter

The transmitter used in the pulsed radar system is controlled by a modulator which is nothing but a pulser. The control is made in such a way that periodic pulses of high power but of short duration are produced.

Antenna system

The antenna system is highly directional and is usually capable of rotating in azimuth or in vertical plane or both. As a result, the antenna system is capable to direct the beam as per need. The output of the transmitter is fed to the antenna.

Trans-receive switch (T.R. switch) or Duplexer

The duplexer connects the transmitter to the antenna and isolates the sensitive receiver from the damaging effects of high power transmitter pulses. As a result, the duplexer controls the transmitting and receiving operations and allows only one antenna for both transmitting and receiving purposes. The duplexer usually connects the antenna to the receiver in the interval pulse during which the reflected energy comes back.

Timer

Timer controls the generation of pulses in the transmitter. Over and above, the receiver and the indicator are synchronized to the timer.

Receiver

The radar receiver is a high sensitivity UHF or microwave receiver. Its noise figure is very low. It must have adequate bandwidth for handling the pulses. The receiver is usually capable of detecting signals of small power of the order of 10^{-12} watt.

Indicator

The indicator displays the output on a cathode ray tube screen. The receiver output is fed to the indicator. The cathode ray tube shows the difference between the outgoing pulse and the returning echoes. The voltage of cathode ray tube display is synchronized with the transmitted pulses.

Scanner

The scanning system rotates both the antenna system and deflection coils of an indicator. When the deflection coil is not magnetic deflection coil type and the same is electrostatic deflection system, a rotating sweep voltage is generated and controlled by the scanning circuit.

5.2.1   Operation of Pulsed Radar

The operation of pulsed radar can be described stagewise as follows:

- The transmitter sends a train of high-power, high frequency short duration pulses through the trans-receive switch to the antenna.
- The echo pulse comes back to the antenna and then through the T.R. switch to the receiver.
- The design of T.R. switch is such that for the outgoing pulse from the transmitter, it connects the transmitter to the antenna and very little energy is allowed to reach the receiver.
- Again, the T.R. switch connects the antenna to the receiver in case of incoming echo pulse from the antenna and very little echo pulse energy reaches the transmitter.
- The echo pulse is amplified before it is received.
- The detected echo pulse in the receiver is displayed on the indicator screen.

5.2.2   Waveforms of the Pulsed Radar System

Figure 5.2(a), (b), (c), (d) and (e) show the time relation in the radar set.
Figure 5.2(a) describes transmitted output voltage.
Figure 5.2(b) describes receiver input voltage.
Figure 5.2(c) describes receiver output voltage.
Figure 5.2(d) describes synchronizing pulses.
Figure 5.2(e) describes sweep voltage.

5.2.3   Some Important Terms Used in Pulse Radar

The following terms are used in pulsed radar.

1. **Pulsed durations or pulse width:**   This is the period for which the transmitter transmits the pulse. Obviously, this is also the duration of the received pulse. Generally, this pulse duration varies form one radar set to another. The typical value of pulsed durations is 1 μs. In Figure 5.2(a) and 5.2(b), it is shown by 'T'.

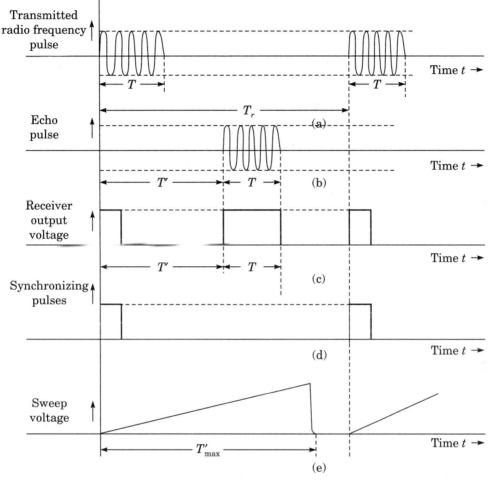

Figure 5.2 Waveforms indicating the time relation in radar set.

2. **Pulse repetition time:** It is the time interval between the starting of the transmission of pulse of the Ist pulse and the starting of the transmission of pulse of the second consecutive pulse. This also varies from one radar set to another according to the purpose of the set. Its typical value is 2000 μs. In Figure 5.2(a) it is shown by 'T_r'.

3. **Pulse repetition frequency (F_r):** This is reciprocal of pulse repetition period 'T_r'. This is the frequency at which the pulse repeats itself.

4. **Duty ratio:** Duty ratio is the ratio of the pulse width 'T' and pulse repetition period 'T_r'. The typical value of ratio is $\dfrac{1\,\mu s}{2000\,\mu s} = 0.0005$.

5. **Peak power (P_p):** Peak power is the output power of the radar transmitter during the pulse interval T. The typical value of peak power is 100 kW.

6. **Average power (P_{av}):** This is the transmitter output power which is average over the pulse repetition interval.

The average power is

$$P_{av} = P_p \times \text{Duty ratio}$$

$$= P_p \times \frac{T}{T_r}$$

Typical value of average power is = 100 kW × .0005 = 50 W.

7. **Travel time in pulsed radar:** It is the ratio of twice the range of the radar and the velocity of propagation of electromagnetic waves.

Hence,

$$T' = \frac{2r}{C}$$

where r is the range of the target and C is the velocity of propagation of electromagnetic waves.

T' is shown in Figure 5.2(b) and Figure 5.2(c).

∴

$$r = \frac{C}{2} T'$$

$\frac{C}{2}$ is equal to 150 m/μs. Therefore, the range of the target is 150 m when $T' = 1$ μs.

5.2.4 Indicator of Radar

The video pulse is fed to the indicator to provide a visual presentation of the target. In A-type of indicator the video pulse found at the output of the radar receiver is applied to the y-deflection plates of a cathode ray oscillograph. Again a linear sweep voltage of the same repetition frequency as the radar pulse possesses is applied to the x-deflection plates. Figure 5.2(e) describes the sweep voltage. The radar receiver amplifies the echo pulse, detects it and further amplifies the detected video pulse. The detected video pulse is the envelope of the radio frequency waves. Figure 5.3 shows the general appearance of 'A' indicator screen.

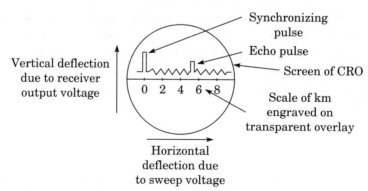

Figure 5.3 Display in pulsed radar on 'A' indicator screen.

The approximate range of the target can be read from a scale engraved on a transparent overlay placed on the face of the C.R. tube.

5.2.5 Synchronizing Voltage Pulse and Sweep Voltage

The indicator receives a synchronizing voltage pulse from the transmitter. This voltage occurs at the same instant as the radio frequency transmits pulse. The leading edge of the synchronization pulse marks the beginning of the time interval and the leading edge of the echo pulse marks the end of the interval. Again, the time at which the sawtooth sweep voltage begins, is controlled by the leading edge of the synchronizing pulse. Over and above, the value of the sweep voltage at the starting instant is so chosen that the spot on the indicator screen is at a position nearly to the left hand edge of the indicator screen. The sweep voltage rises at a constant rate after the starting instant and the movement of the spot across the screen occurs at constant speed. Adjustment of the rate of rise of sweep voltage is made, such that the spot is nearly at the right hand edge of the screen at the end of the time interval T'_{max} according to the maximum range at which objects are to be located.

5.2.6 Range Resolution

The range resolution is the ability to identify separately the objects that are close together. If two objects are separated by less than 150 metres, their echo pulses run together and the radar set cannot show them separately when the transmitted pulse is 1 μs since twice the range is equal to the product of the velocity of light and the two way travel time.

(i.e. $t = \dfrac{150 \times 2}{3 \times 10^8} = 1$ μs). The above is the reason for the importance of range resolution.

5.2.7 Frequency of Radar Transmitter

Frequency of radar transmitter varies according to the types of practical utility. For example, in case of air borne radar, high frequency radar transmitter is essential because large structures cannot be used for air borne radar. On the other hand, ground based radar is used for lower frequencies due to the following facts.

- Larger power can be obtained;
- Inherent noise of the receiver can be decreased.

Merits of high frequency for radar

- For locating small targets, the frequency used should be high.
- It is easier to have a narrower beam for higher frequencies. Hence, low power is needed.
- Narrow beam avoids reflection from the ground surface. Thus, the medium near the ground is illuminated.

Merits of low frequency for radar

- It is easier to generate higher powers at lower frequencies.
- The receiver sensitivity falls with the increase of carrier frequency.

Factors for selection of radar frequency

The frequency of radar set is fixed depending on the following factors.

- Dimensions of the radiating structure
- Range
- Dimensions of the target
- sensitivity of the receiver.

5.2.8   Free Space Radar Range Equation

The radar range equation is based on the following conditions.

- Along an optical line of sight, no large obstacles lie between antenna and the target
- There shall not be any alternative transmission path via any reflecting surface. Any substantial fraction of the total radiated energy should not follow the alternative transmission path.
- The intervening medium should be transparent. It should not absorb any energy from the electromagnetic waves at the frequency utilized.
- The intervening medium should be homogeneous with respect to the refractive index at the radar frequency.

Basing on the above conditions, the radar range equation is dervied as follows:
Power density (P_d) at a distance d from antenna is expressed as,

$$P_d = \frac{P_T}{4\pi d^2}$$

where, P_T represents the peak power transmitted by the transmitter in watt. The entire power P_T is distributed over the surface $4\pi d^2$.

If P_G is the power gain of the transmitter antenna in the direction of the target relative to isotropic radiator, then power density at a distance d will be

$$P_d = \frac{P_T P_G}{4\pi d^2} \text{ W/sq.m.}$$

The power gain P_G depends on the directivity of the aerial. The energy which is incidental to the target gets scattered in various directions. A part of the energy returns in the direction of the radar antenna. The target is generally described in terms of an equivalent cross-section A_s. If the total power possessed by the section of the incident wavefront having the area A_s were radiated by an isotropic radiator placed at the target, the strength of the radio wave reaching the radar receiving antenna would be equal to the strength of the echo produced by the target. Area 'A_s' will then be the effective echo area of the target.

Echo power per square metre at receiver will be $\dfrac{P_d \cdot A_s}{4\pi d^2}$

$$= \frac{P_T P_G A_s}{(4\pi d^2)^2}$$

The power delivered to the receiving antenna will be

$$P_R = \frac{P_T P_G A_s}{(4\pi d^2)^2} A_R$$

where A_R is the capture area of receiving antenna

or

$$d^4 = \frac{P_T P_G A_s \, A_R}{(4\pi)^2 \, P_R}$$

or

$$d = \sqrt[4]{\frac{P_T P_G A_s A_R}{(4\pi)^2 P_R}}$$

Let us assume that $P_{R_{min}}$ is the minimum value of available received power P_R. Then,

$$d_{max} = \sqrt[4]{\frac{P_T P_G A_s A_R}{(4\pi)^2 P_{R_{min}}}}$$

P_G depends on the type of antenna system. For the microwave radar, generally, circular paraboloid is used.

$$P_G = \frac{8\pi A_T}{3\lambda^2}, \text{ where } A_T \text{ is the transmitted area}$$

whereas, for dipole radiator, the gain is increased by 50%. Therefore, the effective value of power gain is

$$P_G = \frac{3}{2} \times \frac{8\pi A_T}{3\lambda^2} = \frac{4\pi A_T}{\lambda^2}$$

Therefore, the free-space radar range equation becomes

$$d_{max} = \sqrt[4]{\frac{P_T P_G A_s A_R}{(4\pi)^2 P_{R_{min}}}}$$

$$= \sqrt[4]{\frac{P_T 4\pi A_T A_s A_R}{\lambda^2 (4\pi)^2 P_{R_{min}}}}$$

Usually, the same antenna is utilized for reception and transmission, therefore, power gain of the transmitter antenna will be equal to the power gain of receiver antenna.

Therefore, the transmitted area will be equal to the capture area of the receiving antenna

$$A_T = A_R = A$$

$\therefore$

$$d_{\max} = \sqrt[4]{\frac{P_T A^2 A_s}{\lambda^2 \, 4\pi \, P_{R_{\min}}}}$$

Again

$$P_G = \frac{4\pi A}{\lambda^2}$$

$\therefore$

$$d_{\max} = \sqrt[4]{\frac{P_T \lambda^4 P_G^2 A_s}{\lambda^2 (4\pi)(4\pi)^2 \, P_{R_{\min}}}}$$

Hence,

$$d_{\max} = \sqrt[4]{\frac{P_T \lambda^2 P_G^2 A_s}{(4\pi)^3 \, P_{R_{\min}}}}$$

5.2.9 Effects of Noise on Radar

Noise affects the maximum radar range when it determines the minimum power that the receiver can handle. To study the above factor, we review the fundamentals of noise.

Thermal noise

The thermal noise, agitation noise, white noise or Johnson noise is the random noise developed in a resistor or the resistive component of a complex impedance on account of rapid and random motion of the molecules, atoms and electrons. The expression of the maximum noise power output of a resistor is

$$P = kTB$$

where k is Boltzmann's constant (1.38×10^{-23} Joules/degree Kelvin)
        T is the absolute temperature
        B is the bandwidth in hertz.

Figure 5.4 describes an equivalent circuit of a resistor as a noise generator. The resistor's equivalent noise voltage is V_p. A noiseless load resistor R_L is connected across the noise generator. When $R_L = R$, the maximum power transfer will occur from noise source V_p to load resistor R_L.

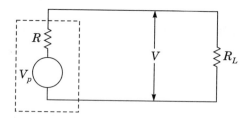

Figure 5.4   Resistor as noise generator.

Hence, the maximum transfer of noise power is

$$P = \frac{V^2}{R_L} = \frac{V^2}{R} = \frac{(V_p/2)^2}{R} = \frac{V_p^2}{4R}$$

∴ $$V_p^2 = 4RP = 4RkTB$$

Hence, $$V_p = \sqrt{4\,RkTB}$$

When there are two sources of thermal agitation noise, then there will be two sources of thermal agitation noise generators in series.

Let the sources be $V_{p_1} = \sqrt{4kTBR_1}$ and $V_{p_2} = \sqrt{4kTBR_2}$. The sum of the two such rms voltages in series is given by the square root of the sum of their squares.

$$V_R = \sqrt{V_{p_1}^2 + V_{p_2}^2}$$

$$= \sqrt{4\,kTBR_1 + 4\,kTBR_2}$$

$$= \sqrt{4\,kTB\,(R_1 + R_2)}$$

Figure 5.5 describes several amplifying stages. Two stages of amplification are shown. The gain of the first stage is A_1 and the gain of the second stage is A_2. The first stage has total input-noise resistance R_1 and the second stage has a total input noise resistance R_2. The output resistance is R_3.

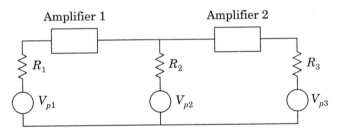

Figure 5.5 Noise of several amplifying stages.

Figure 5.5 indicates the noise circuit of two amplifying stages. The rms noise voltage at the output on a ccount of R_3 is

$$V_{p3} = \sqrt{4\,kTB\,R_3}$$

So, $$V'_{p3} = \frac{V_{p3}}{A_2} = \frac{\sqrt{4\,kTB\,R_3}}{A^2} = \sqrt{4\,kTB\,R'_3}$$

where $$R'_3 = \frac{R_3}{A_2^2}$$

V'_{p3} is the voltage referred to the input end of the amplifier 2 and R'_3 is its corresponding resistance from the point of view of noise.

Hence, the equivalent noise resistance at the input of the second stage is $R_2 + \dfrac{R_3}{A_2^2}$

Similarly, at the input stage of the first amplifier, the referred resistance is

$$\frac{R_2 + \dfrac{R_3}{A_2^2}}{A_1^2}$$

Hence, the equivalent noise resistance of the whole cascaded amplifier is

$$R_1 + \frac{R_2}{A_1^2} + \frac{R_3}{A_1^2 A_2^2}$$

In this way, calculation of equivalent noise resistance can be made for n-stage cascaded amplifier.

Noise in reactive circuit

Figure 5.6 describes a reactive circuit. Since the inductor 'L' possesses a small resistive element R_1, it is non-ideal tuned circuit at the input. That is why, R_1 generates noise voltage V_p.

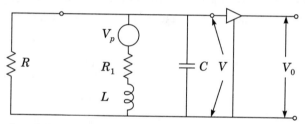

Figure 5.6   Amplifier circuit with non-ideal tuned circuit in the input.

The noise current in the RLC circuit will be

$$I_p = \frac{V_p}{R_1 + j\,(X_L - X_C)}$$

At the resonance condition, $X_L = X_C$

$$I_p = \frac{V_p}{R_1}$$

The magnitude of the noise voltage which appears across the capacitor 'C' will be

$$V = I_p \cdot X_C = \frac{V_p Q R_1}{R_1} = Q V_p$$

Since $X_C = Q R_1$ at resonance

Again, $V^2 = Q^2 V_p^2$

$$= Q^2 4kTBR_1$$

$$= 4kTBQ^2 R_1$$

$$= 4 \, kTBR_p$$

where

$$Q^2 R_1 = R_p$$

∴

$$V = \sqrt{4 \, kTBR_p}$$

Therefore, it is now very clear for the reactive circuit, the equivalent parallel impedance of the tuned circuit at resonance will be $Q^2 R_1$. Hence, the final noise equivalent circuit will be as shown in Figure 5.7.

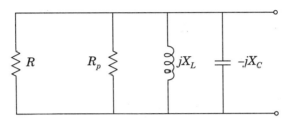

Figure 5.7 Noise equivalent circuit for non-ideal tuned circuit in the input.

Concept of noise figure

The noise figure is the ratio of signal to noise power supplied to the input terminals of the system to the signal to noise power supplied by the system to the output load impedance. That means,

$$N_F = \frac{\text{Signal/Noise at the input}}{\text{Signal/Noise at the output}}.$$

Figure 5.8 describes the noise circuit between antenna and receiver.

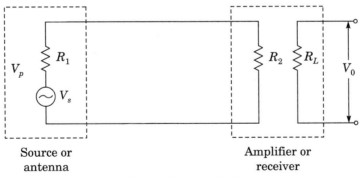

Source or antenna

Amplifier or receiver

Figure 5.8 Noise figure calculation circuit.

Antenna is the source. The receiver is the amplifier. The input source voltage is, $V_{si} = \dfrac{V_s R_2}{R_1 + R_2}$

where V_s is the source voltage
R_2 is the input resistance
R_1 is the source internal resistance.

Hence, the input signal power is $P_{si} = \dfrac{V_{si}^2}{R_2} = \dfrac{V_s^2 R_2^2}{(R_1 + R_2)^2 \, R_2}$

$$= \dfrac{V_s^2 R_2}{(R_1 + R_2)^2}$$

Again, the input noise voltage is

$$V_{pi}^2 = 4 \, kTB \; . \; \dfrac{R_1 R_2}{R_1 + R_2}$$

because, for noise voltage the equivalent resistance will be the outcome of the two resistances R_1 and R_2 in parallel.

Therefore input noise power is

$$P_{ni} = \dfrac{V_{pi}^2}{R_2} = \dfrac{4 \, kTBR_1 R_2}{(R_1 + R_2) \, R_2}$$

$$= \dfrac{4 \, kTBR_1}{R_1 + R_2}$$

Hence, input signal to noise power will be,

$$\dfrac{P_{si}}{P_{ni}} = \dfrac{\dfrac{V_s^2 R_2}{(R_1 + R_2)^2}}{\dfrac{4 \, kTBR_1}{R_1 + R_2}}$$

$$= \dfrac{V_s^2 R_2}{(R_1 + R_2)^2} \times \dfrac{(R_1 + R_2)}{4 \, kTBR_1}$$

$$= \dfrac{V_s^2 R_2}{4 \, kTBR_1 \, (R_1 + R_2)}$$

The output signal power is given by,

$$P_{so} = \dfrac{V_{so}^2}{R_L}$$

where V_{so} is the output signal voltage.

$$P_{so} = \dfrac{(AV_{si})^2}{R_L}$$

where 'A' is the gain of the amplifier.

$$= \dfrac{A^2 V_{si}^2}{R_L} = \dfrac{A^2}{R_L} \cdot \left(\dfrac{V_s R_2}{R_1 + R_2} \right)^2$$

$$= \dfrac{A^2 V_s^2 R_2^2}{R_L (R_1 + R_2)^2}$$

If P_{no} indicates the noise output power, then output signal to output noise power is

$$\frac{P_{so}}{P_{no}} = \frac{A^2 V_s^2 R_2^2}{R_L (R_1 + R_2)^2 P_{no}}$$

$\therefore$ The noise figure $= \dfrac{\dfrac{P_{si}}{P_{ni}}}{\dfrac{P_{so}}{P_{no}}}$

$$= \frac{V_s^2 R_2}{4 \, kTBR_1 \, (R_1 + R_2)} \frac{R_L (R_1 + R_2)^2 P_{no}}{A^2 V_s^2 R_2^2}$$

$$= \frac{R_L (R_1 + R_2) P_{no}}{4 \, kTBR_1 A^2 R_2}$$

Again, we know that the equivalent noise resistance of an amplifier or receiver is the combination of

(i) input resistance of the first stage
(ii) the equivalent noise resistance of the first stage
(iii) noise resistances of the subsequent stage referred to the first stage.

Therefore, all these noise resistances will be added up to the parallel combination of R_1 and R_2. Let the value of the equivalent resistance be 'R_3'. If the resistance R_2 is not included in the above equivalent resistance R_3, then the corresponding resistance will be

$$R_4 = R_3 - R_2$$

The total equivalent noise resistance of the receiver will be

$$R_r = R_4 + \frac{R_1 R_2}{R_1 + R_2}$$

Hence, the equivalent noise voltage at the input of the receiver will be

$$V_{ni} = \sqrt{4 \, kTBR_r}$$

Hence, the output noise power will be

$$P_{no} = \frac{V_{no}^2}{R_L}$$

$$= \frac{(A V_{ni})^2}{R_L}$$

$$= \frac{A^2 \, 4 \, kTBR_r}{R_L}$$

Hence, the noise figure will be

$$\frac{R_L (R_1 + R_2) P_{no}}{4 kTB R_1 A^2 R_2}$$

$$= \frac{R_L (R_1 + R_2) A^2 \, 4 \, kTBR_r}{4 \, kTB \, R_1 A^2 R_2 R_L}$$

$$= R_r \frac{R_1 + R_2}{R_1 R_2}$$

$$= \left(R_4 + \frac{R_1 R_2}{R_1 + R_2} \right) \frac{(R_1 + R_2)}{R_1 R_2}$$

$$= \frac{R_4 \, (R_1 + R_2)}{R_1 R_2} + 1$$

Now, to minimize the noise figure for a particular value of antenna resistance, the ratio $\frac{R_1 + R_2}{R_1 R_2}$ should be minimum. That means, R_2 should be made much larger than R_1.

$\therefore$ Noise figure $= 1 + R_4 \left(\frac{1}{R_2} + \frac{1}{R_1} \right)$.

When R_2 is very large, then noise figure $\approx 1 + \frac{R_4}{R_1}$.

Of course, in case of $R_1 \neq R_2$, an impedance mismatch occurs. As a result, the transfer of power from source (antenna) to the system (receiver) is not maximum. Thus, the noise is reduced with the condition of impedance mismatch.

EXAMPLE 5.1   A resistor of value 25 kΩ is connected to the input of an amplifier. The amplifier is performing at the frequency range of 11 to 12 MHz. Determine the rms noise voltage at the input of the amplifier if the ambient temperature is 25°C.

Solution

$$\text{RMS noise voltage} = \sqrt{4 kTRB}$$

$$k = 1.38 \times 10^{-23} \text{ (Boltzmann's constant)}$$

$$T = 273 + 25°C = 298$$

$$R = 25 \times 10^3 \ \Omega$$

$$B = 12 - 11 = 1 \text{ MHz} = 1 \times 10^6 \text{ Hz}$$

$\therefore$ RMS noise voltage

$$= \sqrt{4 \times 1.38 \times 10^{-23} \times 298 \times 25 \times 10^3 \times 1 \times 10^6} \ \text{volt.}$$

$$= \sqrt{4 \times 1.38 \times 298 \times 25 \times 10^{-14}}$$

$$= \sqrt{41124 \times 10^{-14}}$$

$$= 202.79 \times 10^{-7} = 20.279 \ \mu V.$$

EXAMPLE 5.2 A system is described as follows:

(a) gain of a noiseless amplifier = 50
(b) Bandwidth = 50 kHz
(c) Meter reading at the output of the amplifier = 5 mV rms.
(d) operating temperature of resistor = 27°C

Find out the value of the resistance.

The bandwidth of the amplifier is reduced by 30 kHz, find out the meter reading when the gain of the amplifier is kept constant.

Solution

$$V_p = \text{Noise voltage} = \sqrt{4kTRB}$$

$$V_p^2 = 4kTRB$$

Hence,

$$R = \frac{V_p^2}{4 \ kTB}$$

RMS noise voltage developed in the resistor $= \dfrac{5 \times 10^{-3}}{50} = 10^{-4}$

∴

$$R = \frac{(10^{-4})^2}{4 \times 1.38 \times 10^{-23} \times (273 + 27) \times 50 \times 10^3} \ \Omega$$

$$= \frac{10^{-8}}{4 \times 1.38 \times 10^{-23} \times 300 \times 50 \times 10^3}$$

$$= \frac{10^{12}}{4 \times 1.38 \times 300 \times 50}$$

$$= \frac{10^9}{4 \times 1.38 \times 3 \times 5}$$

$$= \frac{10^7 \times 10^2}{82.8}$$

$$= 1.208 \times 10^7 \ \Omega$$

$$= 12.08 \times 10^6 \ \Omega$$

In the second case, bandwidth becomes 50 − 30 = 20 kHz

∴

$$V_n = \sqrt{4 \ kTRB}$$

The output voltage $= A\sqrt{4kTRB}$

A is the amplifier gain, i.e. 50.

∴ Output voltage will be recorded by the meter

$$= 50\sqrt{4\times1.38\times10^{-23}\times(273+27)\times12.08\times10^{6}\times20\times10^{3}}$$

$$= 50\sqrt{4\times1.38\times300\times12.08\times20\times10^{-14}}$$

$$= 50\sqrt{4\times1.38\times3\times12.08\times20\times10^{-12}}$$

$$= 50\sqrt{4000.896\times10^{-12}}$$

$$= 50\times63.253\times10^{-6}$$

$$= 3162.65\times10^{-6}$$

$$= .00316265 \text{ volt}$$

EXAMPLE 5.3 A parallel tuned circuit is provided with the following data:

(a) The 'Q' of the circuit is 12
(b) Resonating frequency is 12 MHz
(c) The value of capacitor is 11 pF
(d) Temperature = 27°C.

Find out the noise voltage which a wide band voltmeter records when the same is connected to the tuned circuit.

Solution

$$\frac{1}{\omega C}=\frac{R}{Q}$$

or

$$R=\frac{Q}{\omega C}=\frac{12}{(2\pi\times12\times10^{6})\times11\times10^{-12}}$$

$$= .0145\times10^{6}$$

$$B=\frac{f}{Q}=\frac{12\times10^{6}}{12}=10^{6}\text{ Hz}$$

∴ Noise voltage which will be recorded $= V_n = \sqrt{4kTRB}$

$$= \sqrt{4\times1.38\times10^{-23}\times(273+27)\times.0145\times10^{6}\times10^{6}}$$

$$= \sqrt{24.012\times10^{-11}}$$

$$= \sqrt{24.012\times10^{-1}}\times10^{-5}$$

$$= \sqrt{2.4012} \times 10^{-5} \text{ volt}$$

$$= 1.5496 \times 10^{-5} \text{ volt}$$

EXAMPLE 5.4 A video amplifier circuit is provided with the following data:

(a) 350 Ω equivalent noise resistance
(b) input resistance 450 Ω
(c) bandwidth of the amplifier = 8 MHz
(d) Ambient temperature = 27°C.

Find out the noise voltage at the input of a video amplifier.

Solution

$$\text{Resistance} = 350 + 450 = 800 \ \Omega$$

$$T = 273 + 27 = 300$$

$$\text{Noise voltage} = \sqrt{4 \, kTBR}$$

$$= \sqrt{4 \times 1.38 \times 10^{-23} \times 300 \times 8 \times 10^{6} \times 800}$$

$$= \sqrt{1059.84 \times 10^{-13}}$$

$$= \sqrt{105.984} \times 10^{-6}$$

$$= 10.295 \times 10^{-6} \text{ volt.}$$

EXAMPLE 5.5 A two stage amplifier circuit is described as follows:

(a) First stage output resistance = 25 kΩ
(b) Voltage gain of 1st stage = 12
(c) Input resistance of 1st stage = 600 Ω
(d) Equivalent noise resistance of 1st stage = 2100 Ω
(e) Second stage output resistance = 450 kΩ
(f) Voltage gain of 2nd stage = 22
(g) Second stage input resistance 100 kΩ
(h) Second stage equivalent noise resistance = 12 kΩ.

Find out the equivalent input noise resistance of two stage amplifier. If the bandwidth of the amplifier is 12 kHz and the ambient temperature is 300 K, find the equivalent input noise voltage.

Solution

$$R_3 = 450 \text{ k}\Omega \quad \text{(as per Figure 5.9)}$$

$$R_2 = \frac{25 \times 100}{25 + 100} \text{ k}\Omega + 12 \text{ k}\Omega$$

$$= 20 + 12 = 32 \text{ k}\Omega$$

$$R_1 = 600 + 2100 = 2700 \ \Omega$$

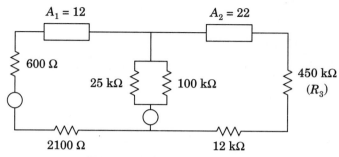

Figure 5.9 Example 5.5.

∴ R_{eq} = equivalent input noise resistance

$$= R_1 + \frac{R_2}{A_1^2} + \frac{R_3}{A_1^2 A_2^2}$$

$$= 2700 + \frac{32000}{(12)^2} + \frac{450000}{(12)^2 \, (22)^2} \; \Omega$$

$$= 2700 + 222.22 + \frac{450000}{69696}$$

$$= 2700 + 222.22 + 6.457$$

$$= 2928.677$$

Equivalent input noise voltage $= \sqrt{4k \, TB \, R_{eq}}$

$$= \sqrt{4 \times 1.38 \times 10^{-23} \times 300 \times 12 \times 10^3 \times 2928.677}$$

$$= \sqrt{581986.69 \times 10^{-18}}$$

$$= 762.88 \times 10^{-9} \text{ volt}$$

EXAMPLE 5.6   A three stage amplifier circuit is described as follows:

(a) 1st stage
   (i) voltage gain = 22
   (ii) input resistance = 650 Ω
   (iii) equivalent noise = 1550 Ω
   (iv) output resistance = 32 kΩ

(b) 2nd stage
   (i) voltage gain = 27
   (ii) input resistance = 42 kΩ
   (iii) equivalent noise resistance = 6.2 kΩ
   (iv) output resistance = 102 kΩ

(c) 3rd stage
  (i) voltage gain = 28
  (ii) input resistance = 82 kΩ
  (iii) equivalent noise resistance = 10.2 kΩ
  (iv) output resistance = 1.2 MΩ

Find out the equivalent input noise resistance of the overall 3 stage amplifier. Consider the bandwidth of operation 12 kHz at a temperature of 300 degree kelvin. Also determine the equivalent noise voltage of the Ist stage.

Solution

$$R_1 = 650 + 1550 \; \Omega \text{ (As per Figure 5.10)}$$

$$= 2200 \; \Omega$$

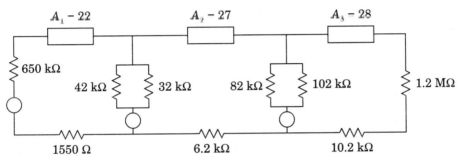

Figure 5.10

$$R_2 = \frac{42 \times 32}{42 + 32} \; k\Omega + 6.2 \; k\Omega$$

$$= 18.162 + 6.2$$

$$= 24.362 \; k\Omega$$

$$R_3 = \frac{82 \times 102}{82 + 102} \; k\Omega + 10.2 \; k\Omega$$

$$= 45.46 \; k\Omega + 10.2 \; k\Omega$$

$$= 55.66 \; k\Omega$$

$$R_4 = 1.2 \; M\Omega$$

∴ Equivalent input noise resistance

$$R_{eq} = R_1 + \frac{R_2}{A_1^2} + \frac{R_3}{(A_1 A_2)^2} + \frac{R_4}{(A_1 A_2 A_3)^2}$$

$$= 2200 + \frac{24362}{(22)^2} + \frac{55660}{(22 \times 27)^2} + \frac{1.2 \times 10^6}{(22 \times 27 \times 28)^2}$$

$$= 2200 + 50.3347 + \frac{55660}{(594)^2} + \frac{1.2 \times 10^6}{(16632)^2}$$

$$= 2200 + 50.3347 + 0.1578 + .004338$$

$$= 2250.496838$$

equivalent noise voltage of the 1st stage

$$= \sqrt{4\,kTBR_{eq}}$$

$$= \sqrt{4 \times 1.38 \times 10^{-23} \times 300 \times 12 \times 10^3 \times 2250.496838}$$

$$= \sqrt{447218.7316 \times 10^{-18}}$$

$$= 668.744 \times 10^{-9}$$

$$= 0.668744 \times 10^{-6} \text{ volt}$$

EXAMPLE 5.7 The amplifier circuit is described as follows:

(a) First stage
   (i) voltage gain = 12
   (ii) input resistance = 650 Ω
   (iii) equivalent noise resistance = 1650 Ω
   (iv) output resistance = 28 kΩ

(b) Second stage
   (i) voltage gain = 26
   (ii) input resistance = 82 kΩ
   (iii) equivalent noise resistance = 12 kΩ
   (iv) output resistance = 1.2 MΩ

Find out the equivalent input noise resistance of the above two stage amplifier. Also find out the noise figure of the amplifier if it is driven by a generator whose output impedance is 55 Ω.

Solution

$$R_1 = 650 + 1650 \text{ (As per Figure 5.11)}$$

$$= 2300 \ \Omega$$

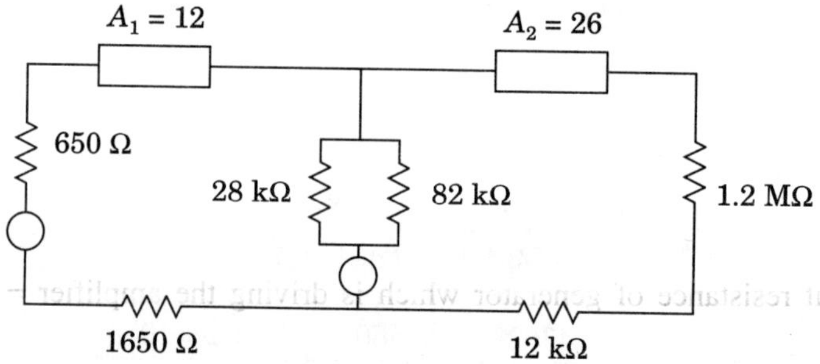

Figure 5.11 Example 5.7.

$$R_2 = \frac{28 \times 82}{28 + 82} + 12$$

$$= \frac{28 \times 82}{110} + 12$$

$$= 20.87 + 12$$

$$= 32.87 \text{ k}\Omega$$

$$R_3 = 1.2 \text{ M}\Omega$$

$$\therefore \quad R_{eq} = 2300 + \frac{32870}{12^2} + \frac{1200000}{(12)^2 \times (26)^2}$$

$$= 2300 + 228.264 + 12.33$$

$$= 2540.594 \ \Omega$$

Noise figure calculation

$$R'_{eq} = R_{eq} - 650$$

$$= 2540.594 - 650$$

$$= 1890.594$$

$$\text{Noise figure} = 1 + R'_{eq} \ \frac{55 + 650}{55 \times 650}$$

$$= 1 + 1890.594 \times \frac{705}{55 \times 650}$$

$$= 1 + 37.28 = 38.28$$

EXAMPLE 5.8 A two stage amplifier is described as follows:

(a) 1st stage
  (i) output resistance = 26 kΩ
  (ii) voltage gain = 14
  (iii) input resistance = 650 Ω
  (iv) equivalent noise resistance = 2450 Ω

(b) 2nd stage
  (i) output resistance – 350 kΩ
  (ii) voltage gain = 26
  (iii) input resistance = 120 kΩ
  (iv) equivalent noise resistance = 10 kΩ

(c) The output resistance of generator which is driving the amplifier = 52 Ω

Find out:

    (i) Equivalent input resistance

    (ii) Equivalent input noise voltage when the bandwidth of the amplifier is 12 kHz and the ambient temperature is 300 K.

    (iii) Noise figure of the system

Solution

As per Figure 5.12

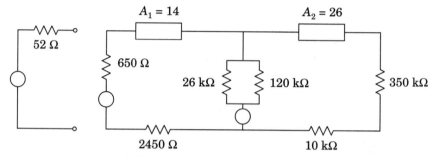

Figure 5.12 Example 5.8.

$$R_3 = 350 \text{ k}\Omega$$

$$R_2 = \frac{26 \times 120}{26 + 120} + 10 = 21.37 + 10 = 31.37 \text{ k}\Omega$$

$$R_1 = 650 + 2450 = 3100 \ \Omega$$

Equivalent input resistance, $R_{eq} = R_1 + \dfrac{R_2}{A_1^2} + \dfrac{R_3}{(A_1 A_2)^2}$

$$= 3100 + \frac{31370}{(14)^2} + \frac{350 \times 10^3}{(14 \times 26)^2}$$

$$= 3100 + 160.05 + 2.642$$

$$= 3262.692 \ \Omega$$

Equivalent input noise voltage

$$= \sqrt{4 \, kTB \, R_{eq}}$$

$$= \sqrt{4 \times 1.38 \times 10^{-23} \times 300 \times 12 \times 10^3 \times 3262.692} \ \text{volt}$$

$$= \sqrt{648362.1542 \times 10^{-18}}$$

$$= 805.2094 \times 10^{-9}$$

$$= .8052094 \times 10^{-6} \ \text{volt}$$

$$R'_{eq} = R_{eq} - 650$$
$$= 3262.692 - 650$$
$$= 2612.692 \ \Omega$$

$$\therefore \quad \text{Noise figure} = 1 + 2612.692 \times \frac{52 + 650}{52 \times 650}$$

$$= 1 + 54.264 = 55.264$$

Mathematical relation of noise effect on radar

Noise effect on radar can be calculated in the following manner.

It is possible to calculate the equivalent noise power generated at the input of the receiver from the definition of noise figure.

$$\text{Noise figure} = \frac{S_i}{N_i} \bigg/ \frac{S_o}{N_o}$$

$$= \frac{S_i N_o}{S_o N_i}$$

where S_i = input signal power
S_o = output noise power
N_i = input noise power
N_o = output noise power

$$\therefore \quad \text{Noise figure} = \frac{S_i N_o}{S_o N_i}$$

$$= \frac{S_i}{GS_i} \frac{G(N_i + N_r)}{N_i}$$

where G = power gain of the receiver
N_r = power generated at the input of the receiver.

We already know

$$\frac{N_r}{N_i} = F - 1 \quad \text{where } F \text{ is the noise figure}$$

$$N_r = (F - 1) \ N_i = kTB \ (F - 1)$$

where k = Botzmann's constant
T = Standard ambient temperature
B = Bandwidth of the receiver.

When the same antenna is used for both reception and transmission, the maxium power gain is given by the condition

$$\text{Maximum power gain,} \quad P_{g\max} = \frac{4\pi \times \text{Capture area of the receiving antenna}}{\lambda^2}$$

Thus, in case of maximum power gain

$$P_R = \frac{P_T A_s}{(4\pi d^2)^2} \times \frac{4\pi A_R}{\lambda^2} \times A_R$$

$$= \frac{P_T A_s \times 4\pi A_R \times A_R}{(4\pi d^2)^2 \, \lambda^2}, \quad \text{when } A_R = A_s$$

$$P_R = \frac{P_T \, 4\pi A_R^2 A_s}{(4\pi)^2 \, d^4 \lambda^2}$$

$$= \frac{P_T A_R^2 A_s}{4\pi \lambda^2 d^4}$$

or

$$P_{R\min} = \frac{P_T A_R^2 A_s}{4\pi \lambda^2 d_{\max}^4}$$

or

$$d_{\max} = \sqrt[4]{\frac{P_T A_R^2 A_s}{4\pi \lambda^2 P_{R\min}}}$$

$$= \sqrt[4]{\frac{P_T A_R^2 A_s}{4\pi \lambda^2 \, kTB(F-1)}}$$

where

$$N_r = P_{R\min} = kTB \, (F-1).$$

Usually, the capture area is taken in terms of antenna diameter ($A_R = 0.65 \ \pi D^2/4$)

Putting all the values of the constant, $d_{\max} = 48\left[\dfrac{P_T D^4 A_s}{B\lambda^2 (F-1)}\right]^{1/4}$

when T is taken = 273 + 17 = 290 K

EXAMPLE 5.9 Find out the minimum receivable signal in a radar receiver which has IF bandwidth of 1.6 MHz. Consider noise figure 9 dB. The ambient temperature is 27°C.

Solution

Noise figure (expressed as a ratio) = antilog $\dfrac{9}{10}$ = 7.943.

Minimum receivable signal = $P_{R\min} = kTB(F-1)$

$$k = 1.38 \times 10^{-23} \text{ (Boltzmann's constant)}$$

$$B = \text{Bandwidth} = 1.6 \times 10^6$$

$$T = 273 + 27 = 300 \text{ K}$$

$$P_{R\,min} = 1.38 \times 10^{-23} \times 300 \times 1.6 \times 10^6\,(7.943 - 1)$$

$$= 4599.0432 \times 10^{-17}\ \text{W}.$$

EXAMPLE 5.10 Find out the maximum range of radar system operating at 4 cm with a peak pulse power 550 kW. The minimum receivable is 10^{-14} W.

The capture area of the antenna is 5.5 m². The radar cross-sectional area of the target is 22 m².

Solution

$$d_{max} = \left(\frac{P_T A_R^2 A_s}{4\pi\lambda^2 P_{R\,min}}\right)^{1/4}$$

$$= \left(\frac{550 \times 10^3 \times 5.5 \times 22}{4\pi \times (.04)^2 \times 10^{-14}}\right)^{1/4}\ \text{metre}$$

$$= 75.8594 \times 10^4\ \text{metre}$$

EXAMPLE 5.11 The overall noise figure of a radar system is 4.77 dB. The following data are available

(a) The antenna diameter = 1.2 m
(b) The IF bandwidth = 550 kHz
(c) The operating frequency = 8.5 GHz
(d) It is capable of detecting targets of 5.5 m² cross-sectional area
(e) Maximum distance = 12.5 km.

Find out the peak transmitted pulse power. Consider standard ambient temperature 17°C.

Solution

$$d_{max} = 48\left[\frac{P_T D^4 A_s}{B\lambda^2 (F-1)}\right]^{1/4}$$

$$\therefore \qquad \left(\frac{d_{max}}{48}\right)^4 = \frac{P_T D^4 A_s}{B\lambda^2 (F-1)}$$

$$P_T = \frac{B\lambda^2 (F-1)}{D^4 A_s}\left(\frac{d_{max}}{48}\right)^4$$

$$\lambda = \frac{3 \times 10^8}{8.5 \times 10^9}\ \text{metre}$$

$$F = \text{antilog}\ \frac{4.77}{10} = 3$$

$$\therefore \qquad P_T = \frac{550 \times 10^3 \left(\dfrac{3}{8.5 \times 10}\right)^2 (3-1)}{(1.2)^4 \times 5.5} \times \left(\frac{12.5}{48}\right)^4 \ \text{W}$$

$$= 0.5526 \ \text{W}$$

5.3 MOVING TARGET INDICATOR (MTI)

The moving target indicator system eliminates the permanent echoes and retains echoes from the moving target. Specially, difficulty arises in mountainous regions and near cities. That is why, separate identification of moving target is made with the help of Doppler effect.

5.3.1 Doppler Effect

The Doppler effect states that the apparent frequency of the electromagnetic or sound waves depends on the relative radial motion of the source and observer. If the source and observer are moving away from each other, the apparent frequency will decrease. On the other hand, if they are moving toward each other, the apparent frequency will increase. In case of radar, the target becomes the source of the reflected waves. The radar receiver is the stationary observer. Hence, the above two are approaching each other. Let us assume that a moving target covers a distance Δd in time interval Δt. As a result the relative phase to the returned echoes shifts by an amount $\Delta \phi$ radians.

For wavelength λ the phase angle is 2π

For unit length the phase angle is $\dfrac{2\pi}{\lambda}$

Hence, for Δd distance the phase angle is $\dfrac{2\pi}{\lambda} \Delta d$

$$\therefore \qquad \Delta \phi = 2 \times \frac{2\pi}{\lambda} \Delta d$$

For 2π angle cycle is 1

For 1 angle cycle is $\dfrac{1}{2\pi}$

So, for angle $\Delta \phi$ the cycle is $\dfrac{\Delta \phi}{2\pi}$

Hence, the corresponding frequency is $\Delta f = \dfrac{1}{2\pi} \dfrac{\Delta \phi}{\Delta t}$

$$= \frac{1}{2\pi} \frac{2 \times 2\pi \times \Delta d}{\lambda \Delta t}$$

$$= \frac{2}{\lambda} \frac{\Delta d}{\Delta t}$$

$$= \frac{2}{\lambda} V_r$$

where V_r is the radial velocity.

5.3.2 Block Diagram of MTI Radar System

Figure 5.13 shows the block diagram of MTI radar.

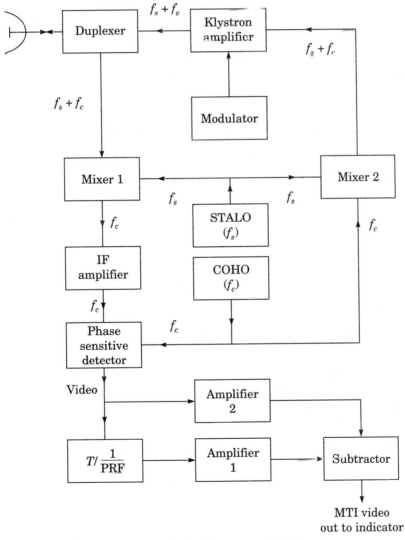

Figure 5.13 Block diagram of MTI radar.

In the block diagram two oscillators are shown. The first is termed STALO (STABLE LOCAL OSCILLATOR). The second is termed COHO (COHERENT OSCILLATOR). Mixer 1 and Mixer 2 are identical. Both of them use the same local oscillator, i.e., STALO.

Phase sensitive detector consists of a circuit similar to the phase discriminator. The frequency of IF is equal to the frequency of coherent oscillator. The modulator produces the train of pulses of appropriate amplitude. The pulses are usually applied between the anode and cathode of the oscillator tube, i.e. klystron.

The power output of the modulator needed is very large. Hence, one megawatt radar operating with 50% efficiency needs the modulator to feed 2 megawatt peak power to the oscillator tube. The COHO is used for generation of RF signal and for reference in the phase detector. The transmitted and reference signals are locked in phase and are termed to be coherent.

The MTI system compares a set of received echoes with those received during the previous sweep. Those echoes whose phase are constant, will be cancelled out. These are nothing but the echoes for the stationary objects. Those echoes which are coming from the moving objects will not be cancelled out. Thus, it becomes easier to find out which targets are moving and that also reduces the time taken by the operator to display accurately. In this system the phase of the echo signal which exists in the IF amplifier system of a conventional radar receiver is being compared to a phase detector with the phase of a reference oscillator. The reference oscillator is operated in such a manner that its phase is related to a fixed manner to the phase of the transmitted pulse. Hence, the permanent echoes have the same constant relative phase from pulse to pulse and develops identical voltage for successive pulse at the phase detector output. Now, subtracting the pulse detector output for the first pulse from that for the second pulse, second pulse from the third pulse, the outcome will be zero in case of permanent echoes. Thus, they will not be visible in the radar screen.

5.3.3 Blind Speed

If the moving target has a velocity whose radial component appears in a phase difference of exactly 2π radians between successive pulses, then no phase shift will be observed. Then the moving target will be observed stationary since the echoes from it will be cancelled by the MTI action. In this condition, the radial velocity is termed as blind speed. Even the target happens to have a velocity whose radial component results in a phase difference of exactly integral multiples of '2π' radians between successive pulses will be also termed blind speed. The blind speed is expressed mathematically as follows:

V_B = Blind speed = pulse repetition frequency × $n\lambda$
λ = wavelength of transmitted signal
n = any integer

Suppose, for one transmitted pulse to second transmitted pulse, the distance covered is Δd.

Hence, the change in frequency is $2 \times \dfrac{\text{Velocity}}{\lambda}$ [where λ is the wavelength.]

If Δt is the pulse repetition time, then velocity is $\dfrac{\Delta d}{\Delta t}$.

Therefore the change in frequency is $\dfrac{2}{\lambda}\dfrac{\Delta d}{\Delta t}$

Again the change in angle is $2 \times 2\pi \dfrac{\Delta d}{\lambda}$

For change in angle $2 \times 2\pi \dfrac{\Delta d}{\lambda}$ the change in frequency $\dfrac{2}{\lambda}\dfrac{\Delta d}{\Delta t}$

Hence, for the change in angle 2π, the change in frequency $= \dfrac{\dfrac{2}{\lambda}\dfrac{\Delta d}{\Delta t}}{\dfrac{2 \times 2\pi\,\Delta d}{\lambda}} \times 2\pi$

$$= \dfrac{2}{\lambda}\dfrac{\Delta d}{\Delta t} \times \dfrac{\lambda}{2 \times 2\pi\,\Delta d} \times 2\pi$$

$$= \dfrac{1}{\Delta t} = \text{Pulse repetition frequency}$$

That is why the blind speed becomes equal to the pulse repetition frequency $\times \dfrac{n\lambda}{2}$.

EXAMPLE 5.12   An MTI radar is described as follows:

(a) It operates at 6 GHz
(b) The pulse repetition frequency = 900 pulse per second.

Find out the lowest three blind speeds of radar.

Solution

$$\text{Wavelength} = \lambda = \dfrac{\text{Velocity of light}}{\text{Operating frequency}}$$

$$= \dfrac{3 \times 10^8}{6 \times 10^9} = \dfrac{1}{2 \times 10} = \dfrac{.1}{2} = .05$$

$$\text{Blind speed} = \text{P.R.f.} \times \dfrac{n\lambda}{2}$$

when $\qquad\qquad n = 1$

$$\text{Blind speed} = 900 \times \dfrac{.05}{2}$$

$$= \dfrac{45}{2} \text{ m/s} = 22.5 \text{ m/s}$$

$$= 81 \text{ km/hour}$$

when $\qquad\qquad n = 2$

$$\text{Blind speed} = 2 \times 900 \times \frac{.05}{2} \text{ m/s}$$

$$= \frac{90}{2} \text{ m/s} = 45 \text{ m/s}$$

$$= 162 \text{ m/s}$$

When $n = 3$

$$\text{Blind speed} = 3 \times 900 \times \frac{.05}{2}$$

$$= \frac{135}{2} \text{ m/s} = 67.5 \text{ m/s}$$

$$= 243 \text{ km/hour}$$

5.4 CONTINUOUS WAVE RADAR (C.W. RADAR)

Figure 5.14 shows the block diagram of continuous wave radar.

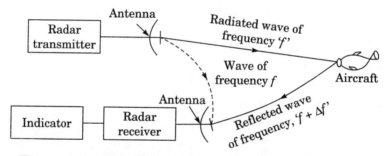

Figure 5.14 Block diagram of continuous wave radar.

It is also possible to detect moving targets by radiating unmodulated continuous wave energy. Here, the radiated wave moves towards the target from radar transmitter with frequency 'f'. The part of energy reflected by the moving target moves towards the radar receiver with frequency $f + \Delta f$ as shown in Figure 5.14. According to Doppler's effect, the frequency of received signal varies from $f + \Delta f$ to $f - \Delta f$.

The main uses of the C.W. radar are:

(a) To measure the speed of automobiles,
(b) To measure the speed shells,
(c) To measure the speed of guided missiles,
(d) To detect moving objects such as automobile, people, etc.
(e) It is useful in military work because it functions satisfactorily in the dark, bad weather, etc.
(f) To detect aircraft even in the presence of fixed objects.

The main limitations of the C.W. radar are as follows:

(a) Several targets at a given bearing tends to cause confusion
(b) Range discrimation is only obtained with the help of very costly circuit complexity.

5.5 FREQUENCY MODULATION RADAR (F.M. ALTIMETER)

The F.M. radar arrangement is similar to that of C.W. radar. The difference is that the transmitted wave is frequency modulated in such a way that the instantaneous frequency on an average changes many cycles per microsecond.

Hence, the direct wave and reflected wave will have different frequencies. The frequency difference indicates the time delay in the reflected wave. Finally, the distance to the reflecting point will be indicated. During the modulation cycle, the difference frequency will vary with sinusoidal modulation. The average value of this difference frequency over a modulation cycle will be proportional to the distance of the target from the transmitter. Average difference frequency at the receiver output is

$$\frac{8(f_m)(\Delta f)(\Delta d)}{c}$$

where f_m — modulating frequency
Δf — frequency deviation
Δd — distance to target
c — velocity of light

The use of frequency modulation radar is altimeter. *Altimer* is an instrument for measuring the height of the aircraft above the ground during landing. The typical operating values of the F.M. altimeter are as follows.

(a) carrier frequency – 440 MHz
(b) modulating frequency – 120 c/s
(c) frequency deviation – 2 to 20 MHz
(d) usual equipment power – less than 1 W.

The procedure of measuring the altitude of the aircraft can be described as follows:

- In an altimeter, the output of the receiver is applied to a frequency meter.
- The frequency meter develops a dc output current proportional to the average frequency.
- The dc current is passed through a dc meter.
- The dc meter is already calibrated to read the altitude in metres directly.

■ SUMMARY ■

Radar systems are subdivided into two categories.

- Continuous wave radar
- Pulsed radar.

Pulsed radar is practically used for detection of targets in most of the cases. A block diagram of pulsed radar system is described. Radar components are transmitter, antenna system, transreceiver switch or duplexer, timer, indicator, scanner and receiver. An idea has been given on them. Operation of pulsed radar has been described. Waveforms of the pulsed radar system have been drawn and described. Pulsed durations, pulse repetition time, pulse repetition frequency, duty ratio, peak power, average power, travel time in pulsed radar have been defined in the context of some important terms utilized in pulsed radar. The video pulse is fed to the indicator to provide a visual presentation of the target. The general appearance of 'A' indicator is shown through a diagram. Synchronizing voltage pulse and sweep voltage are explained. An idea about range resolution is also given. Frequency of radar transmitter has been discussed. Merits of high frequency for radar and low frequency of radar are narrated. Factors for selection of radar frequency are discussed. Free space radar range equation is formulated. Effects of noise on radar is explained in detail. A review has also been made on noise. An introduction to thermal noise is given. The maximum transfer of noise power is calculated. Noise of several amplifying stages has been shown with a block diagram. Equivalent noise resistance of the whole cascaded amplifier has been calculated. This methodology can be applied for n-stage cascaded amplifier. Noise in reactive circuit is also discussed. The concept of noise figure is also given. The input noise power is derived. Input signal to noise power is also calculated. Output signal to output noise power is determined. It is also explained how to minimize the noise figure for a particular value of antenna resistance. Some examples are shown for the noise related problems. Mathematical relation is established for noise effect on radar. Maximum power gain relation is shown. Examples related to radar is expressed. The concept of moving target indicator (MTI) is also discussed. Separate identification of moving target is made with the help of Doppler's effect. The theory of Doppler's effect is narrated and relation between frequency and radial velocity is established. A block diagram of MTI radar system is also discussed. An idea is also given on STALO (Stable local oscillator) and COHO (Coherent oscillator). Blind speed is defined. Example is also shown on blind speed for giving clear idea in that context. Continuous wave radar is also discussed. The main uses of the continuous wave radar are also narrated. The main limitations of continuous wave radar are also discussed. An idea is also given on frequency modulation radar (F.M. altimeter). Some typical operating values of F.M. altimeter are also described.

■ QUESTIONS ■

1. What is a radar? What are the different types of radar systems used in practice?
2. What is a pulsed radar? Explain its operation by a block diagram.
3. What are the different components of pulsed radar?
4. Describe the waveforms of the pulsed radar system.
5. Define the following of a pulsed radar system:
    (a) pulsed durations or pulse width
    (b) pulse repetition time
    (c) pulse repetition frequency
    (d) duty ratio

(e) peak power

(f) average power

(g) travel time in pulsed radar.

6. Describe the indicator of a pulsed radar.

7. What do you understand by synchronizing voltage pulse and sweep voltage in pulsed radar system?

8. Explain the range resolution in pulsed radar system.

9. What are the merits of high frequency for radar system and also the merits of low frequency for radar system?

10. What are the factors to be considered for selection of radar frequency?

11. Establish a free space pulsed radar range equation.

12. Establish the mathematical relation of noise effect on pulsed radar.

13. What is moving target Indicator? How does Doppler's effect help in this respect?

14. Explain the MTI radar with a block diagram.

15. What is blind speed? Explain it clearly.

16. Describe a continuous wave radar with a block diagram.

17. What are the main uses of continuous wave radar?

18. What are the limitations of continuous wave radar?

19. What is frequency modulation radar?

20. What is the procedure of measuring the altitude of the aircraft?

6 ■■■ Television

6.1 INTRODUCTION

The basic features of a television system are explained in Figure 6.1.

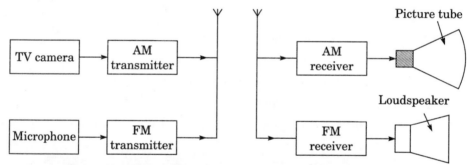

Figure 6.1 Elementary block diagram of a television system.

The optical information of a moving picture is taken by the TV camera and transformed into electrical or video signals and those signals are amplitude modulated by a radio frequency carrier wave and finally radiated by transmitting the antenna. Similarly, the voice is transformed by a microphone into the electrical or audio signals and the same is frequency modulated by another radio frequency carrier wave and radiated by the same transmitting antenna. The receiving antenna receives and sends the above signals to AM and FM receivers for demodulation. Both the AM and FM receivers are housed in the same cabinet. The AM receivers output is sent to the picture tube for optical reproduction and the FM receiver output is applied for acoustic reproduction to have the original voice.

6.2 TV TRANSMITTER AND RECEIVER BLOCK DIAGRAM

Figure 6.2 shows a detailed block diagram of TV transmitter. The main components are

- Television camera
- Microphone

- Crystal oscillator
- Different types of amplifiers
- Scanning and synchronizing circuits
- Combining Network
- Transmitting antenna

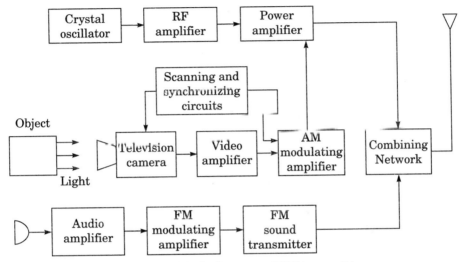

Figure 6.2 Block diagram of TV transmitter.

Figure 6.3 shows a detailed block diagram of the TV receiver.

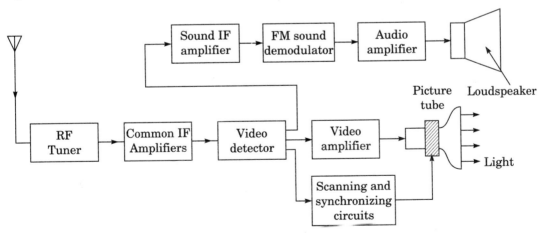

Figure 6.3 A detailed block diagram of TV receiver.

The main components of the TV receivers are:

- Receiver antenna
- RF tuner
- Video detector

- Various types of amplifiers
- FM sound demodulator
- Scanning and synchronizing circuits
- Picture tube

In the transmitter a series of electrical impulses are developed from the camera and ultimately a video signal is developed. The video signal impulses are amplified and then amplitude is modulated by radio frequency carrier wave and the same is radiated through antenna. For synchronizing the electron beam in the receiver picture tube, the synchronizing pulses are introduced into the video signal. Hence, at the end of scanning each horizontal line, a horizontal synchronizing pulse is incorporated and at the end of the image, a vertical synchronizing pulse is incorporated. For sound signal audio amplifier, an FM modulated arrangement is shown in Figure 6.2.

In the receiver circuit, the received signal is passed through the common IF amplifier that is nothing but the heterodyne mixer. With the help of the video detector, the sound and video signals are separated. Synchronizing signals are also separated and applied to the scanning and synchronizing circuits.

The pulses developed from these circuits help to keep the scanning beam at the receiver to be in step with that at the transmitters.

6.3 TELEVISION CAMERA

Figure 6.4 describes a TV camera tube. The major components of TV camera are as follows:

- Focusing lens
- Glass plate
- Conductive coating
- Photoconductive surface
- Cathode
- Electron gun
- Magnetic deflection and focusing coils.

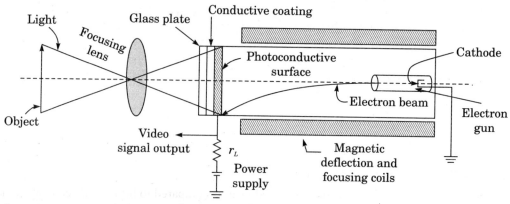

Figure 6.4 TV camera tube.

The lens of the television camera focuses the object to be shown on television on a photo sensitive plate termed *mosaic* which is available in the camera tube. The photo layer has resistance when no light falls on it, but the same decreases depending on the intensity of light falling.

A thin pencil of electrons from an electron gun in the camera tube travels along successive horizontal lines on the mosaic screen. Hence, the electron beam is used to pick up the picture information available on the target plate in terms of varying resistance at each point. The beam on the way to the inner side of the glass plate, where the transparent conductive coating exists, is being deflected by a pair of magnetic deflecting and focusing coils being mounted on the glass envelope and kept mutually perpendicular to each other for achieving scanning of the entire target area. The scanning process releases a series of electrical impulses that produce the video signal. The video signal impulses are amplified and then amplitude modulated by radio frequency carrier wave and then the same is radiated through antenna. For synchronizing the electron beam in the receiver picture tube, the synchronizing pulses are introduced into the video signal. Hence, at the end of scanning each horizontal line, a horizontal synchronizing pulse is incorporated and at the end of the image, a vertical synchronizing pulse is incorporated.

6.4 SCANNING IN THE TELEVISION SYSTEM

Scanning is process by virtue of which a series of electrical impulses is released to form the video signal. The complete frame of a television picture is scanned thirty times per second in such a way, which is very similar to read the page. The beam in the camera or picture tube moves at a constant velocity across the screen. When it reaches the end of the screen on the right hand side, it whips back to the left hand edge of the screen and continues in this manner. When the beam reaches the bottom of the screen, it whips back to the top of the screen.

6.4.1 Horizontal and Vertical Scanning

Horizontal scanning (Figure 6.5) is the process by virtue of which reading from line to line is made. The time taken from the beginning of one line to the instant when the next line begins to be scanned is 63.5 μs, which is termed H. The above time includes the scanning of the picture from left to right and the rapid return retrace from right to left. The retrace also takes 10.2 μs. In other words, retrace takes 16% of the time allocated for horizontal scanning. The retrace is to be made invisible. That is why, the scanning beam current is to be made zero from the beginning of the retrace to just after its end. The process is termed blanking in case of horizontal scanning. Therefore, a pulse is to be added to the video waveform at the right moment and for the correct period ensuring that the signal level has been raised to that state of blanking. Then the blanking voltage is applied and the horizontal scanning generator receives a synchronous pulse and retrace will be intimated. The retrace continues for a period of time indicated by the time constant of the oscillator generating the scanning waveform. As soon as the retrace ends, the scanning of the next line starts. Hence, after a lapse of 0.16 H (H–time allocated for scanning of one line), the picture will be visible.

Vertical scanning (Figure 6.5) is more or less similar to the horizontal scanning. Only the difference is in the direction of movement. The vertical scanning is made to lift the beam up as and when desired. The vertical scanning is slower as compared to horizontal scanning. When the horizontal scanning takes place 15750 times per second, the vertical scanning takes place

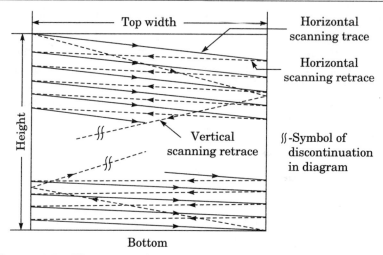

Figure 6.5 Elementary drawing of horizontal scanning and vertical scanning beam on the picture frame.

60 times per second. Suppose, by performing horizontal scanning, the beam has reached the midway of the line 'x', and at that time the vertical blanking is applied. The vertical scanning generator will receive a synchronous pulse and the vertical retrace will be started after a certain time and during that period, the horizontal scanning has brought the beam down to line 'y' where 'y' is obviously greater than 'x'. During the time of vertical retrace, the horizontal will be also continued. The vertical retrace continues until the beam reaches the top of the picture, the beam starts to descend. Usually, about 21H (21 × time allocated to scan one line) time is required for the vertical blanking operation and afterwards it is removed. The above procedure of horizontal and vertical blanking is repeated as and when it is required to obtain the actual picture. The basic important point is that blanking is applied sometimes before the retrace begins and removed sometimes after it has ended. Both the above margins are used safely and to provide individual designers some flexibility.

The frame repetition rate for scanning as per Indian standard is 25 per second. That means, with horizontal 625 lines in each frame, 25 frames are being scanned per second. The total number of horizontal lines scanned per second is 625 × 25 = 15625 lines. Figure 6.5 describes elementary diagram of horizontal and vertical scanning.

6.4.2 Interlaced Scanning

Interlaced scanning is that type of scanning where each field consists of one half of the total number of lines available. For example, if there are 625 lines per frame, then the first scan or field will cover 312.5 lines and the second scan or field will start from half way across the top of the picture and covers alternate lines, which are omitted by the first field. If the frame repetition rate is standardized at 25 per second, then the repetition rate of field will be 50 per second. Since the ac power line frequency in India is 50 c/s, the 50 cycle scanning frequency helps the design of transmitter, receiver and power supply filters. The image formed on the retina of the eye of a human being is retained on it for a short period. The rapid flashing picture frame creates illusion of continuity to the eye. If the number of frames is large enough, the flicker is not observed and the flashes appear continuous. The minimum rate of flashes at which the flicker disappears is termed the critical flicker frequency.

Figure 6.6 describes the interlaced scanning with first field and second field.

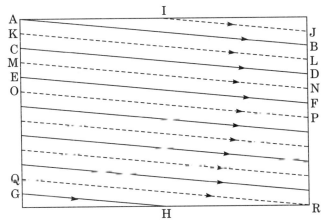

Figure 6.6   Interlaced scanning on a frame. (Continuous line—first field, dashed line—second field).

Figure 6.7 describes the vertical retrace of interlaced scanning. The main points are as follows.

- AB — One horizontal scanning line (Figure 6.6)
- BC — Blanked out
- CD — Next horizontal scanning line
- The point C is almost at the same height as B since the retrace is very quick.
- The scanning point moves to and fro across the frame, the spot moves downward at constant but slow rate. Hence, the scanning lines are slightly sloped and each forward scanning line is a little below the preceding line.
- At the point H_1, only half the horizontal scanning has completed.
- After that quick vertical upwards flyback begins from point H_1 to I (Figure 6.7). During this time the spot is blanked out.

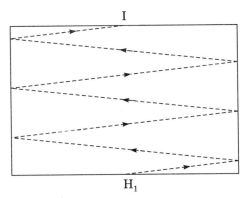

Figure 6.7   Vertical retrace of interlaced scanning.

6.4.3 Vertical Resolution

The vertical resolution means the ability of a scanning system to resolve or identify separately the vertical details of the picture. It is expressed mathematically as follows:

$$n = \frac{H}{\alpha D}$$

n — no. of lines of vertical resolution
H — height of the picture
D — distance for watching
α — minimum angle of vertical resolution in radians.

For a visual angle 10°, the D/H ratio is six. The resolving capability of the human eye is about 1 minute of visual angle 10°.

That means $\alpha = \dfrac{1}{60}$ degree.

Therefore, $n = \dfrac{1}{6} \times 60° \times \dfrac{180}{\pi} = 600$ lines

Figure 6.8 shows the white and black lines.
Figure 6.9 shows the minimum vertical angle α.

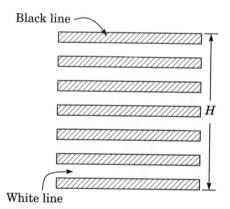

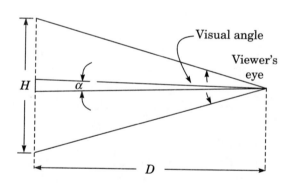

Figure 6.8 White and Black lines of vertical resolution.

Figure 6.9 Minimum vertical viewing angle.

In case of visual angle 15°, $D/H = 4$.

Hence, $$n = \frac{1}{4} \times 60 \times \frac{180}{\pi} = 900 \text{ lines}$$

In practice, the maximum vertical resolution is reduced below the active number of lines used for scanning. The reasons are:

(i) The scanning beam is not aligning with the resolution lines.
(ii) The finite beam width.

It is generally found that the average number of effective lines gets reduced to 0.7 times the total active scan line present. The reduction factor is termed kell factor. The value of scale factor lies between 0.64 to o.85. In case of 625 line system, if we assume that 40 lines will be lost in vertical retrace, the number of active scanning reduces to (625 – 40) = 585 lines. Considering the kell factor 0.7, the vertical resolution becomes 585 × 0.7 = 410 lines.

6.4.4 Horizontal Resolution

The horizontal resolution is the ability of the scanning system to resolve or identify separately the horizontal details of the picture. It classifies the changes in brightness levels of elements along a horizontal scanning line. Usually, for 625 lines system, 40 lines are lost in vertical retrace. Moreover, the statistical analysis shows that average number of effective lines is reduced to 0.7 times the active scan lines present. The effective lines of vertical resolution come as (625 – 40) × 0.7 = 410 lines. The horizontal resolution will have the same value. But considering the aspect factor, which is width to height ratio of the rectangular format of TV, as 4:3, the number of white and vertical lines for matching horizontal resolution will be $410 \times \dfrac{4}{3} = 546$.

This is obviously equivalent to 273 cycles of black and white elementary areas. The time period of one horizontal line will be

$$\frac{1}{15625} \text{ second} = 64 \ \mu s.$$

Since the horizontal line frequency is equal to the line per picture × picture per second, i.e. 625 × 25 = 15625 lines/second.

12 μs are lost in horizontal retrace (64 – 12) = 52 μs completes the active horizontal line scanning. Figure 6.10 shows alternate white and black elements. Figure 6.11 shows video signal on scanning. The video signal is square wave.

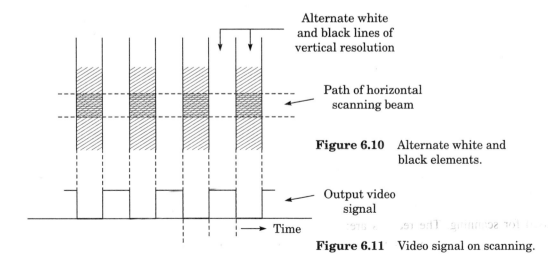

Alternate white and black lines of vertical resolution

Path of horizontal scanning beam

Figure 6.10 Alternate white and black elements.

Output video signal

Time

Figure 6.11 Video signal on scanning.

The periodic time of the square wave is $\dfrac{52}{273}\,\mu s = 0.2\,\mu s$.

Hence, the highest fundamental frequency $= \dfrac{1}{0.2 \times 10^{-6}} = \dfrac{10^6}{0.2} = 5$ MHz.

Hence, the highest fundamental video frequency $= \dfrac{\text{Active lines} \times \text{Kell factor} \times \text{Aspect ratio}}{2 \times \text{Line forward scan period}}$

That means, in case of 625 line system

$$\text{Active lines} = 625 - 40 = 585$$

$$\text{Kell factor} = 0.7$$

$$\text{Aspect ratio} = \dfrac{4}{3}$$

Line forward scan period = Total time period of one horizontal line – Horizontal retrace period

$$= 64\ \mu s - 12\ \mu s = 52\ \mu s$$

6.5   SYNCHRONIZATION IN TELEVISION

Synchronization is a process in television by virtue of which the correct timing of vertical and horizontal sweep motion is maintained and at the same time the receiver and transmitter are locked in step. The synchronization signals are sent out alongwith the information of the picture. These are sent out periodically at the line and field scanning frequencies in the form of rectangular pulses. Usually, the horizontal line frequency is given by $625 \times 25 = 15625$ lines/second; hence, the horizontal synchronous pulse is transmitted for each horizontal line at a frequency of 15625 Hz. In this way, a vertical synchronous pulse is sent for each field to keep the vertical scanning in step. Thus, the vertical scanning frequency becomes 50 Hz. To avoid interference with the picture on TV screen, the synchronous pulses are transmitted during the scanning retrace time, because, at that time, the screen is blanked out and no information of the picture is transmitted.

6.6   RANGE OF TELEVISION BANDWIDTH

It has been observed that 625 lines per picture frame possess 15625 horizontal lines scanning per second. Since large information is being transmitted in an extremely short time, very high video signal frequencies up to 5 MHz are produced.

Over and above, FM sound channel is to be added to the overall TV bandwidth. A channel of 7 MHz width is to be provided for transmitting the complete TV signal. Hence, this large frequency range cannot be superimposed upon the carrier in the broadcast frequency range from 500 to 1600 kHz. That is why, the Federal Communication Commission has provided 13 television channels. Each channel is provided with 7 MHz wide in the VHF bands from 54 to 88 MHz and from 174 to 216 MHz.

6.7 BANDWIDTH IN CASE OF SEQUENTIAL SCANNING AND INTERLACED SCANNING

In case of sequential scanning the bandwidth is calculated in the following manner:

It is known that the number of picture frames/second is to be made at least 50 to avoid fickering. Hence, the horizontal scanning frequency is $50 \times 625 = 31250$ lines/second for 625 line system. This is equivalent to a line period of 32 μs. Therefore, for the requisite horizontal resolution of $546/2 = 273$ pairs of black and white alterations in one horizontal line, the bandwidth requirement will be

$$\frac{273}{(32-6)} \text{ MHz} = 10 \text{ MHz}.$$

Here, it is assumed that 6 alterations out of 32 are lost in horizontal retrace.

In case if interlaced scanning, the entire picture is divided into sets of fields. Each field contains half of the total number of lines per picture frame and the two fields are scanned alternately.

The first field of 312.5 lines is the odd field and is scanned sequentially as shown by the continuous line in Figure 6.6. The odd field starts from A and terminates at point I. The second field of 312.5 lines starts at point I and terminates at point A. Each field of 312.5 lines is completed in (1/50) second. Hence, the complete picture frame is scanned in (1/25) second. Hence, in interlaced scanning, a frame rate of only 25 frame/second is used but an effective flicker rate of 50 cycles/second is achieved. Hence, in case of interlaced scanning, the bandwidth requirement reduces to half, i.e. 5 MHz because 312.5 lines are scanned in (1/50) second. The flyback from bottom of a field to the top of a field needs a time interval equal to 20 lines. Therefore, $(625 - 40) = 585$ lines carry the picture information. These lines are termed active lines.

6.8 COMPOSITE VIDEO SIGNAL

The composite video signal in the TV is the combination of the following:

    (a) video signal
    (b) horizontal blanking pulse
    (c) horizontal synchronizing pulses
    (d) vertical blanking pulses
    (e) vertical synchronizing pulses
    (f) equalizing pulses

Video signal is the electrical signal corresponding to the information of the picture at the output of the TV camera which scans the picture. *Horizontal synchronizing pulses* are required at the end of the horizontal scan. *Vertical synchronizing pulses* are required at the end of the horizontal scanning. The picture tube is kept inoperative during the horizontal and vertical retrace intervals with the help of blanking pulses. The *blanking pulses* are developed at the transmitting station and are added to the video signal. The actual horizontal retrace takes a small fraction of the line interval '*h*' as shown in Figure 6.12.

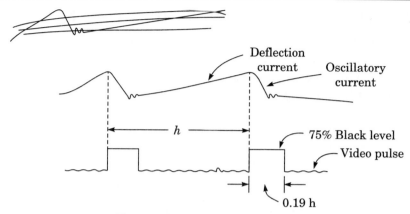

Figure 6.12 Blanking signal.

At the time of retrace, damped oscillatory current in the deflection coil will be developed. As a result, the horizontal pulses at the black level will provide 75% blank and the interval taken will be 0.19 h as shown in Figure 6.12. In case of vertical blanking, the picture tube is made inoperative.

Figure 6.13 shows the horizontal synchronizing and blanking pulse.

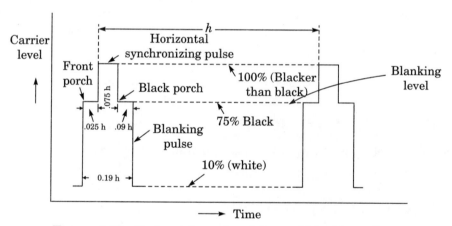

Figure 6.13 Horizontal synchronizing and blanking pulse.

The total line period $h = \dfrac{1}{625 \times 25} = 64\ \mu s$

Horizontal synchronizing pulse duration = 0.075 × 64 = 4.7 μs with a tolerance ± 2 μs.
Blanking pulse duration = 0.19 h = 0.19 × 64 = 12 μs with a tolerance of + 3 μs to – 2 μs.
Front porch = 0.025 × 64 = 1.5 μs.
Back porch = 0.09 × 64 = 5.76 μs.

Front porch: The horizontal synchronizing pulse starts .025 h (=1.5 μs) later than the blanking pulse. This period is termed front porch.

Back porch: The synchronous pulse terminates about 0.09 h = 0.09 × 64 μs = 5.76 μs before the end of the blanking pulse. This is termed the back porch. Due to early termination of back porch, the line retrace is completed itself and all oscillations in the deflection circuit dies down before the next forward deflection starts. In case of colour TV, the back porch helps to accommodate the burst of colour subcarrier.

The levels in the composite video signals are maintained as follows by using the negative modulation.

(i) Tips of the synchronizing pulses – 100% level
(ii) Blanking level – 75%
(iii) Peak white level – 10%

At the end of each field (consisting of 625/2 = 312.5 lines) vertical synchronizing waveform is inserted in the composite video signal.

Figures 6.14(a) and 6.14(b) show the field synchronizing pulses, equalizing and blanking pulses. Figure 6.14(a) shows the odd field. Figure 6.14(b) shows the even field. The vertical field blanking period is usually twenty times the line period '*h*'. In other words, it is 20 × 64 = 1280 μs. The vertical synchronizing pulse duration is 2.5 h. For maintaining the horizontal synchronization during the vertical synchronization pulse, the vertical synchronizing pulse is split up by serrations of 4.7 μs wide into five narrow pulses. This serrated vertical synchronization pulse occurs for 0.5 h, i.e. 0.5 × 64 = 3 μs interval and width of each pulse is equal to (32 – 4.7) = 27.3 μs. The timing of the serrations is made in such a way that the leading edges of alternate half line pulse coincide with the leading edges of horizontal synchronizing pulse if they would exist. The field retrace begins at the middle of the horizontal scanning line in the case of an odd field and at the end of a horizontal scanning line in the case of even field. That is why, half line rhythm is essential.

Equalizing pulses: The field synchronizing pulses are separated from the line synchronous pulses in the TV receiver. To produce the composite single field pulse, the serrated vertical synchronization pulses are integrated. The composite single field pulse is used for triggering and synchronizing the vertical oscillator. The integrated vertical synchronizing pulses are produced at the ends of odd and even fields and these should be identical for perfect interface. On the other hand, the line period preceding the vertical synchronizing pulses for odd and even field are found unequal. It is being observed that same is *h*/2 before an odd field and *h* before an even field.

Hence, by using five narrow pulses each 2.3 μs wide occurring at *h*/2 rhythm preceding the field synchronizing pulses, the interval preceding the vertical synchronizing pulse can be made *h*/2 in the odd and even field. These five pulses are termed pre-equalizing pulses and they equalize the integrated vertical synchronizing for odd and even fields. Similarly, the post equalizing pulses are also required as shown in Figures 6.14(a) and 6.14(b).

6.9   VESTIGIAL SIDEBAND TRANSMISSION SYSTEM IN THE TELEVISION SYSTEM

If a television system develops video frequencies up to 5 MHz, the two sidebands of the amplitude modulated video carrier will occupy a band of 10 MHz.

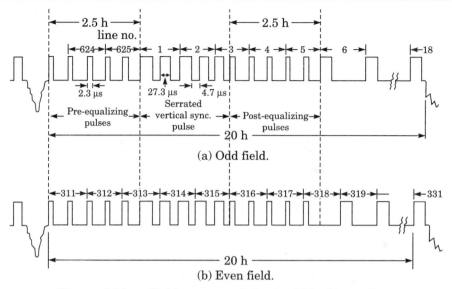

Figure 6.14   Field sync equalizing and blanking pulses.

This is actually more than the bandwidth of the entire video pulse sound channel. Since the channel bandwidth is small, the video carrier is transmitted with a single sideband. For avoiding distortion a small vestigial portion of the lower video-sideband is transmitted. This is termed vestigial sideband transmission as shown in Figure 6.15. In case of 7 MHz standard television channel, the limit of the lower sideband is arbitrarily labelled zero frequency and the vestigial sideband is extended up to 1.25 MHz where the video carrier is located. From 1.25 MHz to 6.25 MHz, the upper video-sideband is extended to full amplitude and the same is extended up to 6.75 MHz at reduced amplitude. The frequency modulated sound carrier is placed at a centre frequency of 6.75 MHz having two sidebands with bandwidth 100 kHz.

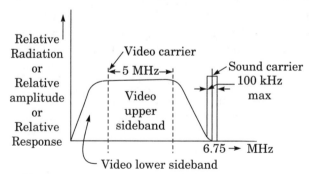

Figure 6.15   Vestigial sideband transmission.

6.9.1   Demerits of Vestigial Sideband Transmission

The demerits of the vestigial sideband are as follows:

(a) The power of the transmitter although small is wasted in the vestigial sideband filters. Because these filters remove the remaining lower sideband.

(b) There occurs a loss of about 6 dB in the signal to noise voltage ratio relative to what would be available it double sideband transmission is used because the attenuation slope of the receiver to correct the boost at lower video frequencies keeps the carrier at 50% output voltage and that creates the loss.

(c) Phase and amplitude distortion of the picture signal are found in spite of very good filter design at the transmitter.

Over and above, if is really difficult to tune IF stages of the receiver corresponding to the ideal needed response. Even for this some phase and amplitude distortion occur.

(d) For given amount of local oscillator mismatch or drift after initial tuning, more critical tuning at the receiver is necessary. Of course, for British 625 line system this is better because it permits 1.25 MHz unattenuated lower sideband transmission instead of 0.75 MHz for other system.

In spite of all the above demerits, vestigial sideband is utilized in all television systems since large saving is possible if the bandwidth is made required for each channel in case of non-use of vestigial sideband transmission.

6.10 FREQUENCY MODULATION IN TELEVISION

The sound signal is frequency modulated because it provides interference free reception. The amplitude of the modulated carrier is found constant and the frequency is varied according to the variations in the modulating signal. The variation in the carrier frequency will be proportional to the instantaneous value of the modulating voltage. Obviously, the rate at which the frequency variation will take place, will be equal to the modulating frequency. Let us assume that the modulating signal is sinusoidal. Figure 6.16 shows the modulating voltage and the frequency modulated wave.

6.10.1 Mathematical Analysis of Frequency Modulated Wave

Let us consider the ac wave as $e = a \sin \theta(t)$

where e — instantaneous amplitude

$\quad a$ — peak amplitude

$\quad \theta(t)$ — total angular displacement at time 't'.

The instantaneous angular velocity ω_i will be $\dfrac{d\theta(t)}{dt}$

so,
$$\omega_i = \frac{d\theta(t)}{dt}$$

Again
$$\theta(t) = \omega_c t + \theta$$

where ω_c = constant angular velocity

i.e.
$$\omega_c = 2\pi f_c$$
$$\theta = \text{angular position at } t = 0$$

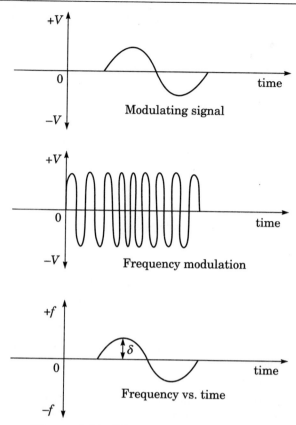

Figure 6.16 FM modulation waveform.

$$\therefore \qquad \frac{d\theta(t)}{dt} = \omega_c$$

Hence
$$\omega_i = \omega_c$$

Therefore, a frequency modulated wave with sinusoidal modulation can be described as follows

$$\omega_i = \omega_c + 2\pi \, \Delta f \cos \omega_m t$$

where ω_c = angular velocity of carrier wave

ω_i = instantaneous angular velocity

$\omega_m = 2\pi \cdot f_m$ where f_m is the frequency of modulating signal

Δf — maximum deviation of instantaneous frequency from the average value.

Now,
$$\omega_i = \frac{d\theta(t)}{dt} = \omega_c + 2\pi \, \Delta f \cos \omega_m t$$

Integrating the above

$$\theta(t) = \omega_c t + \frac{2\pi \, \Delta f}{\omega_m} \sin \omega_m t + \theta$$

where θ is the angular position at time $t = 0$.

Since $\qquad\qquad\qquad\qquad e = a \sin \theta(t),$

instantaneous amplitude will be $\qquad e = a \sin \left\{ \omega_c t + \dfrac{2\pi \, \Delta f}{\omega_m} \sin \omega_m t \right\}$

Assume $\qquad\qquad\qquad\qquad\qquad \theta = 0$

∴ $\qquad\qquad\qquad\qquad\qquad e = a \sin\{ \omega_c t + m_f \sin \omega_m t \}$

where $\qquad\qquad\qquad\qquad\qquad m_f = $ modulation index

$$= \frac{\Delta f}{f_m} = \frac{2\pi \, \Delta f}{\omega_m}$$

since modulation index is the ratio of frequency deviation and modulating frequency.

The sine of a sine function can be described as

$$e = a \,[(\sin \omega_c t \, \cos \, (m_f \sin \omega_m t) + \cos \omega_c t \, \sin \, (m_f \sin \omega_m t)]$$

The term cos$t$ ($m_f \sin \omega_m t$) can be expressed by Bessel function.

$$J_0 \, (m_f) + 2J_2(m_f) \cos 2\omega_m t + 2J_4 \, (m_f) \cos 4\omega_m t + \cdots$$

similarly, $\quad \sin \, (m_f \sin \omega_m t)$ will be $2J_1 \, (m_f) \sin \omega_m t + 2J_3 \, (m_f) \sin 3\omega_m t + \cdots$

Therefore,

$$e = a \, \{J_0 \, (m_f) \sin \omega_c t + J_1 \, (m_f) \, [\sin \, (\omega_c + \omega_m)t - \sin \, (\omega_c - \omega_m)t]$$
$$+ J_2 \, (m_f) \, [\sin \, (\omega_c + 2\omega_m)t - \sin \, (\omega_c - 2\omega_m)t]$$
$$+ J_3 \, (m_f) \, [\sin \, (\omega_c + 3\omega_m)t - \sin \, (\omega_c - 3\omega_m)t] + \cdots$$

6.10.2 Outcome of the Analysis of Frequency Modulated Wave

The outcomes coming out from the above instantaneous voltage equation are as follows:

- A large number of sidebands exist with the carrier. Over and above, the sidebands are separated from the carrier by integer multiples of 'f_m'.
- For a given m_f, the values of the Bessel functions are narrated in Table 6.1.

Table 6.1 The values of the Bessel functions

m_f	J_0	J_1	J_2	J_3	J_4	J_5	J_6	J_7	J_8
0	1.0	—	—	—	—	—	—	—	—
0.25	0.98	0.12	—	—	—	—	—	—	—
0.5	0.94	0.24	0.03	—	—	—	—	—	—
1.0	0.77	0.44	0.11	0.02	—	—	—	—	—
2.0	0.22	0.58	0.35	0.13	0.03	—	—	—	—
3.0	−0.26	0.34	0.49	0.31	0.13	0.04	—	—	—
4.0	−0.40	−0.07	0.36	0.43	0.28	0.13	0.05	—	—
5.0	−0.18	−0.33	0.05	0.36	0.39	0.26	0.13	0.05	—
6.0	0.15	−0.28	−0.24	0.11	0.36	0.36	0.25	0.13	0.06
7.0	0.30	0.00	−0.30	−0.17	0.16	0.55	0.34	0.23	0.13

It is clear that the value of J_n decreases as number 'n' increases. The values of J_n may be positive or negative.

- The sideband distribution is symmetrical about the carrier frequency.
- If the amplitude of the modulating signal increases for a given modulating frequency, there will be increase in 'Δf'. Thus, m_f will increase. That makes larger no. of sidebands to get significant amplitudes. Therefore, higher amplitude signal would require more sidebands for transmission without distortion. Although the total transmitted power will remain constant.
- It is also observed from the tabulated result (Table 6.1) of Bessel coefficients, when the frequency is half the modulating frequency, the second and higher order sideband components relatively small. Over and above, the frequency band needed to accommodate the essential part of the signal is the same as in amplitude modulation. When m_f exceeds unity, some important higher order sideband components exist and as a result, larger bandwidth is needed for obtaining distortion free transmission as far as possible.

Usually, for calculating channel bandwidth, J coefficients having magnitude less than 0.05 for a calculated value of m_f may be neglected, because a lot of higher sidebands have insignificant relative amplitudes.

6.10.3 Bandwidth of FM Channel

The FM channel bandwidth is expressed as $2\pi f_m$; where f_m is the frequency of modulating wave and n is the number of significant side frequency components. The value of 'n' is obtained from the value of modulation of index. Generally, the channel bandwidth is estimated for the worst case where even the highest frequency to be transmitted causes maximum allowed frequency deviation.

The maximum frequency deviation of commercial FM is limited to 75 kHz. The modulating frequency generally covers 25 Hz to 15 kHz. Say, 15 kHz tone has unit amplitude, which is equal to the maximum permitted amplitude.

So, in this case $m_f = \dfrac{75}{15} = 5$.

For $m_f = 5$, the Bessel function (Table 6.1) shows $J_n = J_7$, i.e. $n = 7$.

Therefore, bandwidth = $2 \times 7 \times 15 = 210$ kHz. In the 625 – B television system the maximum deviation (Δf) should not exceed ± 50 Hz for the highest modulating frequency of 15 kHz.

So,
$$m_f = \frac{50}{15} \approx 3.$$

From Table 6.1, it is found $n = 5$.

Hence, the bandwidth = $2 \times 5 \times 15 = 150$ kHz.

The estimation of the bandwidth can also be made from Carson's rule. Carson's rule describes that the bandwidth needed to pass an FM wave is equal to the twice the sum of the deviation and the highest modulating frequency.

Hence, for the standard transmission the bandwidth needed is $2(75 + 15) = 180$ kHz. Similarly for 625–B system, the Carson's rule describes bandwidth requirement as $2(50 + 15) = 130$ kHz.

6.10.4 Detail of Different Television Systems

The main data of television systems being utilized in different countries are described in Table 6.2.

Table 6.2 Principal television systems

Items	Western Europe, Middle East, India and most Asian countries	North and South America including US, Canada, Mexico and Japan	USSR	France	England
Lines per frame	625	525	625	625	625
Frames per second	25	30	25	25	25
Field frequency (Hz)	50	60	50	50	50
Line frequency (Hz)	15625	15750	15625	15625	15625
Video bandwidth (MHz)	5 or 6	4.2	6	6	5.5
Channel bandwidth (MHz)	7 or 8	6	8	8	8
Video modulation	Negative	Negative	Negative	Positive	Negative
Picture modulation	AM	AM	AM	FM	AM
Sound signal modulation	FM	FM	FM	AM	FM
Colour system	PAL	NTSC	SECAM	SECAM	PAL

6.11 MONOCHROME PICTURE TUBE

The monochrome picture tube, as shown in Figure 6.17, produces a picture in black and white. It actually consists of electron gun with continuous phosphor coating. The elements of the picture tube are as follows:

(a) Cathode with base
(b) Control grid
(c) Accelerating anode
(d) Focusing anode
(e) Two centering magnets
(f) Two pincushion error magnets
(g) Deflection windings
(h) Deflection yoke
(i) Final anode (18 kV and HT connector)
(j) Inner aquadag conductive coating (18 kV)
(k) External conductive coating
(l) Glass envelope
(m) Glass face plate
(n) Phosphor coating
(o) Aluminized coating

Figure 6.17 describes all the elements of a picture tube.

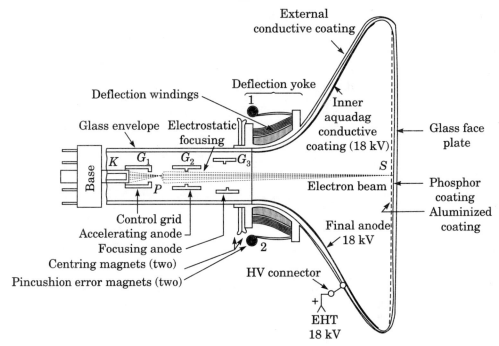

Figure 6.17 Monochrome picture tube.

6.11.1 Electron Gun

In the electron gun, cathode is indirectly heated. It consists of a cylinder of nickel. It is coated at its end with thoriated tungsten or barium and strontium oxides. The emitting materials have low work function. When the same is heated, there will be a release of sufficient electrons to form the necessary stream of electrons within the tube. Figure 6.17 describes the electron gun. Here the control grid G_1 is kept at a negative potential with respect to the cathode. As a result, it controls the flow of electrons from the cathode. It is a cylinder with a small circular opening to keep the electron stream in a small area.

The grid G_2 is the accelerating or screen grid. The grid G_3 is the focusing grid. These grids are kept at different potentials with respect to the cathode. The range varies from 200 volt to 600 volt. All the elements of the electron gun are connected to the base pins. Through the tube socket, the elements receive their rated voltage. P is termed the crossover point. All the electrons are turned into a tiny spot, i.e. crossover point, by applying suitable field. The screen grid and focus electrode draw electrons from cross over point and bring them to a focus at the viewing screen. The focus anode is larger in diameter and is kept at a higher potential than the accelerating anode. Most important point is that the electrode voltages are so chosen and electric field is varied such that all the electrons get focussed on the screen of the picture tube.

6.11.2 Aquadag Conductive Coating

The electron stream should acquire sufficient velocity to reach the picture tube screen material. As a result, the online picture can be exhibited properly. That means, proper energy can be achieved. This anode is the conductive coating with colloidal graphite on the inside of the wide bell of the tube. This coating is termed *aquadag*. This exists from almost half way into the narrow neck to within 3 cm of the fluorescent screen. This is connected through a specially connected pin at the top or side of the glass bell to a very high potential of over 15 kV. The exact voltage, of course, depends on the tube size and is about 18 kV for 48 cm monochrome tube. When the electrons are accelerated under the influence of high voltage anode area, they acquire tremendous high velocity before they hit the screen. Again, for the very high velocities of the electrons, the secondary emission will take place from the screen. There may be a chance of accumulation of negative space charge for the secondary emitted electrons near the screen. That will ultimately prevent the arrival of the primary beam. But, this does not occur due to the fact that the conductive coating being at a very high positive potential collects the secondary emitted electrons.

Thus, both the purposes are served. The beam velocity is increased and unwanted secondary electrons are removed.

6.11.3 Electromagnetic Deflection Device

Since it is much more advisable to generate large currents than high voltages, electromagnetic deflection scheme is applied to all the picture tubes. In a picture tube with 15 kV at the final anode, about 7500 volt is necessary to get full deflection on a 50 cm screen. It is really very difficult to generate such high voltages at the deflection frequencies. On the other hand, with magnetic deflection, large current is necessary to obtain the same deflection. That is why, both electric and magnetic fields are utilized for deflecting the electron beam. In the magnetic deflection, much larger deflection angles can be obtained without defocusing. On the other hand, in electrostatic deflection, the larger deflection angles tends to defocus the beam. Over and above, the deflection plates are required to be placed further apart since the deflection is made larger. Hence, higher voltages are to be required to produce the same deflection field.

For magnetic deflection two pairs of deflecting coils are mounted outside and close to the neck of the tube. This makes the system more economical and more rugged, whereas, in case of electrostatic deflection, two delicate pairs of deflecting plates are required inside the picture tube.

6.11.4 Deflection Yoke

Figure 6.18 describes cross-sectional view of a yoke showing location of vertical and horizontal windings about the neck of the picture tube.

Figure 6.19 shows the orientation of the magnetic fields developed. The magnetic field of the coils reacts with the electron beam and accordingly deflection occurs. The horizontal deflection coil sweeps the beam across the face of the tube from left to right. It is actually split into two sections and mounted above and below the beam axis. The vertical deflection coil is also similarly split into two sections and placed left and right on the neck for pulling the beam gradually downward as the horizontal coils sweep the beam across the tube face. Actually, each coil obtains its respective sweep input from the associated sweep circuits and finally they form

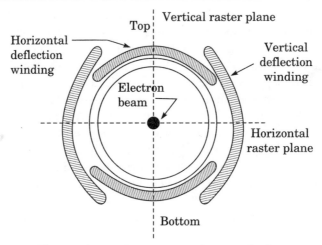

Figure 6.18 Cross-sectional view of yoke.

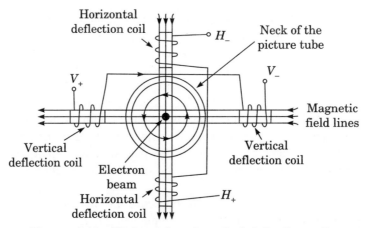

Figure 6.19 Horizontal and vertical deflecting coils.

the raster upon which the picture information is traced. Typical values of deflection angles are 70°, 90°, 110° and 114°.

Figures 6.20 and 6.21 show short picture tube with 110° deflection angle and long picture tube with 55° deflection angle respectively. A large deflection angle needs more power from the deflection circuits. As a result, the tubes are made with a narrow neck for putting the deflection yoke closer to the electron beam. A 110° yoke has a smaller hole diameter in comparison with neck diameters for tubes with lesser deflection angles. The hole diameter of 110° yoke is above 3 cm. The merit of the large deflection angle is that for equal picture size, the picture tube is shorter and can be installed in a smaller cabinet. For larger deflection angles, it is necessary to use a special type of winding for generating uniform magnetic fields for linear deflection. Here, the thickness of the deflection winding varies as the cosine of the angle from a central reference line. This type of winding is termed cosine winding.

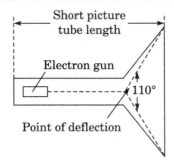

Figure 6.20 Short picture tube length with 110° deflection angle.

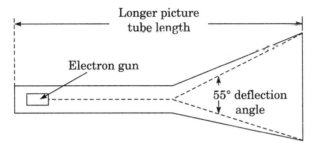

Figure 6.21 Long picture tube length with 55° deflection angle.

6.11.5 Screen Phosphor

The phosphor chemicals are usually light metals, for example zinc and cadmium in the form of sulphide, sulphate and phosphate compounds. The material is processed for developing very fine particles. These fine particles are applied on the inside of the glass plate. The high velocity electrons of the beam hit the phosphor and excite its atoms with the result that the corresponding spot fluoresces and emits light. The phosphorescent characteristics of the chemicals utilized are such that an afterglow remains on the screen for a short while after the beam leaves from the screen spot. The afterglow characteristic is termed *persistence*. Medium persistence is needed to increase the average brightness and to reduce flicker. Of course, the persistence must occur less than (1/25) second for picture tube screens, otherwise if one frame persists into the next, blurring of objects in motion will occur. The decay time of picture tube phosphors is approximately 5 millisecond and its persistence is referred to as P_4 by the industry.

6.11.6 Rectangular Face Plate Picture Tube

A rectangular image on a circular screen is the wastage of screen area. That is why, all the modern picture tubes have rectangular face plates. The breadth to height ratio is maintained 4 : 3. A rectangular tube with 54 cm screen indicates that the distance between the two diagonal points is 54 centimetre. The thickness of the plate is approximately 1.5 cm. This thickness is sufficient to withstand air pressure on the evacuated glass envelope. Previously, special glass or plastic shields were placed in the cabinet in front of picture tube for preventing any glass from hitting the viewer in case of an implosion. Modern picture tube incorporates integral implosion protection. Different systems are used in this connection. For example, one of the arrangements is termed *Kimcode*. A metal rim band (Figure 6.22) is held around the tube by a tension strap or with a layer of epoxy element in Kimcode. Another example is Panpoly. Here, a special faceplate is held in front of the tube by epoxy cement. Of course, in all cases, it is customary to check for implosion proofing in case of replacing any picture tube.

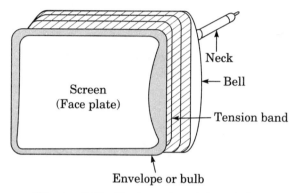

Figure 6.22   Rectangular picture tube.

6.11.7   Yoke and Centring Magnets

The positioning of the yoke is very important aspect. The yoke on all the black and white tubes is positioned right up against the flare of the tube for achieving complete coverage of the area of full screen. The yoke is moved as far forward as possible, otherwise the electron beam will strike the neck of the picture tube and develops a shadow near the corners of the face plate. The mounting system allows positioning of the yoke against the tube funnel and permits rotation of the yoke for ensuring horizontal lines to run parallel to the natural horizontal axis.

Through the horizontal and vertical deflection coils direct current is supplied to accomplish electrical centring of the beam. Of course, for low voltage power supply, this method is not utilized, otherwise added current drain will occur. In case of modern tubes, a pair of permanent magnets exists for centring as shown in Figure 6.17. They are generally mounted in the form of rings on the yoke cover. Poles of both the magnets can be properly moved with a pair of projecting tube being provided on the magnetic rings. Two tabs, i.e. one from each ring coincide with each other and the strongest field is obtained. That means, the beam will be pushed furthest off centre. Minimum field is obtained when the two tabs are kept 180° apart, i.e. they are placed on opposite sides. The two rings are rotated together for changing the direction in which decentring is observed. Figures 6.23(a) and 6.23(b) describe the above.

The edge of the yoke liner shown in Figure 6.17 is utilized for holding small permanent magnets. These are positioned for correcting any pincushion error as shown in Figure 6.23.

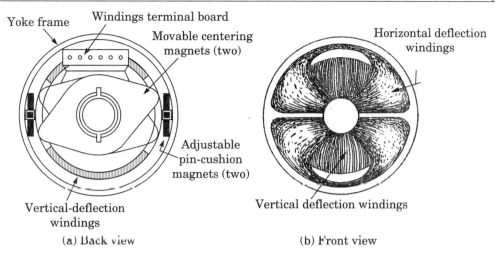

Yoke frame Windings terminal board Movable centering magnets (two) Horizontal deflection windings Adjustable pin-cushion magnets (two) Vertical-deflection windings Vertical deflection windings

(a) Back view (b) Front view

Figure 6.23 Details of deflection yoke.

6.11.8 Screen Brightness

It is observed that approximately fifty per cent of the light emitted at the screen during the time of striking of electron beam turns back into the tube. Approximately another twenty per cent is lost in the glass of the tube on account of internal reflection. Actually, approximately twenty per cent reaches the viewer. Even image contrast is impaired on account of interference developed by the light that is returned to the screen after reflection from some other points. Over and above, a dark brownish patch on the screen is observed due to the following fact.

Ions in the beam existing in spite of the best precautions at the time of degassing damage the phosphor material striking it. This particular area generally centers around the middle of the screen since the greater mass of the ions prevents appreciable deflection at the time of their transit. As a result, they reach almost at the centre of the screen. To avoid the above problem, all modern picture tubes are provided with a very thin coating of aluminium on the back surface of the screen phosphor. The aluminized coating is made very thin and with a final anode voltages of 10 kV, the electrons of the beam will get sufficient velocity to penetrate the coating and excite the phosphor. Thus, the major portion of the light which would normally travel back and get lost in the tube is now reflected back to the screen by metal backing. As a result, much improved brilliancy is observed. The connection is made with aluminized coating with high voltage anode coating. That helps in draining off the secondary emitted electrons at the screen. As a result, the brightness is further improved. In earlier picture tubes, a magnetic beam, bender usually termed ion-trap was used to deflect the heavy ions away from the screen. But recently, in the picture tubes, there is no necessity of ion-trap, because they are provided with metal coating on the screen. Moreover, the ions due to their greater mass fail to penetrate the metal backing and do not reach the phosphor screen. Therefore, providing aluminized coating on the phosphor screen, the screen brightness and contrast are not only improved, but also, they help us not to provide ion-trap.

6.11.9 Filter Capacitor

The filter capacitor for high voltage supply is formed in the following manner:

On the outer surface of the picture tube, a grounded coating is provided. This maintains shielding from stray fields. This also acts as one plate of the capacitor. The other plate is of inner anode coating. The glass bulb serves as the insulator between the two. This is capacitor which is actually the filter capacitor for the high voltage supply. This capacitor holds charge for a long time after the 'switching off' of the anode voltage. That is why, proper precaution is to be taken from the point of view of safety. Before handling the picture tube, the capacitor should be discharged by shorting the anode button to the grounded wall coating.

6.11.10 Spark Gap

There is every possibility of arcing or flashover in the electron gun especially at the control grid because of close spacing between the various electrodes and the utilization of very high voltages. Obviously, voltage surges will be developed on account of arcing. That will damage the associated circuit components. Hence, to protect the receiver circuit on account of the above arcing, metallic spark gaps are provided as shunt paths for surge currents. In some cases, neon bulbs are utilized as spark gaps. The gas in the neon tube ionizes while the potential crosses a certain limit. As a result, a shunt path is provided for the high voltage arc current.

6.12 PICTURE TUBE CIRCUIT AND ASSOCIATED CONTROLS

Figure 6.24 shows the picture tube circuit and its associated controls. Most important items of the above circuit are:

- The dc voltages to the screen grid and focus grid are taken from the horizontal stage and adjusted to suitable values by resistive potential divider networks.
- Sufficient high voltage to the second anode of the picture tube is provided for producing proper screen brilliancy for normal visualization. From the output of the horizontal deflection circuit, this voltage is found.
- The variable bias control is made in the cathode circuit or control grid circuit. This helps to control the electron density. That will certainly control the brightness on the screen. Usually, brightness control is kept at the front panel of the receiver so that the spectator can adjust the brightness.
- For modern picture tubes, critical focus adjustment is not required.
- The contrast control is generally the part of the cathode or control grid circuit. At the front panel, the control is kept for the adjustment of contrast in the reproduced picture.

6.13 SAFETY IN PICTURE TUBE OPERATION

- There is every possibility of implosion of the tube if the tube is hit with a hard object because of high vacuum in the modern picture tube.
- There is also possibility of implosion if the tube is made to rest on its neck.

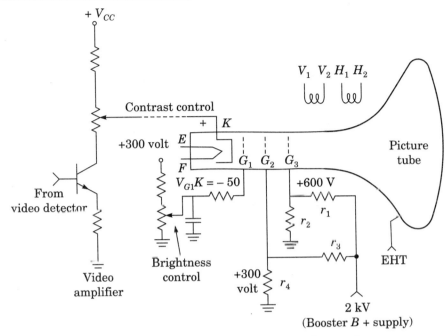

Figure 6.24 Picture tube circuits and controls.

- There is also every chance of injury of the person who are struck by the tube fragments when the implosion occurs due to breakage of the tube.
- The most important safety of human being is protective goggles. Even gloves should also be used by the person who handles the picture tube.
- The tube neck should be properly handled because the tube neck is fragile.

6.14 IMAGE ORTHICON CAMERA

Figure 6.25 describes the image orthicon camera.

It image orthicon camera has the following three main sections.

- Image section
- Scanning section
- Electron gun-cum-multiplier section.

6.14.1 Image Section

The important descriptions of image section are:

- The inside of the glass face plate at the front is coated with a silver antimony coating sensitized with cesium for serving as photocathode.
- From the object light is focused on the photocathode surface with the help of a lens system.

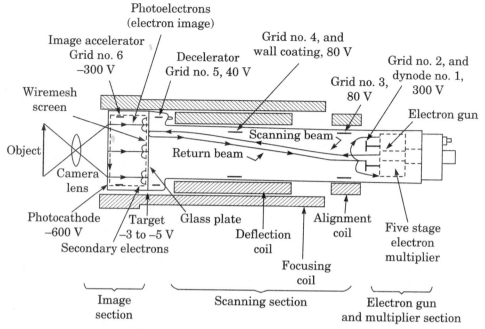

Photoelectrons
(electron image)

Image accelerator
Grid no. 6
−300 V

Decelerator
Grid no. 5, 40 V

Grid no. 4, and
wall coating, 80 V

Grid no. 2, and
dynode no. 1,
300 V

Grid no. 3,
80 V

Wiremesh
screen

Electron gun

Object

Scanning beam

Return beam

Camera
lens

Photocathode
−600 V

Target
−3 to −5 V

Glass plate

Alignment
coil

Secondary electrons

Deflection
coil

Five stage
electron
multiplier

Focusing
coil

Image
section

Scanning section

Electron gun
and multiplier section

Figure 6.25 Image orthicon camera.

- Now there will be release of electrons from each point of the photocathode in proportion to the incident light intensity.
- Photocathode surface is semitransparent and the light rays penetrate it to attain the inner surface from where electron emission takes place.
- An electron image of the scene or picture is developed on the target side of the photocoating and extends towards it because the number of electrons emitted at any point in the photocathode has a distribution corresponding to the brightness of the optical image.
- Since the photo cathode is a conductor, it cannot store charge although the conversion efficiency of the photo cathode is very high.
- Due to the above problem, the electron image developed at the photo cathode is shifted towards the target plate situated at a short distance from it.
- Usually the target plate is built from a very thin sheet of glass and can store the charge obtained by it.
- The target plate is kept at about 400 volts more positive with respect to the photocathode. The resultant electric field provides the desired acceleration and motion to the emitted electrons towards it.
- During the motion of the electrons, they have an affinity to repel each other, and, as a result, the distortion of information is being observed.
- For preventing the divergence effect an axial magnetic field, developed in this region by the long focus coil, is applied.

- The above magnetic field provides helical motion of increasing pitch and focuses the emitted electrons on the target into a perfect electron image of the original optical image.
- Since the image side of the target has a very small deposit of cesium, it has a high secondary emission ratio.
- Since the high velocity is obtained by the electrons during its motion from photocathode to the target plate, secondary emission occurs, as the electrons bombard the target surface.
- The above secondary electrons are taken by a wire-mesh screen.
- the wire-mesh screen is placed in front of the target on the image side and is kept at a slightly higher potential with respect to the target.
- This screen consists of 300 meshes per cm^2 with an open area of 50 to 75 per cent. As a result, the screen wires do not interfere with the electron image.
- The secondary electrons leave behind on the target plate surface. As a result, there occurs a positive charge distribution corresponding to the light intensity distribution on the original photocathode.
- It is to be seen that for storage action this charge on the target plate should not go forward laterally over its surface. Otherwise, the resolution of the device would be destroyed. To obtain the above, the target is made of very much thin sheet of glass.
- The positive charge distribution occurs during the frame storage time say 40 ms, and, as result, the sensitivity of the tube increases.
- The intensity of the positive charge distribution is four to five times more than the charge coming out from photocathode.
- The increase in charge density relative to the charge coming out at the photocathode is termed 'image multiplication'. This ultimately helps in the increase of sensitivity of image orthicon.
- Figure 6.25 describes the two sided target having charge image on one side and electron beam scanning the opposite side.
- The target plate has high resistivity laterally for storage action and low resistivity along its thickness. This helps the positive charge to conduct to the other side which is scanned. That is why the thickness of the target plate is about 0.004 mm.
- Whatever charge distribution develops on one side of the target plate on account of the focused image, becomes available on the scanned side. Finally, the video signal is found from here.

6.14.2 Scanning Section

The important descriptions of scanning section are as follows:

- The electron gun structure develops a beam of electrons which is accelerated towards the target.
- The positive accelerating potentials of 80 to 330 volts are provided to grid 2, grid 3 and grid 4 which is connected internally to the metalized conductive coating on the inside wall of the tube (as shown in Figure 6.25).

- The electron beam is focused at the target by magnetic field of the external focus coil and also by voltage applied to grid 4.

- The alignment coil gives magnetic field which can be varied for adjusting the position of scanning beam for accurate location.

- Vertical and horizontal deflecting coils are mounted on yoke external to the tube. The magnetic fields developed by the above produce the deflection of electron beams to scan the entire target

- The vertical and horizontal deflecting coils are fed from two oscillators, one is working at 15625 Hz for horizontal deflection and the other is operating at 50 Hz for vertical deflection.

- The target plate is approximately at zero potential, and, hence, the electrons in the scanning beam should not be allowed for forward motion at the surface of target plate and then return towards the gun structure.

- The grid 4 voltage is adjusted to develop uniform deceleration of electrons for the entire target area. That is why, the electrons in the scanning beam are slowed down near the target. Over and above, this removes any possibility of secondary emission from the side of the target plate.

- If a certain element area on the target plate attains a potential of say, 2 volts during the storage time, then, on account of its thinness, the scanning beam finds the charge deposited on it, part of which is diffused to the scanned side and equal number of negative charges will be deposited on the opposite side.

- Therefore, out of total electrons in the beam, some is deposited on the target plate and the rest of the portion stops at its surface and turns back to move towards the first electrode of the electron multiplier.

- On account of the low resistivity across the two sides of the target, the deposited negative charge neutralizes the existing positive charge in less than a frame time.

- The target can again be charged due to the availability of the incident picture information, which will be scanned during the successive frames.

- The target is scanned element by element. Hence, if there are no positive charges at certain points, all the electrons in the beam return towards the electron gun and there will be no deposit on the target plate.

- The number of electrons, which leaves the cathode of the gun, is constant and out of this some is deposited and the rest travels back and provide signal current. This signal current varies in amplitude according to the information of the picture.

- The signal current is maximum for black areas on the picture. The reason is that the absence of light from black areas on the picture does not develop any emission on the photocathode and there is no secondary emission at the corresponding points on the target. Hence, electrons are not required from the beam to neutralize them. On the other hand, for high light areas on the picture, maximum loss of electrons occurs from the target plate on account of secondary emission. Therefore, there occurs large deposition of electron from the beam. This, finally, reduces the amplitude of the returning beam current.

- Thus, it is observed that the resultant beam current which turns away from the target is maximum for black areas and minimum for bright areas on the picture. High intensity light provides large charge imbalance on the glass target plate. As a result, the scanning beam is unable to neutralize it completely in one scan. Moreover, the earlier impression exists for several scans.

- The loss of resolution occurs due to the following fact:
  The beam is of low velocity type. The velocity is reduced to near zero in the region of target. it is subjected to stray electric fields in its vicinity. This causes defocussing and loss of resolution.

- On the other hand, the beam must hit the target at right angle at all points of the target for better resolution.

- The above problems are solved in the image orthicon due to the combined action of electrostatic field developed on account of the potential and magnetic field of the long focussing coil. The interaction of two fields raises cycloidal motion to the beam in the vicinity of target. That hits it at right angle irrespective of the point being scanned. Thus, resolving capability of the picture tube is improved.

6.14.3   Electron Multiplier

The important descriptions of electron multiplier are as follows:

- The returning stream of electrons reach the gun which is close to the aperture from which electron beam emerged.

- A part of a metal disc covering the gun electrode is the aperture.

- The secondary emission is developed when the returning electrons strike the disc since the disc is at positive potential of about 300 volt with respect to the target.

- The first stage of the electron multiplier is served by the disc.

- Successive stages of electron multiplier are made symmetrically around and back of the first stage.

- The secondary electrons are attracted to the dynodes at progressively larger positive potentials.

- Five stages of multiplication are utilized. Figure 6.26 describes the same.

- The total gain obtained at the electron multiplier is $(4)^5 \approx 1000$ since each multiplier stage gives a gain of approximately 4.

- High signal to noise ratio is obtained due to this signal multiplication.

- The secondary electrons are collected by the anode finally.

- The anode is connected to the highest supply voltage of +1500 volts in series with a load resistance.

- The anode current which is passing through the above load resistance has the same variations which are present in the return beam from the target and amplified by the electron multiplier.

- The voltage across the load resistance is the required video signal.

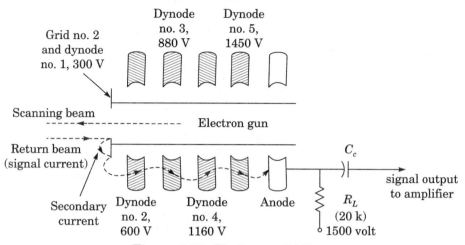

Figure 6.26 Electron multiplier.

- The amplitude of the above signal varies according to the light intensity variations of the scene being displayed.
- The output across the load resistance is coupled capacitively with the signal amplifier of the camera.
- The camera output signal will have an amplitude of 500 mV peak to peak when the load resistance is 20 kΩ and typical dark and high light currents are 30 μA and 5 μA respectively.

6.15 VIDICON

Vidicon is another very useful camera. The important points of vidicon camera are as follows:

- Vidicon is of small size camera.
- Its operation is very easy.
- It works on the principle of photoconductivity. Here, the resistance of the target material shows a remarkable decrease when exposed to light.
- Figure 6.27 shows the structural drawing of a typical vidicon.
- Figure 6.28 describes the circuit arrangement for obtaining camera signal output.
- The target possesses a thin photoconductive layer of either selenium or antimony compounds. This is actually deposited on a transparent conducting film which is coated on the inner surface of the face plate. The conductive coating is termed *signal electrode* or *plate*.
- The image side of the photolayer is in contact with the signal electrode. This is connected finally to the dc supply through the load resistance R_L as shown in Figure 6.28.
- The beam that comes out from the electron is focussed on surface of the photo conductive layer by combined action of uniform magnetic field of an external coil and electrostatic field of grid no. 3 as shown in Figure 6.27.

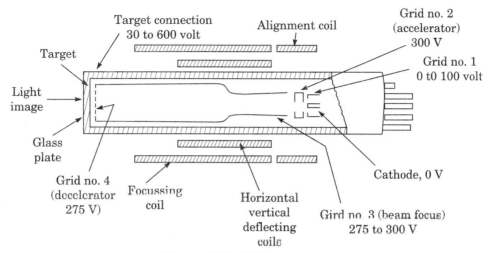

Figure 6.27 Vidicon camera.

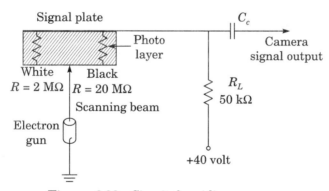

Figure 6.28 Circuit for vidicon camera.

- Grid no. 4 gives a uniform decelerating field between itself and the photoconductive layer, and, as a result, the electron beam moves towards the layer with a low velocity for preventing any secondary emission.

- For scanning the target, deflection of the beam is found by vertical and horizontal coils which are placed around the tube.

- The thickness of the photolayer is 0.0001 cm. The photolayer acts like an insulator having approximate resistance 20 MΩ during dark period.

- When the light is focussed on the photolayer, the photon energy helps more electrons to go to the conduction band and as a result resistivity is reduced.

- When bright light falls on any area of photoconductive coating, resistance across the thickness of the portion is reduced to about 2 MΩ. Hence, with an image on the target, each point on the gun side of photolayer takes a certain potential with respect to the dc supply. This assumed potential depends on its resistance of the signal plate. For example, with a source potential of 40 volts an area with high illumination may come across a potential of approximately 39 volts on the beam side. Again, dark areas may attain a potential of 35 volts due to high resistance of the photolayer. Therefore, a pattern of positive potential is observed on the gun side of the photolayer developing a charge image which corresponds to the incident optical image.

- Light from scene falls continuously on the target, but each element of the photocoating is scanned at intervals equal to the frame time. As a result, there occurs storage action and the net change in resistance, at any point or element on the photoconductive layer, depends on the time. This time elapses between two successive scannings and the intensity of incident light. The net change in resistance of all elementary areas is proportional to the variation of light intensity in the scene being displayed.

- The beam encounters different positive potentials on the side of the photolayer which faces the gun since the beam scans the target plate.

- Sufficient number of electrons from the beam are deposited on the photolayer surface for reducing the potential of each element towards the zero cathode potential.

- The rest of the electrons, which are not deposited on the target return back and are not used in the vidicon.

- During the scanning of the beam, the sudden change in potential on each element develops a flow of current in the signal electrode circuit. That produces a varying voltage across the load resistance R_L.

- The amplitude of current and the corresponding output voltage across R_L is directly proportional to the light intensity variations on the scene.

- The output voltage is found negative for white areas because a large current would develop a higher voltage drop across R_L.

- The developed video output voltage across the load resistance 50 kΩ is sufficient. It does not require any image or signal multiplication as it is found in image orthicon.

- The conventional amplifier is utilized for further amplification of output signal. Finally, the signal leaves the camera unit. This makes the vidicon a simple picture tube compared to others.

- Figure 6.29 describes vidicon output characteristics.

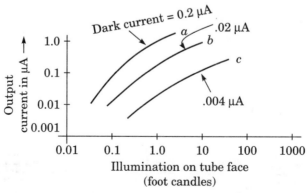

Figure 6.29 Light transfer characteristics of vidicon.

The curves *a*, *b*, *c* are shown for different values of dark current. The dark current is the output with no light. The setting of the dark current is made by adjusting the target voltage. Sensitivity and dark current increase when the target voltage is increased. The typical value of the output for vidicon is 0.4 µA for bright light and for dark current it is 0.02 µA.

- Vidicon has been modified a lot. Previously it was used only where there was no fast movement on account of inherent lag. The application was restricted to slides, pictures of closed circuit TV. Now, with the improved version, it has wide application in education, medicine, industry, aerospace and oceanography. Now-a-days, it is a short tube with a length of 12 to 20 cm and diameter between 1.5 and 4 cm.
- The estimated life of vidicon is between 5000 and 20,000 hours.

6.16 SILICON DIODE ARRAY VIDICON

A modification of vidicon is silicon diode array vidicon (Figure 6.30). The important discussion of the silicon diode array vidicon is as follows:

- Here, the target is manufactured from a thin '*n*' type silicon wafer instead of deposited layers on the glass faceplate. The final outcome is an array of silicon photodiodes for the target plate.
- One side of the substrate (*n*-type silicon) is oxidized to form a film of silicon dioxide acting as an insulator.
- An array of fine openings is made in the oxide layer by photomasking and etching processes.
- These openings are utilized as a diffusion mask for developing corresponding number of individual photodiodes.

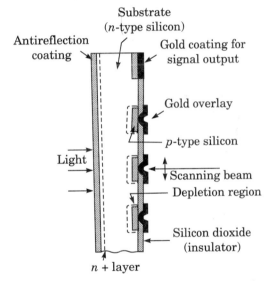

Figure 6.30 Silicon diode array target plate.

- Boron, which is used as dopent, is vapourized through the array of the holes. It forms islands of *p*-type silicon on one side of *n*-type silicon substrate.
- In fact, a very thin layer of gold is deposited on each *p*-type opening for formation of contacts for signal output.
- The other side of the substrate is provided with an antireflection coating.
- As a result, the dimension of the *p–n* photodiodes is about 8 µm in diameter.
- The typical dimension of the silicon target plate is 0.003 cm thick, 1.5 cm square having an array of 540 × 540 photodiodes.
- The target plate is mounted in a vidicon type of camera tube.

6.16.1 Operation of Silicon Diode Array Vidicon

The scanning and operation of the vidicon can be explained as follows:

- The photodiodes are reverse biased. The typical value of voltage being applied is +10 volts to $n+$ layer on the substrate.
- This side is illuminated by the light focussed on to it from the image.
- The incidence of light develops electron-hole pairs in the substrate.
- Holes are swept over to the 'p' side of the depletion region due to the application of the electric field. This reduces reverse bias on the diodes.
- The procedure will continue to produce storage action till the scanning beam of electron gun scans the photodiode side of the substrate.
- The scanning beam deposits electrons on the p-side. Hence, the diodes come back to their original reverse bias.
- Thus, the video signal is established due to the sudden increase in current across each diode developed by the scanning beam.
- Hence, the current flows through a load resistance in the battery circuit and develops a video signal which is proportional to the intensity of light falling on the array of photodiodes.
- The typical value of peak signal current is usually 7 μA for bright white light.
- The advantage of this vidicon with multidiode silicon target is that it is less susceptible to damage or burns on account of excessive high lights.
- It has low lag time and high sensitivity to visible light. This can be extended to the infrared region.
- The particular name of such vidicon has the trade name of 'Epicon'.
- These types of camera tubes have wide application in industrial, educational and CCTV services.

6.17 SOLID STATE IMAGE SCANNERS

The concept of this device depends on the technology and applications of charge coupled devices. The salient features of this system are as follows.

- The charge coupled devices (CCDs) is a new technology in metal oxide semiconductor (MOS) circuitry.
- The CCD can be assumed as shift register formed by a string of very closely spaced MOS capacitors.
- It has the capability of storing and transferring analog charge signals, i.e. electrons or holes, which can be introduced optically or electrically.
- Figure 6.31 describes the construction of the above device. It consists of a p-type substrate. The one side of the substrate is oxidized for the formation of film of silicon dioxide. This is obviously an insulator.

- The photolithographic processes are applied. An array of metal electrodes, termed gates, are deposited on the insulator film.

- As a result, a very large number of tiny MOS capacitors on the entire surface of the chip are formed.

- The application of small positive potentials to the gate electrodes makes the development of depletion regions just below them.

- These are termed potential wells.

- The depth of each well (depletion region) varies with the magnitude of the applied potential.

- The gate electrodes operate in groups of three, with every third electrode connected to a common conductor. This is shown in Figure 6.31.

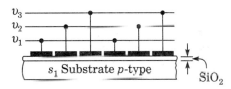

Figure 6.31   Three phase n-channel MOS charged couple device.

- At the time of focussing the image onto the silicon chip, electrons are generated within it, but very close to the surface.

- The number of electrons usually depends on the intensity of incident light.

- The developed electrons are collected in the nearby potential wells.

- The pattern of collected charges represents the optical image.

- The charge of one element is transferred along the surface of the silicon chip with the help of a more positive voltage to the adjacent electrode or gate and reducing the voltage on it.

- The minority carriers, i.e. the electrons are being accumulated in the wells and reduce their depths.

- The accumulation of charge carriers under the first potential wells of two consecutive trios is shown in Figure 6.32. It indicates the transfer of electrons between wells. Figure 6.33 shows different phases of clocking voltage waveform.

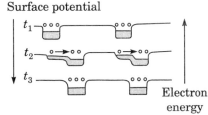

Figure 6.32   Transfer electrons between potential wells.

- In practice, the charge transfer is effected by multi phase clock voltage pulses as shown in Figure 6.33. The clock voltage pulses are applied to the gates in a suitable sequence.

- Figure 6.32, actually, shows the manner through which the transition takes place from potential wells under v_1 to those under v_2. Similarly, from v_2 to v_3 and v_3 to v_1, similar transfer movement of charges occurs under the influence of continuing clock pulses.

- In this way, after one complete clock cycle, the charge pattern moves one stage to the right.

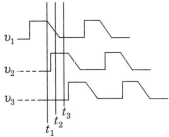

Figure 6.33   Clocking voltage waveform of different phases.

- Thus, clocking sequence continues and the charge finally reaches the end of the array and the collection of the same forms the signal current.
- A large number of CCD (charge coupled devices) arrays are packed together to form the image plate.
- The advantage is that it does not require an electron gun, scanning beam, high voltage or vacuum envelope of a conventional camera tube. The potential needed to move the charge is only 5 to 10 volts.
- The spot under each trio performs as the resolution cell.
- When light image is focussed on the chip, electrons are developed in proportion to the intensity of light falling on each cell.
- The above principle of one dimensional charge transfer can be integrated in many ways to render a solid state area image device.
- Usually, a set of linear imaging structures are arranged. As a result, each one correspond to a scan line in the display.

- The lines are, then, independently addressed and read into a common output diode with the help of driving pulses through a set of switches controlled by an address register which is shown in Figure 6.34.
- The output can be a small diffused diode in one corner of the array for reduction of capacitance.
- The charge packets getting out of any line are taken to this diode by an additional vertical output register.

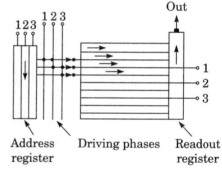

Figure 6.34 A line addressed structure.

- The sequence of addressing the lines is found out by the driving circuitry in the above type of addressed structure. Obviously, interlacing can be performed in a natural way.
- CCD is a very important device in the field of solid state imaging.
- Full TV line-scan arrays have already been manufactured for TV cameras.
- Of course, the quality of such sensors is not yet suitable for normal TV studio use.
- RCA SID 51232 is one such 24 lead dual-in-line image senser.
- The above is a self-scanned senser intended primarily for utilization in generating standard interlaced 525 line television pictures.
- The device possesses 512×320 elements and is manufactured with a 3-phase n-channel, vertical frame transfer organization using a sealed silicon gate structure.
- Figure 6.35 describes the above.
- The overall picture performance of image scanner is comparable to that of 2/3 inch vidicon camera tubes. But undesirable characteristics, for example, lag and microphonics are removed.

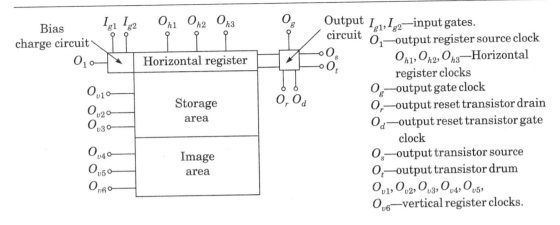

Figure 6.35 Chips block diagram of A 512 × 320 element sensor.

I_{g1}, I_{g2}—input gates.
O_1—output register source clock
O_{h1}, O_{h2}, O_{h3}—Horizontal register clocks
O_g—output gate clock
O_r—output reset transistor drain
O_d—output reset transistor gate clock
O_s—output transistor source
O_t—output transistor drum
$O_{v1}, O_{v2}, O_{v3}, O_{v4}, O_{v5},$ O_{v6}—vertical register clocks.

- The SID 51232 is available in a hermetic, edge contacted, 24-connection dual-in-line package. Over and above the package consists of an optical glass window as shown in Figure 6.36. This helps an image to be focussed into senser's 12.2 mm image diagonal.

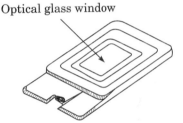

Optical glass window

Figure 6.36 Optical glass window.

6.18 CABLE TELEVISION

The cable television system can be broadly categorized as follows:

(a) Master antenna television system (MATV)
(b) Community Antenna television system (CATV)

The objective of MATV is to deliver a strong signal (over 1 mV) from one or more antennas to every television receiver connected to the system. Usual applications of MATV system are hotels, motels, school, apartment buildings, etc.

The CATV is a cable system that distributes good quality television signal to a very large number of receivers throughout the entire community. In other words, the CATV system feeds increased TV programmes to subscribers. It has many more active VHF and UHF channels than a receiver tuner can directly select. This actually needs utilization of special active converter in the head end.

6.18.1 MATV

MATV is designed to have a 75 Ω impedance. Usually, the antennas have 300 Ω impedance. So, to make the impedance to 75 Ω, a balun is used.

The above allows a convenient match between the coaxial transmission line and components that make up the system. As shown in Figure 6.37, antenna outputs fed into a 4-way hybrid.

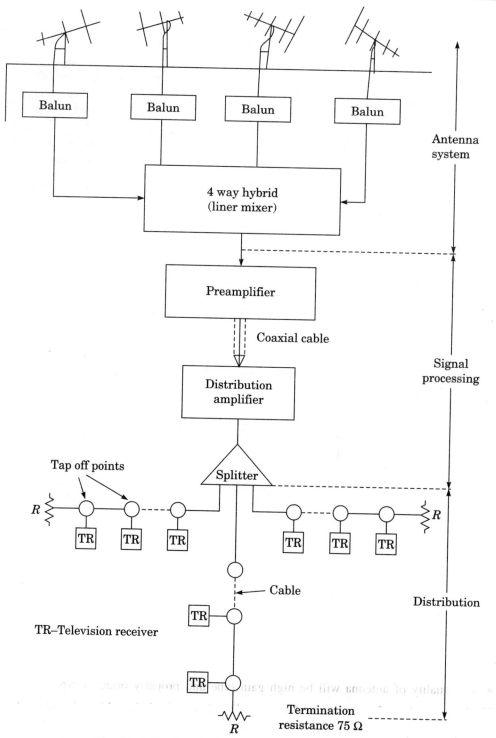

Figure 6.37 Block diagram of a MATV system.

The hybrid is generally a signal combining linear mixer that provides suitable impedance matches for preventing development of standing waves.

The distribution amplifier is fed by the output from the hybrid through a preamplifier. These amplifiers raise the signal amplitude to a level which is sufficient for overcoming the losses of the distribution system at the time of providing an acceptable signal to every receiver in the system. The splitters receive the output from the distribution amplifier via the co-axial trunk line.

Actually, the purpose of the splitter is to provide trunk line isolation and impedance match. This is simply a resistive inductive device. Then the splitters send the signal to tap-offs. These tap-offs are point of delivery.

The subscriber taps are shown in the following figures.

Figure 6.38 transformer coupled.

Figure 6.39 capacitive coupled.

Figure 6.40 resistive coupled.

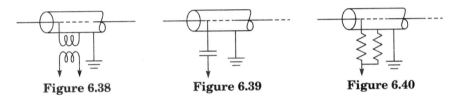

| **Figure 6.38** | **Figure 6.39** | **Figure 6.40** |

The subscriber taps provide isolation between receivers on the same line. Hence, mutual interference is prevented. The taps are usually mounted on the wall. They look like ac outlets. Wall taps are found with 300 Ω output, 75 Ω output and a dual output. The best method is to use a 75 Ω type with a matching transformer. The matching transformer is generally mounted at the antenna terminals of the receiver. The system will have a VHF output and a UHF output. The improperly terminated lines will produce standing waves. To avoid this, the end of each 75 Ω distribution is terminated with a 75 Ω resistor which is termed by the word 'terminator'.

6.18.2 CATV

The important features of a CATV are described below.

- The CATV system are used in remote areas or in valley areas being surrounded by mountains. Since the signal is not received properly, CATV can help in this purpose.
- Now-a-days, CATV is also used in big cities because tall buildings make the signal weak. Troubles are created due to multipath reflections.
- For CATV, a single antenna site is selected. This site is usually on the top of a hill, mountain or sky-scraper.
- The quality of antenna will be high gain type and properly oriented type.

If a large number of signals come from one direction, a single broad based antenna is used to cover those channels.

- Cable television installations help in the following ways
  - Household service
  - Business service
  - Educational service
  - Commercial TV and FM broadcast programmes.
- Usually, news, local sports and community programmes, burgler, fire alarms, weather reports, commercial data retrieval, meter readings, document reproduction, computer aided instructions, centralized library services are the major duties of CATV.
- For many of the services, extra subscription fee is charged from the subscriber.
- The co-axial distribution network has a large number of cable pairs, in general it becomes 12 or 24. This helps to select any channel or programme out of the many which are available at a given time.
- Figure 6.41 describes the CATV. Here, the signals from various TV channels are collected in the same way as in case of MATV system.
- A CATV system is combined with a MATV set-up.
- If UHF exists in addition to VHF at the reception, the signal from each UHF channel is processed by a translator.
- The translator heterodynes the UHF channel frequencies down to a VHF channel being a frequency converter.
- The CATV system operates with large co-axial cables. Again the transmission loss through the cable is much greater at UHF than at VHF. Hence, translation at CATV system is advantageous.
- As shown in Figure 6.41, the set-up from the antennas to the combiner is called head end.
- CATV outputs from the combining network are fed to a number of trunk cables through a broadband distribution amplifier.
- The trunk cables take signals from the antenna site to the utilization site. The distance may be several kilometres away.
- Feeder amplifiers are provided at several points along the line for overcoming progressive signal attenuation. The signal attenuation occurs on account of cable losses. High band attenuation is greater than the low band attenuation because cable losses are greater at high frequencies. To equalize the above, the amplifiers and signal splitters are sometimes replaced by equalizers.
- The signal distribution from splitters to tap-off points is made through multicore co-axial cables in the same manner as it is being done in an MATV system.
- The signal level utilized to a television receiver is of the order 15 mV. This is quite good from the reception point of view without producing accompanying radiation problem from the CATV system.

6.18.3 Closed Circuit Television (CCTV)

Closed circuit television is a special type of system. Here, camera signals are made available to a limited number of monitors or receivers. Different types of links are made according to the following:

(a) Distance between the two locations

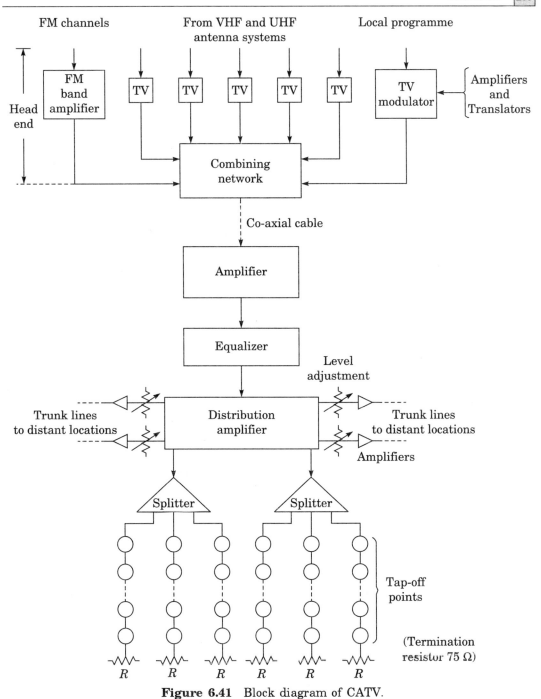

Figure 6.41 Block diagram of CATV.

(b) The number and dispersion of receivers

(c) Mobility of either camera or receiver.

Figures 6.42 to 6.45 describe different link arrangements being used for CCTV. The easiest link is a cable where video signal from the camera is connected directly through a cable to the receiver. The television monitor means the receiver without RF and IF circuits.

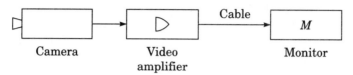

Figure 6.42 CCTV with direct camera link to one monitor.

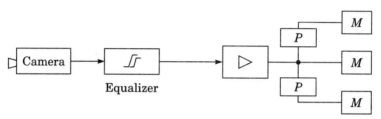

Figure 6.43 CCTV with direct camera link to several monitors.

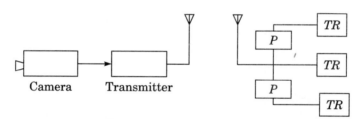

Figure 6.44 CCTV with wireless link to several receivers.

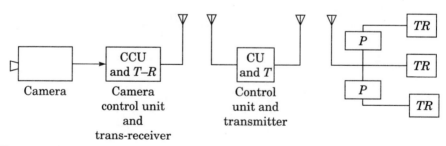

Figure 6.45 CCTV with remotely controlled camera feeding several TV receivers located at a distance.

It is only needed for reception in such a link arrangement. Approximately, one volt peak-to-peak signal is needed by the monitor. CCTV, generally, does not follow television broadcast standards because of the following:

- The video signal is generally delivered through cables.
- In case of transmission, it is over a limited region and for restricted use.

Applications of CCTV

- **Education:** A teacher may deliver lecture to a large number of students sitting at different locations.
- **Medicine:** For observing seriously ill patients in intensive care units, several monitors and camera units can be installed. Even operations can be shown to the medical students from distance places without assembling them in front of the operation table.
- **Business:** To keep an eye over customers and sales personnel, television cameras can be installed at different locations in big departmental stores.
- **Surveillance:** Closed circuit TV can be utilized for surveillance in banks, railway yards, ports, traffic points and different other similar locations.

Industry: Nuclear reaction and other such phenomena cannot be observed without the help of CCTV. CCTV also helps in the scanning of earth's surface and probing other planets.

Home: With the help of CCTV, it is very easy to see the visitor before opening the door.

Aerospace and oceanography: For aerospace and oceanography a carrier is used for transmitting the signal and a complete receiver is needed for reception. Figure 6.44 describes this system. A wireless link is used between the transmitter and receiver. In some cases, camera is remotely controlled over a microwave radio link.

6.18.4 Picture Phone and Facsimile

This is an important application in television where two people can see each other while discussing over the telephone line. This consists of the following.

- Small picture tube
- Miniature TV camera

Facsimile is, of course, another application of electronic transmission of visual information over telephone lines. Usually, a still picture can be transmitted in this manner at a slow scanning rate. Facsimile is also utilized for sending copies of documents over telephone lines.

6.18.5 Video Tape Recording (VTR)

The VTR is the improvement over the previous method of recording motion pictures taken from the screen of the television receiver. Video tape keeps the line quality of broadcasting and it has the strength of being edited and duplicated without delay. The advantages of VTR are:

- It has the strength of immediate playback.
- The recorded material can be repeated for viewing many times without any problem.
- Duplication of it for distribution to a large number of users can be made very easily.

The main features of a VTR are:

- The video signal is recorded on a magnetic tape for picture reproduction.
- This is similar to the audio tape being used for reproduction of sound.

- Here, the plastic tape is made to move in physical contact with the tape head.
- The plastic tape has a very fine coating of ferric oxide.
- The magnetic particles on the tape are magnetized when electrical signal is applied to the tape head.
- Two tiny bar magnets are developed on the tape for each cycle of the signal.
- The length of the bar magnets is inversely proportional to the frequency of applied signal.
- Hence, these bar magnets form a chain with like poles adjacent to each other.
- Since these bar magnets are on recorded tape, these move across the playback head and there occurs a change in flux linkages with the head. Thus, a voltage is developed across the coil terminals.
- Figure 6.46 describes the electrical signal being recorded in the form of bar magnets on the magnetic tape. Figure 6.47 describes the development of signal during playback.

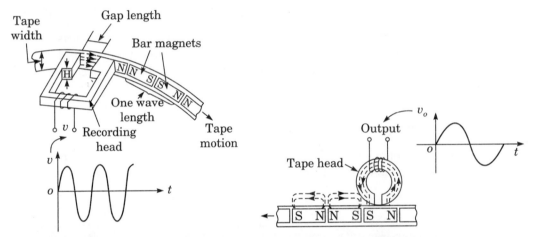

Figure 6.46 Signal recorded in the form of bar magnets on the magnetic tape.

Figure 6.47 Signal development during playback.

- As the recording frequency increases, the length of the bar magnets decreases. But each head has a certain gap length. When the limiting frequency is attained at a given tape speed, total length of the two adjacent bar magnets becomes equal to the gap length.
- Actually, output of the playback head will be zero at this frequency because each bar magnet will develop equal and opposite voltage in the coil. As a result, no net flux passes through core of the head.
- The typical example is that for a tape speed of 19 cm per second and gap length of 6.3 microns (0.00025″), the usable frequency attains to the value of 15 kHz and that is enough for audio recording.
- The output voltage from a playback head is directly proportional to the rate of change of flux, and, as a result, for every doubling of frequency the output voltage will become twice.
- Each time the frequency gets halved, i.e. one octave lower and the output falls by 6 dB.

- This discrepancy is overcome by providing equalizing circuits in the playback amplifier.
- The signal which is to be recorded is not generally applied directly to the record head. If it is made so, then the output will be highly distorted on account of non-linearity of B–H curve of the core material around its zero axis.
- The above problem is solved by superimposing the recording signal on a high frequncy ac voltage.
- The amplitude of the high frequency bias is considered such that its positive and negative peaks lie within the linear portions of the B–H curve.
- Figure 6.48 shows the two outputs (X and Y) being added up to give linear output with improved signal to noise ratio.
- The ac bias frequency is made large, and, as a result, the beat signal between the highest signal frequency and bias frequency does not fall in the audio range.
- The typical value of ac bias frequency is 60 kHz.

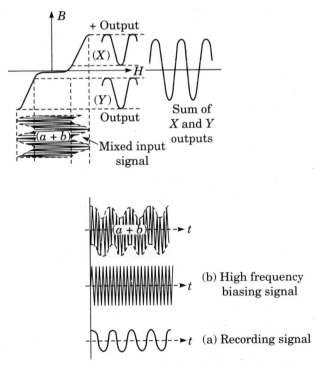

Figure 6.48   AC biasing in audio tape recording.

6.19 TELEVISION THROUGH SATELLITE

The usual method for extended coverage of TV by microwave space communication and co-axial cable links is very expensive. Satellite communication is contributing a lot in this respect. Geostationary communication satellites have been launched into synchronous orbits around the earth in recent years. These satellites help communicate national and international television programmes around the world. Three artificial satellites placed in equatorial orbits at 120° from each other cover the whole land area of the world. The main features of the above television system are as follows:

- Highly directive, high power, land based transmitters transmit wideband microwave signals to the geostationary satellite above the transmitter.
- Each microwave channel has a bandwidth of several tens of megahertz. It can accommodate many TV signals and telephone channels.
- The satellites get power from solar batteries.
- The satellites receive the transmitted signal, demodulate and amplify.
- The amplified demodulated signal is remodulated on a different carrier and then, again, the same is transmitted.
- The transmitting antenna on the satellite directs the radiated beam to a narrow region on the earth. Suitable reflector is used for this purpose.
- Higher power satellites usually provide large power flux densities. As a result, smaller size antennas can be used for reception.
- In case of national distribution, the transmission is made downwards from a wide angle antenna. Hence, generally, the whole national area is illuminated by the transmission.
- In case of international distribution, the transmission is towards the other one or two satellites from highly directive antennas.
- Same demodulation, amplification and remodulation transmission process is repeated in the next satellite in case of international distribution.
- The final 'down channel' transmission is received either in the same country or different country with the help of a large cross-section antenna.
- The same is processed in low noise receivers.
- Finally, reradiation takes place from the regular TV transmitters.
- There are a number of 'INTELSAT' satellites over the Atlantic, Pacific and Indian oceans being operated as relay stations to some forty ground stations around the world.
- The international system of satellite communication caters to the continental 625/50 and the American 525/60 systems.
- So, in case of the above two different systems of television standards, the ground station converts the received signal with the help of digital international conversion equipment to the local standards before the relay of it.
- Frequency modulation is utilized for both 'up channel' and 'down channel' transmission.
- The frequency modulation helps in providing good immunity from interference and it requires less power in the satellite transmitter. Of course, FM needs a larger bandwidth.

6.19.1 Uses of Satellites

Satellites are used for international TV relaying. Over and above, satellites are also used for distributing national programmes over extended regions in large countries. Satellites are generally used in three following ways.

- Rebroadcast system

- Limited rebroadcast system
- Direct transmission.

The main features of rebroadcast system are as follows:

- The emission from a low power satellite is received with the help of a high sensitivity medium size antenna on a high sensitivity low noise earth station. The medium size antenna is of a metre.
- The received satellite programme is again sent over the high power terrestial transmitter for reception on conventional TV receivers.
- This procedure is suitable for metropolitan areas where a large number of TV receivers are in operation.
- This procedure also helps on national hook up of television programmes on all distantly located television transmitters.
- Of course, in our large country it is expensive to do so by microwave or co axial cable links.

The main features of limited rebroadcast system are as follows:

- Low power transmitters can be utilized to cover the limited area in rural areas where clusters of villages and towns exist, and the receiver density is moderate.
- The satellite Instructional Television Experiment programme conducted by India in cooperation with NASA of USA in 1975–1976 was a limited rebroadcast system.
- A high power Application Technology satellite-6 (ATS-6) placed at a height of 36000 km in a geostationary synchronous orbit with sub-satellite longitude of 33° East was utilized for beaming TV programmes over most parts of the country.
- Figure 6.49 describes the above.
- TV programmes from the earth station at Ahmedabad were transmitted to ATS-6 at 6 GHz FM carrier with the help of a 14 m parabolic dish antenna.
- The bandwidth of FM carrier was 40 MHz.
- The down transmission from the satellite was made from a 80 W FM transmitter at 860 MHz.
- The video band of transmitted signal was 5 MHz.
- The transmitted signal consisted of two audio signals frequency modulated on two audio subscribers of 5.5 MHz and 6 MHz.
- This enabled transmission in two different languages. Reception of any one of these would be acceptable.

The main features of Direct Transmission are as follows:

- Direct reception of broadcast programme is possible in areas which are remote from terrestial broadcast stations.
- The cost of reception in this system is very high even in case of high power satellite transmissions.
- Here, special antenna is required to receive the signals and front end convertor unit for modifying the signals into conventional broadcast standards.

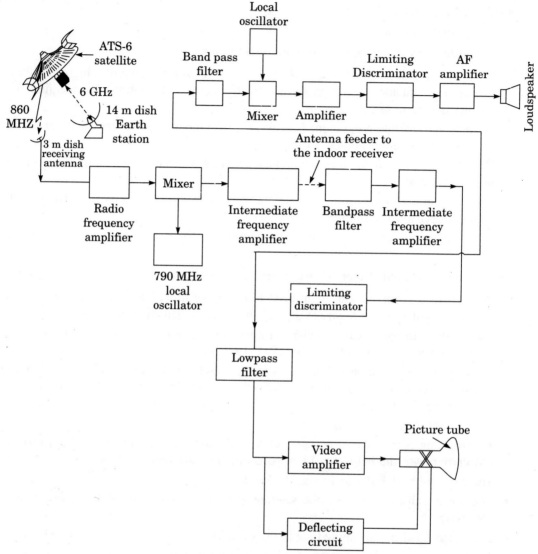

Figure 6.49 ATS-6 satellite.

- Research is going on in this respect. The cost of low noise front end for receivers is reducing. Probably, in future direct individual reception will be practically feasible.

6.20 COLOUR TELEVISION

Introductory part of colour television is based on the theory of additive colour mixing. Here, all the colours including white can be developed by mixing red, green and blue lights. The colour camera gives video signals for the red, green and blue information. Each colour TV system is compatible with the corresponding monochrome system. This means that colour broadcasts can be received as black and white on monochrome receivers. On the other hand, colour receivers are able to receive black and white TV broadcasts. Figure 6.50 describes the above. The three colour signals are separated and fed to the three electron guns of colour

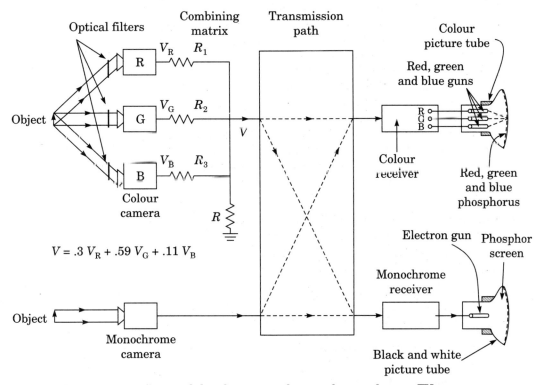

$$V = .3 \, V_R + .59 \, V_G + .11 \, V_B$$

Figure 6.50 Compatibility between colour and monochrome TV systems.

picture tube at the receiver end. The screen of the picture tube has red, green and blue phosphors being arranged in alternate dots. Each gun develops an electron beam for illuminating the three colours separately on the fluorescent screen. The red, green and blue colour information is integrated by the eye. As a result, their luminance perceives the actual colour and brightness of the picture which is being televised.

Usually, there are two systems:

(i) American 525 line monochrome and NTSC colour systems.
(ii) 625–B monochrome (black and white) and the compatible PAL–B colour systems.

India and many European countries use the second one. NTSC colour television receivers have two additional controls, which are known as colour and Hue controls. Both are placed at the front panel alongwith other controls. The intensity or amount of the colour in the reproduced picture is varied by the colour or saturation control. Actually, the hue control selects the correct colour which is to be displayed. For setting the correct skin colour, this is utilized. On the other hand, PAL colour receivers do not require any tint control. IN SECAM colour receivers, both tint and saturation controls are not needed.

6.20.1 Concept of Compatibility

The concept of compatibility lies on the following factors:

1. The colour television signal must develop a normal black and white picture on a monochrome receiver without any modification in the circuit.
2. A colour receiver should be able to develp a black and white picture from a normal monochrome signal. This is termed *reverse compatibility*.

For maintaining full compatibility the composite colour signal must need the following:

- It must occupy the same bandwidth as that of the corresponding monochrome signal.
- The location and spacing of the picture and sound carrier frequencies will remain the same.
- The colour signal must have the same brightness information as that of a monochrome signal which transmits the same scene.
- The composite colour signal must contain colour information alongwith the ancillary signals required for allowing this to be decoded.
- The system should use the same deflection frequencies and synchronizing signals as utilized for monochrome transmission and reception.
- The colour information must be taken in such a way that it does not affect the picture reproduced on the screen of a monochrome receivers.

To meet the above factors, it is essential to encode the colour information of the scene in such a manner that it can be transmitted within the same channel bandwidth of 7 MHz and without disturbing the brightness signal. At the same time, receiving end will be provided with a decoder to recover the colour signal back in the original form to feed it to the tricolour picture tube.

6.20.2 Properties of Light

On the analysis of white light from the sun, it is observed that the radiation is not simply a single wavelength, but it consists of a band of frequencies. Spectrum of electromagnetic radiation consists of

- Radio waves (frequency -10^5 Hz, wavelength $- 3 \times 10^3$ m)
- Infra red (frequency $- 10^{10}$ Hz, wavelength $- 3 \times 10^{-2}$ m)
- Ultra violet (frequency $- 10^{15}$ Hz, wavelength $- 3 \times 10^{-7}$ m)
- X-rays (frequency $- 10^{20}$ Hz, wavelength $- 3 \times 10^{-12}$ m)
- Cosmic rays (frequency $- 10^{25}$ Hz, wavelength $- 3 \times 10^{-17}$ m)
- Visible spectrum (frequency $- 5 \times 10^{14}$ Hz)

Visible spectrum consists of the following colours:

- Red
- Orange
- Yellow
- Green   Wavelength range
- Blue   From 780×10^{-9} m to 380×10^{-9} m
- Indigo
- Violet

When radiation from entire visible spectrum reaches the eye in suitable proportions, white light is being observed. On the other hand, if the part of the range is filtered out, the remainder of the visible spectrum provides us the sensation of colour. All objects, which we see, are focussed sharply by the lens system of the eye on its retina. The retina is situated at the back side of eye and it has light sensitive organs that measure the visual sensations. There lies connection between retina and optic nerve. The optic nerve transmits the light stimuli, which is sensed by the organs, to the optical centre of the brain. The light sensitive organs are of two types

- rods
- cones

The rods perceive objects in various shades of grey from black to white. The cones are broadly categorised into three groups

- One set of cones finds out the presence of blue colour in the object focussed on the retina
- The second set detects red colour
- The third set checks the green range.

The combined relative luminosity curve is shown in Figure 6.51.

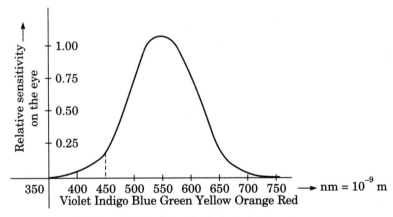

Figure 6.51 Wavelength in nanometres.

A curve is developed between relative sensitivity of human-eye and wavelengths of colours from violet to red. As shown in Figure 6.51, the sensitivity of the human eye is greatest for green light. But the same is decreasing towards both the red and blue ends of the spectrum. Actually, the maximum sensitivity occurs at the range of 550 nm wavelength. This is a yellow, green colour.

6.20.3 Colour Theory

Red, green and blue colours are termed *primary colours*. With the help of adjustable intensities, red, green and blue colours can develop most of the colours found in everyday life. Even white light can also be developed by adjusting suitable intensities of these colours. In television, red green and blue are utilized as basic colours. Even pair wise mixing of primary colours, the following complementary colours are developed.

- Red + Green = Yellow
- Red + Blue = Magenta (purplish red shade)
- Blue + Green = Cyan (greenish blue shade)

Figure 6.52 describes additive colour mixing. Here each circle corresponds to one primary colour.

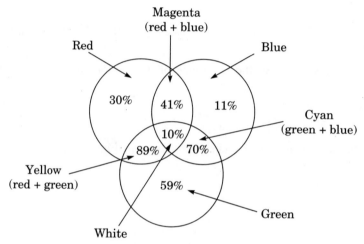

Figure 6.52 Additive colour mixing.

Figure 6.53 describes the subtractive mixing. Here, the subtractive mixing of three primary colours develops black.

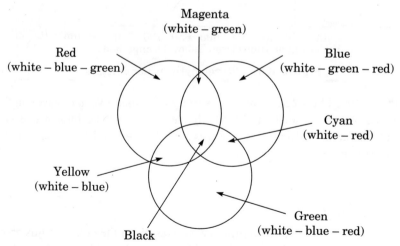

Figure 6.53 Subtractive colour mixing.

Grassman's law

The eye is not able to differentiate each of the colours which mix to develop a new colour. It perceives the resultant colour. Hence, the eye assumes that the output of three types cones is additive. The subjective impression which is obtained when green, blue and red lights attain the eye simultaneously, may be matched by a single light source possessing the same colour. The impression of brightness developed by the combined light source is numerically equal to the sum of the luminances of the three primaries which constitute the single light. The property of the eye of developing a response that depends on the algebraic sum of the red, green and blue inputs is termed *Grassman's Law*. For example, white has been observed to be reproduced by adding red, green and blue lights Usually, the reference white for colour television has been a mixture of 30% red, 59% green and 11% blue. Therefore, one lumen of white light = 0.3 lumen of red + 0.59 lumen of green + 0.11 lumen of blue.

Similarly, as per Figure 6.52 and law of colour is additive mixing.

$$1 \text{ lumen of white light} = 0.89 \text{ lumen of yellow} + 0.11 \text{ lumen of blue}$$
$$= 0.7 \text{ lumen of cyan} + 0.3 \text{ lumen of red}$$
$$= 0.41 \text{ lumen of magenta} + 0.59 \text{ lumen of green.}$$

If the concentration of luminous flux is reduced by a common factor from all the component colours, the resultant colour will be white, but the level of brightness will be reduced.

In general, a colour has three characteristics for specifying its visual information. These are as follows:

- Luminance or brightness
- hue or tint
- saturation

Luminance or brightness: This is the amount of light intensity which is experienced by the eye irrespective of the colour of light.

Hue or tint: The colour of any object is identified by its hue or tint. For example, the green leaves have green hue.

Saturation: Saturation is the spectral purity of colour light. The saturation is taken as an indication of how little the colour is diluted by white. That means, a fully saturated colour does not possess any white. Vivid green is fully saturated whereas light green is nothing but the dilution with white. Chrominance is the hue and saturation of a colour being put together. It is also termed chroma.

Figure 6.54 shows chromaticity diagram.

Here X and Y indicate colour coordinates. The relative brightness of the colour is indicated by Z-coordinates in three dimensional representation. Here white lies on the central point 'C' where 'X' is 0.31 and Y is 0.32. The wavelength of white in TV transmission and reception is the mixture of 30 per cent of red colour, 59 per cent green colour and 11 per cent blue colour.

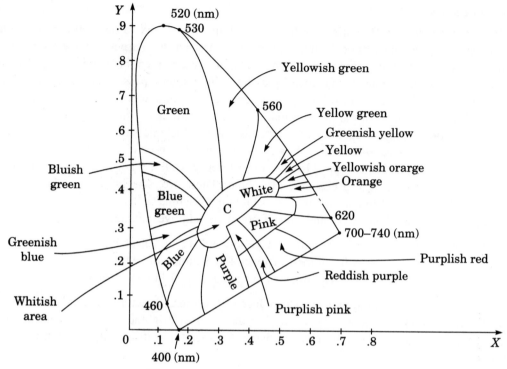

Figure 6.54 Chromaticity diagram.

6.20.4 Colour Television Camera

Figure 6.55 describes schematic Block diagram of TV camera. The main features of its operation are as follows.

- It consists of three camera tubes
- Each tube receives selectively filtered primary colours.
- Each camera tube produces a signal voltage proportional to respective colour intensity being received by it.
- The image developed by the lens is divided into three images with the help of glass prisms.
- The three prisms are termed dichroic mirrors.
- The dichroic mirror passes one wavelength and rejects other wavelength. In this way, red, green and blue colour images are developed.
- Afterwards, the rays are passed through colour filters. These filters are called trimming filters.
- The filters develop highly precise primary colour images.
- These primary colour images are converted in video signals with the help of image–orthicon or vidicon camera tubes.

- In this way, three colour signals are developed. The signals are termed Red, Green and Blue signals.
- Simultaneous scanning of the three camera tubes is made by a master deflection oscillator and synchronous generator which drives all the three tubes.
- Three video signals developed by the camera represent three primaries of the colour diagram.
- With the help of selective use of these signals, all colours in the visible spectrum can be developed on the screen of a special picture tube.

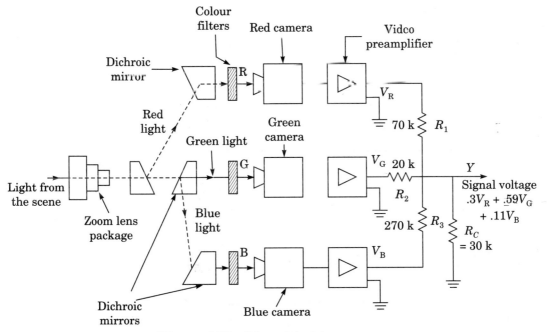

Figure 6.55 Colour television camera.

- For generating the monochrome or brightness signal which represents the luminance of the scene, the addition of three camera outputs through the resistance matrix is in the proportion of 0.3, 0.59 and 0.11 of Red, Green and Blue respectively.
- The signal voltage which comes across the common resistance R_C indicates the brightness of the scene and is termed 'Y' signal. Hence,

$$Y = 0.3 \text{ Red} + 0.59 \text{ Green} + 0.11 \text{ Blue}$$

6.20.5 Colour Voltage Amplitudes

Figure 6.56 indicates the nature of output from the three cameras when a horizontal line across a picture having vertical bars of red, green and blue colours is scanned. At any one instant, only one camera delivers output voltage corresponding to the colour being scanned. Different values of red colour voltage are shown in Figure 6.57. Red, pink and pale pink having different shades of red have decreasing values of colour intensity. The corresponding output voltages have decreasing amplitudes. Hence, Red, Green or Blue voltage provide information of the specific colour. On the other hand, their relative amplitudes depend on the level of saturation of that colour.

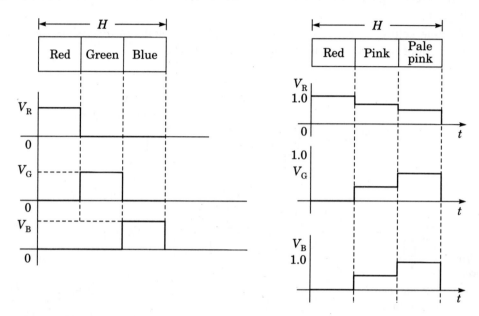

Figure 6.56   Camera video output voltage for red, green and blue colour bars.   **Figure 6.57**   Effect of colour desaturation.

Figure 6.58 describes the voltages of the three camera outputs which are drawn below the colour bar pattern.

6.20.6 Development of Colour Difference Voltages

In monochrome television system Y signal is modulated and transmitted. Generally, all the three colours signals are not transmitted separately. The red and blue camera outputs are combined with Y signal for obtaining colour difference signals. The colour difference voltages are developed by subtracting the luminance voltage from the colour voltages. As a result, (R–Y) and (B–Y) are developed. It is only needed to transmit two of the three colour difference signals as the third may be derived from the other two. This circuit is shown in Figure 6.59.

The output voltages are as follows.

$$Y = 0.3R + 0.59G + 0.11B$$
$$(R - Y) = 0.7R - 0.59G - 0.11B$$
$$(B - Y) = 0.89B - 0.59G - 0.3R.$$

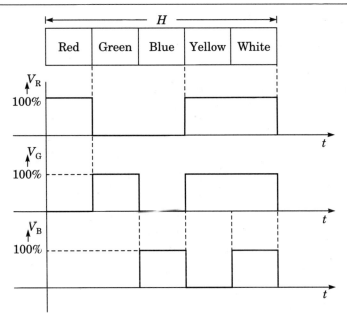

Figure 6.58 Red, green and blue camera video output voltages.

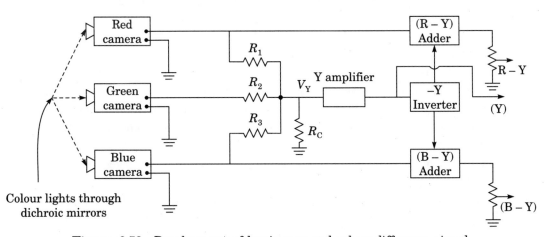

Figure 6.59 Development of luminance and colour-difference signal.

The voltage V_Y as developed from resistance matrix is low since R_C is taken small for avoiding cross talk. Therefore, it is amplified before it leaves the camera subchassis. Again, the amplified Y signal is inverted to find $-Y$ as the output. Here, one adder circuit adds the red camera output to $-Y$ for obtaining the $(R - Y)$ signal. Again, the second adder combines the blue camera output to $-Y$ and delivers $(B - Y)$ as its output. The difference signals which are found in this manner carry information both about the hue and saturation of different colours.

6.20.7 Colour Television Picture Tubes

Colour television picture tubes are classified into three categories.

- Delta gun colour picture tube
- Guns in-line or precision in-line colour picture tube
- Single gun or Trintron colour picture tube.

Delta-gun colour picture tube

The main features of delta-gun colour picture tube are as follows (Figure 6.60)

- It consists of three separate guns as shown in Figure 6.60(a).
- The guns are equally spaced at 120° interval with respect to each other. They are tilted inwards in connection to the axis of the tube.
- The guns develop an equilateral triangular configuration.
- Figure 6.60(b) describes the tube employing a screen where three colour phosphor dots being arranged in groups termed *triads*.
- Each phosphor dot consists of one of the three primary colours.
- There are repetition of triads.
- The number of phosphor dots depends on the size of the picture tube.
- Approximately 10,00,000 dots are available. That means, nearly 3,33,000 triads exist.
- Figure 6.60(c) describes shadow mask which is located about one cm behind the tube screen.
- The shadow mask is a thin perforated metal sheet.
- The mask has one hole for every phosphor dot triad on the screen.
- The various holes are so arranged that electrons of the three beams on passing through any one hole will hit only the corresponding colour phosphor dots on the screen.
- The ratio of electrons passing through the holes to these reaching the shadow mask is approximately twenty per cent.
- The rest eighty per cent of the total beam current energy is dissipated as a heat loss in the shadow mask.
- All the three colour difference signals are fed to the three grids of colour picture tube.
- The inverted luminance signal (−Y) is applied at the junction of the three cathodes.
- The signal voltages subtract from each other for developing control voltages for the three guns.

$$V'_{G1} - V_K = (V_R - V_Y) - (-V_Y) = V_R$$
$$V''_{G1} - V_K = (V_G - V_Y) - (-V_Y) = V_G$$
$$V'''_{G1} - V_K = (V_B - V_Y) - (-V_Y) = V_B$$

- In some cases, the Y signal is subtracted in the matrix and the final colour voltages are directly applied to the corresponding control grids.

Thus, the cathode is returned to a fixed negative voltage. The problems of the Delta-gun tube are as follows:

- A large amount of circuit complexity and service adjustments are needed for proper convergence. Usually four static convergence magnets and a dynamic convergence

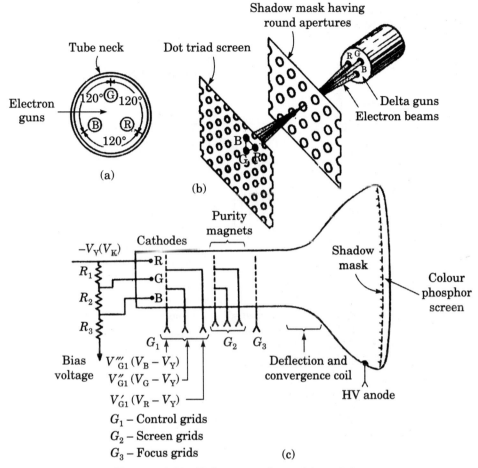

G_1 – Control grids
G_2 – Screen grids
G_3 – Focus grids

Figure 6.60 Delta-gun colour picture tube.

assembly are applied. Approximately, about 12 pre-set controls are essential for achieving proper vertical and horizontal convergences over the whole screen.

- The focus and convergence planes cannot be kept coincidental for the three beams and, as a result, the focus cannot be sharp over the whole screen.
- The mask intercepts over 80% of the beam currents, and, as a result, electron transparency of the mask is very low.

Precision-in-line (PIL) colour picture tube

The main features of PIL are as follows:

- In this colour picture tube, there are three guns which are aligned precisely in a horizontal line.
- Figure 6.61 describes the precision-in-line colour picture tube with a yoke.
- The colour phosphors are deposited on the screen in the form of vertical strips in triads (R, G, B). These are repeated along the breadth of the tube.

- The aperture mask has vertical slots corresponding to colour phosphor strips as shown in Figure 6.61(b).

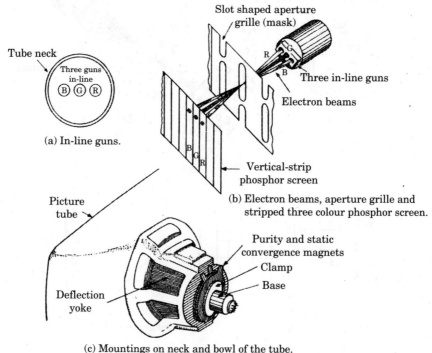

(a) In-line guns.

(b) Electron beams, aperture grille and stripped three colour phosphor screen.

(c) Mountings on neck and bowl of the tube.

Figure 6.61 Precision-in-line colour picture tube.

- One vertical line of slots is for one group of fine strips of red, green and blue phosphors.
- The beam in the centre, i.e. green moves along the axis of the tube, because all the three electron beams are on the same plane.
- The slots in the mask are designed in such a way that each beam strikes its own phosphor and is prevented from landing on other colour phosphors.
- This tube has higher electron transparency. Over and above, it requires fewer convergence adjustments because of the in-line gun structure.

Trintron colour picture tube

The main features of Trintron colour picture tube are as follows:
- Trintron colour picture tube has a single gun having three in-line cathodes.
- The three phosphor triads are arranged in vertical strips.
- Each strip is only a few thousandth of a centimetre wide.
- A metal aperture grille-like mask is kept very close to the screen.
- It has one vertical slot for each phosphor triad.
- It has greater electron transparency compared to those of delta gun and PIL tubes.

- The details of the trintron colour picture tube are shown in Figure 6.62. Figure 6.62(a) describes the gun structure, Figure 6.62(b) shows the electron beams, and vertical stripped three colour phosphor screen and Figure 6.62(c) indicates the focus and convergence details.

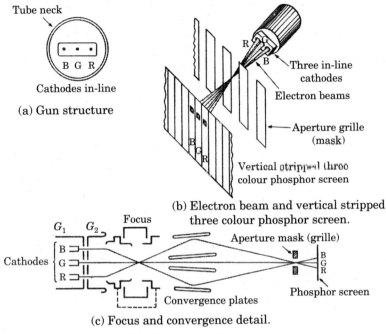

(a) Gun structure

(b) Electron beam and vertical stripped three colour phosphor screen.

(c) Focus and convergence detail.

Figure 6.62   Trintron colour picture tube.

- Here, the three beams are bent by an electrostatic lens system and it appears that they emerge from the same point in the lens assembly.
- A sharper image is found with good focus over the entire picture area because the beams have a common focus plane. As a result, convergence problems are reduced and adjustments which are necessary are very few.
- The trintron system has been modified by incorporating a low magnification electron gun assembly, long focusing electrodes and a large aperture lens system.
- It has a high precision deflection yoke with minimum convergence adjustments.
- It gives a high quality picture with very good resolution over large screen display tubes.

■ SUMMARY ■

First of all, the basic features of the television are explained with elementary block diagram. Then the same is explained by detailed block diagram of TV transmitter and receiver. Detailed description is made on television camera tube. Scanning in the television system is also discussed. Both horizontal and vertical scanning are elaborately discussed. An idea is also given on interlaced scanning. Expression of vertical resolution is shown. An idea is also given about horizontal resolution. Importance of synchronization is explained clearly. The range of television bandwidth is discussed. The bandwidth in case of sequential scanning and interlaced scanning are elaborately discussed. Detailed idea is given about composite video signal. Video signal, horizontal blanking pulse, horizontal synchronizing pulse, vertical blanking pulse, vertical synchronizing pulse, and equalizing pulse are discussed. The need for vestigial sideband transmission system in the television system is also explained. Demerits of vestigial sideband transmission are also explained.

The sound signal of the television system is frequency modulated. The mathematical analysis of frequency modulated wave is also reviewed. Principal television systems are tabulated.

Monochrome picture tube is explained with diagrams. Several components such as electron gun, aquadag conductive coating, electromagnetic deflection device, screen phosphor, rectangular face plate picture tube, yoke and centring magnets, screen brightness, filter capacitor, spark gaps are described in detail. Picture tube circuit and associated controls are shown through diagrams. An idea is also given on safety in picture tube. Image orthicon camera is described in detail. The concept of electron multiplier is also discussed in this context. Another very useful camera, vidicon is elaborately described. Circuit diagram for obtaining vidicon camera signal output is also shown. Light transfer characteristics of vidicon camera is also explained graphically. Salient features of silicon diode array vidicon are also given. Operation of silicon diode array vidicon is also discussed. The salient features of solid state image scanners are described. The cable television system are broadly categorized as follows.

(a) Master antenna television (MATV) system
(b) Community antenna television (CATV) system

The MATV system is explained with a block diagram. The important features of CATV systems are also described. An idea about closed circuit television (CCTV) is also given. The applications of CCTV are also described.

The most important applications of television, where two people can see each other while talking over the telephone, is explained through picture phone and facsimile. Video tape recording is improvement over this method. The advantages of VTR are narrated. The main features of VTR are also discussed. An idea regarding television through satellite is also given. 'INTELSAT' satellite has been described. A TS–6 satellite is also discussed.

Comptability between colour and monochrome TV systems is discussed. In this connection properties of light are explained. And above all, colour theory is also discussed. Chromaticity diagram is also described. Schematic diagram of colour television camera is also shown. Colour voltage amplitudes are also discussed.

In this connection, development of colour difference voltages is explained. Detailed idea about coloured television picture is also presented. Delta gun colour picture tube is described. The salient features of precision-in-line (PIL) colour picture tube are mentioned. The main features of Trintron colour picture tube are discussed.

■ QUESTIONS ■

1. Explain the principle of TV-transmitter and TV-receiver through a block diagram.

2. Explain the principle of operation of a television camera.

3. Describe the horizontal and vertical scanning of a television system.

4. What is interlaced scanning?

5. What do you mean by vertical resolution and horizontal resolution of the TV system. Explain clearly.

6. Why synchronization process is needed in television system?

7. How do you calculate bandwidth in case of sequential scanning and interlaced scanning in television system?

8. What is composite video signal? What is the need of equalizing pulses in television system? Explain clearly.

9. What is vestigial sideband transmission system in television? What are the demerits of vestigial sideband transmission system?

10. Describe a monochrome picture tube with a diagram.

11. Describe the picture tube circuit and its associated controls.

12. What are the safety measures to be adopted for picture tube?

13. Describe the image orthicon camera.

14. What is electron multiplier? Explain with a diagram.

15. Describe a vidicon camera.

16. Silicon diode array vidicon is the modification of vidicon. Explain.

17. Describe the solid state image scanners.

18. What is 'MATV'? Explain its operation with a block diagram.

19. What is 'CATV'? What is CCTV?

20. Describe the applications of CCTV.

21. Write a short note on (a) picture phone (b) facsimile.

22. What is video tape recording? What are the main features of VTR?

23. What are the advantages of satellite communication?

24. Describe the operation of ATS-6 satellite through a block diagram.

25. Each colour TV system is compatible with the corresponding monochrome system. Explain the same with a diagram.

26. Describe the colour theory and how is it related with colour television?

27. Describe the block diagram of a colour television camera.

28. What do you mean by colour voltage amplitudes?

29. Describe delta-gun colour picture tube.

30. Describe precision-in-line (PIL) colour picture tube.

31. Describe the main features of Trintron colour picture tube.

7. ■■■ Network Management in Communication

7.1 INTRODUCTION

Four words are very common in the present advanced communication engineering. These words are 'Network', 'Terminal', Link' and 'Node'. These can be explained as follows.

Network	Terminal	Link	Node
Telephone	Subscriber set	Line/radio	Exchange
Telex	Teleprinter	Line/radio	Exchange
Computer	Data terminal	Digital link	Computer

Terminal means the point from where the message is originated. Link means the device through which the message is being carried.

Node means the point where the same is received.

7.2 SWITCHED NETWORK

Most networks are based on circuit switching. In message switched networks, the entire message is stored at every node. Message transmission is possible only when a free link is available. Over and above, error control is made at every node. Generally, the link utilization is high but the corresponding time delay can be considerable from a few seconds to several minutes. Whereas in packet switched network, action is taken to combine the merits of circuit switching and message switching. Messages are divided into smaller units which are called packets. Moreover, each packet has error control facility. The length and structure of the packet are matched for meeting the characteristics of the lines, data, rates, delays, buffer storage for achieving maximum through-put. Of course, delays are withstandable for a few seconds that allow good interactive operation. The computer networks use packets for intercommunication. The comparison of circuit switching, message switching and packet switching can be made as follows.

Item	Circuit switching mode	Message switching mode	Packet switching mode
Delay	It is negligible	It is high	It is tolerable
Error control	It is poor	It is good	It is good
Interactive communication	It is feasible	It is not feasible	It is feasible
Data rates	These are low	These are high	These are high
Line utilization	It is poor	It is good	It is good

Switching can be categorized as follows:

- Space switching
- Time switching

In *space switching*, there lies a path between the input and the output. In *time switching*, there lies a virtual connection between the input and the output. For example, analogue signals are switched exclusively by space switching networks, i.e. cross bars, semiconductor cross points, etc. On the other hand, digital signal can be switched by both space switches and time switches. Space switches are gates and time switches are memories.

Since the time switching is memory-oriented, it needs less hardware and at the same time full non-blocking switching networks can be easily realized. Large digital networks are developed by the combination of space and time switches.

7.3   NEED FOR A NUMBER OF CHANNELS

The bandwidth of a given link means information carrying capacity. Generally, the bandwidth of a given link is much higher than that needed for transmission of a single channel of information. Hence, it is economic to divide the capacity of the link into a number of channels— termed *multiplexing*. Multiplexing is generally categorized as follows:

- Frequency-division multiplexing (FDM)
- Time-division multiplexing (TDM)

In *frequency-division multiplexing*, frequency band is splitted into a number of smaller frequency bands. Each band carries one channel. Generally, in public telephone systems for transmission of a large number of telephone channels this method is used. Whereas, in *time-division multiplexing* the time period, i.e. the 'frame' time is splitted into a number of time slots. One time slot is kept for one channel. This method is largely used with digital signals. It is very convenient for digital interfacing. These two multiplexing methods are also termed *transparent multiplexing*.

7.4   DATA TRANSMISSION

In case of data transmission, amplitude modulation can be utilized with the amplitude of the carrier tone being varied according to the data bit. It is used generally for low bit rate applications. Moreover, it has poor noise immunity. On the other hand, frequency modulation has better noise immunity. In data transmission, frequency modulation is also termed *frequency shift keying* (FSK).

In this type of modulation, the carrier frequency is changed as per data bit. The frequency modulation is suitable for low speeds up to 1200 bps. In the data transmission, the phase modulation is termed *phase shift keying* (PSK). Phase modulation modems usually operate in 4 or 8 phases allowing bit-rate transmission over the same narrow band telephone channel. For short range transmission or transmission over cable/twisted pair, baseband transmission is also applied. In case of baseband transmission, transmission of digital signal is made without any modulation of a carrier signal.

The data transmission is categorized as follows:

- Asynchronous transmission
- Synchronous transmission.

Asynchronous transmission means transmission of data in units of characters. The transmitted character is recovered by scanning the line at a higher rate and detecting the start and stop bits. In ASCII code format, the arrangement is as follows:

- 11 bits are transmitted per character.
- 7 information bit
- 1 parity bit
- '0' start bit
- two '1's stop bits.

The speed is variable up to 2400 bps.

The merits of asynchronous transmission are as follows:

- Simple transmission and detection
- Hardware is simple.

The demerits are

- High overheads
- Poor error control
- Low through-put
- Not suitable for high-speed, high volume transmission.

In case of *synchronous transmission,* messages are sent in blocks of fixed or variable length up to 10,000. Blocks are called packets. Each packet consists of one or more characters for synchronization and error control utilizing the cyclic redundancy check. Synchronization actually makes recovery of clock pulses from the incoming bit stream for regeneration and recovery of the signal which is received. The maximum length of the packet is found by the network characteristics, for example, the delay, the error rates, turn around time, etc.

The modulation and demodulation processes needed for data transmission are carried out through modems. Some modems also help in the process of associated control functions besides modulation and demodulation processes. The main features of the functions can be described as follows:

- Transmitting the signalling conditions.
- Detecting the presence of these on the incoming line.
- Phase encoder-decoder is applied.
- The received signal is filtered.
- It is passed on to an equalizer.

- Balanced demodulators gives coherently demodulated signals.
- The inphase and quadrature demodulated signals give data with timing and carrier-recovery information.

Complexity in this system of modem depends on the following:

- The speed of operation
- Simplex operation/duplex operation
- 2 wire/4 wire circuits
- Simple ICs are needed for low speed 300 bps operation, whereas very elaborate signal processing circuits are needed for high speed 32 kbps modems being operated in satellite networks.

Modems also require echo-cancellation circuit in high speed long distance links. For better capabilities, sometimes switched lines or dedicated lines are used. These lines have controlled characteristics. Involvement of modem can be summarized as follows:

- Secondary channel
- Equalization
- Soft carrier disconnection
- Scrambling
- Testing
- Transmit only/receive only
- Originate only/answer only
- Attended/unattended operation
- Forward error control
- Switching to lower speed
- Elastic buffer storage
- Alternate voice/data operation
- Multiplexing and line protection

7.5 NETWORK

Networks can be broadly classified as follows:

- Star network
- Tree structure
- Mesh network
- Ring structure

Terminals and processors are connected in different methods for meeting the specific requirements of traffic and geographical distribution. In case of *star network*, a number of terminals are connected to one single central processor. But, the *tree structure* is the combination of several stars. *Mesh network* gives one or more alternate paths like a grid. Whereas, the *ring structure* possesses all the terminals being connected in the form of a loop.

Organization of a network consists of the following considerations.

- System performance requirement
- User interface

- Expandability
- Modularity
- Performance criterion
- System utilization
- Queues

A data call is generally routed through the complex communication network. Over and above, the problem of routing a packet is much more complex than that of routing a telephone call. Routing generally assumes existence of alternative path at a node. For finding out routing, the route finding algorithm is not adaptive towards the changing pattern of traffic. The random routing strategy gives fixed decision rules as to which neighbouring node the message is to be routed. Here, source or destination information is not needed. The merits of the above are as follows:

- No directory is required
- It is robust and insensitive to the network structure

The demerit is that it is highly inefficient and long time delays may occur.

On the other hand, in case of adaptive routing strategy, the choice of node depends upon the outcome of commutation on the basis of locally found condition of arriving at a minimum delay route.

Even congestion may occur in the network. To control the congestion, a constraint is imposed on the rate of flow of messages of each source/destination pair. Sometimes, by limiting the number of characters on node with buffer, control is applied locally. Moreover in some cases global constraint is imposed on the total number of messages which may come across anywhere in the network.

7.6 NETWORK PROTOCOLS

Rules are provided for the flow of data in the network. These are called *network protocols*. The main objective of network protocols is to transfer data quickly and reliably between two specified points. The network protocols perform the following:

- Error detection
- Correction of error
- Recovery procedure being adopted as a result contingencies can be handled in proper manner.

Levels of protocols are explained as follows:

Level 1: The lowest level protocol is generally at the hardware level. It is the physical interface between the terminals and the network. It also explains the linking characteristics and procedures issued for establishing, maintaining and disconnecting the communication between the terminals and the network or between any two terminal units.

Level 2: This is the data link control for exchange of data between the terminals and network or between any two of the terminal units and is called *line control* or *line discipline*. This protocol certifies the following:

- A block of data is received from one end of a data link to the other end.
- The data is received correctly.

The main features of level 2 are as follows:

- A connection between the two stations is established and terminated.
- Message integrity is certified through error detection, request for retransmission, and positive or negative acknowledgement.
- The sender and receiver are identified through polling or selection.
- Requests for status, station reset, reset acknowledgement, start, start acknowledgement, and disconnection are the control functions being handled.

Level 3: Level 3 is the *network control protocol*. It explains the format and control procedures for the transfer of user data through a communication network. It is made through software whereas the level 1 and level 2 are done through hardware.

Level 4: Level 4 performs the following functions:

- Message reconstruction from data blocks.
- Data block/virtual message connection.

Level 5: Level 5 is used for the following:

- To initialize run
- To terminate sessions

Level 6: Level 6 is used for handling the following:

- Interpretation of data exchanged
- Control of data structure
- Display of data
- Character codes and formats.

Level 7: Level 7 is used for the following:

- Deadlock recovery
- File access
- Industry standard

Here the operational procedures are made flexible. These depend on the following:

- The organization and functions being performed are remote latch processing, control, file transfer protocol, civil aviation protocol, etc.

7.7 ERROR DETECTION AND CORRECTION TECHNIQUES

The error detection and correction techniques consist of

- Error detection
- Parity checks
- Single error detection in the caracter and redundancy checks.

For *error checking* in a block of data, a block check character (BCC) is utilized. In case of *cyclic redundancy check* (CRC), the check character is found by dividing all the serial bits of block by a pre-determined binary number. The remainder of this division is nothing but the check character. The same is matched with the check character developed at the receiver. The error is indicated by the mismatch. A 16-bit cyclic redundancy check is utilized in synchronous protocols. The error correction is obtained by retransmission of the message. An automatic repeat request (ARQ) is needed for the purpose. These are three types

- Stop and wait
- Continuous repeat ARQ
- Selective repeat ARQ.

Error-correcting codes (ECC) may be utilized for correcting up to a given number of errors. This needs addition of sufficient redundant bits to the message for allowing both detection and correction of errors at the receiver. The redundancy may be made up to 100% extra. Error rate improvement may be obtained with the help of a factor of 10^2–10^3. The above technique is applied to the following:

- channels having poor signal/noise ratio
- data broadcasting networks
- space communication links.

7.8 MULTIPLEXERS AND CONCENTRATORS

Multiplexer is a device which divides the capacity of communication line among a number of terminals. As already discussed there are two main techniques.

- Time-division multiplexing (TDM)
- Frequency-division multiplexing (FDM)

In case of TDM technique, a multidrop connection is realizable for serving a number of terminals on one link. On the other hand, a concentrator is a device which combines data from a number of sources of different speeds into high speed for transmission to a host computer. This is also called *communication processor*. Concentrators generally utilize mini or micro computer for this objective. The intelligent time division multiplexer allows the sum of the channel data rates to be higher than its multiplex link data rate. Statistical nature of data traffic is used in this case. The outcome is the excellent use of channel capacity.

7.9 SATELLITE COMMUNICATION

Satellite circuits usually operate at a high bit rate, for example 56 kbps. That is why, these are very important to have an optimum choice of frame size and error control procedure. The errors in satellite links are randomly distributed. Hence, the error detection techniques should be made quite impressive. Forward error correction (FEC) techniques are generally used. For satellite networks, the main problem is delay. Direct substitution of terrestrial link by a satellite link would reduce the through-put substantially. That is why, selective automatic repeat request is essential for this purpose. FEC schemes allow the receiver to correctly decode a message even if some of the packets are lost. This is done by adding redundant information to the system.

7.10 DATAGRAM

A datagram consists of the address of destination computer. It is nothing but a packet of data. The packet switching network considers the datagram as an individual element and passes it on to the destination. It is used for the following:

- Cash dispenser
- Credit validation
- Electronic funds transfer (EFT)

The electronic fund transfer is the computer-based systems which are used to perform financial transactions electronically. It is actually used for the following:

- Cardholder-initiated transactions where a cardholder makes use of a payment card.
- Direct deposit payroll payments for a business to its employees through a payroll services company.
- Direct debit payments from customer to business, where the transaction is initiated by the business with customer's permission.
- Electronic bill payment in on-line banking, that may be delivered by EFT or paper check.
- Transactions involving stored value of electronic money, possibly in a private currency.
- Wire transfer via an international banking network.
- Electronic benefit transfer.

7.11 VIRTUAL CALL

Virtual call is a point to point connection between sending and receiving terminals. Packet switched based resources are not permanently assigned to the virtual circuit. Otherwise, it is similar to a circuit switched call. The network delivers packets in the same manner in which they are received by the network. It takes responsibility for recovering lost packets and for not delivering duplicate packets.

7.12 LOCAL AREA NETWORK (LAN)

Local area network operates in a small local area. In fact, it is characterized by a very high speed communication between processors and terminals/devices. They are interconnected by a bus of a single conductor or group of conductors. Their applications consist of distribution, sharing and optimal use of computer resources.

7.13 INTEGRATED NETWORKS

Integrated networks perform integration of voice and data. The 64-kbps, PCM channel gives a very good carrier for data and systems with facilities for both voice (64-kbps) and data (9.6 kbps). The organization of the electronic office is developed. More research is going on for the development of techniques for handling voice in packets in data networks.

7.14 NEED OF MODULATION FOR DATA SIGNALS

Basic data signals do not exist in a form which is suitable for direct transmission over telephone circuits. A typical data signal has significant frequency components near to dc, and, that is why, it would be impossible to carry such signals directly over the telephone network. That is why modulation/demodulation equipment is needed. The modem actually converts data signals to frequencies, in the voice band and these can be transmitted over the telephone network. Frequency shift keying (FSK) is reliable for low speed data applications. The binary data 0s and 1s are expressed by two frequencies f_1 and f_2 respectively.

FSK is a type of frequency modulation where the modulating signal is a binary data sequence. It produces a large number of significant sidebands. It does not make optimum use of the available bandwidth. As a result, it cannot be used for high speed data applications. Of course, the alternatives of frequency shift keying are amplitude modulation (AM) and phase shift keying (PSK). Amplitude modulated signals are developed by multiplying the baseband signal by a cosine carrier frequency. The carrier frequency is the arithmetic mean of the edge frequencies of the available transmission bandwidth.

In this way, we can develop a double sideband suppressed carrier (DSBSC) signal.

Figure 7.1(a) indicates baseband signal. Figure 7.1(b) indicates carrier frequency and Figure 7.1(c) indicates AM signal generated. Here,

$$f_c = \frac{f_h + f_l}{2}$$

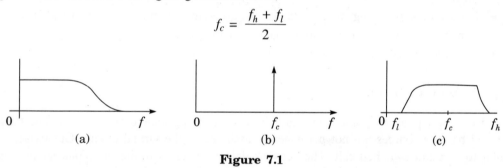

Figure 7.1

The original baseband signal can be recovered by multiplying the baseband signal with a cosine carrier and applying low fass filter. Figure 7.2(a) shows AM signal generated. Figure 7.2(b) signal shows carrier frequency. Figure 7.2(c) shows the recovered signal.

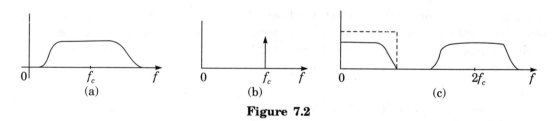

Figure 7.2

Figures 7.3(a) and (b) describe the equivalent complex baseband channel and equivalent baseband channel respectively. The above behaves like a low pass channel. Amplitude modulation may be performed at two levels.

• By direct modulation with the binary data stream.

- By multilevel modulation with digits taken from the data stream 'n' at a time and then transmitted as a 2^n amplitude modulated signal. Here, bandwidth utilization can be improved by the use of single sideband techniques because amplitude modulation develops two sidebands having identical information. It is worthwhile to use vestigial sideband amplitude modulation instead of suppressing a complete sideband because the modulating frequency band may contain significant low frequency components. Phase shift keying takes n-bits at a time from the data sequence and encodes them into 2^n phase shifts.

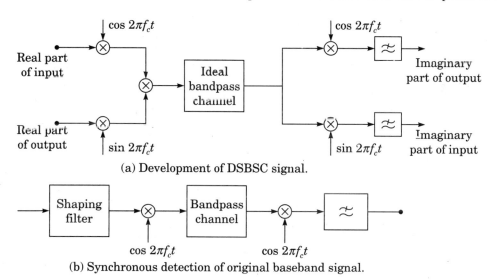

(a) Development of DSBSC signal.

(b) Synchronous detection of original baseband signal.

Figure 7.3

7.14 DATA TRANSMISSION

Data transmission services were introduced in the name of 'Datel services'. FSK modems were also introduced. The advantages of the FSK were,

- It gave good performance
- It was very simple to implement
- It gave a stable operation over a wide variety of channels
- It also allowed asynchronous operation
- The modem performance was not affected by the data sequence because the time signal is always present with amplitude whatever pattern of 1s and 0s may be. Of course, two standard FSK systems are in practice. The first was developed for enabling keyboards and similar machines to communicate with one another over the public switchboard telephone network which is termed PSTN, and private speech circuits at signalling rates of up to 200 bits/second in a full duplex mode. The CCITT recommendation was encashed to cover 300 bits/second in each direction. Channel 1 is utilized for the transmission of the caller's data and channel 2 is utilized for transmission in other direction. There is no problem for using these modems in asynchronous or synchronous working. The United Kingdom version of this modem is termed as Datel Modem No. 2. In the United States of America the Bell system device, known as Dataset No. 103 gives same facilities.

7.15 TELEMATIC SERVICE

With the advancement in the field of data communication and on account of microprocessors, telematic services have been developed. The several versions of the above services are,

- electronic mail
- electronic fund transfer
- videotex
- teletex
- facsimile

Use of videotex services has been restricted to commercial purposes. These services are very much lucrative for private users because they require low budget system with no need of hard copy.

Figure 7.4 shows a videotex terminal. This is the application of domestic TV. It consists of the following equipment.

- Videotex adaptor
- Modem
- Keypad
- TV set

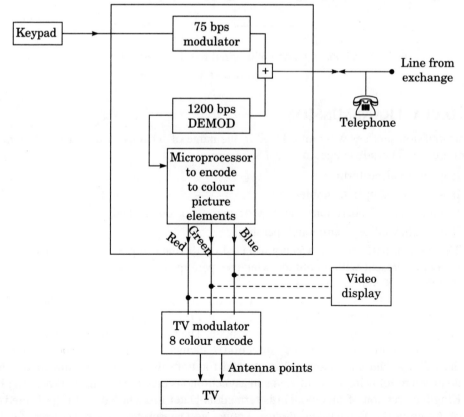

Figure 7.4 Videotex terminal.

There are two types of users in this service

- Information seekers
- Information providers

The *information seekers* can go to the system by a switched telephone network with dialling mechanism. With the help of keypad, and dials, the number of database is dialled by the user, and afterwards, the user reaches the screen of the terminal to get a display contents page of database and specific page of information can also be obtained by providing further command to the keyboard. On the other hand, the information provider can edit/update their databases independently by providing connection through either the telephone network or leased lines with special terminals or similar to others. Figure 7.5 describes the data communication path for the above.

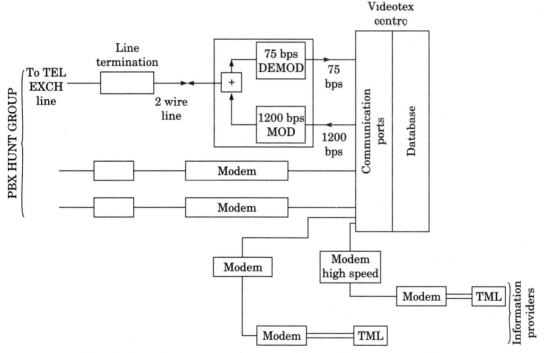

Figure 7.5 Data communication path for information providers.

Different databases can be switched through a simple switching arrangement at the videotex centre depending on the queries of user.

The call from a user is taken as in case of other calls to the PBX type numbers of database. Then the same is terminated by modems with autoanswering features.

Figure 7.6 describes this operation. The modems are connected with the switch and then in turn collects information from different databases on higher speed lines and the message will be received by the telephone line. Generally, the speed for transmission from user to database/switch is 75 bps. On the other hand, in the reverse direction, the speed is 1200 bps.

Figure 7.7 describes the same. The 75 bps transmit and 1200 bps receive are used at the user's end and the 1200 bps transmit and 75 bps receive are used at the videotex centre end.

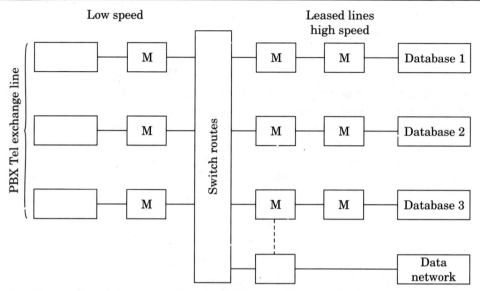

Figure 7.6 Information from different databases on higher speed lines.

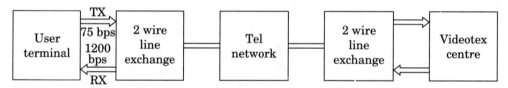

Figure 7.7 Block diagram between user terminal and videotex centre.

7.16   TELETEX

Teletex is simply a slow speed text communication service. The main objectives of this system are as follows:

- Its speed of transmission is of the order of 10 seconds per A4 page.
- Various national typewriter alphabets are available in this system.
- It has also text editing capability.
- Any public telecommunication network can be used for this purpose.

Figure 7.8 describes the teletex system. It is a memory transfer with built-in error connection. The terminals are the same to those of world processors with all editing capacities. The terminal of this system is similar to an office typewriter with the following devices.

- Typewriter with storage
- Video display
- Independent transmit and receive transfers for messages.

The networks to which teletex is connected are as follows

- Telephone network (PSTN)
- Circuit switched data network
- Packet switched data network.

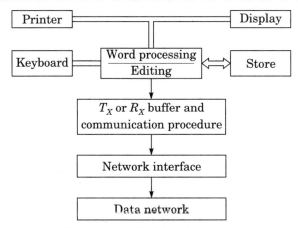

Figure 7.8 Teletex terminal.

For PSTN access, the CCITT has recently standardized the 2400 bps full duplex and 1200 bps duplex modems for working on PSTN in synchronous and asynchronous modes. For circuit and packet switched data networks, standard procedures are followed. Fundamentally, the telex is developed for becoming network independent. Therefore, the standards developed in the terminals are as per session and document levels of a protocol hierarchy. The main feature of the service is the need of a centralized telex to telex and vice versa interface for enhancing universality and speed.

Figure 7.9 describes the teletex networking.

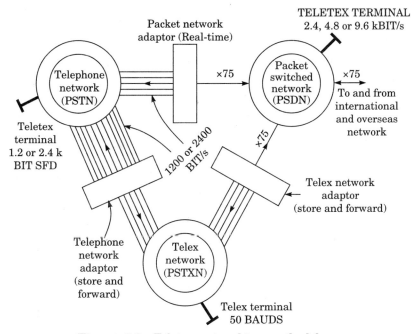

Figure 7.9 Teletex networking methodology.

Figure 7.10 describes telex service.

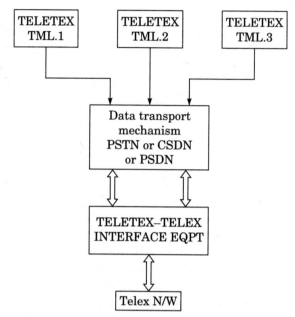

Figure 7.10 Block diagram of telex service.

7.17 FACSIMILE SERVICE

The main objective of facsimile service is to develop capability of transmitting copies of any script (latin or non-latin), diagrams, signatures, etc. There are four categories of machine.

- **Group 1:** 6 minutes for standard one A4 page.
- **Group 2:** 3 minutes for standard one A4 page.
- **Group 3:** 1 minute for standard one A4 page.
- **Group 4:** less than 1 minute for standard one A4 page.

Generally, Group 1 and Group 2 are slow machines. Group 3 is the standardized machine for public telephone networks. Group 4 is used for public data networks.

The group 1 machine takes AM or FM signals for modulation to compatible line signals. The group 2 utilizes AMVSB with phase modulation. In case of Group 3 machine, the picture is digitized. Here, the signals utilize the standard CCITT modems at speeds having range from 2400 bps to 9600 bps.

Figure 7.11 describes fundamental schematic circuit of a Fax M/C. Picture scanning may be of drum or flat bed type. Modulator may handle AM, FM, AMVSBPM or PSK signals.

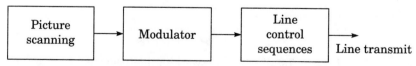

Figure 7.11 Fundamental schematic circuit of a Fax M/C.

The line control sequences indicate

- Choice of speed
- Configuration
- Phasing information
- Status of device
- Start of transmission
- End of transmission.

In case of drum type scanner, the document which is to be transmitted is tightly fixed to a drum. The drum rotates at a specified speed and the scanning beam of light travels along the drum. The reflected light is measured from element. Then the same is encoded. The encoded elements modulate a carrier. Finally, the same is sent on line.

In case of flat-bed scanners, the movement of the document becomes horizontal. It is scanned line by line depending on the density of the picture elements.

Figure 7.12 describes receiving end of facsimile system. The printing process is either thermal or electrosensitive. That is why, special paper is required for printing. Usually for small portable desk top versions, thermal printing is used.

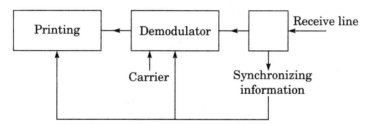

Figure 7.12 Block diagram of receiving end of facsimile system.

The types of CCITT standard facimile equpments are as follows.

- Group 1
- Group 2
- Group 3

In case of *Group 1* amplitude modulation is done for leased circuits only. The carrier frequency is generally in the range of 1300–1900 Hz. It is corresponding to black or white signals. Frequency modulation is also done in leased and switched connections. The carrier is at 1700 Hz for switched access. The maximum black signal is at 2100 Hz and the maximum white signal is at 1300 Hz.

In case of *Group 2*, the type of equipment takes AM with vestigial sideband filtering cum phase modulation and with a carrier frequency of 2100 Hz. The density of scanning is 3.85 lines/mm length.

Group 3 makes digital scanning using 3.85 lines/mm or higher resolution of 7.7 lines/mm. Each line contains black and white picture elements of 1748 elements. The digital information can be transmitted taking standard voice-band modems at 24 W, 48 W and 96 W bps.

7.18 DATA NETWORK BASING ON SATELLITE

History says that the beginning of the data communication was through start-stop telegraphy. That was the concept of Morse key. Morse key was replaced by Teleprinters. The teleprinter service was extended to subscriber's premises by Telex. Gradually, the range of the data rates became 9.6 kbit/s to 300 kbit/s. This was made possible from the concept of line modems. Dedicated voice circuits are now being replaced by public switched telephone network (PSTN).

Of course, the data rate is limited on account of impulse noise.

There are there categories of data networks

- Circuit switched
- Message switched
- Packet switched

The circuit switch network requires development through connection before data is passed. This is similar to PSTN. The message switched system makes message transportation with one link at a time. In packet switched system alternate routing is available for averaging of channel utilization. These networks are dependent on standardized protocols for physical/electrical interface, with packet switch and transportation schemes. Hence, virtual circuit and datagram facilities are available here. That is why, packet switched scheme is the most efficient from consideration of network resources.

The availability of satellite gives a viable alternative with much increased capacity. The satellite or any other broadcast medium can be utilized on

- fixed basis
- demand basis
- random assignment basis.

The *fixed* assignment scheme is just like the same being used for terrestial media. The *demand* assignment helps channel utilization on flexible basis. *Random assignment* scheme helps a large number of users with poor predictability of channel utilization.

The main demerit of the use of the satellite medium is the increased cost of terminal equipment. The merits, of course, can be described as follows.

(a) Its performance is excellent for large distances.
(b) It has inaccessible terrain
(c) It possesses large capacity
(d) It has multi-drop applications
(e) It has considerations of short time availability for installation and operation.

The facility of data or digital mode of information communication can be utilized for a variety of applications by variety of users. These can be described as follows.

- It can be used for remote accessing of computer facilities and databases. Specially for R & D organizations and academic institutions interactive terminals are available. It is also used for various transport agencies, hotels and police.
- It has large file transfers for sharing of computer hardware/software and databases for urgent applications.

- It has messaging facility for urgent communications demanded by a large users.
- It helps interconnection of regional terrestrial networks for telegraphy and telex.
- It also helps in News/FAX exchange and distribution for PTI/UNI.

The following points are to be considered for the above system

- Performance
- Overall capacity
- Satellite availability with frequency/power coordination
- Terminal configuration/cost.

From the point of view of performance, the considerations are different for two different applications, i.e. Network application and interactive application. In case of network application, the performance consideration is throughput efficiency and in case of interactive application; two, important considerations are delay rate and error rate.

Delay may be limited

- by propagation time
- by retransmission strategy and processing time
- by retransmission energy and processing time in communication controller.

With the help of microprocessor for communication controller, the delay may not exceed 3 seconds for 75% throughput efficiency. A channel error rate of 10^{-4} is expected.

The overall capacity can be described as follows:

- The total requirements add up to peak traffic of approximately 80 kb/s
- With 40% data efficiency, the needed channel rate is rendered at 290 kb/s on account of overhead bits and clashes
- If 25% more capacity is added, then 256 kb/s transmission rate would be adequate for unexpected growth
- A bandwidth of 150 kHz would be needed utilizing 4 phase modulation.

The Indian National Satellite (INSAT) is provided with twelve communications transponders of 32 dBW EIRP (edge of coverage) in the C band and one direct broadcasting transponder of 42-dBW EIRP (edge of coverage) in the c/s band. The frequency plan, for these transporters, is available.

It has been estimated that 4.5 metre (19.7 G/T) terminal, with direct modulation scheme having minimal redundancy, can be built at a cost of Rs. 10 lakhs. Similarly chicken-mesh terminals, with analogue modem, may cost within Rs. 30,000.

7.19 NETWORK MANAGEMENT

Office automation and data application are very important phenomena in network management. Over and above, information technology has become a key factor in this area. Specially, organizations utilize information processing systems for providing essential support facilities. The information processing system management is integrated in the overall management structure of the organization for deriving maximum benefit. The information processing system consists of the following.

- hardware

- software
- procedural facilities.

Figure 7.13 describes information processing system. It consists of the following:

- Application system
- Distributed processing support system
- Communication system.

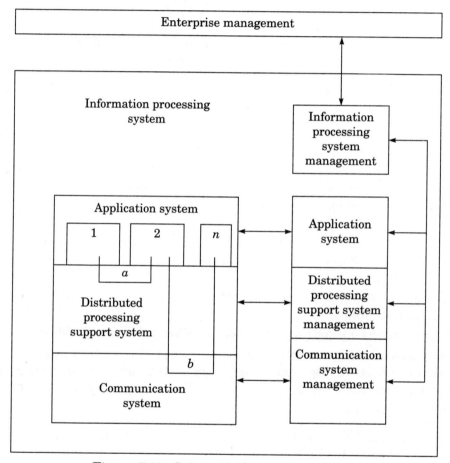

Figure 7.13 Information processing system.

Figure 7.14 describes application system management. This takes care of all the user applications and relationships among them which develops interactions among user applications. Bank service is one of the examples. The application system consists of banking applications which mean accounting, bookkeeping, etc. Relations among applications mean account manipulation. Standardization bodies, such as ISO (International Standard Organization) have understood the merit of distributing processing support and are trying to develop a proper network.

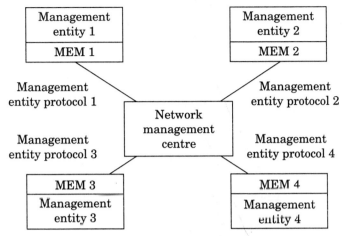

Figure 7.14 Block diagram of application system management.

7.19.1 Communication Network

The ISO and CCITT are setting up standards for making communication easy. Communication system management is needed to co-ordinate and control network operation. That is termed *network management*. A communication network is controlled by an organization and is defined as the network management. The examples of networks are:

- Public switched telephone network
- Public packet switching network
- Local area network (LAN)
- Integrated services digital network (ISDN)
- Proprietary network depending on typical network architectures.

Figure 7.15 describes network management from the communication point of view. It is a customer network. ME1, ME2, ME3, ME4, ME5, ME6, ME7 are management entities. Management entities are of two types.

- Passive management entities
- Active management entities.

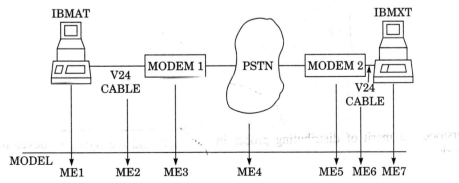

Figure 7.15 Network management.

Passive management entities are managed remotely and they are simple devices or complex systems for example cables, printed boards, wiring frames, dumb modems and terminals, PABXs which is managed locally. *Active management entities* can be managed by remote control through a communication link. The examples are proprietary networks, PABX networks, protocol handler and intelligent modem.

7.19.2 Approaches to Network Management

In case of centralized approach, all the active management entities are connected to the network management centre (NMC). The 'NMC' carries all managemnt functions. The management data are sent to the 'NMC' utilizing one or more protocols. Figure 7.16 describes the above. If the network management centre fails, all management facilities will be lost.

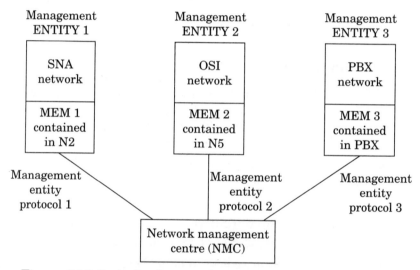

Figure 7.16 Centralized approach towards network management.

Figure 7.17 describes the distributed approach to the network management. In case of distributed approach, all management entities can communicate with one another. NMC functions are distributed over several such entities. A common management protocol is needed so that all management entities can intercommunicate with one another as shown in Figure 7.17. If there is failure of one entity, a part of the NMC functionality will be lost.

Figure 7.18 shows hierarchical approach. In case of hierarchial approach, all management entities are equipped with their own management facilities and they can collect management data.

Here, connection is made in a hierarchial manner. Different communication protocols are used for communication with the NMC. In Figure 7.18, it is shown that ME 11 and ME 12 are managed autonomously by MEM1 when ME1 and ME2 are managed by the NMC.

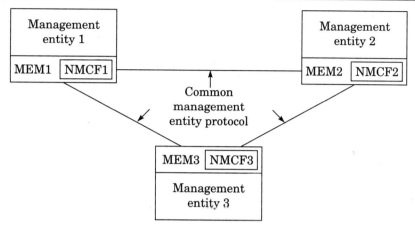

Figure 7.17 Distributed approach towards network management.

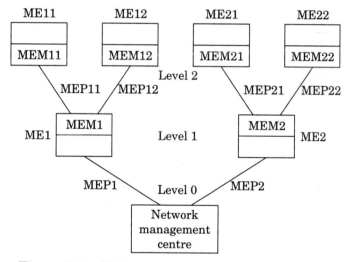

Figure 7.18 Block diagram of hierarchical approach.

7.19.3 Network Model

The components of the network are as follows:

- *Physical components*, e.g., devices, cables, etc.
- *Logical components*, e.g. services provided by ISDN, packet switching network.

Thus, network model should consist of all the above models.

Any relation among the components is also to be shown. Each physical and logical component possesses the following parameters.

- Name
- State
- Physical location
- Last maintenance date.

The idea of network model is found in Figure 7.19.

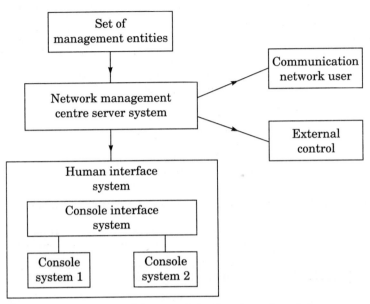

Figure 7.19 Server system and human interface in network management centre.

7.19.4 Architecture of NMC

The network management centre (NMC) architecture comprises the following elements.

- Set of management entities which are required to be managed;
- External agents which can access the NMC databases in a controlled manner and which can control the NMC remotely;
- The NMC server system which deals with management entities;
- Human interface system which helps the NMC personnel to interact with management entities through the NMC server system.

The server system is nothing but the heart of the NMC. The NMC server system exchanges information with management entities at level 1. Management entities at level 2 are managed by the following

- Management entity management at level 1
- NMC server system utilizing facilities provided by level 1 management entity management.

The NMC server system communicates with the set of management entities through interfaces that translate different types of management entity protocols into a common management entity protocol.

The processing units in the server system are as follows:

- Network user interface;
- External control interface.

The network user interface allows a network user to access server system databases in a controlled manner. The external interface allows another NMC to control the network NMC remotely.

Applications of NMC

The main NMC applications are as follows:

- Configuration management
- Performance management
- Fault management
- Security management
- Accounting management
- Recording and replay for the purposes of maintenance and training.

The functions which manage the NMC server are as follows:

- NMC initialization
- NMC control
- Operating system interface
- System help function
- On-line facilities for developing NMC user applications and NMC security applications.

■ SUMMARY ■

This chapter deals with network, terminal, link and node of advanced communication engineering. Terminal means the point from where the message originates. Link means the device through which the message is being carried. Node means the point where the same is received. An idea about switched network is given. Circuit switching mode, message switching mode and packet switching mode are described. Concepts of space switching and time switching are explained. An idea about the concept of number of channels is given. Multiplexing is classified by frequency-division multiplexing (FDM) and time-division multiplexing. Data transmission is discussed. The same is classified by asynchronous transmission and synchronous transmission. The modulation and demodulation processes needed for data transmission are carried out through modems. Some modems also help in the process of associated control functions besides modulation and demodulation processes. The main features of the functions are narrated. Networks are broadly classified as star network, tree structure, mesh network and ring structure. An idea is given about the organization of network. The network protocols are discussed. Levels of protocols are explained, e.g. 1, 2, 3, 4, 5, 6 and 7. The error detection and correction techniques are also described. Comparison of multiplexers and concentrators are made. The concept of satellite communication is described.

Datagram is discussed. It consists of the address of destination computer. It is nothing but a packet of data.

Point-to-point connection between sending and receiving terminals is explained through virtual call. An idea is also given about local area networks (LANs). Integrated networks are also discussed. The need for modulation of data signals is also discussed. With the advancement in the field of data communication and on account of use of microprocessors, telematic services have been developed. Several versions of the above services are narrated. Use of videotex services has been discussed. Data communication path for information providers is explained through block diagrams. Information from different databases on higher speed lines is also explained through a block diagram. Block diagrams between user terminal and videotex centre is also discussed.

An idea is also given about teletex which is a slow speed text communication service. Diagram is also shown on Teletex networking. Block diagrams are also drawn for Telex services. An idea is also given about modernized facsimile service. Fundamental schematic circuit of a fax machine is also exhibited. The types of CCITT standard facsimile equipments are also discussed.

Data network is discussed keeping the base on satellite. In this connection, public switched Telephone network is dealt with. Use of satellite medium for data network has several merits and these have been narrated. The facility of data or digital mode of information communication can be utilized for a variety of applications by a variety of users. Those are also described.

The Indian National Satellite (INSAT) is provided with twelve communication transponders of 32 dBW EIRP (edge of coverage) in the C band and one direct broadcasting transponder of 42-dBW EIRP (edge of coverage) in the C/S band.

Network management is discussed. The information technology (IT) has become a key factor in this area. The information processing system consists of the following.

- hardware
- software
- procedural facilities

Information processing system is discussed with the block diagram. Application system management has also been dealt. Communication system management is needed to co-ordinate and control network operation.

The network management is described from the communication point of view. Both passive management entities and active management entities are explained. Centralized approach towards network management is discussed. Distributed approach to network management is also explained. Hierarchical approach is also shown.

An idea has also been given about network model. Both the physical and logical components are explained. Network management centre indicating the server system and human interface is also shown. Architecture of network management centre is also explained. The functions which manage the NMC server are also mentioned.

■ QUESTIONS ■

1. What do you mean by switched network? Compare circuit switching mode, message switching mode and packet switching mode.

2. What do you mean by data transmission? Compare asynchronous transmission and synchronous transmission.

3. What are broad classifications of network? How are they defined?

4. What are the considerations to be made for the organization of the network?

5. Define the network protocols. How would you explain the levels of protocols?

6. Write a short note on 'Error-correcting codes'.

7. Define the concentrator. How does it differ from multiplexer?

8. What is the main problem of satellite network?

9. Write a short note on 'datagram'.

10. What do you mean by virtual call?

11. What is local area network?

12. Why modulation is needed for data signals?

13. What are the advantages of FSK?

14. What are the several versions of telematic service? Describe the videotex terminal.

15. What are the types of users for videotex terminal? Explain them with a block diagram.

16. What is Teletex? Explain the Teletex terminal with a block diagram.

17. Explain the Teletex networking and telex service with a diagram.

18. What are the different types of machines being used for facsimile services?

19. What are the merits of the use of satellite medium?

20. In satellite network application, how delay rate can be made limited?

21. What is network management? Explain by a block diagram information processing system and application system management.

22. What do you mean by management entities? How many types of management entities are there?

23. What is network management centre? What are the different approaches to network management?

24. What do you mean by network model?

25. What are the different elements of architecture network management centre?

8 ▪▪▪ Advanced Communication Systems

8.1 SOLID STATE RADIO SYSTEM

Modern communication systems possess combined expertise in radio equipment and microprocessor technology. It gives high frequency to the following applications.

- Defence
- Military
- Naval
- Air
- Diplomatic services

These systems are based on a range of quick tuning transmitters and receivers with computerized management and control. These help unmanned transmitting and receiving stations. A slight routine maintenance is enough for these. Remote control facilities can be applied to each equipment. The following units are used to control the fundamental equipment.

- Transmitter control panel (H 101–6812).
- Receiver control panel (H 102–6812).
- Multiple equipment systems
- Status display panel (H 103–6811)
- Equipment selector panel (H 104–6811)
- Operator's control panel (H 105–6811)

Transmitter control panel is microprocessor based unit. It makes all operational controls and revertive displays needed to remotely control a drive/amplifier combination of an H 1542 drive and H 1042/H 1141 amplifier or an H 1082/3 T transmitter. Receiver control panel is a microprocessor based unit. It gives all operational controls. It also gives revertive displays to remotely control a single H 2542 receiver or a diversity pair.

In case of multiple equipment systems, a number of equipment are controlled by one control panel.

Status display panel displays the operational status of the equipment under control. It displays either transmitter status or receiver status.

Equipment selector panel is placed into the system between the control panel and the multiplex. It helps the operator in selecting the equipment to be controlled. Operator's control panel is available for use where operators need access to the equipment which is being controlled from a central point. For completing the system control panels for aerial selection, station alarms and rotable log periodic aerials exist.

8.1.1 Concept of the Basic System

The basic system can be described as follows

- Controllable and revertive data are available over a four wire system through modems.
- In the control direction, its microprocessor gets parallel commands from the panel controls.
- This organizes them into a serial data stream for sending to the controlled equipment.
- The controlled equipment microprocessor reforms the serial information in parallel commands after receiving the serial data stream.
- A change in the equipment occurs.
- Revertive information from the controlled equipment is processed by the microprocessor.
- The same is passed in serial form over the revertive path to the control panels.
- It is then converted into parallel data for the various displays and indicators.
- Data words are the same to a teleprinter character. These consist of 7 bits + 1 bit parity framed by 1 start and 2 stop bits.
- External line signalling rates of 50, 110, 300 and 600 bands exist.
- Of course, the slower speed would cover mostly the requirements.
- Standard CCITT V24/V28 interfaces are utilized throughout.
- Each processor unit possesses two duplex serial input–output ports.
- One is used for control purposes and other is needed for paired equipment. They are self-announcing/interrogating on connection to the system.
- The system gives proper recognition to the changes which are operator induced or spontaneous.
- Standard signalling modems are employed.
- A plug in modem card is added to the processor unit at each end for single equipment systems.

Here, the following equipments will be required.

    (a) Remote control panel
    (b) Two modem cards
    (c) Two low speed intersite lines

Further option is a parallel interface card.

8.1.2 General Features of the Transmitter

General features of the transmitter of solid state devices are as follows:

- Fast frequency changes can be tolerated easily

- Operation is soft soft-fail.
- MTBF (Meantime between failure) is very high and MTTR (Mean time to repair or meantime to recovery) is very low.
- Modular construction is compact.
- There is built-in test equipment and status monitoring scheme is available.
- There is suitable facility for container installation.
- There is arrangement of remote and extended control.
- There will be front access only for easy service and maintenance.
- There should be built in transmit receive aerial switch.

Figure 8.1 describes the block diagram of a fully automatic linear h.f. transmitter. This type of transmitter works in the 1.6–30 MHz frequency band. Its design is of compact modular type. It consists of

- drive unit;
- preamplifier unit;
- two 500 W amplifiers complete with individual switched mode dc supplies; and
- feeder matching unit.

8.2 MULTI-ACCESS RADIO TELEPHONE SYSTEM (MARTS)

'MARTS' can be described as follows:

- Modular construction allowing step by step expansion from 1 subscriber to 60 subscribers.
- It works continuously with proper reliability.
- Physical cables are not present.
- Interfacing is made with any telephone exchange.
- Fault location is checked by automatic or manual system.
- Modems exist for computer hook-up data or link of telecommunication.

8.2.1 Composition of MARTS

The MARTS consists of three sub-systems.

- Exchange terminal equipment (ETE)
- Radio base station (RBS)
- Subscriber radio terminal (SRT)

The ETE is installed in the same location as telephone exchange.

The RBS is installed at an elevation or on a tower and it develops a 2-way radio link between subscribers and the exchange through the ETE.

The SRT develops a radio link to the telephone exchange through RBS and ETE.

8.2.2 Uses of MARTS

- The MARTS helps rural subscriber by providing services which are offered by the national telephone-network.

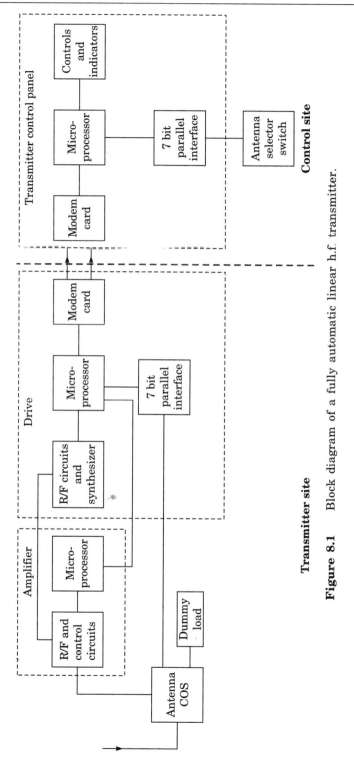

Transmitter site

Figure 8.1 Block diagram of a fully automatic linear h.f. transmitter.

- Utilized by organizations operating in far-flung areas and for ship-to ship and ship to shore communications
- Used in ports, railways, oil fields and mining areas.

8.3 INSTRUMENT LANDING SYSTEM LOCATION (ILSL)

The ILSL has the following features:

- The ILSL satisfies operational performance as laid down in category I/II/III of the International Civil Aviation Organization (ICAO).
- Its reliablity is very high.
- It is a solid state device. It has dual transmitters installed in each localizer and Glide path cabinet.
- It incorporates triple redundancy monitoring with automatic change over and alarm.
- It consists of mechanical modulator of unique design.
- It has a remote control facility on a single pair. It uses FSK multiplexing technique.
- It exhibits a high degree of commonality of units between localizer and glidepath.
- Module exchange service can be made of low cost.
- It is immune to mains power failure.
- It can easily adjust to site conditions with suitable aerials.

Instrument landing system (ILS) is a low approach guidance system. It is fundamentally a system in which ground equipment transmits radio signals on account of guiding an aircraft towards landing. The main important thing is that the ILS will be useful for various conditions of weather.

It will be useful for the following

- The weather exhibits clear skies.
- The weather exhibits limitless visibility to dense clouds.
- The weather may provide blinding blizzards or typhoon like winds.

This instrument should be sophisticated because even a small error in descent rate can develop the outcome in a hard landing short of runway or a late touchdown with a resulting overshoot. The allowable margin between a successful and unsuccessful landing in the vertical and horizontal planes is approximately a quarter of a degree.

Figure 8.2 describes the block diagram of localizer/glidepath equipment.

The main components of this equipment are as follows:

- Transmitter
- Modulator
- RF distribution unit
- Co-axial distribution unit
- Aerial distribution unit
- Monitor units and alarm units
- Local and remote control units
- Power supply unit
- Aerial array

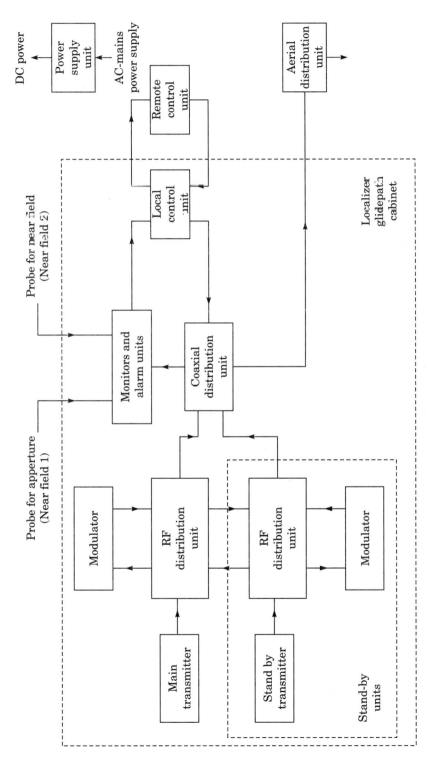

Figure 8.2 Block diagram of localizer/glidepath equipment in flight system.

The transmitter gives the radio frequency power of the localizer/glidepath equipment. It generally operates at the frequency range of 108 MHz to 112 MHz band / 328 MHz to 336 MHz band.

The modulator unit obtains two signals in r.f. phase with each other from the r.f. distribution unit and gives the following modulated signals back to the r.f. distribution unit.

- a double sideband signal being separated from the carrier frequency by 90 Hz;
- a signal in audio frequency phase quadrature with the above;
- a double sideband signal being separated from the carrier frequency by 150 Hz; and
- a signal in audio frequency phase quadrature with the above.

The output of the transmitter is collected in R.F. distribution unit and is divided into two parts. One part is further divided into two equal signals in r.f. phase with each other and taken to the mechanical modulator. The outputs of the mechanical modulator are joined in the R.F. distribution unit with the original and the phase shifted other part of the transmitter r.f. output for providing the following outcomes.

- A carrier frequency with an associated pair of double sidebands. The double sidebands are separated from the carrier frequency by 90 Hz and 150 Hz respectively. The mean frequency of the double sidebands will be in phase with the carrier frequency. This is also termed *course carrier and sidebands* (CSB).
- A *pair of double side bands:* The sidebands are separated from the suppressed carrier frequency by 90 Hz and 150 Hz respectively. The mean frequency components of 90 Hz sidebands are 180° out of phase with those of the 100 Hz sidebands. This is also termed *course sidebands only* (course SBO).
- *Signal being present only in localizer equipment:* It is termed *clearance carrier and sidebands* (Clearance CSB). It is similar to course CSB with all sidebands phase shifted by approximately 22.5° with respect to the carrier. The audio frequency phase of the modulation tone will be in phase quadrature with the audio frequency phase of the corresponding course CSB.
- *Clearance sideband only:* It is termed *clearance SBO*. It is present in localizer equipment. The audio frequency phase of the modulation tone is in phase quadrature with the audio frequency phase of the corresponding course SBO.

Co-axial distribution unit gets r.f. outcomes from the two r.f. distribution connected with the main and standby transmitter units. Under normal scenario, it supplies the aerial distribution unit and the internal r.f. load respectively. The interchanging of load connections is made with specific command from the Local/Remote control unit.

Aerial distribution unit gets the output signals from the co-axial distribution unit. It supplies the aerial system with the combination of the signals at the appropriate power levels and phase relationships needed for obtaining the requisite course and clearance radiation patterns.

Monitor units examine the performance of the localizer/glidepath equipment always.

It also checks the acceptability of the radiation pattern received from the associated aerial array. In case of operation performance category III, four monitor unit sets exist. They monitor the following.

- main transmitter;
- standby transmitter;

- aperture (near field 1); and
- aperture (near field 2).

Each monitor unit set consists of three monitor units. These act as follows:

- one monitoring the width
- one monitoring the position
- one monitoring the clearance of radiation pattern.

The parameters of the signal monitored are:

- r.f. level
- modulation sum and difference in depth of modulation

The above is understood utilizing probes in the equipment and the field. One alarm unit is connected with each monitor unit set.

Local and remote control units give local and remote control facility respectively for the operation of localizer/slide path equipment.

Remote operation, for localizer/glide path is made on a single pair by utilizing FSK multiplexing techniques.

Regarding the power supply unit, the whole equipment gets dc power from six batteries on continuous charge.

The localizer aerial array is a 26 m/56 m wide, 5.4 m/3.6 m high array. It consists of 12/24 dipoles with corner reflectors or reflector fence.

Otherwise, low profile 2.1 m high aerials would be found. Glide path aerials are generally of three types.

- 2–element null-reference array
- 2–element sideband-reference array
- 3–element type *M* with and without quadrature clearance.

Glide path arrays are installed on masts at heights between 9 m and 17 m.

8.4   LOW POWER TV TRANSMITTER

Very low power TV transmitters are needed for the remote, hilly areas and islands under the TV network. The merit of this type of TV system is that it does not require whole time technical staff for operating the system. It can be mounted at any place. The cost is also very modest. The system gets TV reception from INSAT series satellites in the S-Band and then the same is sent in the normal TV Broadcast band after proper processing. The whole system operates on rechargeable battery bank. The battery bank is charged through an array of solar photovoltaic panels. The advantage is that it can serve the rural community living within 5 km radius with the help of an omni-directional aerial. The system has an ability to perform on 230 volts, 50 Hz ac mains supply.

Here, 6.3 m diameter parabolic aerial is used. This aerial receives S-Band satellite TV Broadcast signals from INSAT. The aerial unit amplifies the very weak received signals. The down-converter unit installed at the hub of the aerial converts the amplified signal to 70 MHz IF. The 70 MHz IF signal is passed to an INDOOR UNIT with the help of a coaxial cable. The control unit gives control signals to the down converter and the indoor unit. The indoor unit finally demodulates the satellite FM signal to Video and Audio signals. The control unit gives necessary interface signals and as a result the TV transmitter system becomes on for broadcasting the picture and sound signals.

The unattended dual low power TV transmitter consists of:

- Two 10-W transmitters.
- Automatic changeover unit.

The 10-W transmitter consists of

- TV Exciter
- Low power amplifier
- Notch filter unit
- Auxiliary power supply unit

The automatic change over unit comprises:

- Auto switching unit (ASU)
- Changeover unit (COU)

8.5 HIGH DEFINITION TELEVISION (HDTV)

High definition television has a receiver with more natural and realistic viewing experience. The speciality of this TV can be described as follows:

- *A wide screen presentation.* It has a diagonal display of 40–50 inches.
- It has an aspect ratio 16:9 whereas in the conventional existing TV, it is 4:3.
- The horizontal and vertical resolution is approximately double than that of conventional TV.
- There is an improvement in the quality of picture. The improvement is done by removing some of the artefacts available with today's transmission system.
- The multichannel high quality digital sound is used.

The most important thing of HDTV is that some fairly complex signal processing is made in this TV so that bandwidth compression is possible in this type of TV. Furthermore, the compression can be made by a factor of about four times. As a result, the channels that are found currently do not need large bandwidth for delivering high quality signals to the consumer. For the rapid growth of new algorithms of VLSI, this fairly complex signal processing is now being developed.

8.5.1 Signal Processing and Bandwidth Compression

Here, the television signal is considered as a three-dimensional signal. Time is taken as the third dimension. The horizontal sampling along each TV line produces a signal which is sampled in all three dimensions. The process of bandwidth compression is now obtained by discarding some of the sampling, i.e. by subsampling. The sampling theorem describes that if one-dimensional analogue signal is sampled at a sampling frequency F, the sampling procedure gives rise to an infinite number of repeats of the signal spectrum at multiples of F in the frequency domain. Hence, if the original spectrum is not band limited to $F/2$, the first repeat spectrum would overlap the original spectrum making aliasing. The sampling frequency is reduced and additional repeat spectra are made by reducing the data rate of the original signal by subsampling.

If alternate samples are to be removed, the sampling frequency will be changed to $F/2$. Obviously, at that time the signal is to be band limited to $F/4$ for avoiding aliasing.

The above one-dimensional analysis can be made for other two dimensions, i.e. the second and third dimensions.

8.6 CELLULAR RADIO

Recently, cellular radio telephone services are making rapid headway in providing mobile telephones for automobiles and for use in the home, office and on the street. Cellular radio helps in emergency communications and disaster management. The main difference between the conventional mobile telephone service and the cellular system is in the distribution of service. The cellular techniques help the same frequency to be used several times in the same urban environment. In case of cellular techniques, a specified area is divided into discrete regions or cells. Each of which is acted by a specific band of frequencies. Figure 8.3 describes the cellular system. It is a cellular service formed by hexagonal cells. It is also termed seven cell site. It repeats the pattern with 120° aerials. Each cell has a base station.

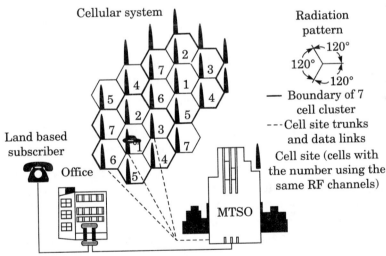

Figure 8.3 Idea of cellular system.

The base station switches transmit/receive calls to and from any mobile unit situated in the cell. Base stations are joined to a mobile telecommunication switching office (MTSO). The objective of MTSO is to record call information for billing purposes.

Figure 8.4 shows the schematic diagram of an MTSO system. In a cellular system, there is provision for future growth in demand. The cells can be divided into smaller cells. The method is called 'cell-splitting'.

The major design features of the cellular systems are as follows:

- Adaptability of the system should be made to traffic density.
- Capability of the system should be there for serving many thousands of uses of mobile.
- At the time of conversation, communication quality is to be monitored.

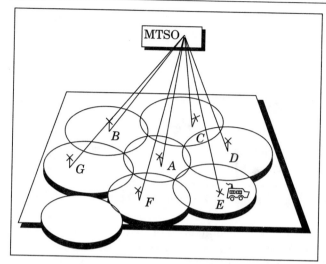

Figure 8.4 Schematic diagram of mobile telecommunication switching office system.

- The system should have the capability to provide service to hand-held portable phones and mobile units.
- A built-in tariff charging system should be supported by the system.
- Any mobile unit can be capable of calling any other unit anywhere in the specified area.
- The design should be such that the quality of service will be similar to as performed by a wired system.
- The arrangement should be such when a mobile leaves a cell to enter another cell, there will be an automatic 'switching on' of the channel for ensuring uninterrupted service.

The World Administrative Radio Conference (WARC) made a new shared allocation for land mobile services in 1979. It has been found that the 900 MHz band gives an optimum channel capacity and frequency reuse capacity. The WARC made the frequency range of 860–960 MHz for land mobile services. In the UK, the frequency band 935–950 MHz is allotted to cellular base station network transmitters. The cellular telephone receives on the above band and transmits at 890–905 MHz band.

Figure 8.5 shows the block diagram of a typical cellular telephone instrument. The same aerial can be utilized for transmitter and receiver with the help of the diplexer (as shown in Figure 8.5). The diplexer is a pair of filters and the filters help in proper tuning.

8.7 INTEGRATED SERVICES DIGITAL NETWORK (ISDN)

ISDN provides network for telephony, telex, teletex, facsimile and data transmission. In other words, ISDN integrates above services economically. Even it can provide services for video telephony. The main merits of ISDN are

- Cost effectiveness
- Capability
- Universality

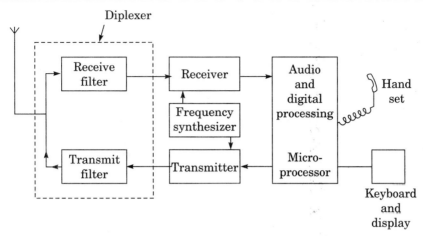

Figure 8.5 Block diagram of cellular telephone instrument.

The first step towards ISDN was taken by A.W. Reewes. Reewes was the discoverer of pulse code modulation (PCM) technique. He invented it in the year 1938. Afterwards, due to the development of semiconductor technology, the concept of ISDN became economically viable. But, it was felt in the year 1964 by the Consultative Committee of International Telegraph and Telephone (CCITT) and the organization of International Telecommunication Union (ITU) of the United Nations that there was no demand for an integrated network at that time. But, now it is felt that the demand of non-voice services are gradually increasing like anything due to the rapid growth of information technology.

Digitization of the network is the only first step in the direction of ISDN. For the development of ISDN, the most important thing is switching system. The ISDN commercial services in the USA and the UK are given in Table 8.1

Table 8.1 ISDN commercial services in the USA and the UK

Characteristics standard	AMPS (USA)	TACS (UK)	NMT	HCMTS
Frequency band	800 MHz	900 MHz	450 MHz	900 MHz
No of channels	666	1000	200	1000
Peak deviation	12 kHz	9.5 kHz	5 kHz	5 kHz
Control channels	21	21	Variable	1
Channel spacing	39 kHz	25 kHz	25 kHz	25 kHz
Signaling rate	10 kbps	8 kbps	1.2 kbps	300 bps
First implemented	1979	1985	1981	1979

AMPS — Advanced mobile phone service

TACS — Technical advanced communication services

NMT — Nordic mobile telephone

HCMTS — High capacity mobile telephone service

Even today, there are no reliable estimates of the costs for the countries developing ISDN. It is still under confusion whether flat rate is advisable or there should occur different rates for voice and non-voice services.

The comparative study of satellite technology and ISDN is given is Table 8.2.

Table 8.2 Comparative study of satellite technology and ISDN

Satellite technology	*ISDN*
Satellite systems can never meet the exceptionally high standards for the effective and reliable functioning.	The functioning of ISDN is much effective and reliable.
For echo elimination technique and data protocols, the satellite systems are really reliable and effective.	For realization of global ISDN, distance independent nature of satellite system is really essential.
A satellite helps in horizontal spread of ISDN by giving network connectivity to remote business subscriber.	The conventional ISDN link is found uneconomic many times.
The flexibility of satellite system is excellent. In case of emergencies and natural disasters the traffic can be routed from fixed and mobile locations easily.	The flexibility is not very good.
It can carry heavy traffic to the tune of 280 Mbps and also it is found economically viable for lighter traffic.	It is not excellent for both heavy traffic and low traffic compared to those of satellite system.
In data transmission packet switching it has major limitation.	There is less limitation in this case.

8.8 OPTICAL FIBRE COMMUNICATION

The main components of optical fibre communication system are shown in Figure 8.6

- Source
- Modulation
- Transmission medium
- Repeaters
- Detector
- Amplification
- Demodulation

Source

Generally the following sources are used.

- LED
- Laser

For low-bit rate systems using multimode fibre, LED is generally chosen as source. The choice of source generally depends on the choice of medium. LED is a pin junction device.

It emits light and that depends on the forward bias current through the junction. The light output is proportional to the diode current and that is why, modulation is a very simple procedure. Generally, where reasonably wideband non-coherent light is required, LED source is applied. In case of high speed system using mono mode fibre, a coherent light source is needed. In that case *laser* source is required. Gallium arsenide laser is generally used. Lasers are generally more expensive than light emitting diodes. Lasers need more expensive drive circuits. Lasers are less reliable than LED and that is why, these require more frequent servicing and replacement.

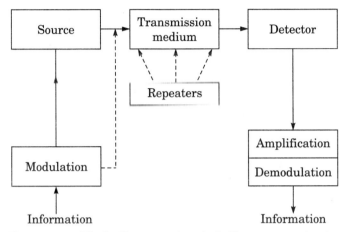

Figure 8.6 Block diagram of optical fibre communication.

Transmission medium

Transmission medium can be categorized as follows.

- Multi mode
- Monomode
- Graded-index fibre
- Fibre bundle

For data rates up to about 10 Mbits/s, a multimode fibre is utilized due to the following reasons:

- Ease of termination
- Lower cost per metre of fibre.

In many applications bit rates exceeding 10 Mbits are needed. Monomode fibre is used in that case. Digital television is one of the examples. In many cases, it is found better and at the same time cheaper to use a bundle of multi-mode fibres rather than a single monomode fibre for higher transmission rates. Digital telephony is one of such examples. It also enchances the reliability, otherwise it is also not advisable to make serveral thousand telephone calls to one single fibre strand which is not even thicker than a human hair.

Detector

The detectors can be categorized as follows:

- *P-i-n* photodiode

- Avalanche photodiode
- Photomultiplier

The *P-i-n* photodiode is used as detector for low speed inexpensive system. The advantages of the *P-i-n* photodiode as detector are:

- Temperature and bias stability is quite appreciable
- Cost is low

The main disadvantage is that it is less sensitive.

Modulation

The light source is modulated by variation in current through the device junction. The light emitted from the junction is approximately proportional to the device current. This is the method of analogue modulation.

Digital modulation is performed by using binary signalling. It is done by switching the current between zero and the value of current providing emission without the overload of junction. Actually, the current becomes zero when there is no emission. But the fact is that, in practice, the current is never found zero because of faster switching. Therefore, a higher modulation rate can be obtained if the minimal flow of current is kept. In the digital system, modulation of the light beam is possible in a way external to the emitting device. The light beam is deflected opto-electronically. As a result, it does not couple into the fibre for generating the zero transmission signal state. Suitable devices for the above technique is under development. That is why, direct electrical modulation technique is preferred. In case of analogue modulation, the external modulation of the light beam does not claim feasible technique.

Demodulation

In case of light detector, the output current is approximately proportional to the power of the light signal falling on the photosensitive junction of the detector device. The signal is then amplified and processed for getting an estimate in the receiver of the transmitted signal.

Repeaters

The repeaters are nothing but detection and retransmission of the information bearing light beam. These are required depending on the following:

- Length of the fibre connection
- Loss coefficient of the fibre connection.

Standard of repeater spacings for different systems is given in Table 8.3

Table 8.3 Standard of repeater spacings for different systems

System	Information rate (Mbits/s)	Repeater spacing (km)
LED and multi-mode	2.048	10.0
optical fibre of loss	8.448	6.0
3dB/km	34.368	1.7
LASER and monomode	2.048	15
optical fibre of loss	8.448	13
3 dB/km	34.368	10.4
	139.264	8.5
	565.000	6.5

8.9   SATELLITES TRACKING THROUGH EARTH STATION TECHNOLOGY

The main features of earth station technology from the point of view of satellite in our country are as follows:

- India has more than 400 earth stations in the INSAT network.
- These are used for different purposes, such as
    - (a) Telecommunications
    - (b) TV networking
    - (c) Radio networking
    - (d) Weather data gathering from unmanned stations
- Three earth stations are used for overseas communications using Intelsat
- Twenty Indian ships have a marine communication service utilizing Immersat network.
- Community TV through satellite is of immense importance.

Earth stations are used alongwith space crafts in orbit for various applications in different frequency bands. Major earth stations are now going to use microcomputer controlled subsystems being monitored and operated remotely with advanced data logging facilities. Small earth stations even act with demand assigned multiple access (DAMA) for optimal use of transponder on board in satellites. Advances in earth station technology have been in progress in the last ten years. The reasons for the above achievement are as follows.

- Development in VLSI
- Development in signal processing
- Development in digital speech interpolation and spread spectrum techniques
- Development in military communication.

8.10   ADVANCES IN SATELLITE NETWORKING

Research is going on to improve the potentialities of satellite communications. The attention is given to the following aspects.

- Since operation is to be made with a large number of very small earth stations, larger transmit power and more complex aerials are needed.
- Efficient signal processors and switching equipment are needed.
- Reduction of the transmission routes is needed for direct connections between satellites.
- Higher frequency bands are necessary for enlarging the available bandwidth and the transmission capacity.

The development of technology will help to use telecommunication satellites for critical signal processing. Further research is going on for extending and improving terrestrial telecommunication technology. The vital work is the digitization of the signals and the merging of processing with the transmission of information. A creation of a world wide service integrated telecommunications network is being established. The ultimate goal of this research is to provide users with all the telecommunications services being desired through a single network in space communications technology. The work to be done on manned and unmanned missions is increasing constantly. Hence, the demands on the telecommunication transmissions are also increasing. Attention is provided towards the competition between satellite and optic fibre technology. Truly, a future world wide terrestrial network will be provided by the satellite network. The work to be done by future satellites can be categorized as follows:

- The work includes services for the transmission of telephone calls and television signals over long distances. The above telecommunication satellite services will be mostly performed by fibre optic cables.

This work consists of the following:

  (a) Communications services with different needs from the point of view bandwidths, partner stations and transmission lines.
  (b) Data collection and data distribution services for large areas and telecommunications services for countries where it would be very difficult, expensive and technically critical to construct terrestrial networks.
- The work connected with application of terrestrial mobile services to areas which are not served by proper terrestrial infrastructure. Rather the spacecraft in the planned global telecommunications is to be included.

Figure 8.7 describes an integration of satellites into an information satellite network. Satellites are generally classified according to their performance as follows:

- *Satellites for national and regional use:* These are developed for operation with small and extremely small earth stations.
- *Satellites for international use:* These connect terrestrial networks through broadband transmission channels.
- *Relay satellites:* These satisfy the requirements of manned and unmanned space travel. These allow communication with space stations, space transporters and platforms. These are also used for continual connections, for example, Earth observation.

A lot of research is in progress for information satellites (INFOSAT). The satellites of the above three areas would be interconnected permanently. Applying time-division and space division multiplexing techniques, the signals can be exchanged between the satellites and the terrestrial subscribers. Exchanges in the terrestrial networks can also be connected to the national information satellites. Mobile subscribers can also be connected to the national/regional information satellites in the frequency ranges required for these services.

Radio and TV services can also be integrated into the information satellite network. The connections among the satellites help the programmes to be broadcast live from one country to another. Moveover, it can be also possible to transmit high definition television (HDTV) signals. Radio-paging systems can be extended for covering the whole world. By this method, it is possible to contact subscribers anywhere. Of course, the caller must have an approximate idea of the location of the subscribers. With the help of a simple transmitter available in the papers and a location finding system integrated in the satellite, it will not also be difficult to attain the subscribers even if their location are not known. Even, with the help of excellent processors, information satellites can do complicated measuring and control work. Sensors in the satellites and on the earth can visualize processes on the surface of earth and in inner space. By direct processing, the results can be obtained. The signal processing unit on board helps the evaluated results to be processed for meeting the requirements of different users by feeding into the proper transmit channels of the satellite.

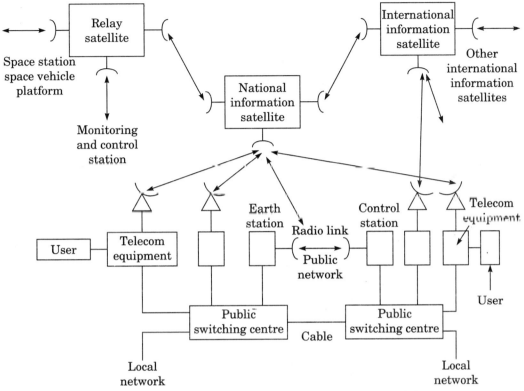

Figure 8.7 Information satellite network in integrated form.

The main features of the design of INFOSATs can be described as follows:

(a) The connections to different users are performed through several aerials and transmitters/receivers in different frequency ranges.

(b) Transmitter and receiver converters transmit the signal in the intermediate frequency ranges with the help of switching matrix.

(c) The terminals for communication among the satellites are also joined directly to the switching matrix.

(d) The modulators and demodulators are required for signal processing on board. They are connected to the switching matrix.

(e) The control and monitoring equipment examines all the subsystems and equipment and assure that they are functioning accurately. Hence, the sensors can also be installed on the satellites. They help to visualize the processes on the earth and in inner space and finally transfer the measured data to the evaluation equipment.

Through information satellite (INSAT) network following services can be performed:

- Data collection services for large areas with many data transmitter stations.
- Radio and distribution services to many users over a large area.
- Mobile radio services being combined with location finding services.
- Earth observation services up to the extent of environmental protection services.

- Telecommunication services among subscribers, for example on ships, in aircraft and space vehicles.
- Telecommunication services among subscribers with a low volume of traffic.
- Covering entire world radio-paging services.

It will be possible to supply all the subscribers with a future global network with all required information by integrating INFOSATs into the global terrestrial network. Obviously, at that time it is not the point where the subscribers are situated, because all the information is obtained by the user terminal from satellite directly or through the terrestrial network.

The integral part of the planned, world wide broadband telecommunication network is the information satellite network. That is why, a planning is to be made such that the satellite network and terrestrial network can be closely co-ordinated. Since signal processing takes place in the satellite itself and many small earth stations work directly with the information satellites, modification in the arrangement is being made. The most important initial point being stressed upon is to examine in detail the possibilities and limits of information satellite. The operation of an open network complemented by information satellites will be obviously complex. There is no doubt that information satellites play an essential role in the world wide telecommunication system. A pilot programme is needed to facilitate the introduction of the technologies and techniques in which many promising services would be available on a trial basis and tested. Broadband space and environmental monitoring services are generally suitable for this purpose. The objective of the pilot programme is to develop and test an intelligent experimental satellite with terminals for communication satellites. At the time of the test, several partial trial networks are to be connected to one another and to other satellite systems and also to terrestrial networks. For establishing information satellite technology as an entirely operation system, the pilot design is being implemented for confirming whether the proposals can be practically applied and to find out difficulties which we have to face and the necessary remedy for the same.

8.11 TECHNOLOGICAL GROWTH OF SATELLITE COMMUNICATION TECHNOLOGY

With the development in satellite technology, weight, size and RF power, a logical amount of increase of available channel capacity is being observed. Presently, very small aperture earth terminals (VSATs) called microstations with aerials of 1.5 m–2.5 m are available. Several thousand such terminals are being used for business communications. The trend for utilizing very small earth stations in customer houses for all types of business communication will continue. Even the microstations will be utilized for interconnection of personal computers and for other personal communications. Satellite capacity is increasing day by day. Widespread utilization of 6/4 GHz for satellite communication is the cause of severe interference co-ordination problems with other satellite systems and terrestrial systems. In future 14/11 GHz and 30/20 GHz band will appear in common use. Higher bandwidth will be available at higher frequency bands and interference co-ordination will be quite easier because a few satellite systems and terrestrial systems are being planned to be under operation. Even it will be possible to utilize certain portions of the frequency band for satellite services only.

Moreover, for higher frequencies, the aerial size will be smaller. Presently, satellite repeater is fundamentally a simple combination of amplifier and frequency changer. Regenerative repeaters can be utilized with digital transmission for isolating up link and down link noise.

This will increase the channel capacity and link performance. Sufficient amount of multiplexing/switching functions can be adopted on board. Earth station size, complexity and costs will decrease. Even unattended microearth stations can be designed for adjusting particular applications for voice, video or data.

Technology in this respect is more advanced due to the development of digital signal processing techniques. It offers remarkable advantages for processing of voice signals, for encoding, error correction, multiplexing and modulation. Quality of voice can be available at bit ratio as low as 4.8 kb/s to 9.6 kb/s. The following applications are praiseworthy for the contribution of digital signal processing.

- Teleconferencing which is highly economical with the use of bandwidth compression techniques.
- Full motion video teleconferencing becomes possible at 64 kb/second.
- Error coding gives a powerful tool for trading earth station size, bandwidth and link performance.
- Different types of modulation schemes can be economically implemented using DSP.
- Digital multiple access techniques such as SSMA and TDMA help in realizing higher capacity and considerable flexibility.
- Digital circuit multiplication equipment helps in obtaining large channel capacities.

Here the advantages of digital speech interpolation with low bit rate encoding can be combined.

Mobile satellite communication is developing day by day through a wide research. Presently, several thousand ships are linked through the INMARSAT (International Maritime Satellite) Organization system for voice, telegraph and data with public telecommunication networks. Aeronautical satellite service has been implemented through the INMARSAT system.

8.12 ADVANCEMENT OF COMMUNICATION IN RURAL AREA

The general structure of a rural telecommunication network is shown in Figure 8.8.

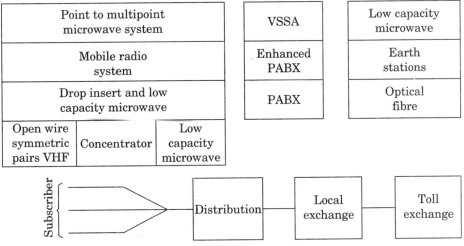

Figure 8.8 VSSA exchange general structure.

The very small stand alone (VSSA) exchange has been shown. Digital technology is the basis of rural networks. It actually integrates a wide range of services. It has the following merits

- It is flexible.
- It is economic.
- It has a range of capacities which can satisfy the present needs and the future growth.
- Services, centralized operation and maintenance are very good.
- It is suitable for outdoor operation under severe climate conditions.
- Different types of electric power sources including solar cells can be utilized.
- Transmission subsystems are being operated over long distances.
- Transmission subsystem is reliable. Even it can be operated unattended. The remote control and supervision of operation and maintenance can be done.
- The transmission subsystem is suitable for crossing difficult areas such as wild forests, swamps and mountain ranges with the help of low capacity point-to-point microwave link or small earth station.
- Many systems are used for subscriber distribution, for example open wire, cable, UHF radio, microwave drop/insert systems, multiaccess radio systems.

The switching of the above scheme has the following important features.

- A full range of exchange equipment for rural networks is being utilized. The range of the same starts from medium/large exchanges to very small stand alone systems.
- The above includes an enhanced PABX (FASTCOM switch). This is used in various activities. Even it is integrated into satellite based networks.
- The modular architectures of the digital switching systems permit exchange equipment to be placed in remote areas nearer to subscribers.
- The remote units are connected through optical fibre or microwave links to help exchanges. The exchanges give the call handling administration and operation and maintenance.
- Subscriber services are more or less same as those of large exchanges in urban areas. Trunks may be either digital or analogue. For this, an additional analogue digital converter is taken.
- The very small stand alone (VSSA) exchange is used in the signalling systems. The above helps to fit into any type of rural network.
- The VSSA exchange is generally of following types.
  - It is housed indoors in standard switching racks
  - It may be housed in a weather proof cabinet for outdoor use.

The main features of the transmission system can be narrated as follows:

- Long haul digital radio relay systems are utilized to link rural switches to the main network over distances up to 50 km in a single hop and up to a few hundred kilometres utilizing relay stations. The common frequencies are 0.45 GHz, 0.9 GHz, 1.5 GHz and 2.5 GHz.
- The cost effective Fastcom small earthstation is made for connecting remote, isolated areas through satellite.

- Earthstations are arranged in a star or mesh configuration linking several rural networks.
  - The above structure may cover the whole country and that is why, a domestic satellite (DOMSAT) network is needed. Figure 8.9 describes the above.
  - Fastcom stations can give telephone, telegraph and data transmission links and receive audio and video broadcasts.
  - Transmission is generally made utilizing the frequency division multiple access/ single channel per carrier mode (FDMA/SCPC). SCPC modulation may be either analogue or digital. In case of the demand of medium and high capacity routes, channels are usually multiplexed on to one or more synchronous carriers (64 kbits/s to 2 or 8 Mbit/s carriers) utilizing multiple channel per carrier (MCPC) techniques. The above systems are generally used to link the main stations of a meshed or semi meshed DOMSAT network. Earthstations channel equipment is made such as to interface with circuit multiplication equipment that will allow the capacity of each MCPC channel being multiplied by a factor of 5 or even more. For illustration it can make 150 voice channels utilizing a 2 Mbits/modem. A Fastcom station fundamentally consists of two assemblies
  - Aerial system
  - Telecommunication equipment

The aerial system consists of the following.

- A main and secondary reflector
- Primary feed and duplexer
- Low noise amplifier
- Automatic tracking device

The size of the aerial is based on the following factors

- Equivalent isotropic radiated power or the transmit power multiplied by the aerial gain obtained from the satellite.
- Equivalent isotropic power transmitted by the stations.
- Authorized power transmitted in sidelobes, which are the lobes of the far field radiation pattern that are not the main beam. Actually, the terms 'beam' and 'lobe' are synonyms. An antenna radiation pattern is more commonly termed *beam pattern*. The power density in the sidelobes is generally much less than that in the main beam. Figure 8.10 describes the sidelobes.

The main features of the telecommunication equipment can be described as follows.

- This equipment is kept in a small house. This can work outdoors in severe climatic conditions.
- The transmitted signal modulates a carrier. The frequency of the same is obtained by a synthesizers within the 121–158 MHz intermediate frequency band. Synthesizers are tuneable in 0.5 MHz steps.
- Different single channel per carrier (SCPC) frequencies are added in a combiner and then the same is transformed to the RF band. Then the RF carriers are amplified in a power amplifier.

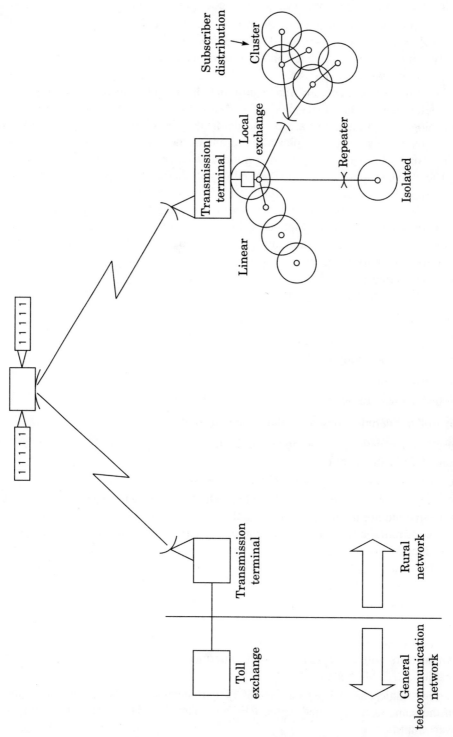

Figure 8.9 Domestic satellite (DOMSAT) network.

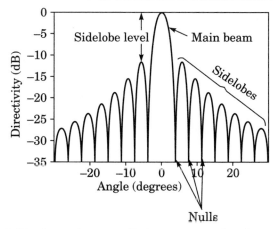

Figure 8.10 An antenna radiation pattern showing sidelobes.

Again on the receiving side, the single channel per carrier (SCPC) signal from the satellite is amplified by the low noise amplifier and then down converted utilizing a dual frequency changer.

- After developing 121–158 MHz band, the carriers are distributed to the various SCPC channel units by the intermediate frequency divider. Each channel unit obtains all SCPC carriers but synthesizer selects one of them.

- Fastcom stations can be installed rapidly even on roughly prepared sites. Small diameter aerials can be placed on a simple concrete slab. Even building is not needed since the equipment is contained in a sand proof housing which helps it to bear severe climatic conditions. No local operator is needed since the station is entirely stand alone and remote supervision is possible. Even in the area where electrical power is not available, the low power consumption of the equipment allows power to be delivered from solar cells.

The distribution of the rural system has the following important features.

- Rural areas require longer subscriber lines. When the distance exceeds three kilometres, point to multipoint access radio systems give the best ways of implementing local networks.

- RURTEL system can work up to 320 subscribers spreadover a long area with repeaters. The following performances are being made.

  (a) subscriber line connections for conventional and coin box-telephones;
  (b) data transmission;
  (c) telex operation at up to 300 baud.

- RURTEL acts as a concentrator utilizing time division multi-access techniques. 1.5 or 2.4 GHz bands are used for transmission over point to multipoint radio links. High quality transmission is obtained with the help of digital modulation and regeneration in repeater stations.

8.13   SPEECH PROCESSING TECHNOLOGIES

Speech is the most important form of communication between human beings. Speech recognition and synthesis technologies have been developed a lot due to the improvement in VLSI technology. Speech processing algorithms have also been progressed much. Universal high performance multiprocessor system is also used for isolated and connected speech recognition, speech coding and speech synthesis.

Three basic speech processing algorithms have been in utilization in the microprocessor system.

- Speech recognition algorithm.
- Speech coding algorithm.
- Text to speech algorithm

The main features of *speech recognition algorithm* can be described as follows:

- It depends on single stage dynamic time warping for connected word recognition.
- This can also be applied to isolated words.
- Feature vectors, i.e. selected measurement are found out from the digitized input signal.
- The feature vectors of the unknown utterance are compared with the speech patterns of all reference templates.
- The reference templates are based on the accumulated Euclidian distance among unknown words and the reference templates.
- This is done utilizing dynamic time warping.
- Finally, the reference word with the smallest accumulated distance is selected as the recognized word. The capacity of the system for real time speech recognition is approximately 1000 reference templates.
- For connected word recognition the syntax has to be realized.
- A finite state syntax is to be used.
- The finite state syntax is entered by the user through an interactive programme.
- The ending node of the syntax is attained.
- The best matching phrase is found out by analyzing the words being stored in the phrase buffer for selecting the best phrase from among all the possible stored phrases.
- The above type of phrase selection is termed *backtracing* since it starts with the last word and goes back to the first.
- The analysis depends on the minimum accumulated distance between the stored templates and unknown utterance.
- Silence templates are also kept in the algorithm for the comparison between the speech and silence.

In the clear explanation, the process of electronically converting a speech waveform into words is being followed. It can be more generalized as the process of extracting a linguistic notion from a sequence of sounds. This is an acoustic event which may encompass linguistically relevant components. Such as words or phrases and irrelevant components, for example, ambient noise, extraneous and partial words in an utterance.

To convert a speech waveform into a sequence of words, involves several important steps.

- A microphone picks up the acoustic signal of the speech to be recognized and converts it into an electrical signal.
- A modern speech recognition system requires the electrical signal being represented digitally with the help of analogue to digital converter. Then it can be processed by digital computer or microprocessor.
- The speech signal is then analyzed for producing a representation consisting of salient features of the speech.
- The feature of the speech is derived from its short-time spectrum which is measured successively over short-time windows of length 20–30 milliseconds overlapping at intervals of 10–20 ms. Each short-time spectrum is transformed into a feature vector.
- The temporal sequence of the above feature vectors form a speech pattern.

Several algorithms are available for speech analysis and synthesis. How do we choose a particular algorithm depends on the bit rate and quality constraints. For example, a 32-kbit/second adaptive differential pulse code modulation (ADPCM) is taken for high quality speech coding.

A diphone concatenation approach is utilized for text to speech synthesis. This methodology is being used effectively in many different languages. Of course, for each language, a different phonetic and linguistic analysis is to be undertaken for identifying the optimal set of diphones. Diphones are obtained from natural speech by a segmentation programme. This will identify the steady state parts of speech. The text to speech conversion consists of two main parts.

- Linguistic processing
- Speech synthesis

The *linguistic processing* means the segmentation of written text into diphones and development of the prosodic contour. On the other hand, *speech synthesis* is possible by concatenating the code diphones.

Figure 8.11 describes the block diagram of speech processing system interfaced to a host computer. The host computer may be VME system or personal computer. The high performance speech processing system is interfaced to a host computer, through a standard VME bus or PC bus.

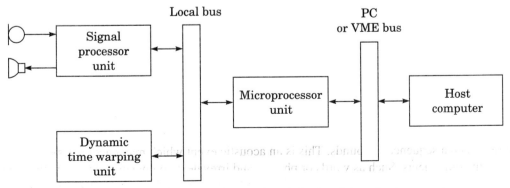

Figure 8.11 Speech processing system interfaced to a host computer.

The VME bus is a computer bus standard. It is originally developed for the motorola 68000 line of CPUs. VME is the acronym for VERSA-module Europe. The hardware for the multiprocessor speech processing system has three main functional units.

- A front end unit for digital signal processing
- A dynamic time warping unit for fast template matching
- A microprocessor for system control

Figure 8.12 describes a block diagram of the front end board of digital signal processing.

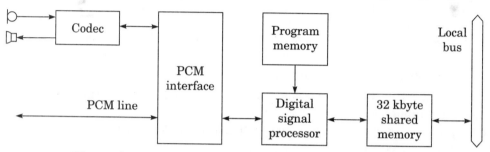

Figure 8.12 Digital signal processing board with CODEC.

The main elements of digital signal processing board with CODEC are as follows

- 'CODEC' for analogue bandpass filtering and analogue/digital conversion of the audio signal;
- A digital signal processor;
- A shared memory for rapid data exchange between the signal processor and microprocessor.

The CODEC is a device or program which is capable of encoding and/or decoding a digital data stream or signal. The analogue signal is sampled at 8 kHz and digitized by a standard PCM codec to develop log coded samples. These samples are transformed to a 12 bit linear scale by a table look up in the DSP. The DSP calculates the short-term energy densities utilizing a digital filter bank and transforms them into the mel cepstrum domain. The mel cepstrum coefficients are sent to the microprocessor and DTW board for matching with the reference vector sequences. Figure 8.13 describes the DTW unit.

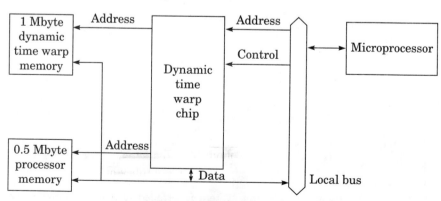

Figure 8.13 DTW unit.

The DTW is constructed as a 2 μm CMOS standard cell gate array with a power consumption of approximately 100 mW. It is a chip which gives the high throughput rate needed for vocabulary of about 1000 words. CMOS is the complementary metal oxide semiconductor. Usually, the CMOS technology is used in microprocessor. The DTW unit interfaces with the general purpose central processing unit, i.e. CPU. The CPU actually controls the DTW chip. In case of pattern comparison in speech recognition, the chip makes the Euclidean distance calculation and finds the DTW path.

The dynamic time warping (DTW) is an algorithm for measuring the similarity between two sequences which may vary into time or speed. For example, similarities in walking patterns would be detected, even if in one video the person is walking slowly and if in another he is walking more quickly or even if there are accelerations or decelerations during the course of one observation. Truly, the DTW is a method that permits a computer to find an optimal match between two given sequences with certain restrictions. Since the chip clock frequency is 10 MHz, the basic DTW cycle for processing one template frame takes 450 ns. Approximately, one thousand templates can be processed in real time, with an average length of forty frames and frame duration 20 ms. The DTW chip can address up to 1 Mbyte of DTW memory.

A standard 16 bit microprocessor is utilized for the CPU. It is operated at 10 MHz. Microprocessor can address up to 512 kbytes of programme and data memory. The CPU performs the following basic tasks

- Bootstrapping of the system;
- Initialization and start up of the signal processor. That is on the front-end board and of the DTW chip;
- Exchange and management of data between the front end and DTW unit;
- To download or upload reference templates or synthesis data from the host computer or to the host computer.

Software for the microprocessor system can be categorized into two main parts

- speech recognition and synthesis programmes.
- application software.

Programmes for the signal processor are implemented in TMS assembly. The software for the microprocessor is developed in both C and assembler languages.

The control and application software is written in C with time critical routines being produced in assembler. In other words, software for speech recognition is developed at SEL and the application software is written by research centres. The SEL offers development services to a wide range of industries.

SEL software private limited is the development arm in India of a Global Technology Group.

The high performance multiprocessor system has been utilized for demonstrating the advantages of speech input/output equipment in modern office communication services. The application to office communication includes the following.

- An automatic voice controlled telephone operator.
- A voice-activated voice mail system developed by SEL.
- A voice actuated sorting machine and telecommunication system.

Figure 8.14 describes the system for voice control of an operator console function. The speech processing system is connected to the operator console through a 2/4 wire interface.

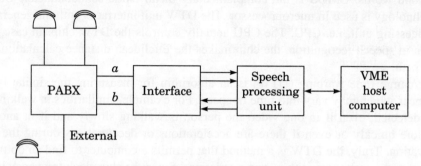

Figure 8.14 Block diagram of voice controlled telephone operator console.

This is controlled by application software running on a VME host computer. The main features of the system are as follows:

- Speech input for dialling;
- Access to PABX features by spoken command;
- Speech output for user guidance and replaying telephone message.

The methodology of operation can be described as follows:

- When the automatic telephone exchange operator is called, the system asks the user to state the name of the called party;
- After getting the confirmation of the recognized party's name, the system converts the name into DTMF tones for the PABX DTMF tone which is the dual tone multifrequency. It is used for telephone signalling over the line in the voice frequency band to the call switching centre;
- If the called subscriber is busy or not available, the caller can keep a message on the speech processing system. This would be delivered automatically and repeatedly to the called party.

This operation occurs at programmable time intervals until it is responded. A total number of 300 names and command can be implemented in the speaker-independent recognition system. Figure 8.15 describes the block diagram of a voice activated sorting machine in a mail room.

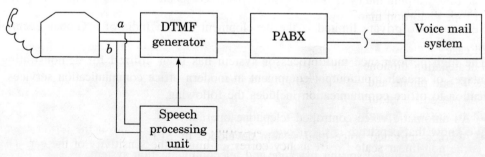

Figure 8.15 A voice activated sorting machine in a mail room.

Here, the speech processing unit is utilized for controlling a voice mail system by voice commands. Here DTMF (Dual tone multi frequency) signals are transmitted either by local or long distance telephone line. The major benefit of speech recognition in this case is the facility for assigning a voice command or command string to a sequence of key strokes by controlling the operation of the voice mail system.

Figure 8.16 describes the system for permitting handicapped persons for communicating with others by telephone. Here the messages are entered through the Braille terminal and converted to speech so that those can be listened in the normal way by the called subscriber. The handicapped person may also get a telephone call through the portable tactile radio paging facility that is connected to the system. Sixty speaker-independent templates can be loaded into the system.

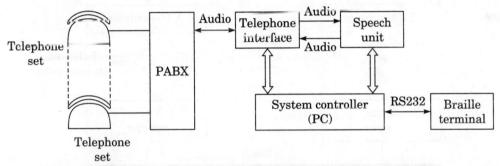

Figure 8.16 System of communications of handicapped persons.

The following terminologies are often used in the speech processing technologies.

- Isolated word recognition
- Accumulated Euclidean distance
- Time warping
- Diphone concatenation
- Prosodic contour
- Mel cepstrum

Isolated word recognition means words or phrases spoken with pauses between words.

The distances are termed Euclidean when the sum of the squarred differences between the components of the feature vectors are considered.

The time warping indicates the warping of one speech pattern on to the other in accordance with a time distortion map between the two patterns. The map is defined as the time warping path.

In case of diphone concatenation, all the possible words in a language can be developed by concatenating diphones. The *diphone* is a speech segment which starts at the steady-state centre of one phone and ends at the steady-state centre of the next phone.

The prosodic contour expresses the intonation of a phrase. Intonation is given by developing the pitch contour depending on the punctuation.

We know that cepstrum is the inverse spectrum of the logarithm of the power spectrum. Mel is the non-linear scale for frequency corresponding to the sensitivity of the ear. The log scale is nothing but non-linear scale.

8.14 TELECOMMUNICATION APPLICATION WITH MULTI-PROCESSOR SYSTEM

A dynamically reconfigurable multiple bus and multiple architecture permit system resources to be shared by all the processors. Figure 8.17 shows a multibus structure.

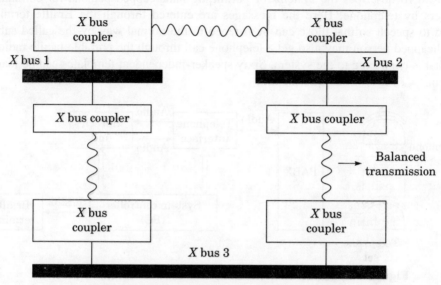

Figure 8.17 Multibus structure with X bus.

The hardware architecture is arranged around a minibus which is termed the *X-bus*.

Now, the capacity of the bus is limited with respect to the data rate and the number of processors can be connected, the system can be extended by coupling several X-buses utilizing X-bus couplers. All the hardware resources, for example, memory, telecommunication devices, disk controllers can be accessed by any processor. It does not depend on the position of structure. The multibus structure helps by developing configurations requiring a large amount of memory. Two X-buses are connected by a pair of identical CBX bus couplers. It has two functions.

- It decouples the two buses, and, as a result, these can operate simultaneously and independently.
- It provides address filtering. It is nothing but the control of access to the memory.

The X bus is generally shared by several processors. This is to be utilized when the same is needed and as small as possible for repetitive and local tasks. For obtaining this objective, each processor is equipped with a local bus for accessing local memory. Figure 8.18 describes the above. The local memory can be accessed by any other system processor through the X-bus.

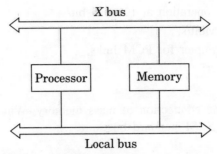

Figure 8.18   Block diagram of local bus for accessing each processor with a local memory.

The memory board is arranged with an address filter which helps local memory to be accessed by the X-bus or by the local bus or both. Each processor possesses an addressing space of 4 Gbytes, arranged into pages. Pages are described as follows.

- The first part is private and cannot be accessed by any other processor.
- The next part is the address accessed by each processor through local bus.
- The last part consists of the general memory address space accessible by the processors through the main bus.

Figure 8.19 describes an input–output structure.

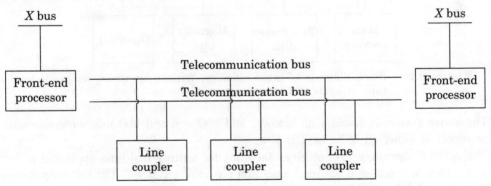

Figure 8.19   Block diagram of an Input–output structure.

With front-end processor, about 128 telecommunication lines can be connected. The interface for these lines is made by transmission coupling boards. Each of which is connected to two telecommunication buses for giving additional security. The operation range of front-end processor is 2 Mbit/s simultaneously in both directions of transmission.

The main transmission couplers consist of

- High level data link control (HDLC);
- Low and medium speed couplers which are capable of managing up to 48 kbits/s lines;
- HDLC high-speed couplers for interfacing up to four 1 Mbit/second lines;
- Asynchronous line couplers which have eight lines/board;
- BSC couplers for facsimile;

- Videotex coupler for operation at 1200/75 bit/s;
- ISDN coupler for 2 Mbit/s;
- Telephone network coupler for PCM links;
- 2 Mbit/s PCM coupler;
- X.21 coupler.

Figure 8.20 describes the connection of mass memory, Winchester disks, magnetic tape and tape streamers through SCSI standard buses.

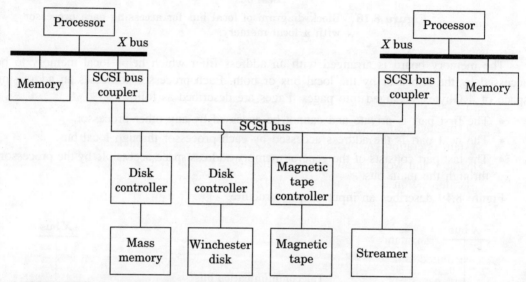

Figure 8.20 Block diagram of mass memory, Winchester disks, magnetic tape and tape streamers.

The above system is found with a tower and 600 mm and 900 mm wide cabinets. The power supply is either 48 V dc or 220 V ac.

The ATHOS operating system gives facilities for writing real-time applications for data communication networks and on-line transaction processing systems. The software description consists of the following.

- *Virtual memory management:* This helps in simplifying user interfaces. It also protects an application against interference from other applications running on the same system.
- *Efficient file management:* The efficient file management offers the following.
  (a) optimized disk access;
  (b) flexible management of physical media;
  (c) control of shared partitions;
  (d) files and records and data integrity within a transaction processing environment
- *Operator and terminal management system:* This gives the following.
  (a) multiple sessions;
  (b) multiple windows;
  (c) user-friendly man-machine interface.

- *ANIX, a UNIX port on the system:* Anix software develops slide show software, photo album, presentation and video software for digital camera users. UNIX is a more secured operating systems.
- Transaction processing monitor.
- Access to the UNIFY and ORACLE rational databases.

Athos is a multiprocessor operating system. It supports virtual memory management. Its main work is to control the system hardware during system initialization, reconfiguration and operations and maintenance.

Task management mechanisms support good performance. It gives security and a reconfiguration capability. Several programmes can be grouped into higher level functions, termed a logical processor. ATHOS operating system applications are run in virtual memory, and, as a result, they are fully protected against the other applications. Memory space is arranged in logical segments identified by their protection attributes and size.

High level system services are accepted by high level language run-time interfaces. The main high level service consists of

- File management system (FMS) and that is mandatory;
- System operation and maintenance (SOM) and this is also mandatory;
- Operator and workstation access method (WAM) and this is optional;
- Communication access method (CAM) and this is also optional;
- Extended communication access method (ECAM) and this is optional;
- File transfer access method and this is optional;
- Application management system and this is optional;
- Distributed and secured transactional access method (DISTRAM) and this is optional.

In file management system, the stress is given on the easy evaluation of performance and facilities being offered to application to control performance utilizing parameters. The other file management items describe:

(a) Catalogue facilities at several levels;
(b) Mirrored disk mechanism for ensuring that the data does not get deleted in the event of hardware failure;
(c) transactional multiple file open close facilities for ensuring data consistency in a transactional environment.

In case of system operation and maintenance, a full screen menu-mode, multiwindow, manmachine interface is provided for permitting remote operators to access the system.

For minimizing the load on the control system, some part of the required processing capacity can be distributed to intelligent workstations. That is why, workstation access is so important.

Application management system gives facilities for developing new services for downloading them from the software development system to the target machine and finally for integrating them with the available application.

The main requirements of DISTRAM are as follows

- To facilitate design;
- To implement secure non-stop transactional services;
- To permit an application to be distributed over several sites in a network.

The ANIX operating system has the following main advantages:

(i) It is possible to use the wide range of high quality softwares.
(ii) Applications running under ANIX can take the benefit of ATHOS facilities for communication and secure file management.

ANIX is a multiprocessor adaption of UNIX.

Multiprocessor system can really give the high performance needed in today's sophisticated applications.

■ SUMMARY ■

Solid state radio system is described. The main applications are at defence, military, naval, air and diplomatic services. This helps unmanned transmitting and receiving stations. Different units of the above are described. The salient features of the basic system are discussed. A block diagram of a fully automatic linear h.f. transmitter is shown.

Multi-access radio telephone system (MARTS) is discussed. Composition of MART is also dealt. Use of MART system is also described.

Instrument landing system localizer (ILSL) is discussed. ILSL should be sophisticated because even a small error in descent rate can develop the outcome in a hard landing short of runway or a late touchdown with a resulting overshoot. A block diagram of localizer/glidepath equipment is shown and described in detail.

An idea is also given about low power TV transmitter. Very low power TV transmitters are needed for the remote, hilly areas and islands under the TV network. The unattended dual low power TV transmitter is also discussed.

High definition television (HDTV) is also dealt. It has a wide screen presentation. It has a diagonal display of 40–50 inches and an aspect ratio of 16:9. The most important thing of HDTV is that some fairly complex signal processing is made in this TV so that bandwidth compression is possible in this type of TV. An idea has also been given in detail about signal processing and bandwidth compression.

The concept of cellular radio is introduced. Cellular radio telephone services are making rapid headway in providing mobile telephones for automobiles and for use in the home, office and on the street. The major design features of the cellular system are discussed. A block diagram of the typical cellular telephone instrument is explained.

Integrated services digital network (ISDN) provides network for telephony, telex, teletex, facsimile, data transmission and video telephony. The merits of ISDN are also described. The ISDN commercial services in the USA and UK are also tabulated. The comparative study of satellite technology and ISDN is described.

A block diagram of optical fibre communication is discussed. Transmission medium is categorized as multimode, monomode, graded-index fibre and fibre bundle. In this connection, an idea about detector, modulation, demodulation, repeaters is introduced.

Satellites tracking through earthstation technology is dealt with. The main features of earthstation technology from the point of view of satellite in our country are described. The reasons for the achievement in earthstation technology are narrated. Advancement in satellite networking is also discussed. The main features of the present research are described. Satellite services will be performed mostly by fibre optic cables. Information satellite network in integrated form is described through a block diagram.

A lot of research is in progress for information satellites (INFOSATs). The main features of the design of INFOSATs are also discussed. An idea about technological growth of satellite communication technology is given. The concept of very small earthstations is also explained. Technology in this respect is more advanced due to the development of digital signal processing techniques.

A discussion has also been made on advancement of communication in the rural area.

The general structure of a rural telecommunication network is shown through a block diagram. Very small stand alone exchange (VSSA) is described and its merits are also discussed. Domestic satellite network (DOMSAT) is also described. The switching of the VSSA includes an enchanced PABX (FASTCOM switch). A detailed idea is given on Fastcom stations. An idea is also given on RURTEL which can work up to 320 subscribers.

A discussion has also been made on speech processing technologies.

The main features of speech recognition algorithm have been described. Speech processing system interfaced to a host computer is also explained. Digital signal processing board with CODEC is shown. The CODEC is a device or program which is capable of encoding and/or decoding a digital data stream or signal. DTW unit is also described. Truly, the dynamic time warping (DTW) is a method that permits a computer to find an optimal match between two given sequences with certain restrictions. The DTW chip can address up to 1 Mbyte of DTW memory. Voice controlled telephone operator console is also described. The main features of the above system are discussed. Description is also given for the system of communications of handicapped persons. A voice activated sorting machine in a mail room is shown. Here, the speech processing unit is utilized for controlling a voice mail system by voice commands.

Telecommunication application with multiprocessor system is discussed. Multibus structure is shown. Input–output structure is also described in this connection. The connections of mass memory, Winchester disks, magnetic tape, and tape streamers through SCSI standard buses are shown. An idea about virtual memory management, ANIX is given. ATHOS which is a multiprocessor operating system is also discussed. The advantages of ANIX operating system are also narrated.

■ QUESTIONS ■

1. What are the general features of the transmitter of solid state radio system?

2. What is multiaccess radio telephone system. Describe its composition.

3. What are the main features of instrument landing system?

4. What are the main components of localizer/glidepath equipment? Describe them.

5. What is low power TV transmitter? What are its advantages?

6. What is high definition television? What are its specialities?

7. What are the major design features of the cellular system?

8. What are the merits of integrated services digital network? Describe ISDN Commercial services in the USA and the UK.

9. Develop a comparative study between satellite technology and ISDN.

10. What are the main components of optical fibre communication system? Describe them.

11. What are the main features of earthstation technology from the point of view of satellite in our country?

12. What are the main features of the present research on satellite communications? What are the works to be expected to be done by future satellites.

13. How would you integrate satellites into an information satellite network? What are the services to be performed through information satellite network?

14. What are the satellite applications where digital signal processing is contributing much?

15. What is VSSA exchange? What are its merits?

16. Write a short note on 'FASTCOM'.

17. Write a short note on 'RURTEL'.

18. What are the main features of speech recognition algorithm?

19. What is DTW unit? Write a short note on it.

20. What are the applications of office communication? Describe them.

21. What is multibus structure? Write a short note on it.

22. What is ATHOS? Explain its work.

23. What are the advantages of ANIX operation system?

Appendix

1. For 50 kHz frequency of electromagnetic wave the height of the vertical antenna required will be
   (a) 1500 m   (b) 6000 m   (c) 150 m   (d) 600 m.

2. Modulation means
   (a) Multiplication of a low frequency signal with a high frequency signal
   (b) Superimposition of a low frequency signal with a high frequency carrier signal
   (c) Division of a low frequency signal with a high frequency signal
   (d) Addition of a low frequency signal with a high frequency signal.

3. The voltage of a voice signal is termed
   (a) carrier voltage   (b) main voltage
   (c) modulating voltage   (d) primary voltage.

4. The translated signal is
   (a) modulated signal   (b) carrier signal
   (c) basic signal   (d) modulating signal.

5. The amplitude modulation is defined as,
   (a) the amplitude of a carrier signal being varied by the modulating voltage whose frequency is much higher than that of carrier
   (b) the amplitude of a carrier signal being varied by the modulating voltage whose frequency is much lower than that of carrier
   (c) the amplitude of a carrier signal being varied by the modulated voltage whose frequency is much higher than that of carrier
   (d) the amplitude of a modulated signal being varied by modulating voltage whose frequency is much higher than that of modulated.

6. The amplitude modulated voltage will be expressed as

   (a) $V_c (1 + m \sin \omega_m t)$ where m is a constant and is equal to $\dfrac{V_m}{V_c}$

   (b) $mV_c^2 \sin \omega_m t$

   (c) $mV_c \sin \omega_m t$

   (d) none of the above.

7. The process of amplitude modulation gives following sideband frequencies

   (a) $\omega_c + \omega_m, \omega_c + 2\omega_m$

   (b) $\omega_c + \omega_m, \omega_c - \omega_m$

   (c) $\omega_c + 2\omega_m, \omega_c - 2\omega_m$

   (d) $\omega_c + \omega_m, \omega_c - \omega_m, \omega_c + 2\omega_m, \omega_c - 2\omega_m.$

   where ω_c is the carrier angular frequency.

   ω_m is the angular frequency of modulating signal.

8. The bandwidth of amplitude modulated signal is

   (a) $2(f_c + f_m)$ (b) $2f_m$ (c) $f_c + f_m$ (d) $f_c - f_m.$

   where f_c is the frequency of carrier signal and f_m is the frequency of modulating signal.

9. The modulation index of an amplitude modulated signal is

   (a) $\dfrac{V_{\max} + V_{\min}}{V_{\max} - V_{\min}}$ (b) $\dfrac{V_{\max} - V_{\min}}{V_{\max} + V_{\min}}$ (c) $\dfrac{V_c}{V_m}$ (d) $\dfrac{V_c - V_m}{V_c + V_m}.$

   where $V_{\max}$ is the maximum voltage

   $V_{\min}$ is the minimum voltage

   V_c is the carrier voltage

   V_m is the modulating voltage.

10. The basic circuit of the collector modulation in amplitude modulation consists of

    (a) Class 'AB' amplifier

    (b) Class 'B' amplifier

    (c) Class 'C' amplifier

    (d) Class 'A' amplifier.

11. In case of collector modulation for amplitude modulation, the modulated amplifier is a

    (a) Push–pull amplifier

    (b) Class AB amplifier

    (c) Class A amplifier

    (d) Class B amplifier.

12. Find which of the following statements is correct.

    (a) The modulation is much more linear in case of base modulation compared to collector modulation

    (b) The power output per transistor is higher in case of collector modulation compared to base modulation

    (c) The collector circuit efficiency is higher in case of base modulation compared to collector modulation

    (d) The base modulation requires higher modulating power than collector modulation.

13. The double sideband suppressed carrier modulation consists of

    (a) the product of modulating signal and carrier wave signal

    (b) the division of modulating signal and carrier wave signal

(c) the addition of modulating signal and carrier wave signal

(d) the subtraction of carrier wave signal and modulating signal.

14. For single sideband modulation, the saving of the power in the practical application

(a) decreases   (b) increases

(c) remains the same   (d) none of the above.

15. The frequencies of the two sideband signals of the output of the balanced modulator are 10 MHz + 100.3 kHz and 10 MHz – 100.3 kHz, the selectivity percentage is

(a) 2%   (b) 20%   (c) 100%   (d) 1%.

16. The output of the balanced modulation provides

(a) Carrier signal frequency

(b) Two sidebands and carrier signal frequencies

(c) Two sidebands and modulating frequencies

(d) Two sidebands.

17. In case of vestigial sideband,

(a) The part of one sideband is suppressed

(b) The parts of both the sidebands are suppressed

(c) The parts of one sideband and carrier are suppressed

(d) The parts of both sidebands and carrier are suppressed.

18. Multiplexing means

(a) Many individual messages can be transmitted over a large number of communication channels

(b) Any individual message can be transmitted over a large number of communication channels

(c) Many individual messages can be transmitted simultaneously over a single communication channel

(d) An individual message can be transmitted over a single communication channel.

19. The time division multiplexing utilizes

(a) analogue modulation system

(b) pulse modulation system

(c) both analogue and pulse modulation systems

(d) none of the above.

20. The term *heterodyning* is involved in

(a) Amplitude modulation   (b) Frequency modulation

(c) Amplitude demodulation   (d) Frequency demodulation.

21. The recovery of the translated signal can be made by the following manner.

(a) Dividing the translated signal with $\cos \omega_c t$

(b) Multiplying the translated signal with $\cos \omega_c t$

(c) Adding the translated signal with $\cos \omega_c t$

(d) Subtracting the translated signal with $\cos \omega_c t$.

where ω_c is the carrier angular frequency.

22. The baseband signal strength is reduced during reverse translation of amplitude modulated signal due to the following fact.
    (a) The auxiliary signal used in the initial translation differs by a phase angle from the auxiliary signal used in the recovery translation
    (b) The difference in frequency of auxiliary signal used in the initial translation and recovery translation
    (c) The difference in amplitude of auxiliary signal used in the initial translation and recovery translation
    (d) None of the above.

23. In case of square law diode detector, the diode is operating
    (a) in the non-linear region of dynamic current–voltage characteristic
    (b) in the linear region of dynamic current–voltage characteristic
    (c) both in the linear and non-linear region of dynamic current–voltage characteristic
    (d) in negative bias.

24. In case of linear diode detector, the modulated carrier voltage should have
    (a) very high modulating voltage   (b) very high carrier voltage
    (c) very high baseband voltage   (d) none of the above.

25. The frequency modulation keeps
    (a) the amplitude of modulated carrier varying
    (b) the amplitude of modulated carrier constant
    (c) the frequency of modulated carrier constant
    (d) both amplitude and frequency varying.

26. The mathematical expression of frequency modulated signal is
    (a) $f = f_c(1 + k \cos \omega_m t)$ (b) $f = f_c(1 + kV_m \cos \omega_m t)$
    (c) $f = f_c(1 + kV_m \cos \omega_c t)$ (d) $f = f_c(1 + V_m \cos \omega_m t)$.

    where f_c is the carrier frequency
    V_m is the maximum modulating voltage
    ω_c is the angular frequency of carrier signal
    ω_m is the angular frequency of modulating signal
    k is the proportionality constant.

27. The maximum frequency deviation in frequency modulated signal is
    (a) $k f_m f_c$ (b) $KV_m f_c$ (c) $kV_c f_m$ (d) $kV_m (f_c + f_m)$.

    where f_c is the carrier signal frequency, f_m is the frequency of modulating signal, V_m is the maximum voltage of modulating signal and V_c is the maximum voltage of carrier signal.

28. The instantaneous value of the FM voltage is
    (a) $A \sin \left(\omega_c t + \dfrac{kV_m f_c}{f_m} \sin \omega_m t\right)$ (b) $A \sin \left(\omega_c t + \dfrac{V_m f_c}{f_m} \sin \omega_m t\right)$
    (c) $A \sin \left(\omega_c t + \dfrac{kV_m f_m}{f_c} \sin \omega_m t\right)$ (d) $A \sin \left(\omega_m t + \dfrac{kV_m f_c}{f_m} \sin \omega_c t\right)$

where f_c is the carrier signal frequency, f_m is the modulating signal frequency, V_c is the maximum voltage of carrier signal, V_m is the maximum voltage of modulating signal, k is the constant of proportionality, A is the maximum value of the FM voltage.

29. The solution of the instantaneous value of the FM voltage can be made by
   (a) Legendre polynomial
   (b) Bessel function
   (c) Fourier series
   (d) Z-transform.

30. The value of reactance in a reactance modulator is
   (a) $\dfrac{X_C}{g_m}$
   (b) $\dfrac{X_C}{g_m R}$
   (c) $\dfrac{R}{2\pi f g_m C}$
   (d) $\dfrac{g_m}{X_C R}$.

where X_C is the reactance of the capacitor, R is the resistance of reactance modulator circuit, g_m is the transconductance of the device.

31. In AM transmitter, the ratio of maximum power and average power is
   (a) 2 times
   (b) 4 times
   (c) 3 times
   (d) 1.

32. The noise affection in FM and AM reception can be described as follows
   (a) AM reception is more affected by noise
   (b) FM reception is more affected by noise
   (c) AM and FM are equally affected from the noise point of view
   (d) It depends on the type of signal.

33. The noise can be reduced further by increasing the deviation
   (a) in case of FM
   (b) in case of AM
   (c) in case of both FM and AM
   (d) neither in case of FM, nor in case of AM.

34. Comparison of adjacent channel interference can be described as follows
   (a) The adjacent channel interference in AM station is more compared to FM stations
   (b) The adjacent channel interference in AM stations is less compared to FM stations
   (c) The adjacent channel interference in AM stations is equal to that of FM stations
   (d) The comparison of adjacent channel inference may be in either way and that totally depends on the perfection of the respective modulation.

35. The noise is more in AM because
   (a) AM broadcasts in the MF and HF ranges
   (b) AM broadcast in the VHF range
   (c) AM broadcasts in the UHF range
   (d) None of the above.

36. The ratio of wide channel required by FM with respect to that of AM is
   (a) 2
   (b) 4
   (c) 6
   (d) 10.

37. Indicate which statement is correct
   (a) FM transmitting and receiving equipments are more complex for modulation and demodulation but the area of reception for FM is small
   (b) FM transmitting and receiving equipments are not so complex and the area of reception for FM is small

(c) FM transmitting and receiving equipments are more complex for modulation and demodulation and the area of reception for FM is large

(d) FM transmitting and receiving equipments are not so complex for modulation and demodulation but the area of reception is large.

38. FM transmitter amplifies high frequency more than the low frequency audio signal to reduce the effect of noise

(a) in case of pre-emphasis

(b) in case of de-emphasis

(c) both in case of pre-emphasis and de-emphasis

(d) none of the above.

39. In case of phase modulation

(a) the phase of the carrier is varied but the amplitude of the same remains constant

(b) the phase of the carrier is varied and the amplitude of the same remains varied

(c) the phase of the carrier is constant but the amplitude of the same remains varied

(d) the phase of the carrier is constant and the amplitude of the same remains constant.

40. The phase modulated wave can be represented as

(a) $A \sin (\omega_c t + m_p \sin \omega_m t)$ (b) $A \sin (\omega_m t + m_p \sin \omega_c t)$

(c) $A \sin (\omega_c t - m_p \sin \omega_m t)$ (d) $A \sin (\omega_m t - m_p \sin \omega_c t)$.

where ω_c is the angular frequency of carrier wave

ω_m is the angular frequency of modulating wave

m_p is modulation index

A is the maximum magnitude of amplitude modulated wave

41. Pulse amplitude modulation is defined as

(a) the signal is sampled at random intervals and each sample is kept proportional to the amplitude of the signal at the instant of sampling

(b) the signal is sampled at regular intervals and each sample is kept proportional to the amplitude of the signal at the instant of sampling

(c) the signal is sampled at regular intervals and each sample is kept equal to the amplitude of the signal at the instant of sampling

(d) the signal is sampled at random intervals and each sample is kept equal to the amplitude of the signal at the instant of sampling.

42. In case of single polarity PAM

(a) the fixed dc level is added to the signal

(b) the fixed dc level is multiplied to the signal

(c) the fixed dc level is subtracted to the signal

(d) the fixed dc level is divided to the signal.

43. Frequency modulation is made on PAM due to the fact

(a) to develop varying amplitude pulse (b) to develop constant amplitude pulse

(c) to shape the pulse triangular (d) none of the above.

44. Pulse frequency modulation, pulse width modulation and pulse position modulation are three types of

(a) pulse amplitude modulation   (b) pulse time modulation
(c) delta modulation   (d) pulse code modulation.

45. In case of pulse modulation,
    (a) the starting time and amplitude of each pulse are varying
    (b) the starting time and amplitude of each pulse are kept fixed but the width of each
        pulse is made proportional to the amplitude of the signal at that instant
    (c) the starting time and amplitude of each pulse are kept fixed but the width of each
        pulse is made equal to the amplitude of the signal at that instant.
    (d) the starting time and the amplitude of each pulse are varying, but the width of each
        pulse is made proportional to the amplitude of the signal at that instant.

46. In case of pulse width modulation
    (a) the negative pulse width does not exist
    (b) the negative pulse width exists
    (c) the negative pulse width exists at the start or end
    (d) None of the above.

47. The pulse width modulation is developed as
    (a) It is generated by trigger pulses at the sampling rate by controlling the starting time
        of pulses from a bistable multivibrator and by feeding in the signal for controlling
        the duration of the pulses
    (b) It is generated by trigger pulses at the sampling rate by controlling the starting time
        of pulses from a monostable multivibrator and by feeding in the signal for controlling
        the duration of the pulses
    (c) It is generated by trigger pulses at the sampling rate by controlling the starting time
        of pulses from a monostable multivibrator
    (d) None of the above.

48. The demodulation of the pulse width modulation is made
    (a) by passing the same in an integrating circuit
    (b) by passing the same in a filtered circuit
    (c) by passing the same in multiplexer
    (d) by passing the same in flip-flop circuit.

49. In case of pulse position modulation
    (a) the amplitude of the pulses are kept varying
    (b) the width of the pulses are kept varying
    (c) the position of each pulse in relation to the position of the recurrent reference pulse
        is varied by each instantaneous sampled value of the modulating wave
    (d) the amplitude of the pulses is kept constant but the width of the pulses varies.

50. For developing pulse position modulation
    (a) Integrator is essential
    (b) Differentiator and diode clipper are essential
    (c) Only differentiator will serve the purpose
    (d) Integrator and clipper are essential.

51. In case of demodulation of PPM

  (a) Monostable multivibrator is needed

  (b) Bistable multivibrator is needed

  (c) Both monostable and bistable multivibrator are need

  (d) None of the above.

52. The PWM input is given to an XOR directly and also through a delay circuit.

  (a) The output will be PAM signal

  (b) The output will be PPM signal

  (c) The output will be PCM signal

  (d) None of the above.

53. The clock input to the flip-flop is made by passing PPM through a NOT gate.

  (a) The output is a PAM wave

  (b) The output is PCM wave

  (c) The output is PWM wave

  (d) None of the above.

54.

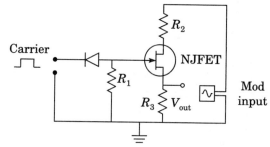

  In the above figure,

  (a) V_{out} will be PAM

  (b) V_{out} will be PWM

  (c) V_{out} will be PPM

  (d) V_{out} will be PCM.

55. PAM demodulator requires

  (a) an integrator

  (b) an envelope detector

  (c) a single toggle filp-flop

  (d) a decoder.

56. In PCM, 7 digit will be termed

  (a) OPPP   (b) OOPP   (c) OPOP   (d) POPP.

57. Distorted PCM signal can be converted to regenerated PCM signal by

  (a) Filter

  (b) Regenerative repeater

  (c) Decoder

  (d) Reconstruction filter.

58. Three basic functions, i.e. equalization, timing and decision making are performed by

  (a) Regenerative repeater

  (b) Reconstruction filter

  (c) Decoder

  (d) Quantizer.

59. The PCM signal is developed by

  (a) sampling and encoding

  (b) sampling, quantizing and encoding

  (c) sampling and quantizing

  (d) sampling, filtering and quantizing.

60. The sampling theorem describes that if the sampling rate in any modulation system

  (a) exceeds 1.5 times the maximum signal frequency, the original signal can be developed in the receiver with minimal distortion

(b) exceeds 1.75 times the maximum signal frequency, the original signal can be developed in the receiver with minimal distortion

(c) exceeds twice the maximum signal frequency, the original signal can be developed in the receiver with minimal distortion

(d) None of the above.

61. A 300 watts carrier is modulated to a depth of 80%, the total power in the modulated wave will be

(a) 396 W (b) 200 W (c) 500 W (d) 356 W.

62. The low pass signal can be sampled by using

(a) op-amp (b) An analogue switch CD4016
(c) PCM (d) none of the above.

63. The components of transmitter in a radio communication are

(a) Transducer, audio amplifier, aerial
(b) Transducer, frequency compensator, audio amplifier, aerial
(c) Audio amplifier, aerial
(d) Transducer, aerial.

64. The components of the receiver in radio communication are

(a) Aerial, amplifier, demodulator, transducer
(b) Aerial, amplifier, transducer
(c) Aerial, demodulator, transducer
(d) Aerial, demodulator.

65. The function of the RF buffer amplifier in a high level broadcast transmitter is

(a) to isolate the oscillator from the modulation phenomenon
(b) for high amplification
(c) for modulation
(d) none of the above.

66. The function of the master oscillator in a high level broadcast transmitter is

(a) to develop stable carrier voltage of desired frequency
(b) to isolate the oscillator from the modulation phenomenon
(c) for amplitude modulation
(d) none of the above.

67. The type of oscillator used for maintaining the generated frequency constant within close limits even for voltage variation, ambient temperature variation, and variation of temperature components of load, is

(a) Master oscillator (b) Buffer oscillator
(c) Harmonic oscillator (d) None of the above.

68. The best choice of oscillator for master oscillator in case of high level broadcast transmitter is

(a) Hartley oscillator (b) Colpitt oscillator
(c) Crystal oscillator (d) None of the above.

69. The harmonic generator of a radio transmitter is

(a) Class C tuned amplifier   (b) Class B amplifier

(c) Class A amplifier   (d) None of the above.

70. The demerit of the harmonic generator in radio transmitter is

(a) heavy damping on the input circuit

(b) high impedance of the tuned circuit

(c) high impedance of the tuned circuit and heavy damping on the input circuit

(d) none of the above.

71. The modulating amplifier in radio transmitter is

(a) Class C amplifier   (b) Class B push-pull amplifier

(c) Class A amplifier   (d) None of the above.

72. The reason for the use of Class B amplifier in the radio transmitter is

(a) high plate circuit efficiency   (b) high grid circuit efficiency

(c) the less distortion   (d) none of the above.

73. For amplitude modulation, now-a-days the mostly used system is

(a) Low power level modulation

(b) High power level modulation

(c) Both low and high power level modulation

(d) None of the above.

74. The harmonic generator is needed in radio transmission for

(a) eliminating subharmonics   (b) eliminating fundamental

(c) eliminating 3rd harmonic only   (d) none of the above.

75. The modification is made in radio transmission by avoiding crystal controlled master oscillator. The reason for the same is

(a) to have readily adjustable carrier frequency

(b) to have required carrier frequency

(c) to have carrier frequency with harmonics

(d) none of the above.

76. The maximum frequency drift allowed for radio transmitter is

(a) ±10 Hz for medium wave transmitter

(b) ±15 Hz for medium wave transmitter

(c) ± 20 Hz for medium wave transmitter

(d) ±30 Hz for medium wave transmitter.

77. Frequency scintillation in the radio transmission is avoided

(a) by applying master oscillator

(b) by applying master oscillator with buffer amplifier

(c) by applying master oscillator with filter

(d) none of the above.

78. In case of radio transmission, the operation of the oscillator is to be made slightly off the resonant frequency of the tank circuit. The reason for the above is

(a) to eliminate the phase shift between the exciting voltage and the output voltage of oscillator transistor

(b) to allow frequency drift in any oscillator

(c) to encourage the phase shift between the exciting voltage and the output voltage of oscillator transistor

(d) none of the above.

79. The reason for keeping the tank circuit for radio transmitter in closed constant temperature chamber is

(a) the reduction in inductance and capacitance variation in the tank circuit

(b) to vary the tuned frequency

(c) to vary the voltage across the tuned circuit

(d) none of the above.

80. The variation in the interelectrode capacitances of the tank circuit of a radio transmitter is compensated by

(a) using low circuit 'Q'

(b) keeping low ratio of mutual conductance to variations in interelectrode capacitance

(c) by allowing large coupling from the tank circuit to the base and collector of the oscillator and transistor

(d) by using low resonant frequency.

81. A high effective Q in the tank circuit of a radio transmitter can be made

(a) through a very largely coupled load

(b) by providing the ratio of L/C of tank circuit low

(c) by coupling the collector to a large part of the tank circuit

(d) none of the above.

82. The sensitivity of a radio receiver is

(a) the ability to pick up and reproduce weak radio signals

(b) the ability of the radio receiver to separate the signal of a required radio station from the signals of the unwanted stations

(c) the quality or precision with which the output is reproduced

(d) the ability of radio receiver to deliver a constant amount of output for a given period of time when the receiver is supplied with a signal of constant amplitude and frequency.

83. A very important aspect, when a large number of radio stations operate on nearly equal frequencies, is

(a) sensitivity of radio receiver   (b) selectivity of radio receiver

(c) fidelity of radio receiver   (d) stability of radio receiver.

84. A straight receiver in which the incoming signal is first of all amplified in one or more tuned radio frequency amplifier stage is called

(a) TRF receiver   (b) superheterodyne receiver

(c) RF receiver   (d) none of the above.

85. A TRF receiver requires

(a) one or two tuned RF amplifier stages from the point of view of sensitivity and selectivity

(b) more than two tuned amplifiers from the point of view of sensitivity and selectivity

(c) more than five tuned amplifiers from the point of view of sensitivity and selectivity

(d) none of the above.

86. The intermediate frequency of a superheterodyne receiver is

    (a) 460 kHz   (b) 450 kHz   (c) 455 kHz   (d) 440 kHz.

87. The fading of the amplitude of IF carrier at the detector can be restricted with the help of

    (a) AVC   (b) AFC   (c) varactor diode   (d) none of the above.

88. The automatic volume control reduces the amplitude variation on account of fading from a high value of 30 to 40 dB

    (a) to a small value 10 to 20 dB   (b) to a small value 3 to 4 dB

    (c) to a small value 10 to 15 dB   (d) none of the above.

89. When the carrier amplitude increases

    (a) the AVC bias increases and the gains in all the tuned stages increase

    (b) the AVC bias increases and the gains in all the tuned stages decrease

    (c) the AVC bias decreases and the gains in all the tuned stages increase

    (d) the AVC bias decreases and the gains in all the tuned stages decrease.

90. The AVC derives a dc voltage by rectification of carrier voltage in a linear diode detector and this dc voltage is proportional to

    (a) the carrier amplitude   (b) the modulating voltage

    (c) the modulated voltage   (d) none of the above.

91. Time constant of AVC filter is to be chosen such that

    (a) all modulation frequency components will be eliminated

    (b) its value lies within 1 second to 2 seconds

    (c) its value lies within 2 seconds to 3 seconds

    (d) its value lies within 3 seconds to 4 seconds.

92. The positive AVC bias is applied at the base of

    (a) NPN transistor   (b) PNP transistor

    (c) Both NPN and PNP transistor   (d) None of the above.

93. The linear diode detector with π filter and simple AVC are used because

    (a) π filter is more reliable from the point of view of removal of radio frequency components

    (b) π filter is the best filter

    (c) AVC becomes non-operative even for weak signals

    (d) none of the above.

94. An ideal AVC system

    (a) should not be operative until the input carrier voltage reaches a reasonably large predetermined voltage

    (b) should be operative until the input carrier voltage reaches a reasonably large predetermined voltage

(c) should not maintain output level constant after the operation

(d) none of the above.

95. Linear diode detector with delayed AVC is needed because

(a) the AVC system suffers from the drawback that the AVC becomes operative even for weak signals

(b) the AVC system suffers from the drawback that the AVC does not become operative for weak signals

(c) the delay diode does not conduct for zero and small signals

(d) the potential of AVC bias is not equal to the potential of cathode of the diode.

96. Tone compensated volume control is provided for

(a) reducing slowly the volumes of low and high frequency terms

(b) enhancing slowly the volumes of low and high frequency terms

(c) enhancing slowly the volume of reproduced programme

(d) none of the above.

97. The amount of compensation of tone compensated volume control is of the order of

(a) 100 dB   (b) 200 dB   (c) 20 dB   (d) 500 dB.

98. In 3-band superheterodyne receiver, the following 3 bands are available.

(a) Broadcast band, medium wave band, short wave band no. 1

(b) Broadcast band, medium wave band, short wave band no. 2

(c) Broadcast band, short wave band no. 1, short wave band no. 2

(d) None of the above.

99. The magnitude of the AFC control voltage depends upon the

(a) frequency difference

(b) voltage difference

(c) the fact that the frequency of the IF (Intermediate frequency) voltage is above or below the standard value

(d) none of the above.

100. The equivalent circuit of a varactor diode is

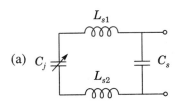

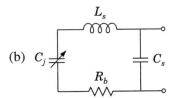

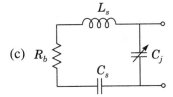

(d) None of the above.

101. The resistive cut-off frequency of the varactor system is

(a) $f_c = \dfrac{1}{2\pi R_b C_{min}}$ (b) $f_c = \dfrac{R_b}{2\pi C_{min}}$ (c) $f_c = \dfrac{2\pi C_{min}}{R_b}$ (d) $f_c = \dfrac{2\pi R_b}{C_{min}}$.

102. The image frequency is

(a) $f_s + f_i$ ''   (b) $f_s - f_i$

(c) $f_s + 2f_i$ (d) $f_s - 2f_i$.

where f_s is the frequency of the signal received in the antenna of the superheterodyne receiver and f_i is the intermediate frequency.

103. The rejection ratio is

(a) $\sqrt{1 + Q^2 \rho^2}$ where $\rho = \dfrac{f_s + 2f_i}{f_s} - \dfrac{f_s}{f_s + 2f_i}$

(b) $\sqrt{1 + Q^2 \rho^2}$ where $\rho = \dfrac{f_s - 2f_i}{f_s} - \dfrac{f_s}{f_s - 2f_i}$

(c) $\sqrt{1 - Q^2 \rho^2}$ where $\rho = \dfrac{f_s + 2f_i}{f_s} - \dfrac{f_s}{f_s - 2f_i}$

(d) $\sqrt{Q^2 + \rho^2}$ where $\rho = \dfrac{f_s + 2f_i}{f_s} - \dfrac{f_s}{f_s + 2f_i}$

where Q is the Q-factor of the tuned circuit of IF stage amplifier.

104. The major factors of antenna system are

(a) Wavelength, antenna impedance

(b) Antenna impedance, directivity

(c) Directivity, wavelength

(d) Wavelength, antenna impedance, directivity.

105. The radio waves propagated outward from an antenna travel at approximately speed of

(a) 186000 miles/second   (b) 18600 miles/second

(c) 1860000 miles/second   (d) 1860 miles/second.

106. Net antenna impedance is

(a) inductive   (b) capacitive   (c) resistive   (d) none of the above.

107. The angular separation between the two half power points on the power density radiation pattern is

(a) the bandwidth of antenna   (b) the beamwidth of antenna

(c) the polarization of antenna   (d) none of the above.

108. The fundamental radio antenna is a metal rod or tubing that has physical length approximately equal to

(a) $\dfrac{1}{4}$ th wavelength in free space at the frequency of operation

(b) $\dfrac{1}{2}$ wavelength in free space at the frequency of operation

(c) full wavelength in free space at the frequency of operation

(d) $\frac{1}{3}$rd wavelength in free space at the frequency of operation.

109. The half wave dipole antenna is also termed
  (a) "zero–dB gain antenna"   (b) "1–dB gain antenna"
  (c) "10–dB gain antenna"   (d) "20–dB gain antenna".

110. Drooping doublet is
  (a) inverted *V*-antenna   (b) half wave dipole
  (c) Yagi antenna   (d) none of the above.

111. The beam antenna consists of
  (a) only resonant half wave dipole
  (b) only director
  (c) only reflector
  (d) resonant half wave dipole, director and reflector

112. The folded dipole is
  (a) full wavelength dipole   (b) two half wavelength dipoles
  (c) single half wavelength dipole   (d) none of the above.

113. Rhombic antenna is termed to be
  (a) double '*V*'   (b) drooping doublet
  (c) folded dipole   (d) none of the above.

114. The transformer in a carbon microphone circuit is required
  (a) to increase the current
  (b) to match the low impedance microphone with the high impedance grid circuit
  (c) to step down the voltage
  (d) none of the above.

115. The microphone current usually varies from
  (a) 200 to 500 mamp   (b) 10 to 100 mamp
  (c) 300 to 1000 mamp   (d) 2 to 5 mamp.

116. The crystal microphone utilizes the property of the certain crystal such as
  (a) rochell salt   (b) barium carbonate
  (c) potassium chlorate   (d) none of the above.

117. In extreme conditions of temperature and humidity
  (a) Crystal microphone is good
  (b) Moving coil microphone is good
  (c) Electrostatic microphone is good
  (d) None of the above.

118. In electrostatic loudspeaker, electrostatic force is developed
  (a) by variation in current   (b) by variation in size of diaphragm
  (c) by variation in inductance   (d) none of the above.

119. In a broadcast superheterodyne receiver, if the intermediate frequency is 455 kHz at 950 kHz, the image frequency will be

    (a) 1800 kHz   (b) 1500 kHz   (c) 1860 kHz   (d) 1600 kHz.

120. In a broadcast superheterodyne receiver, if the intermediate frequency is 455 kHz at 950 kHz, the rejection ratio will be

    (a) 160.703   (b) 144.703   (c) 14.703   (d) 1.4703

121. Three speakers are connected to an amplifier with a line. The power handling capacity of the speakers are 22 watts, 16 watts and 12 watts. The total power delivered by the amplifier is

    (a) $\dfrac{1}{22}+\dfrac{1}{16}+\dfrac{1}{12}$ W   (b) $\dfrac{1}{\dfrac{1}{22}+\dfrac{1}{16}+\dfrac{1}{12}}$ W

    (c) $22 + 16 + 12$ W   (d) 22 W.

122. The attenuation is dB is expressed as

    (a) $10 \log \dfrac{E_1}{E_2}$ (b) $20 \log \dfrac{E_1}{E_2}$ (c) $20 \log E_1 E_2$ (d) none of the above.

123. The output of a microphone in dB is expressed as

    (a) $20 \log_{10} \dfrac{P_2}{P_1}$ (b) $10 \log_{10} \dfrac{P_2}{P_1}$ (c) $20 \log_{10} P_2 P_1$ (d) none of the above.

124. Sidetone in telephone communication system is

    (a) the sound which is heard at the sound generating station
    (b) the sound which is heard at the receiving station
    (c) the sound which is heard at the intermediate station
    (d) none of the above.

125. The quiescent current flowing even in the absence of sound in a telephone communication is due to

    (a) faithful sound reproduction   (b) leakage
    (c) noise   (d) none of the above.

126. The minimum current required for proper operation of carbon microphone in telephone system is

    (a) 100 mA   (b) 50 mA   (c) 23 mA   (d) 10 mA.

127. The maximum resistance allowable in the battery station set loop in a telephone system is

    (a) 500 Ω   (b) 1500 Ω   (c) 1000 Ω   (d) 2200 Ω.

128. The resistance kept at the battery for protecting against short circuits in the wire between local office and subscriber of a telephone system is

    (a) 2200 Ω   (b) 400 Ω   (c) 2000 Ω   (d) 5000 Ω.

129. For a loop distance of about 4 miles telephone connection, the preferred gauge of wire is

    (a) 19 gauge   (b) 10 gauge   (c) 26 gauge   (d) 50 gauge.

130. Varistor is
  (a) a conductor used in telephone system
  (b) a semiconductor in telephone system
  (c) a resistance whose value increases with the increase in current
  (d) a resistance whose value increases with the increase in voltage.

131. In the central exchange system, by central switching, the number of long interconnecting wires is reduced from

  (a) N^2 to N
  (b) $\dfrac{N(N-1)}{2}$ to N

  (c) $\dfrac{N(N+1)}{2}$ to N
  (d) $N(N-1)$ to N.

  where N is the number of stations,

132. In the central exchange system, by central switching, the number of switches is reduced from

  (a) $N(N-1)$ to $\dfrac{N(N-1)}{2}$
  (b) $N(N+1)$ to $\dfrac{N(N+1)}{2}$

  (c) $N(N+2)$ to $\dfrac{N(N+1)}{2}$
  (d) $N^2 + N + 1$ to $\dfrac{N^2+N}{2}$.

  where N is the number of stations.

133. Strowger automatic dialing telephone system is
  (a) a digital system
  (b) an electromechanical switching device
  (c) an electronic system
  (d) a computerized system.

134. The cross bar switch is
  (a) a digital system of telephone system
  (b) an array of horizontal and vertical wires
  (c) an electronic system of telephone system
  (d) a computerized electromagnetic telephone system of exchange

135. In mobile technology, cell is
  (a) the geographical area which is a small region subdivided from a large geographical area
  (b) a very small part of an electronic device
  (c) a small disc
  (d) a small semiconductor.

136. If the bandwidth of a cell of a cellular system is b_c, then the bandwidth provided to each user is

  (a) $n\, b_c$
  (b) $\dfrac{b_c}{n}$
  (c) $n^2\, b_c$
  (d) b_c.

  where n is the number of channels.

137. In mobile to mobile calls, there are
  (a) 100 special set-up channels
  (b) 21 special set-up channels
  (c) 2 special set-up channels
  (d) 10 special set-up channels.

138. Mobile telecommunications, switching office is termed

(a) MTS   (b) MS   (c) MTSO   (d) MO.

139. In mobile to fixed call the local switching office is called

(a) Class 2   (b) Class 3   (c) Class 4   (d) Class 5.

140. In fixed to mobile subscriber calls, the call is routed to

(a) the appropriate MTSO   (b) the appropriate toll office
(c) the appropriate local office   (d) none of the above.

141. In the mobile system, CO is called the

(a) coordinating office   (b) central office
(c) cooperative office   (d) none of the above.

142. In mobile system, NAM means

(a) Non-analogue mobile   (b) Numeric assignment module
(c) Non-analogue module   (d) None of the above.

143. In the mobile system, ESN means

(a) electronic service number   (b) Electromagnetic service number
(c) End service number   (d) None of the above.

144. In the mobile system, when one party hangs up,

(a) the MTSO frees the radio channel and completes the billing information
(b) the CO frees the radio channel and completes the billing information
(c) the NAM frees the radio channel and completes the billing information
(d) the toll office frees the radio channel and completes the billing information.

145. The optical source has a wavelength in the range of 0.85 to 1.6 μm which is about

(a) 10,000 GHz   (b) 77,000 GHz   (c) 1,000 GHz   (d) 30,000 GHz.

146. Solid state lasers produce

(a) non-coherent light
(b) coherent light
(c) both coherent and non-coherent light
(d) none of the above.

147. The design of cladding is made with

(a) lower index of refraction   (b) higher index of refraction
(c) very high index of refraction   (d) none of the above.

148. The bandwidth distance product of the graded index fibre is

(a) 10 Gbps-km   (b) 2 Gbps-km   (c) 4 Gbps-km   (d) 5 Gbps-km.

149. The demerit of avalanche photodiode is that

(a) it requires a high supply voltage to operate
(b) it enhances the receiver sensitivity
(c) it is 10–15 dB more sensitive in detecting low signals at a given error rate
(d) it is less sensitive to temperature.

150. The main difference between the telegraph and telex is

   (a) the signalling method and the procedure of sending the message
   (b) the supply voltage
   (c) the current flowing
   (d) none of the above.

151. Cable code in telegraphy system

   (a) is a type of ac signal   (b) is a type of dc signal
   (c) possesses two signalling conditions (d) none of the above.

152. Cable code in telegraphy system has

   (a) negative voltage to line representing "Dashes"
   (b) positive voltage to line representing "Dots"
   (c) no voltage representing space between words and letters
   (d) none of the above.

153. Morse code

   (a) is not compact   (b) uses high power
   (c) is expensive   (d) none of the above.

154. The letter 'B' is represented in Morse code as

   (a) . ___   (b) ___ ...   (c) ___ . ___ . (d) ___ ..

155. Hyphen is represented in the Morse code as

   (a) . ___ . ___ . ___   (b) ___ . ___ . ___ .
   (c) ___ ___ .. ___ ___   (d) ___ .... ___

156. In the five unit code

   (a) 16 is the total number of combinations available
   (b) 32 is the total number of combinations available
   (c) 64 is the total number of combinations available
   (d) 8 is the total number of combinations available.

157. The letter 'B' is represented in the International Alphabet No. 2

   (a) ● ● ○ ○ ○   (b) ● ○ ○ ● ●   (c) ○ ● ● ● ○   (d) ● ○ ○ ● ○

where ○ — start signal
       ● — stop signal

158. The operating current of non-polarized sounder in telegraph system is

   (a) 100 mA   (b) 55 mA   (c) 10 mA   (d) 5 mA.

159. In the telegraph system, the range of non-polarized relay is

   (a) 25 to 50 mA   (b) 6 to 15 mA   (c) 100 to 150 mA (d) 200 to 250 mA.

160. The coupling of the high frequency apparatus with the power transmission is usually made possible with the help of

   (a) coupling condensers   (b) coupling inductors
   (c) coupling resistors   (d) none of the above.

161. The wave traps in telecommunication in power system
   (a) block the *hf* currents
   (b) block the power frequency current
   (c) provide very high impedance to the passage of power frequency current
   (d) none of the above.

162. In case of telecommunication in power system, the wave trap consists of
   (a) an inductance and a condenser being connected in series
   (b) an inductance and a condenser being connected in parallel
   (c) an inductance and resistance in parallel
   (d) a condenser and a resistance being connected in series.

163. In case of telecommuncation in power system, the resorbit arrestor
   (a) helps as a protective device   (b) acts as a coupling condenser
   (c) acts as an inductor   (d) none of the above.

164. In case of telecommunication in power system, the impedance of the low voltage side of the installation is matched to the impedance of the high voltage side impedance
   (a) to reduce the high frequency power losses to a minimum
   (b) to reduce the low frequency power losses to a minimum
   (c) to develop resonance
   (d) none of the above.

165. For phase to earth coupling in power line carrier system,
   (a) the characteristic impedance is of the order of 800 Ω
   (b) the attenuation for transmission is high
   (c) the cost is more than that of phase to phase coupling in power line
   (d) none of the above.

166. In case of telemetering facilities in power line carrier systems, the total resistance of the instruments and connections should not exceed
   (a) 500 Ω (b) 50 Ω (c) 5,000 Ω (d) 50,000 Ω.

167. In case of power line carrier system protection, the breakers at both ends of the line
   (a) should open and reclose simultaneously
   (b) should not open and reclose simultaneously
   (c) should open and reclose after certain specific time lag
   (d) none of the above.

168. In a picture telegraph system,
   (a) usually 100 lines are traversed per inch
   (b) usually 200 lines are traversed per inch
   (c) usually 300 lines are traversed per inch
   (d) usually 500 lines are traversed per inch.

169. The usual carrier frequency of the amplitude modulated signal of transmitter in photo-telegraph is
   (a) 8500 Hz   (b) 7200 Hz   (c) 1020 Hz   (d) 2500 Hz.

170. In case of transmitter in phototelegraph, the phase difference between the paper clips on the sending and receiving drum does not exceed
    (a) 10°   (b) 15°   (c) 3.6°   (d) 2°

171. In the receiver of the phototelegraph system the picture signal passes through the amplifier, demodulator and then through the low pass filter having f_c
    (a) 1300 Hz   (b) 1000 Hz   (c) 1020 Hz   (d) none of the above.

172. The word Radar means
    (a) Radio signal and reflected wave   (b) Radio detection and ranging
    (c) Radio frequency and ranging   (d) None of the above.

173. When detection of moving targets is made through unmodulated continuous wave energy, then the radar system is termed
    (a) continuous wave radar   (b) pulsed radar
    (c) synchronous radar   (d) none of the above.

174. The periodic pulses of the transmitter of pulsed radar is
    (a) of low power   (b) of low power and large duration
    (c) of low power and short duration   (d) of high power and short duration.

175. The antenna system of pulsed radar is
    (a) non-directional and capable of rotating in azimuth or in vertical plane or both
    (b) highly directional and capable or rotating in azimuth only
    (c) non-directional and capable of rotating in vertical plane only
    (d) highly directional and capable of rotating in azimuth or in vertical plane or both.

176. The duplexer
    (a) connects the transmitter and receiver in radar only
    (b) connects the transmitter to the antenna and isolates the sensitive receiver in radar
    (c) connects the transmitter with the receiver and isolates the antenna in radar
    (d) none of the above.

177. Timer in the radar
    (a) controls the generation of pulses in the receiver of radar
    (b) controls the generation of pulses in the transmitter of radar
    (c) controls the pulses of the duplexer of radar
    (d) none of the above.

178. The pulsed radar receiver is usually capable of detecting signals of small power of the order of
    (a) 10^{-6} W   (b) 10^{-2} W   (c) 10^{-12} W   (d) 10^{-8} W.

179. Pulse repetition time of pulsed radar
    (a) is the time interval between the starting of the transmission of pulse of the first pulse and the starting of the transmission of pulse of the second consecutive pulse
    (b) is the period for which the transmitter transmits the pulse

(c) is the ratio of time interval between the starting of the transmission of pulse of the first pulse and the starting of the transmission of pulse of the second consecutive pulse

(d) none of the above.

180. Duty ratio of a pulsed radar is

(a) the ratio of pulse width and pulse repetition period

(b) the ratio of the pulse repetition period and pulse width

(c) the ratio of time interval between the starting of the transmission of pulse of the first pulse and the starting of the transmission of pulse of the second consecutive pulse

(d) none of the above.

181. Peak power of a pulsed radar is

(a) the output power of the radar transmitter during the pulse interval

(b) the input power of the radar transmitter during the pulse interval

(c) the output power of the radar receiver during the pulse repetition interval

(d) none of the above.

182. The average power of a pulsed radar is equal to

(a) peak power × pulse width

(b) peak power × pulse repetition time

(c) peak power × duty ratio

(d) peak power × pulsed duration.

183. In the pulsed radar,

(a) the leading edge of the synchronization pulse marks the beginning of the time interval

(b) the leading edge of the echo pulse marks the beginning of the time interval

(c) the leading edge of the synchronization pulse marks the end of the time interval

(d) none of the above.

184. In case of airborne radar

(a) high frequency radar transmitter is essential

(b) low frequency radar transmitter is essential

(c) lower frequency radar transmitter compared to that of ground based radar is essential

(d) none of the above.

185. In case of high frequency radar

(a) it is difficult to locate small targets

(b) it is difficult to have a narrower beam

(c) low power is needed

(d) none of the above.

186. Power density (P_d) at a distance d from antenna of a pulse radar is

(a) $P_d = \dfrac{P_T}{d}$ (b) $P_d = \dfrac{P_T}{4\pi d}$ (c) $P_d = \dfrac{P_T}{\pi d}$ (d) $P_d = \dfrac{P_T}{4\pi d^2}$

where P_T represents the peak power transmitted by the transmitter

187. The power density (P_d) at a distance 'd' of a pulse radar will be

(a) $P_d = \dfrac{P_T P_G}{d}$ (b) $P_d = \dfrac{P_T P_G}{4\pi d}$ (c) $P_d = \dfrac{P_T}{P_G d}$ (d) $P_d = \dfrac{P_T P_G}{4\pi d^2}$

where P_T represents the peak power transmitted by the transmitter, P_G is the power gain of the transmitter in the direction of the target relative to isotropic radiator.

188. The maximum value of the distance covered by a pulse radar is

(a) $\sqrt[4]{\dfrac{P_T \lambda^3 P_G^2 A_s}{(4\pi)^3 P_{R\min}}}$ (b) $\sqrt[4]{\dfrac{P_T \lambda^4 P_G^2 A_s}{(4\pi)^3 P_{R\min}}}$ (c) $\sqrt[4]{\dfrac{P_T \lambda P_G^2 A_s}{(4\pi)^3 P_{R\min}}}$ (d) $\sqrt[4]{\dfrac{P_T \lambda^2 P_G^2 A_s}{(4\pi)^3 P_{R\min}}}$

where P_T represents the peak power transmitted by the transmitter, λ represents the wavelength, P_G represents the power gain of transmitter antenna, A_s represents the equivalent cross-section for target, $P_{R\min}$ represents the minimum value of available received power.

189. The value of Boltzmann's constant is

(a) 1.38×10^{-22} (b) 1.38×10^{-23} (c) 1.38×10^{-24} (d) 1.38×10^{20}

190. The equivalent noise voltage of the resistor is

(a) $4RkTB$ (b) $\sqrt{4RkTB}$ (c) $(4RkTB)^2$ (d) None of the above.

where k is the Botzmann's constant
T is the absolute temperature
B is the bandwidth in hertz.

191. The equivalent noise resistance of the two cascaded amplifier is

(a) $R_1 + \dfrac{R_2}{A_1} + \dfrac{R_3}{A_1 A_2}$ (b) $R_1 + \dfrac{R_2}{A_1^2} + \dfrac{R_3}{A_1 A_2}$

(c) $R_1 + \dfrac{R_2}{\sqrt{A_1}} + \dfrac{R_3}{\sqrt{A_1 A_2}}$ (d) $R_1 + \dfrac{R_2}{A_1^2} + \dfrac{R_3}{A_1^2 A_2^2}$.

192. The noise figure is

(a) signal to noise power supplied to the input
(b) signal to noise power supplied by the system to the output
(c) ratio of signal to noise power supplied to the input terminals of the system to the signal to noise power supplied by the system to the output
(d) none of the above.

193. The noise figure of a radar system is

(a) $1 + \dfrac{R_3 - R_2}{R_1}$ (b) $1 + \dfrac{R_3}{R_1}$ (c) $1 + \dfrac{R_1}{R_3 - R_2}$ (d) $1 - \dfrac{(R_3 - R_2)}{R_1}$.

where R_1 is the source internal resistance
R_2 is the input resistance
R_3 is the equivalent noise resistance.

194. The maximum range of a pulsed radar is

(a) $d_{\max} = \left[\dfrac{P_T D^4 A_s}{B\lambda^2 (F-1)}\right]^{1/4}$ (b) $d_{\max} = 48\left[\dfrac{P_T D^4 A_s}{B\lambda^2 (F-1)}\right]^{1/4}$

(c) $d_{max} = 48\left[\dfrac{P_T D^4 A_s}{B\lambda(F-1)}\right]$ (d) $d_{max} = 48\left[\dfrac{P_T D^4 A_s}{B\lambda^3(F-1)}\right]$

where P_T represents the peak power transmitted by the transmitter
  D represents the diameter of capture area
  A_s represents the effective echo area of the target
  B represents the bandwidth
  λ represents the wavelength
  F is the noise figure.

195. Moving target indicator system
  (a) eliminates the permanent echoes and retains echoes from the moving target
  (b) retains the permanent echoes and eliminates echoes from the moving target
  (c) identifies the mountaineous regions effectively
  (d) none of the above.

196. As per the Doppler effect
  (a) if source and observer are moving away from each other, the apparent frequency will increase
  (b) if source and observer are moving away from each other, the apparent frequency will decrease
  (c) if source and observer are moving toward each other, the apparent frequency will decrease
  (d) none of the above.

197. The frequency of IF of MTI radar is equal to
  (a) the frequency of coherent oscillator
  (b) the frequency of stable local oscillator
  (c) the frequency of STALO
  (d) none of the above.

198. The blind speed is equal to
  (a) $\dfrac{1}{3}$ [pulse repetition frequency $\times$ $(n\lambda)$]
  (b) $\dfrac{\text{pulse repetition frequency}}{n\lambda}$
  (c) $\dfrac{1}{4}\left(\dfrac{\text{pulse repetition frequency}}{n\lambda}\right)$
  (d) none of the above.

where n is any interger
  λ is the wavelength of transmitted signal.

199. The main limitation of the continuous wave radar is
  (a) that the range discrimination is only obtained with the help of very costly circuit complexity

    (b) to detect aircraft in the presence of fixed objects

    (c) to detect moving objects such as automobile

    (d) none of the above.

200. The FM radar arrangement is similar to that of

    (a) pulsed radar

    (b) continuous wave radar

    (c) blind speed radar

    (d) none of the above.

201. For aircraft, the operation of altimeter is based on

    (a) pulsed radar

    (b) continuous wave radar

    (c) Frequency modulation radar

    (d) none of the above.

202. In television system, generally,

    (a) the audio signal is transmitted by frequency modulation and video signal is transmitted by amplitude modulation

    (b) the audio signal is transmitted by amplitude modulation and video signal is transmitted by frequency modulation

    (c) the audio signal is transmitted by amplitude modulation and video signal is transmitted by amplitude modulation

    (d) the audio signal is transmitted by frequency modulation and video signal is transmitted by frequency modulation.

203. In television receiver circuit the sound and video signals are separated by

    (a) RF amplifier

    (b) video detector

    (c) scanning circuit

    (d) synchronizing circuit.

204. Mosaic is

    (a) a photo sensitive plate which is available in the camera tube of television

    (b) the name of laser beam

    (c) a plate used in crystal oscillator

    (d) none of the above.

205. The time taken from the beginning of one line to the instant when the next line begins to be scanned is

    (a) 6.35 μs

    (b) 63.5 μs

    (c) 635 μs

    (d) .635 μs.

206. As soon as the retrace ends, the scanning of the next line starts in television system. Hence, after a lapse of

    (a) 0.12 H, the picture will be visible

    (b) 0.14 H, the picture will be visible

    (c) 0.16 H, the picture will be visible

    (d) 0.18 H, the picture will be visible.

    (H —time allocated for scanning of the line.)

207. In the television system, when the horizontal scanning takes place 15750 times per second, the vertical scanning takes place

    (a) 70 times per second

    (b) 60 times per second

    (c) 80 times per second

    (d) 100 times per second

208. In the television system, usually,

(a) about 31 H time is required for the vertical blanking
(b) about 21 H time is required for the vertical blanking
(c) about 41 H time is required for the vertical blanking
(d) about 11 H times is required for the vertical blanking.

(H—time allocated for scanning of the line.)

209. In the television system, the frame repetition rate for scanning as per the Indian standard is

(a) 25 frames per second
(b) 35 frames per second
(c) 50 frames per second
(d) 75 frames per second.

210. In the television system, the Interlaced scanning is that type of scanning where each field

(a) consists of one fourth of the total number of lines available
(b) consists of one half of the total number of lines available
(c) consists of one-eighth of the total number of lines available
(d) consists of one tenth of the total number of lines available.

211. The vertical resolution of a TV system is expressed as

(a) $n = \dfrac{H}{2\alpha D}$ (b) $n = \dfrac{2H}{\alpha D}$ (c) $n = \dfrac{3H}{\alpha D}$ (d) $n = \dfrac{H}{\alpha D}$.

where, n—number of lines of vertical resolution
H—height of the picture
D—distance for watching
α—minimum angle of vertical resolution in radians.

212. It is generally found that the average number of effective lines, in a TV system, gets reduced to

(a) 0.7 times the total active scan line present
(b) 0.4 times the total active scan line present
(c) 0.95 times the total active scan line present
(d) 0.5 times the total active scan line present.

213. In the television system of 625 horizontal lines, the vertical resolution, due to the Kell factor, becomes

(a) 210 lines (b) 310 lines (c) 410 lines (d) 510 lines.

214. The highest fundamental video frequency for a television system is,

(a) $\dfrac{\text{Active lines} \times \text{Kell factor}}{2 \times \text{Line forward scan period}}$

(b) $\dfrac{\text{Active lines} \times \text{Aspect ratio}}{2 \times \text{Line forward scan period}}$

(c) $\dfrac{\text{Active lines} \times \text{Kell factor} \times \text{Aspect ratio}}{2 \times \text{Line forward scan period}}$

(d) $\dfrac{\text{Active lines} \times \text{Kell factor} \times \text{Aspect ratio}}{\text{Line forward scan period}}$.

215. For transmitting the complete TV signal
  (a) a channel of 5 MHz width is to be provided
  (b) a channel of 7 MHz width is to be provided
  (c) a channel of 10 MHz width is to be provided
  (d) a channel of 3 MHz width is to be provided.

216. In case of sequential scanning of a TV system, for 625 lines, the horizontal scanning frequency will be
  (a) 15625 lines/second (b) 31250 lines/second
  (c) 50 lines/second (d) 25 lines/second.

217. For sequential and interlaced scanning the requisite horizontal resolution of 273 pairs of black and white alterations in one horizontal line, the bandwidth requirement will be
  (a) 7.5 MHz (b) 5 MHz (c) 3 MHz (d) 10 MHz.

218. In case of TV system 625 horizontal lines, the horizontal synchronizing pulse duration will be
  (a) 12 μs (b) 4.7 μs (c) 1.5 μs (d) 5.76 μs.

219. The field retrace begins at the Indian television system
  (a) at the middle of the horizontal scanning line in the case of an odd field and at the end of a horizontal scanning line in the case of even field
  (b) at the end of the horizontal scanning line in the case of an odd field and at the middle of a horizontal scanning line in the case of a even field
  (c) at the end of the horizontal scanning line in the case of an odd field and at the end of a horizontal scanning line in the case of even field
  (d) at the middle of the horizontal scanning line in the case of an odd field as well as an even field.

220. The pre-equalizing pulses equalize
  (a) vertical and horizontal pulses
  (b) the integrated vertical synchronizing for odd and even fields
  (c) odd and even fields
  (d) none of the above.

221. In case of 7 MHz standard television channel, the limit of lower sideband is arbitrarily labelled zero frequency and the vestigial sideband is extended up to
  (a) 5 MHz (b) 1.25 MHz (c) 8.25 MHz (d) 6 MHz.

222. The sound signal is frequency modulated because it provides
  (a) interference-free reception

(b) the rate at which the frequency variation will take place, will be equal to the modulating frequency

(c) variable amplitude modulated carrier

(d) none of the above.

223. Carson's rule describes

(a) that the bandwidth needed to pass an FM wave is equal the sum of the deviation and highest modulating frequency

(b) that the bandwidth needed to pass an FM wave is equal to twice the sum of the deviation and highest modulating frequency

(c) that the bandwidth needed to pass an FM wave is equal to thrice the sum of the deviation and highest modulating frequency

(d) none of the above.

224. In the television system lines per frame for north and south America, US, Canda, Mexico and Japan are

(a) 625   (b) 525   (c) 60   (d) 50.

225. The television colour system 'SECAM' is generally followed in

(a) USSR   (b) England   (c) USA   (d) INDIA.

226. For 48 cm monochrome TV, the high voltage applied is

(a) 24 kV   (b) 36 kV   (c) 36 kV   (d) 5 kV.

227. In TV the persistence must occur

(a) less than $\dfrac{1}{25}$ second for picture tube

(b) greater than $\dfrac{1}{25}$ second for picture tube

(c) greater than 0.1 second for picture tube

(d) none of the above.

228. In rectangular face plate picture tube, the breadth to height ratio is

(a) 3 : 2   (b) 2 : 1   (c) 4 : 3   (d) 8 : 5.

229. Without providing ion-trap, the TV screen brightness and contrast can be improved by utilizing

(a) aluminized coating on the phosphor screen

(b) thicker phosphor screen

(c) thinner phosphor screen

(d) none of the above.

230. In the picture tube, spark gap is utilized for

(a) avoiding arcing   (b) enhancing screen brightness

(c) acting as filter capacitor   (d) none of the above.

231. In image orthicon camera, the inside of the glass face plate at the front is coated with a silver antimony coating sensitized with cesium

(a) for serving as photo cathode   (b) for safety

(c) for brightness   (d) for better contrast.

232. In the image orthicon camera, the target plate is kept at

(a) about 200 volts more positive with respect to the photo cathode

(b) about 400 volts more positive with respect to the photo cathode

(c) about 100 volts more positive with respect to the photo cathode

(d) none of the above.

233. In the image orthicon camera, the screen consists of

(a) 400 meshes per cm^2 with an open area of 20 to 30 per cent

(b) 300 meshes per cm^2 with an open area of 50 to 75 per cent

(c) 600 meshes per cm^2 with an open area of 10 to 20 per cent

(d) 200 meshes per cm^2 with an open area of 60 to 70 per cent.

234. The thickness of the target plate of image orthicon camera is

(a) 0.04 mm   (b) 0.02 mm   (c) 0.01 mm   (d) 0.004 mm.

235. The total gain obtained at the electron multiplier is approximately 1000 because each multiplier stage gives a gain of approximately

(a) 5   (b) 4   (c) 3   (d) 2.

236. A vidicon camera works on the principle of

(a) electromagnetism   (b) photo conductivity

(c) photo synthesis   (d) photocell.

237. The thickness of the photolayer in a vidicon camera is

(a) 0.01 cm   (b) 0.001 cm   (c) 0.0001 cm   (d) 0.00001 cm.

238. When the bright light falls on any area of photo conductive coating of a vidicon camera, the resistance across the thickness of the portion is reduced to about

(a) 3 MΩ (b) 1 MΩ (c) 2 MΩ (d) 4 MΩ.

239. The typical value of the output for vidicon camera is

(a) 0.02 μA for bright light   (b) 0.03 μA for bright light

(c) 0.4 μA for bright light   (d) 0.002 μA for bright light.

240. A vidicon is a short tube with a length of

(a) 120 to 200 cm   (b) 12 to 20 cm   (c) 1.2 to 2 cm   (d) 0.120 to 0.200 cm.

241. The typical dimension of the silicon target plate of silicon diode array vidicon is

(a) 0.03 cm   (b) 0.003 cm   (c) 0.0003 cm   (d) 0.3 cm.

242. The charged coupled device is a new technology in

(a) metal oxide semiconductor circuitry   (b) nano technology

(c) VLSI   (d) none of the above.

243. When the light image is focussed on the chip, electrons are developed in proportion to the

(a) intensity of light falling on each cell

(b) square of the intensity of light falling on each cell

(c) cube of the intensity of light falling on each cell

(d) none of the above.

244. RCA SID 51232 is

(a) 24 lead dual-in-line image sensor   (b) opto isolator

(c) device of nano technology   (d) none of the above.

245. MATV is designed to have a

(a) 300 Ω impedance   (b) 75 Ω impedance

(c) 7.5 Ω impedance   (d) .075 Ω impedance.

246. The co-axial distribution network has a large number of cable pairs, in general, it becomes

(a) 10 or 20   (b) 4 or 8   (c) 3 or 6   (d) 12 or 24.

247. The VTR is in a TV system means,

(a) video tape recording   (b) video transmission recording

(c) video transfer recording   (d) none of the above.

248. For a tape speed of 19 cm per second and gap length of 6.3 microns, the usable frequency attains the value of

(a) 15 kHz   (b) 50 kHz   (c) 150 kHz   (d) 200 kHz.

249. The typical value of ac biasing in audio tape recording is

(a) 60 kHz   (b) 100 kHz   (c) 150 kHz   (d) 200 kHz.

250. Satellites get power from

(a) ac generator   (b) dc generator   (c) solar batteries   (d) none of the above.

251. The medium size of antenna in satellite system is

(a) 20 metres   (b) 5 metres   (c) 9 metres   (d) 30 metres.

252. ATS-6 is

(a) Application terrestrial satellite-6   (b) Application technology satellite-6

(c) Application transformed satellite-6 (d) none of the above.

253. TV programmes from earthstation at Ahmedabad are transmitted to ATS-6 at 6 GHz FM carrier with the help of a

(a) 24 m parabolic dish antenna   (b) 14 m parabolic dish antenna

(c) 14 m rectangular dish antenna   (d) none of the above.

254. The down transmission from the satellite is made from a 80 W FM transmitter at

(a) 730 MHz   (b) 860 MHz   (c) 1860 MHz   (d) 2860 MHz.

255. In colour television all colours including white can be developed by mixing

(a) red, yellow, blue   (b) red, green, blue

(c) red, orange, green   (d) red, indigo, green

256. In colour receiver,

(a) both tint and saturation controls are needed if it is SECAM

(b) both tint and saturation controls are not needed if it is SECAM

(c) both tint and saturation controls are not needed if it is PAL

(d) both tint and saturation controls are needed if it is PAL.

257. The colour receiver should be able to develop a black and white picture from a normal monochrome signal and that is termed
(a) reverse compatibility
(b) synchronism
(c) composite compatibility
(d) none of the above.

258. The frequency of cosmic rays is
(a) 10^{20} Hz
(b) 10^{25} Hz
(c) 5×10^{14} Hz
(d) 10^{10} Hz

259. The light sensitive organs are of two types
(a) rods and cores
(b) rods and cones
(c) sticks and cones
(d) sticks and cores.

260. The sensitivity of the human eye is greatest for
(a) red light
(b) blue light
(c) green light
(d) orange light.

261. The maximum sensitivity occurs in the human eye at
(a) 650 nm
(b) 450 nm
(c) 750 nm
(d) 550 nm.

262. In television the basic colours are
(a) red, green and yellow
(b) red, blue and yellow
(c) red, green and blue
(d) none of the above.

263. Pairwise mixing of primary colours develop
(a) Red + green = blue
(b) Red + green = yellow
(c) Blue + green = magenta
(d) Red + green = magenta.

264. The reference white for colour television has been a mixture of
(a) 30% green, 59% red, 11% blue
(b) 30% red, 11% green, 59% blue
(c) 30% red, 59% green and 11% blue
(d) 60% red, 30% green and 10% blue.

265. 1 lumen of white light is equal to
(a) 0.89 lumen of yellow and 0.11 lumen of blue
(b) 0.7 lumen of red + 0.3 lumen of cyan
(c) 0.41 lumen of green + 0.59 lumen of magenta
(d) 0.89 lumen of blue + 0.11 lumen of yellow.

266. Chrominance is
(a) hue
(b) hue and saturation of a colour being put together
(c) saturation
(d) luminance or brightness.

267. Y signal is equal to
(a) $0.3G + 0.59R + 0.11B$
(b) $0.3R + 0.59G + 0.11B$
(c) $0.11R + 0.59B + 0.30G$
(d) $0.70R + 0.20G + 0.10B$.

268. In delta gun colour picturetube, approximately,
(a) 1000 000 dots are available
(b) 1000 00 dots are available
(c) 10 000 dots are available
(d) 1000 dots are available.

269. In case of data transmission,

  (a) amplitude modulation can be utilized with good noise immunity
  (b) amplitude modulation can be utilized with poor noise immunity
  (c) frequency modulation can be utilized with poor noise immunity
  (d) none of the above.

270. In data transmission, frequency modulation is termed

  (a) FSK   (b) PSK   (c) FKS   (d) none of the above.

271. Phase modulation modems usually operate in

  (a) 2 or 4 phases   (b) 4 or 8 phases   (c) 3 or 5 phases   (d) none of the above.

272. In ASCII code format, the speed is variable up to

  (a) 1200 bps   (b) 1800 bps   (c) 2400 bps   (d) none of the above.

273. In case of synchronous transmission, messages are sent in blocks of fixed or variable length up to

  (a) 1000   (b) 10000   (c) 100   (d) 10.

274. In satellite networks

  (a) 16 kbps modems are operated for high speed
  (b) 32 kbps modems are operated for high speed
  (c) 8 kbps modems are operated for high speed
  (d) none of the above.

275. Rules are provided for the flow of data in the network and these are called

  (a) Network topology   (b) Network protocols
  (c) Network laws   (d) None of the above.

276. "A block of data received from one end of data link to the other end" is

  (a) Level 1   (b) Level 2   (c) Level 3   (d) Level 4.

277. 'Interpretation of data exchanged' is handled in

  (a) Level 1   (b) Level 4   (c) Level 5   (d) Level 6.

278. For deadlock recovery

  (a) Level 1 of the network protocol is used
  (b) Level 2 of the network protocol is used
  (c) Level 5 of the network protocol is used
  (d) Level 7 of the network protocol is used.

279. For error checking in a block of data

  (a) BCC is utilized   (b) CRC is utilized
  (c) synchronous protocol is utilized   (d) none of the above.

280. An automatic repeat request is needed for error correction and that is called

  (a) ECC   (b) ARQ   (c) ARR   (d) none of the above.

281. Error rate improvement may be obtained with the help of a factor of

  (a) 10^2–10^3 (b) 10^5–10^6 (c) 10^7–10^8 (d) 10^9–10^{10}.

282. Communication processor is also called
    (a) concentrator
    (b) communication indicator
    (c) signal processor
    (d) none of the above.

283. In satellite communications FEC is termed.
    (a) Front error correction technique
    (b) Forward electronic correction technique
    (c) Forward error correction technique
    (d) Forward error computer technique.

284. Datagram is not used for
    (a) Cash dispenser
    (b) Credit validation
    (c) electronic funds transfer transaction
    (d) None of the above.

285. Virtual call is a
    (a) dummy call
    (b) point-to-point connection between sending and receiving terminals
    (c) perfect call
    (d) none of the above.

286. The 64-kbps, PCM channel gives a very good carrier for data and systems with facilities for both voice of 64 kbps and data of
    (a) 64 kbps
    (b) 32 kbps
    (c) 9.6 kbps
    (d) none of the above.

287. FSK is a type of frequency modulation where the modulating signal is
    (a) an analogue signal
    (b) a sinusoidal signal
    (c) a square wave signal
    (d) a binary data sequence.

288. Phase shift keying takes n-bits at a time from the data sequence and encodes them into
    (a) 2^{n+1} phase shifts
    (b) 2^{n+2} phase shifts
    (c) 2^{n-1} phase shifts
    (d) 2^n phase shifts.

289. In data transmission the CCITT recommend was encashed to cover
    (a) 200 bits/second in each direction
    (b) 100 bits/second in each direction
    (c) 300 bits/second in each direction
    (d) none of the above.

290. Asynchronous or synchronous working between data equipments is possible when the following modem is used
    (a) Datel Modem No. 103
    (b) Datel Modem No. 2
    (c) Datel Modem No. 3
    (d) Datel Modem No. 4.

291. The United Kingdom version of the modem in data transmission is termed
    (a) Dataset No. 103
    (b) Datel modem No. 2
    (c) Datel modem No. 103
    (d) Datel modem No. 4.

292. Videotex services are very much lucrative for private uses because
    (a) they require low budget system with no need of hard copy
    (b) they require no antenna points
    (c) they require no demodulator
    (d) none of the above.

293. The speed for transmission from user to database/switch in videotex system is
     (a) 1200 bps   (b) 75 bps   (c) 12 kbps   (d) none of the above.

294. For PSTN (Public switchboard telephone network) access the CCITT has recently standardized
     (a) 2400 full duplex
     (c) 3600 full duplex
     (b) 1200 full duplex
     (d) none of the above.

295. In facsimile service, Group 1 category machine describes
     (a) 3 minutes for standard one A4 page
     (b) 6 minutes for standard one A4 page
     (c) 1 minute for standard one A4 page.
     (d) less than 1 minute for standard one A4 page

296. In facsimile service,
     (a) group 4 is used for public data networks
     (b) group 3 is used for public data networks
     (c) group 2 is used for public data networks
     (d) group 1 is used for public data networks.

297. In facsimile service, the machine, required for AM or FM signals for modulation to compatible line signals, is
     (a) group 1   (b) group 2   (c) group 3   (d) group 4.

298. In facsimile system, the picture is digitized by
     (a) group 1 machine
     (c) group 3 machine
     (b) group 2 machine
     (d) group 4 machine.

299. As per CCITT standard in facsimile the carrier frequency of group 1 amplitude modulation is
     (a) in the range of 1300–1900 Hz
     (c) 2400 Hz
     (b) 2100 Hz
     (d) 2800 Hz.

300. As per CCITT standards in facsimile, group 3 equipment makes digital scanning using
     (a) 8.5 lines/mm or higher resolution of 17 lines/mm resolution
     (b) 3.85 lines/mm or higher resolution of 7.7 lines/mm resolution
     (c) 1 line/mm or higher resolution or 2 lines/mm resolution
     (d) none of the above.

301. The main demerit of the use of satellite medium in data network is that
     (a) its performance is not good
     (b) it does not possess large capacity
     (c) it has the high cost of terminal equipment
     (d) none of the above.

302. With the help of microprocessor for communication controller, the delay may not exceed
     (a) 2 seconds for 75% throughput efficiency
     (b) 3 seconds for 80% throughput efficiency

(c) 3 seconds for 75% throughput efficiency

(d) 4 seconds for 75% throughput efficiency.

303. In case of satellite in the data network, with 40% data efficiency, the needed channel rate rendered for overhead bits and clashes is

(a) 500 kb/second   (b) 290 kb/second (c) 320 kb/second (d) 400 kb/second.

304. For a 4-phase modulation, in case of satellite in the data network, the bandwidth required is

(a) 200 kHz   (b) 250 kHz   (c) 150 kHz   (d) 175 kHz.

305. The Indian National Satellite is provided with twelve communication transponders of

(a) 42 dBW EIRP in the C band   (b) 32 dBW EIRP in the C band

(c) 52 dBW EIRP in the C band   (d) 36 dBW EIRP in the C band.

306. It is estimated that 1.5 metre (19.7 G/T) terminal, with direct modulation scheme having minimal redundancy, can be built at a cost of

(a) Rs 25 lakhs   (b) Rs 50 lakhs   (c) Rs 10 lakhs   (d) Rs 5 lakhs.

307. In communication network, ISDN is termed

(a) Integrated switch development network

(b) Integrated services digital network

(c) Integrated services development network

(d) None of the above.

308. The proprietory networks are

(a) active management entities

(b) passive management entities

(c) both active and passive management entities

(d) none of the above.

309. In network management, NMC is termed

(a) Network management cell

(b) Network management centre

(c) Network management co-ordinatior

(d) None of the above

310. In the network model, cable is the

(a) physical component of the network

(b) logical component of the network

(c) auxiliary component of the network

(d) none of the above.

311. Services provided by ISDN is

(a) physical component of the network

(b) logical component of the network

(c) auxiliary component of the network

(d) none of the above.

312. Solid state radio system consists of 7 bits + 1 bit parity framed by
   (a) 1 start and 2 stop bits   (b) 2 start and 1 stop bits
   (c) 2 start and 2 stop bits   (d) none of the above.

313. In solid state radio system MARTS is termed
   (a) Main, Access Radio Telephone System
   (b) Multi Access Radio Telephone System
   (c) Multi Auxiliary Radio Telephone System
   (d) None of the above.

314. ETE is the subsystem of MART and that is expressed as
   (a) Exchange terminal equipment   (b) Electro telephone exchange
   (c) External terminal exchange   (d) Exchange telecommunication equipment.

315. SRT is the subsystem of MARTS and that is expressed as
   (a) Standard radio terminal   (b) Subscriber radio terminal
   (c) Server radio terminal   (d) Subsystem radio terminal.

316. RBS is the subsystem of MART and that is expressed as
   (a) Radio bus station   (b) Radio base station
   (c) Radio base server   (d) Radio bus server.

317. ILSL satisfies the operational performance as laid down in category of I/II/III of the international civil aviation organization and it is expressed as
   (a) International landing system localizer
   (b) Instrument landing system localizer
   (c) Instrument landing server localizer
   (d) none of the above.

318. The allowable margin between a successful and unsuccessful landing in the vertical and horizontal planes is
   (a) approximately a half of a degree   (b) approximately a quarter of a degree
   (c) approximately 3/4th of a degree   (d) approximately one degree.

319. The transmitter of the instrument landing system operates at the frequency range of
   (a) 108 MHz to 112 MHz band/528 MHz to 536 MHz band
   (b) 208 MHz to 212 MHz band/328 MHz to 336 MHz band
   (c) 108 MHz to 112 MHz band/328 MHz to 336 MHz band
   (d) none of the above.

320. In the landing system, course CSB is called
   (a) course carrier and sidebands   (b) course carrier and server
   (c) course centre sideband   (d) none of the above.

321. In the landing system the localizer aerial array is generally
   (a) 56 m/112 m wide   (b) 26 m/65 m wide
   (c) 5.4 m/3.6 m wide   (d) 78 m/168 m wide.

322. In the landing system, the localizer array is generally,

(a) 5.4 m/3.6 m high
(b) 2 m/3 m high
(c) 20 m/30 m high
(d) none of the above.

323. In the landing system, generally, there are

(a) 6/12 dipoles   (b) 12/24 diploes   (c) 18/36 diploes   (d) 3/6 dipoles.

324. In the landing system, the glidepath arrays are installed on masts at heights generally between

(a) 9 m and 17 m   (b) 2 m and 10 m   (c) 1 m and 3 m   (d) none of the above.

325. In low power TV transmitter, generally

(a) 6.3 m diameter parabolic aerial is used
(b) 3.3 m diameter parabolic aerial is used
(c) 2.3 m diameter parabolic aerial is used
(d) 1.3 m diameter parabolic aerial is used.

326. For low power TV broadcast,

(a) 455 kHz IF signal is passed to an INDOOR unit with help of a co-axial cable
(b) 70 MHz IF signal is passed to an INDOOR unit with the help of co-axial cable
(c) 30 MHz IF signal is passed to an INDOOR unit with the help of a co-axial cable
(d) none of the above.

327. The unattended dual low power TV transmitter generally consists of

(a) Two 100 W transmitters   (b) Two 10 W transmitters
(c) Three 15 W transmitters   (d) Four 20 W transmitters.

328. In low power TV transmitter, 'ASU' is termed

(a) Analogue switching unit   (b) Analogue server unit
(c) Auto switching unit   (d) Auto server unit.

329. In low power TV transmitter, 'COU' is termed as

(a) control of unit   (b) change over unit
(c) centre of unit   (d) none of the above.

330. The aspect ratio of HDTV is

(a) 4 : 3   (b) 3 : 4   (c) 16 : 9   (d) none of the above.

331. The horizontal and vertical resolution is

(a) approximately three times to that of conventional TV
(b) approximately two times to that of conventional TV
(c) approximately equal to that of conventional TV
(d) none of the above.

332. Generally in HDTV, some fairly complex signal processing is made so that bandwidth compression can be made by an approximate highest factor of about

(a) 2 times   (b) 3 times   (c) 4 times   (d) none of the above.

333. In cellular system, the MTSO is termed

(a) Main telephone switching office

(b) Mobile telecommunication switching office

(c) Main telecommunication server office

(d) Mobile telecommunication server office.

334. In cellular system, the cells can be divided into smaller cells. The method is called

(a) cell division   (b) cell splitting   (c) cell separation   (d) none of the above.

335. A new shared allocation for land mobile services in 1979 had been made by WARC which is called

(a) world analogue radio conference   (b) world administrative radio conference

(c) world administrative radio centre   (d) none of the above.

336. It has been observed that

(a) 1000 MHz band gives an optimum channel capacity and frequency reuse capacity

(b) 900 MHz band gives an optimum channel capacity and frequency reuse capacity

(c) 1600 MHz band gives an optimum channel capacity and frequency reuse capacity

(d) 1200 MHz band gives an optimum channel capacity and frequency reuse capacity.

337. The World Administration Radio Conference made the frequency range of

(a) 860–960 MHz for land mobile services

(b) 1060–1160 MHz for land mobile services

(c) 560–660 MHz for land mobile services

(d) 760–860 MHz for land mobile services.

338. In the UK,

(a) the frequency band 860–960 MHz is allotted to cellular base station network transmitters

(b) the frequency band 935–950 MHz is allotted to cellular base station network transmitters

(c) the frequency band 960–1060 MHz is allotted to cellular base station network transmitters

(d) the frequency band 1000–1060 MHz is allotted to cellular base station network transmitters.

339. In cellular telephone instrument, diplexer is

(a) a pair of filters   (b) a transmitter   (c) a receiver   (d) none of the above.

340. ISDN means

(a) International services digital network

(b) Integrated services digital network

(c) Integrated server digital network

(d) International server digital network.

341. In ISDN, AMPS means

(a) Analogue mobile phone service   (b) Advanced mobile phone service

(c) Advanced mobile phone server   (d) none of the above.

342. In ISDN, TACS means,
   (a) Technical advanced communication services
   (b) Technical analogue communication services
   (c) Technical advanced communication server
   (d) None of the above.

343. In ISDN, NMT means
   (a) Northern mobile telephone   (b) Nordic mobile telephone
   (c) Nano mobile telephone   (d) New mobile technique.

344. In ISDN, HCMTS means
   (a) high capacity mobile telephone server
   (b) high capacity mobile telephone service
   (c) high capacity mobile telephone system
   (d) none of the above.

345. Satellite technology can carry heavy traffic generally to the tune of
   (a) 500 Mbps   (b) 280 Mbps   (c) 120 Mbps   (d) 60 Mbps

346. Compared to LED, laser is
   (a) more reliable
   (b) required more frequent servicing and replacement
   (c) having less expensive drive circuits
   (d) none of the above.

347. For data rates up to about 10 Mbits/second
   (a) a monomode fibre is utilized   (b) a multimode fibre is utilized
   (c) a graded index fibre is utilized   (d) a fibre bundle is utilized.

348. The disadvantage of *p-i-n* photodiode detector is that
   (a) it is less sensitive
   (b) its cost is high
   (c) its temperature and bias stability is not good
   (d) none of the above.

349. For optical fibre system of LED and multi-mode, the information rate and repeater spacing are
   (a) 8.448 Mbits/s, 6.0 km   (b) 34.368 Mbits/s, 1.7 km
   (c) 2.048 Mbits/s, 10.0 km   (d) none of the above.

350. For optical fibre system of LASER and monomode, the information rate and repeater spacing are
   (a) 8.448 Mbits/s, 13 km   (b) 34.368 Mbits/s, 10.4 km
   (c) 2.048 Mbits/s, 15 km   (d) none of the above.

351. Small earthstation even acts with DAMA for optimal use of transponder on board in satellites. DAMA is expressed as
   (a) Demand assigned multiple access   (b) Data assigned multiple access
   (c) Data adjusted mobile access   (d) Data and mobile assignment.

352. VSATs is microstations with aerials of 1.5 m–2.5 m and it is expressed as

  (a) very small aperture earth terminals (b) video of satellites
  (c) very small analogue terminals   (d) none of the above.

353. The severe interference co-ordination problems with other satellite systems and terrestrial systems is happening due to

  (a) widespread utilization of 6/4 GHz for satellite communication
  (b) widespread utilization of 14/11 GHz for satellite communication
  (c) widespread utilization of 30/20 GHz for satellite communication
  (d) none of the above.

354. Due to the development of digital signal processing techniques, quality of voice can be available at a bit ratio as low as

  (a) 4.8 kb/second to 9.6 kb/second   (b) 2.8 kb/second to 5.6 kb/second
  (c) 1.8 kb/second to 3.6 kb/second   (d) none of the above.

355. Due to the contribution of digital signal processing,

  (a) full motion video teleconferencing is possible at 64 kb/second
  (b) full motion teleconferencing is possible at 8 kb/second
  (c) full motion teleconferencing is possible at 6 kb/second
  (d) none of the above.

356. VSSA is termed

  (a) very small stand analogue exchange
  (b) very small stand alone exchange
  (c) very small standard analogue exchange
  (d) very small standard automatic exchange.

357. Long haul digital radio relay systems are utilized to link rural switches to the main network over distances up to

  (a) 50 km in a single hop   (b) 100 km in a single hop
  (c) 200 km in a single hop   (d) 300 km in single hop.

358. SCPC is termed

  (a) standard channel per carrier mode   (b) single channel per carrier mode
  (c) server channel per carrier mode   (d) single carrier per channel mode.

359. MCPC is termed

  (a) mega channel per carrier technique
  (b) multiple channel per carrier technique
  (c) medium channel per carrier technique
  (d) master channel per carrier technique.

360. It can be made

  (a) 500 voice channels utilizing a 2 Mbits/modem
  (b) 1000 voice channels utilizing a 2 Mbits/modem
  (c) 10000 voice channels utilizing a 2Mbits/modem
  (d) 100000 voice channels utilizing a 2 Mbits/modem.

361. In a Fastcom station for telecommunication equipment, the frequency of the transmitted signal modulates a carrier and the frequency of the same is obtained by a synthesizer
   (a) within 60–97 MHz intermediate frequency band
   (b) within 121–158 MHz intermediate frequency band
   (c) within 20–80 MHz intermediate frequency band
   (d) within 221–258 MHz intermediate frequency band.

362. In a Fastcom station for telecommunication equipment, synthesizers are tuneable in
   (a) 0.5 MHz steps   (b) 0.2 MHz steps (c) 0.1 MHz steps (d) 0.05 MHz steps.

363. Fastcom stations
   (a) cannot be installed rapidly on roughly prepared sites
   (b) need local operator
   (c) may allow power to be delivered from solar cells
   (d) none of the above.

364. RURTEL system can work
   (a) up to 1000 subscribers spreadover a long area with repeaters
   (b) up to 500 subscribers spreadover a long area with repeaters
   (c) up to 320 subscribers spreadover a long area with repeaters
   (d) up to 200 subscribers spreadover a long area with repeaters.

365. The feature of the speech is derived from its short time spectrum which is measured successively over short time windows of length
   (a) 50–60 milliseconds overlapping at intervals of 5–10 ms
   (b) 20–30 milliseconds overlapping at intervals of 10–20 ms
   (c) 40–50 milliseconds overlapping at intervals of 12–15 ms
   (d) 100–110 milliseconds overlapping at intervals of 20–30 ms.

366. ADPCM is termed
   (a) additional pulse code modulation
   (b) adaptive differential pulse code modulation
   (c) analogue distribution pulse code modulation
   (d) additive differential pulse code modulation.

367. For high quality speech coding
   (a) a 16 kbit/second adaptive differential pulse code modulation is taken
   (b) a 32 kbit/second adaptive differential pulse code modulation is taken
   (c) an 8 kbit/second adaptive differential pulse code modulation is taken
   (d) a 4 kbit/second adaptive differential pulse code modulation is taken.

368. VME is termed as
   (a) VERSA—module energy   (b) VERSA—module Europe
   (c) Variable module energy   (d) VERSA—mobile Europe.

369. VME bus was originally developed for the
   (a) Motorola 58000 line of CPUs   (b) Motorola 68000 line of CPUs
   (c) Motorola 48000 line of CPUs   (d) Motorola 38000 line of CPUs.

370. The CODEC is a device or program which is capable of encoding and/or decoding a digital data stream or signal. The analogue signal is sampled
    (a) at 16 kHz and digitized by a standard PCM codec to develop log coded samples
    (b) at 8 kHz and digitized by a standard PCM codec to develop log coded samples
    (c) at 32 kHz and digitized by a standard PCM codec to develop log coded samples
    (d) at 64 kHz and digitized by a standard PCM codec to develop log coded samples.

371. DTW is termed
    (a) Dynamic temperature warping
    (b) Dual time warping
    (c) Dynamic time warping
    (d) Digital time warping.

372. The DTW is constructed as a 2 μm CMOS standard cell gate array with a power consumption of approximately
    (a) 200 mW   (b) 300 mW   (c) 100 mW   (d) 500 mW.

373. The DTW is a chip which gives the high throughput rate needed for vocabulary of about
    (a) 2,000 words   (b) 5,000 words   (c) 1,000 words   (d) 10,000 words.

374. CMOS is termed
    (a) combined metal oxide semiconductor
    (b) complementary metal oxide semiconductor
    (c) cumulative metal oxide semiconductor
    (d) coupled metal oxide semiconductor.

375. Usually, CMOS technology is used in
    (a) Digital computer   (b) analogue computer
    (c) microprocessor   (d) none of the above.

376. Since the chip clock frequency is 40 MHz, the basic DTW cycle for processing one template frame takes
    (a) 400 ns   (b) 450 ns   (c) 500 ns   (d) 600 ns.

377. The DTW chip can address up to
    (a) 2 Mbytes of DTW memory   (b) 5 Mbytes of DTW memory
    (c) 1 Mbyte of DTW memory   (d) 10 Mbytes of DTW memory.

378. Microprocessor can address up to
    (a) 1000 kbytes of programme and data memory
    (b) 512 kbytes of programme and data memory
    (c) 10000 kbytes of programme and data memory
    (d) none of the above.

379. The application to office communication includes
    (a) a voice activated voice mail system developed by SEL
    (b) voice controlled telephone operator
    (c) speech input for dialling
    (d) none of the above.

380. The speech processing system is connected to the operator console through
  (a) a 2/4 wire interface
  (b) a 3/6 wire interface
  (c) a single wire interface
  (d) none of the above.

381. PABX means
  (a) public automatic branch exchange
  (b) private automatic branch exchange
  (c) public analogue branch exchange
  (d) private analogue branch exchange.

382. DTMF tones mean
  (a) double tone multi frequency
  (b) dual tone multi frequency
  (c) dual tone mega frequency
  (d) none of the above.

383. The distances are termed enclidean when
  (a) the sum of the difference between the components of the feature vectors is considered
  (b) the sum of the squared differences between the components of the feature vectors is considered
  (c) the multiplication of the squared differences between the components of the feature vectors is considered
  (d) none of the above.

384. The prosodic contour expresses
  (a) the intonation of a phrase
  (b) the inverse spectrum of the logarithm of the power spectrum
  (c) the nonlinear scale for frequency corresponding to the sensitivity of the ear
  (d) none of the above.

385. In multibus structure, the hardware architecture is arranged around a minibus which is termed
  (a) the X-bus
  (b) the X-bus coupler
  (c) balanced transmission
  (d) none of the above.

386. Each processor through X-bus possesses an addressing space of
  (a) 4 Gbytes
  (b) 6 Gbytes
  (c) 8 Gbytes
  (d) 2 Gbytes.

387. In an input–output structure with front end processor,
  (a) about 256 telecommunication lines can be connected
  (b) about 128 telecommunication lines can be connected
  (c) about 64 telecommunication lines can be connected
  (d) none of the above.

388. In an input–output structure, the operation range of front end processor is
  (a) 4 Mbits/s simultaneously in both directions of transmission
  (b) 2 Mbits/s simultaneously in both directions of transmission
  (c) 6 Mbits/s simultaneously in both directions of transmission
  (d) none of the above.

389. For main transmission coupler in input–output structure HDLC means
  (a) High level data link control
  (b) High district link control
  (c) High directional level control
  (d) none of the above.

390. The high level service FMS is described as

    (a) file management system

    (b) file monitoring system

    (c) file mounting system

    (d) none of the above.

391. In high level system WAM means

    (a) working analogue method

    (b) workstation access method

    (c) workstation auxiliary method

    (d) none of the above.

392. ECAM in high level service means

    (a) External communication access method

    (b) Extended communication access method

    (c) Extra communication access method

    (d) none of the above.

393. DISTRAM in high level service means

    (a) Distributed and sectional transactional access method

    (b) Distributed and secured transactional access method

    (c) Disburse and secured transactional access method

    (d) None of the above.

ANSWERS TO OBJECTIVE TYPE QUESTIONS

1. (a)	**2.** (b)	**3.** (c)	**4.** (a)	**5.** (b)	**6.** (a)
7. (b)	**8.** (b)	**9.** (b)	**10.** (c)	**11.** (a)	**12.** (b)
13. (a)	**14.** (b)	**15.** (a)	**16.** (c)	**17.** (a)	**18.** (c)
19. (b)	**20.** (c)	**21.** (b)	**22.** (a)	**23.** (a)	**24.** (b)
25. (b)	**26.** (b)	**27.** (b)	**28.** (a)	**29.** (b)	**30.** (b)
31. (b)	**32.** (a)	**33.** (a)	**34.** (a)	**35.** (a)	**36.** (d)
37. (a)	**38.** (a)	**39.** (a)	**40.** (a)	**41.** (b)	**42.** (a)
43. (b)	**44.** (b)	**45.** (b)	**46.** (a)	**47.** (b)	**48.** (a)
49. (c)	**50.** (b)	**51.** (b)	**52.** (b)	**53.** (c)	**54.** (a)
55. (b)	**56.** (a)	**57.** (b)	**58.** (a)	**59.** (b)	**60.** (c)
61. (a)	**62.** (b)	**63.** (b)	**64.** (a)	**65.** (a)	**66.** (a)
67. (a)	**68.** (c)	**69.** (a)	**70.** (a)	**71.** (b)	**72.** (a)
73. (b)	**74.** (a)	**75.** (a)	**76.** (c)	**77.** (b)	**78.** (a)
79. (a)	**80.** (d)	**81.** (b)	**82.** (a)	**83.** (b)	**84.** (a)
85. (a)	**86.** (c)	**87.** (a)	**88.** (b)	**89.** (b)	**90.** (a)
91. (a)	**92.** (b)	**93.** (a)	**94.** (a)	**95.** (a)	**96.** (a)
97. (c)	**98.** (c)	**99.** (a)	**100.** (b)	**101.** (a)	**102.** (c)
103. (a)	**104.** (d)	**105.** (a)	**106.** (c)	**107.** (b)	**108.** (b)
109. (a)	**110.** (a)	**111.** (d)	**112.** (b)	**113.** (a)	**114.** (b)

115. (b)	**116.** (a)	**117.** (b)	**118.** (a)	**119.** (c)	**120.** (b)
121. (c)	**122.** (b)	**123.** (a)	**124.** (a)	**125.** (a)	**126.** (c)
127. (d)	**128.** (b)	**129.** (c)	**130.** (b)	**131.** (b)	**132.** (a)
133. (b)	**134.** (b)	**135.** (a)	**136.** (b)	**137.** (b)	**138.** (c)
139. (d)	**140.** (b)	**141.** (b)	**142.** (b)	**143.** (a)	**144.** (a)
145. (b)	**146.** (b)	**147.** (a)	**148.** (b)	**149.** (a)	**150.** (a)
151. (b)	**152.** (c)	**153.** (d)	**154.** (b)	**155.** (d)	**156.** (b)
157. (b)	**158.** (b)	**159.** (b)	**160.** (a)	**161.** (a)	**162.** (b)
163. (a)	**164.** (a)	**165.** (b)	**166.** (c)	**167.** (a)	**168.** (a)
169. (b)	**170.** (c)	**171.** (b)	**172.** (b)	**173.** (a)	**174.** (d)
175. (d)	**176.** (b)	**177.** (b)	**178.** (c)	**179.** (a)	**180.** (a)
181. (a)	**182.** (c)	**183.** (a)	**184.** (a)	**185.** (c)	**186.** (d)
187. (d)	**188.** (d)	**189.** (b)	**190.** (b)	**191.** (d)	**192.** (c)
193. (a)	**194.** (b)	**195.** (a)	**196.** (b)	**197.** (a)	**198.** (d)
199. (a)	**200.** (b)	**201.** (c)	**202.** (a)	**203.** (b)	**204.** (a)
205. (b)	**206.** (c)	**207.** (b)	**208.** (b)	**209.** (a)	**210.** (b)
211. (d)	**212.** (a)	**213.** (c)	**214.** (c)	**215.** (b)	**216.** (b)
217. (d)	**218.** (b)	**219.** (a)	**220.** (b)	**221.** (b)	**222.** (a)
223. (b)	**224.** (a)	**225.** (a)	**226.** (c)	**227.** (a)	**228.** (c)
229. (a)	**230.** (a)	**231.** (a)	**232.** (b)	**233.** (b)	**234.** (d)
235. (b)	**236.** (b)	**237.** (c)	**238.** (c)	**239.** (c)	**240.** (b)
241. (b)	**242.** (a)	**243.** (a)	**244.** (a)	**245.** (b)	**246.** (d)
247. (a)	**248.** (a)	**249.** (a)	**250.** (c)	**251.** (c)	**252.** (b)
253. (b)	**254.** (b)	**255.** (b)	**256.** (b)	**257.** (a)	**258.** (b)
259. (b)	**260.** (c)	**261.** (d)	**262.** (c)	**263.** (b)	**264.** (c)
265. (a)	**266.** (b)	**267.** (b)	**268.** (a)	**269.** (b)	**270.** (a)
271. (b)	**272.** (c)	**273.** (b)	**274.** (b)	**275.** (b)	**276.** (b)
277. (d)	**278.** (d)	**279.** (a)	**280.** (b)	**281.** (a)	**282.** (a)
283. (c)	**284.** (d)	**285.** (b)	**286.** (c)	**287.** (d)	**288.** (d)
289. (c)	**290.** (b)	**291.** (b)	**292.** (a)	**293.** (b)	**294.** (a)
295. (b)	**296.** (a)	**297.** (a)	**298.** (c)	**299.** (a)	**300.** (b)
301. (c)	**302.** (c)	**303.** (b)	**304.** (c)	**305.** (b)	**306.** (c)
307. (b)	**308.** (a)	**309.** (b)	**310.** (a)	**311.** (b)	**312.** (a)
313. (b)	**314.** (a)	**315.** (b)	**316.** (b)	**317.** (b)	**318.** (b)
319. (c)	**320.** (a)	**321.** (b)	**322.** (a)	**323.** (b)	**324.** (a)
325. (a)	**326.** (b)	**327.** (b)	**328.** (c)	**329.** (b)	**330.** (c)

331. (b)	**332.** (c)	**333.** (b)	**334.** (b)	**335.** (b)	**336.** (b)
337. (a)	**338.** (b)	**339.** (a)	**340.** (b)	**341.** (b)	**342.** (a)
343. (b)	**344.** (b)	**345.** (b)	**346.** (b)	**347.** (b)	**348.** (a)
349. (c)	**350.** (c)	**351.** (a)	**352.** (a)	**353.** (a)	**354.** (a)
355. (a)	**356.** (b)	**357.** (a)	**358.** (b)	**359.** (b)	**360.** (a)
361. (b)	**362.** (a)	**363.** (c)	**364.** (c)	**365.** (b)	**366.** (b)
367. (b)	**368.** (b)	**369.** (b)	**370.** (b)	**371.** (c)	**372.** (b)
373. (c)	**374.** (b)	**375.** (c)	**376.** (b)	**377.** (c)	**378.** (b)
379. (a)	**380.** (a)	**381.** (b)	**382.** (b)	**383.** (b)	**384.** (a)
385. (a)	**386.** (a)	**387.** (b)	**388.** (b)	**389.** (a)	**390.** (a)
391. (b)	**392.** (b)	**393.** (b)			

Index